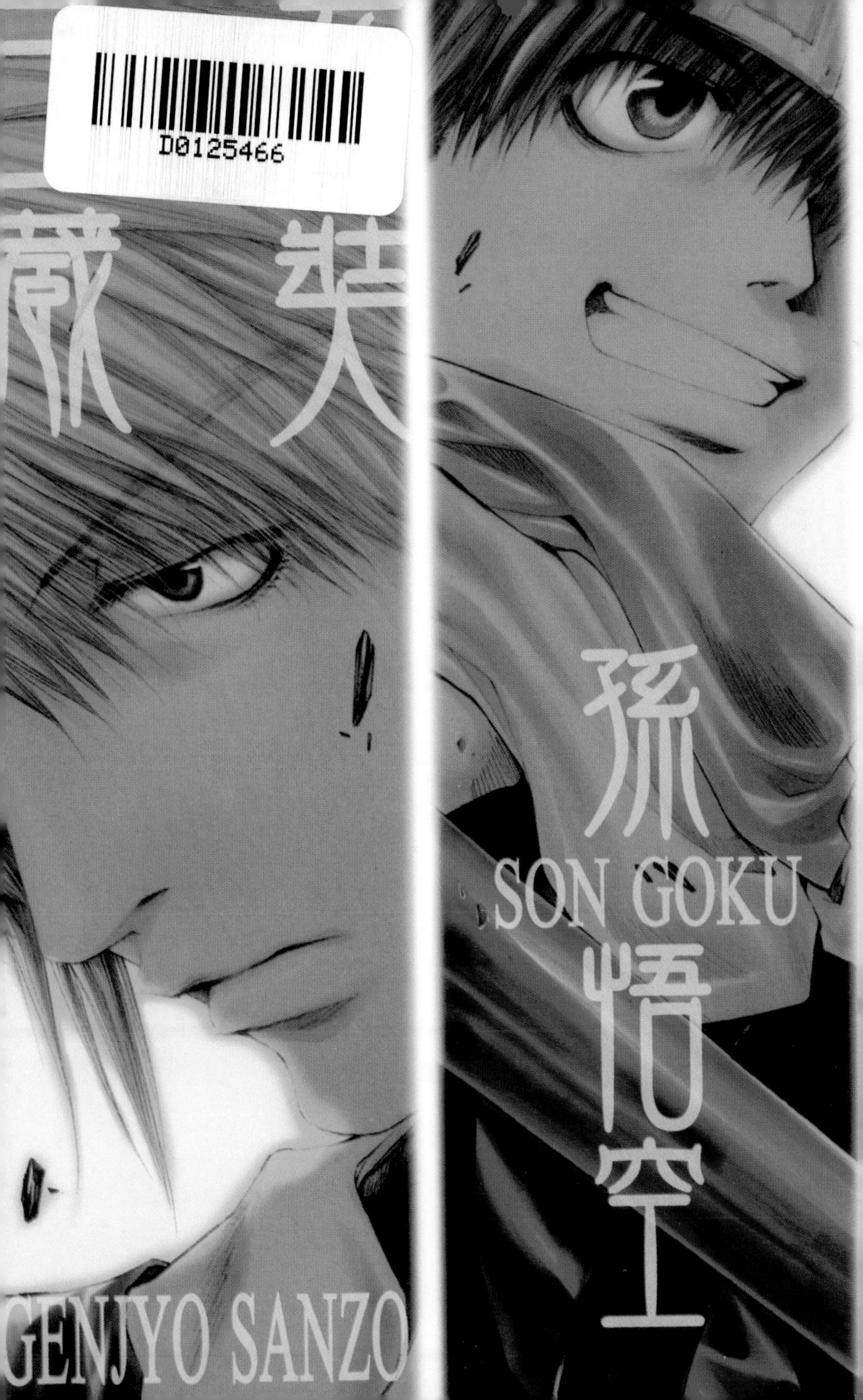

孫悟空
SON GOKU
奘
蔵
GENJYO SANZO

Are you bastards ready yet?

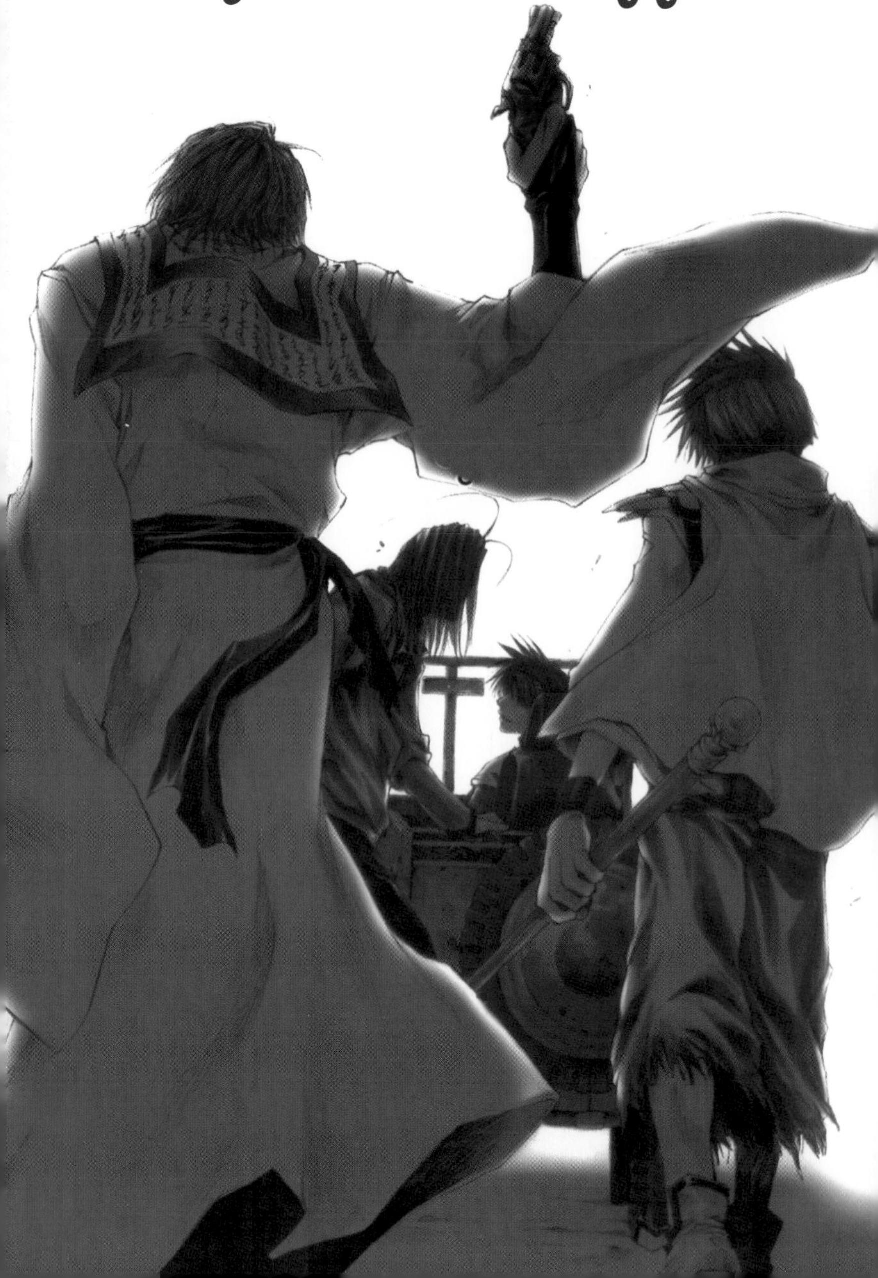

最強伝説 黒沢

福本伸行

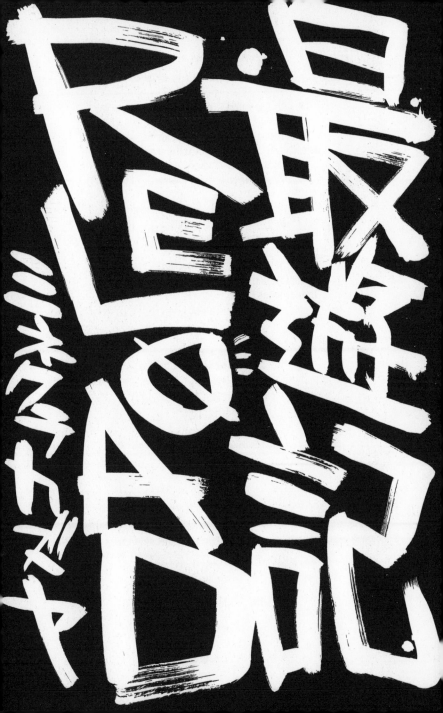

Saiyuki Reload Vol. 1
created by Kazuya Minekura

Translation - Alethena and Athena Nibley
English Adaptation - Lianne Sentar
Associate Editor - Peter Ahlstrom
Retouch and Lettering - Haruko Furukawa
Production Artist - Jason Milligan
Cover Design - Kyle Plummer

Editor - Lillian Diaz-Przybyl
Digital Imaging Manager - Chris Buford
Production Managers - Jennifer Miller and Mutsumi Miyazaki
Managing Editor - Jill Freshney
VP of Production - Ron Klamert
Publisher and E.I.C. - Mike Kiley
President and C.O.O. - John Parker
C.E.O. - Stuart Levy

A  Manga

TOKYOPOP Inc.
5900 Wilshire Blvd. Suite 2000
Los Angeles, CA 90036

E-mail: info@TOKYOPOP.com
Come visit us online at www.TOKYOPOP.com

ISBN: 1-59816-025-7

First TOKYOPOP printing: August 2005
10 9 8 7 6 5 4 3 2 1
Printed in the USA

弾は再び込められた。

Time to reload

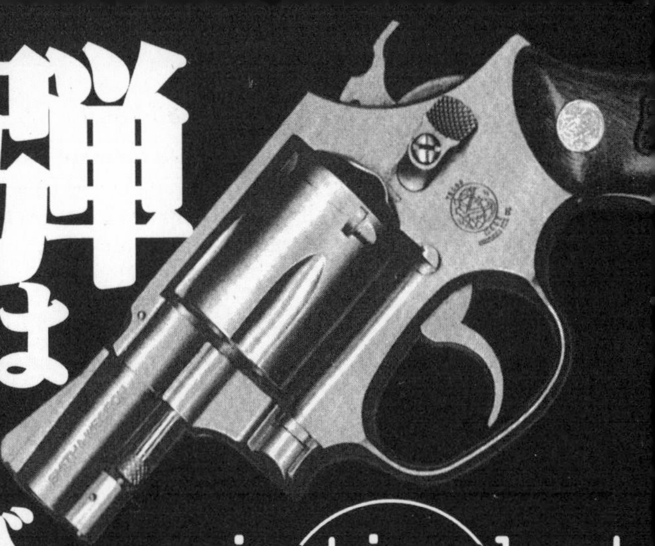

saiyuki-reload 1

KAZUYA MINEKURA

CONTENTS

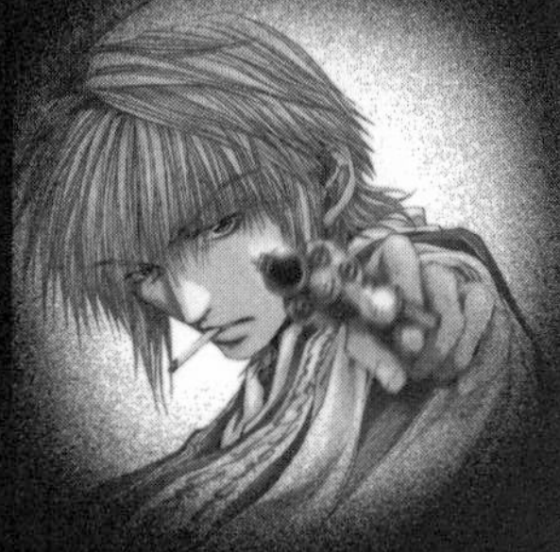

Genjyo Sanzo –

A very brutal, worldly priest. He drinks, smokes, gambles and even carries a gun. He's looking for the sacred scripture of his late master, Sanzo Houshi. He's egotistical, haughty and has zero sense of humor, but this handsome 23-year-old hero also has calm judgment and charisma. His favorite phrases are "Die" and "I'll kill you." His main weapons are the Maten Sutra, a handgun, and a paper fan for idiots. He's 177 cm tall (approx. 5'10"), and is often noted for his drooping purple eyes.

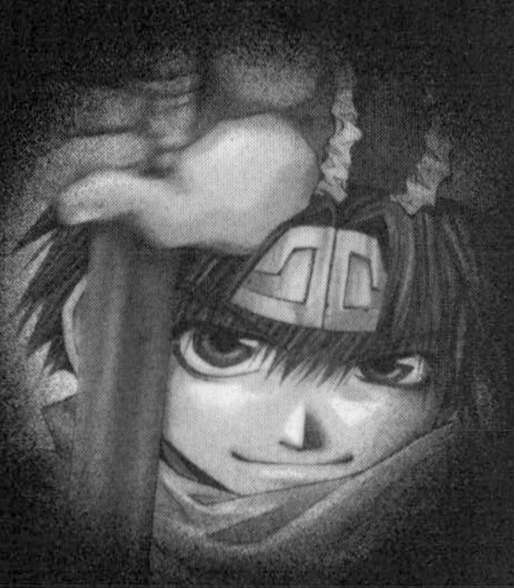

Son Goku –

The brave, cheerful Monkey King of legend, an unholy child born from the rocks where the aura of the Earth was gathered. His brain is full of thoughts of food and games. To pay for crimes he committed when he was young, he was imprisoned in the rocks for 500 years without aging. Because of his optimistic personality, he's become the mascot character of the group; this apparent 18-year-old of superior health is made fun of by Gojyo, yelled at by Sanzo and watched over by Hakkai. He's 162 cm tall (approx. 5'4"). His main weapon is the Nyoi-Bo, a magical cudgel that can extend into a sansekkon staff.

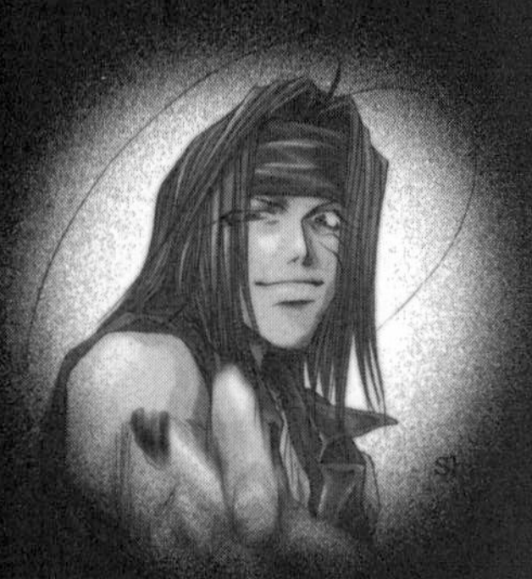

Sha Gojyo –

Gojyo is a lecherous kappa (water youkai). His behavior might seem vulgar and rough at first glance (and it is), but to his friends he's like a dependable older brother. He and Goku are sparring partners, he and Hakkai are best friends and he and Sanzo are bad friends (ha ha!). Sometimes his love for the ladies gets him into trouble. Because of his unusual heritage, he doesn't need a limiter to blend in with the humans. His favorite way of fighting is to use a shakujou, a staff with a crescent-shaped blade connected by a chain; it's quite messy. He's 184 cm tall (approx. 6'), has scarlet hair and eyes and is a 22-year-old chain smoker.

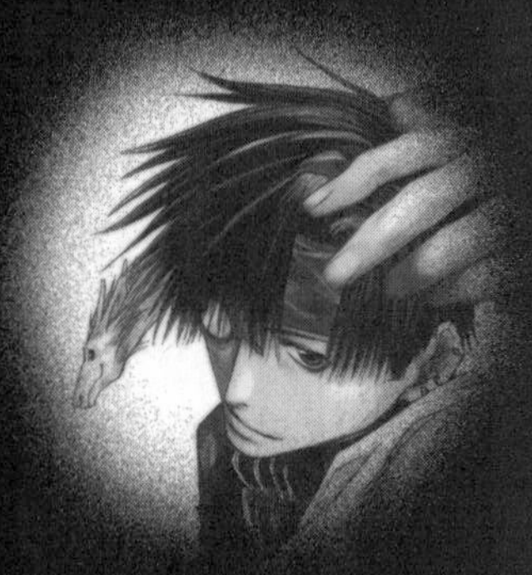

Cho Hakkai –

A pleasant, rather absent-minded young man with a kind smile that suits him nicely. It's sometimes hard to tell whether he's serious or laughing to himself at his friends' expense. His darker side comes through from time to time in the form of a sharp, penetrating gaze, a symbol of a dark past. As he's Hakuryu's (the white dragon) owner, he gets to drive the Jeep. Because he uses kikou jutsu (Chi manipulation) in battle, his "weapon" is his smile (ha ha!). He's 22 years old, 181 cm tall (approx. 5'11"), and his eyes are deep green (his right eye is nearly blind). The cuffs he wears on his left ear are Youkai power limiters.

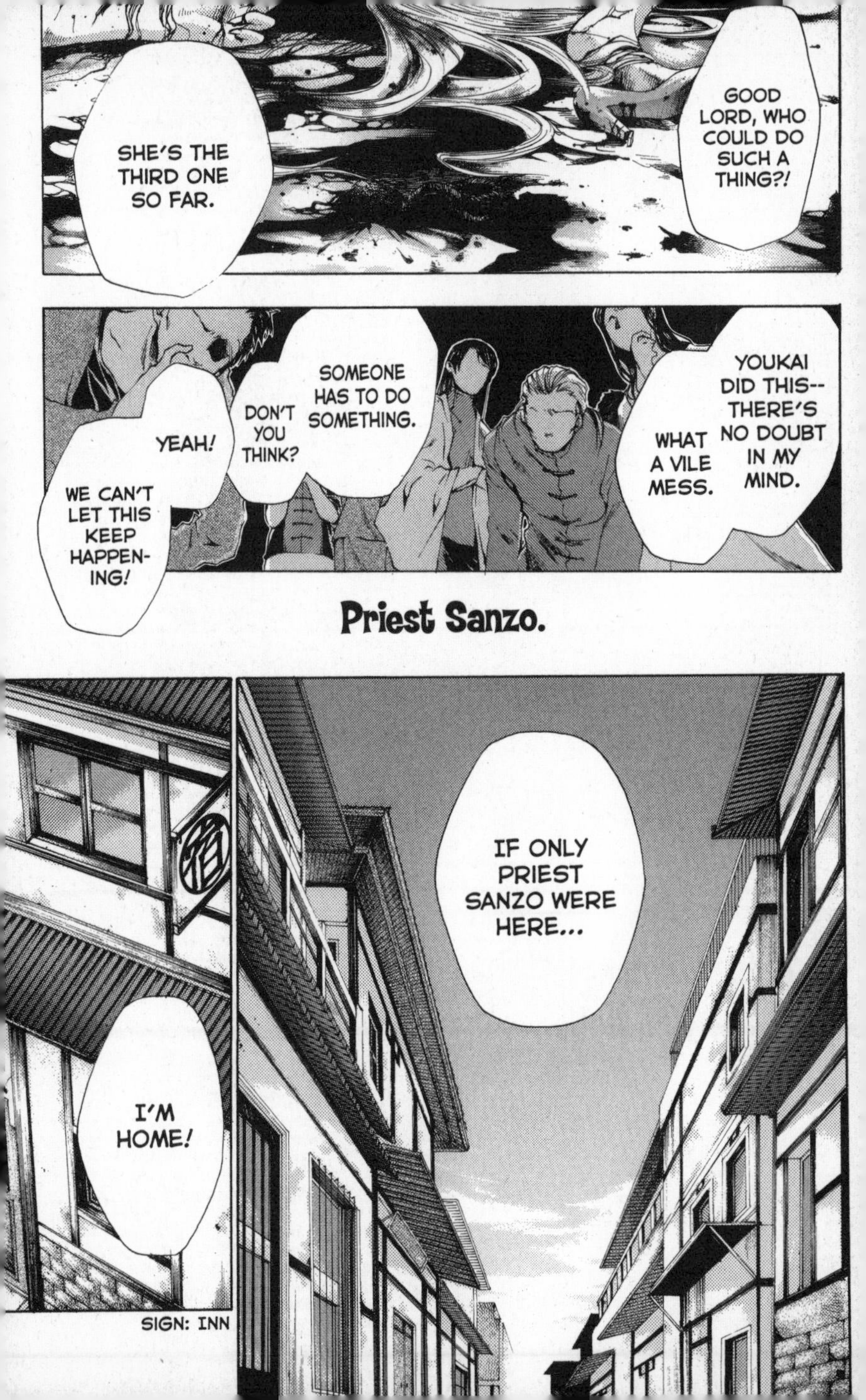
GOOD LORD, WHO COULD DO SUCH A THING?!
SHE'S THE THIRD ONE SO FAR.
YOUKAI DID THIS-- THERE'S NO DOUBT IN MY MIND.
WHAT A VILE MESS.
SOMEONE HAS TO DO SOMETHING.
DON'T YOU THINK?
YEAH!
WE CAN'T LET THIS KEEP HAPPENING!
Priest Sanzo.
IF ONLY PRIEST SANZO WERE HERE...
I'M HOME!
SIGN: INN

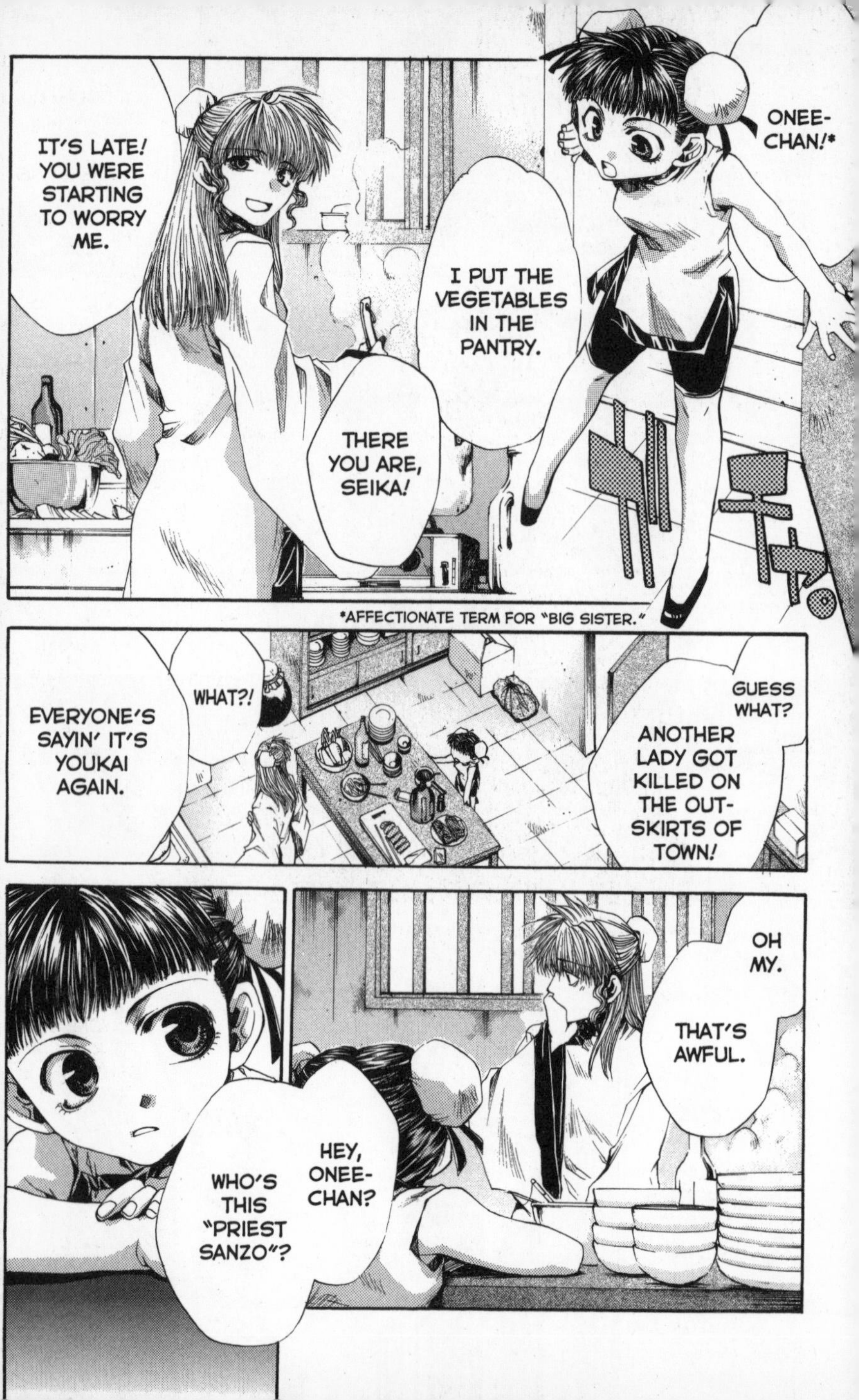
ONEE-CHAN!*
I PUT THE VEGETABLES IN THE PANTRY.
THERE YOU ARE, SEIKA!
IT'S LATE! YOU WERE STARTING TO WORRY ME.
*AFFECTIONATE TERM FOR "BIG SISTER."
GUESS WHAT?
ANOTHER LADY GOT KILLED ON THE OUT-SKIRTS OF TOWN!
WHAT?!
EVERYONE'S SAYIN' IT'S YOUKAI AGAIN.
OH MY.
THAT'S AWFUL.
HEY, ONEE-CHAN?
WHO'S THIS "PRIEST SANZO"?

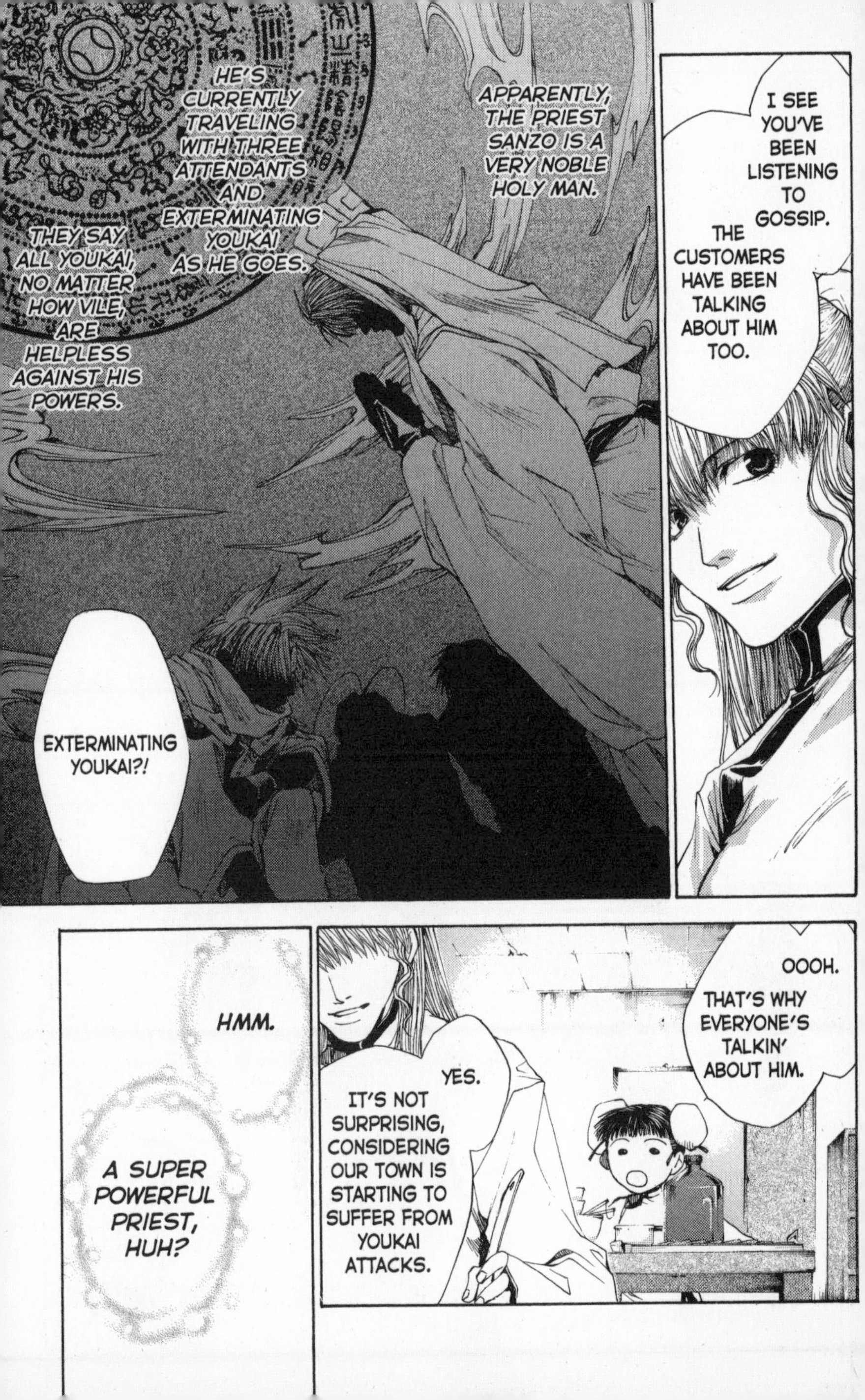
I SEE YOU'VE BEEN LISTENING TO GOSSIP.
THE CUSTOMERS HAVE BEEN TALKING ABOUT HIM TOO.
APPARENTLY, THE PRIEST SANZO IS A VERY NOBLE HOLY MAN.
HE'S CURRENTLY TRAVELING WITH THREE ATTENDANTS AND EXTERMINATING YOUKAI AS HE GOES.
THEY SAY ALL YOUKAI, NO MATTER HOW VILE, ARE HELPLESS AGAINST HIS POWERS.
EXTERMINATING YOUKAI?!
OOOH.
THAT'S WHY EVERYONE'S TALKIN' ABOUT HIM.
YES.
IT'S NOT SURPRISING, CONSIDERING OUR TOWN IS STARTING TO SUFFER FROM YOUKAI ATTACKS.
HMM.
A SUPER POWERFUL PRIEST, HUH?

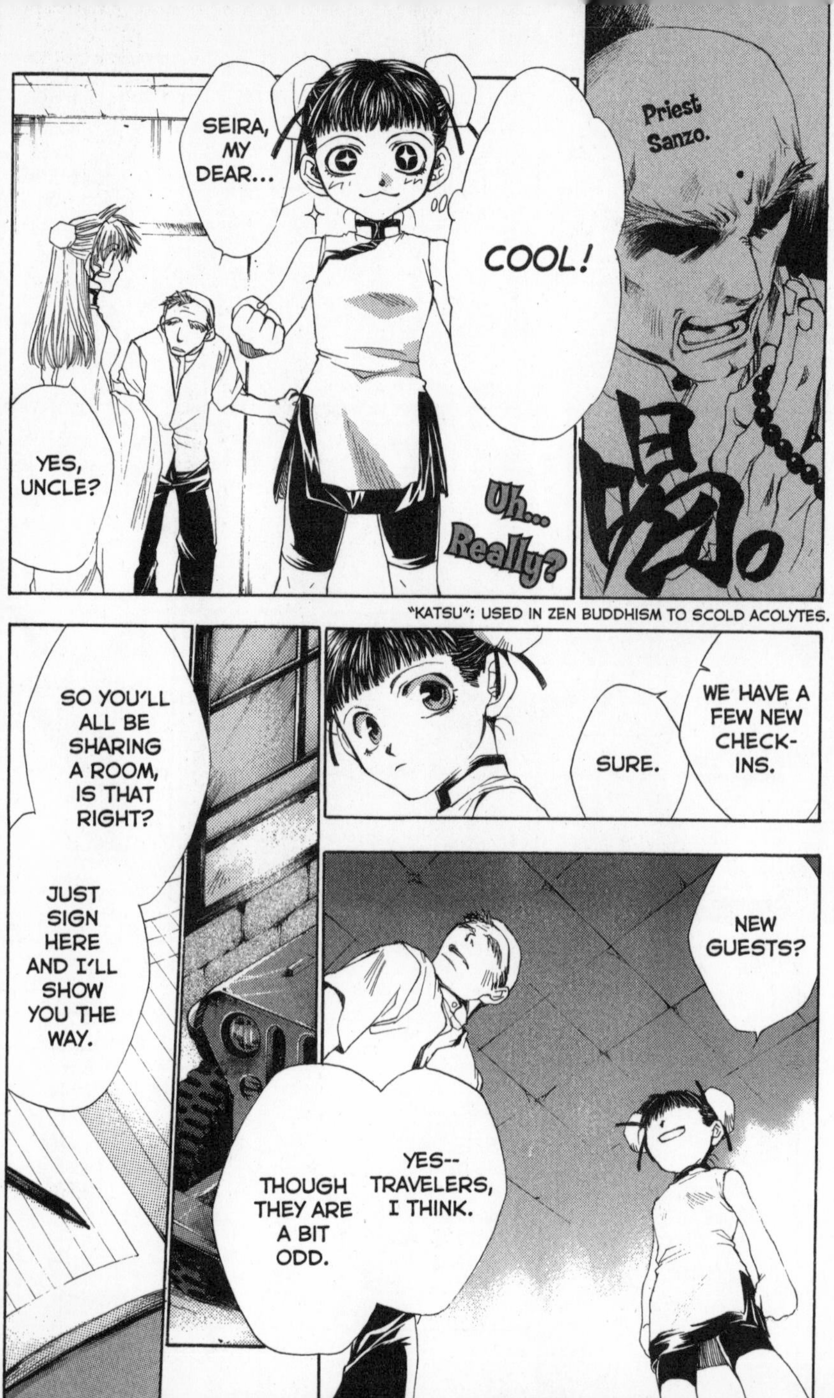
Priest Sanzo.
喝
COOL!
Uh... Really?
SEIRA, MY DEAR...
YES, UNCLE?
"KATSU": USED IN ZEN BUDDHISM TO SCOLD ACOLYTES.
WE HAVE A FEW NEW CHECK-INS.
SURE.
NEW GUESTS?
YES-- TRAVELERS, I THINK.
THOUGH THEY ARE A BIT ODD.
SO YOU'LL ALL BE SHARING A ROOM, IS THAT RIGHT?
JUST SIGN HERE AND I'LL SHOW YOU THE WAY.

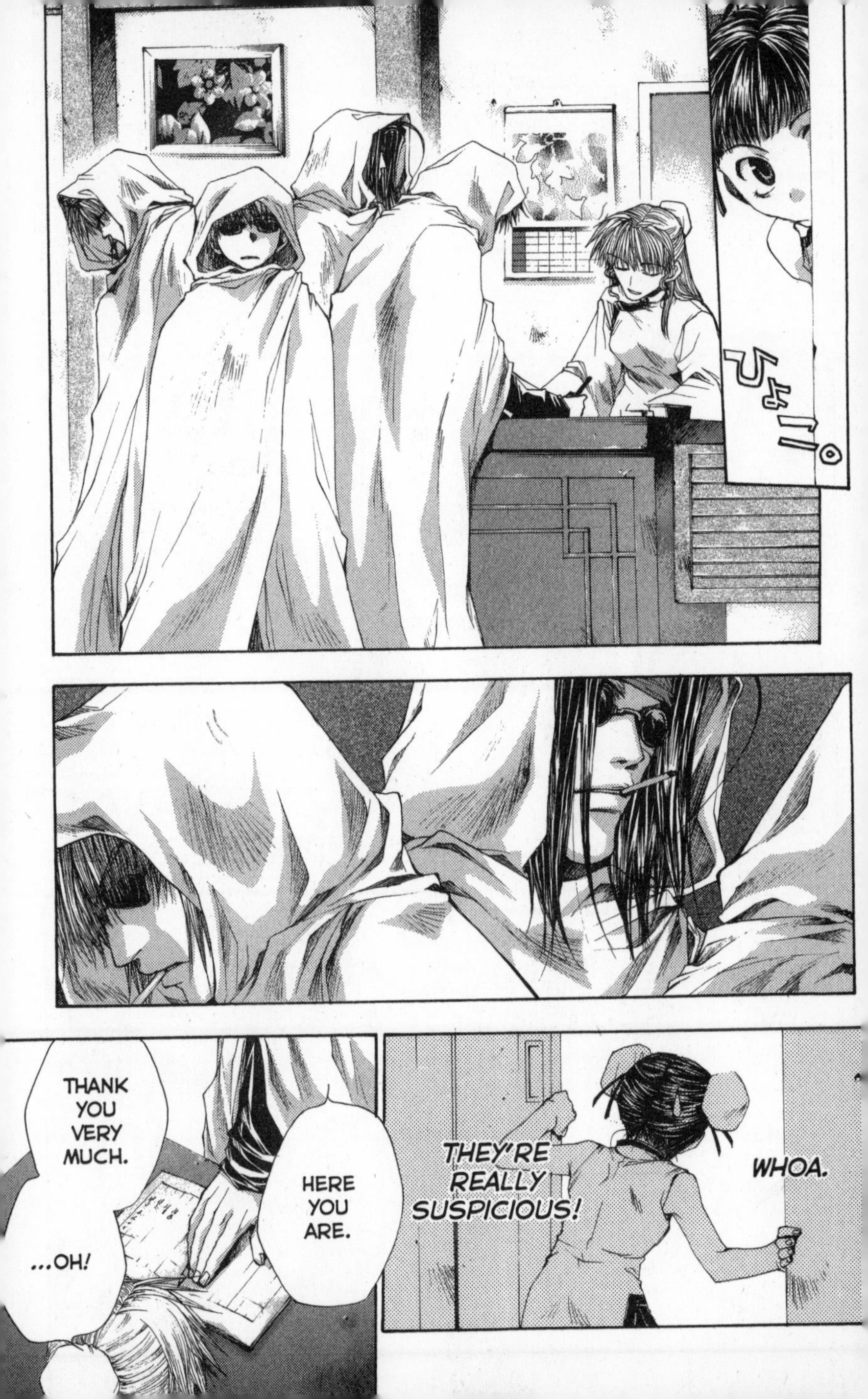
ひょこ。
WHOA.
THEY'RE REALLY SUSPICIOUS!
HERE YOU ARE.
THANK YOU VERY MUCH.
...OH!

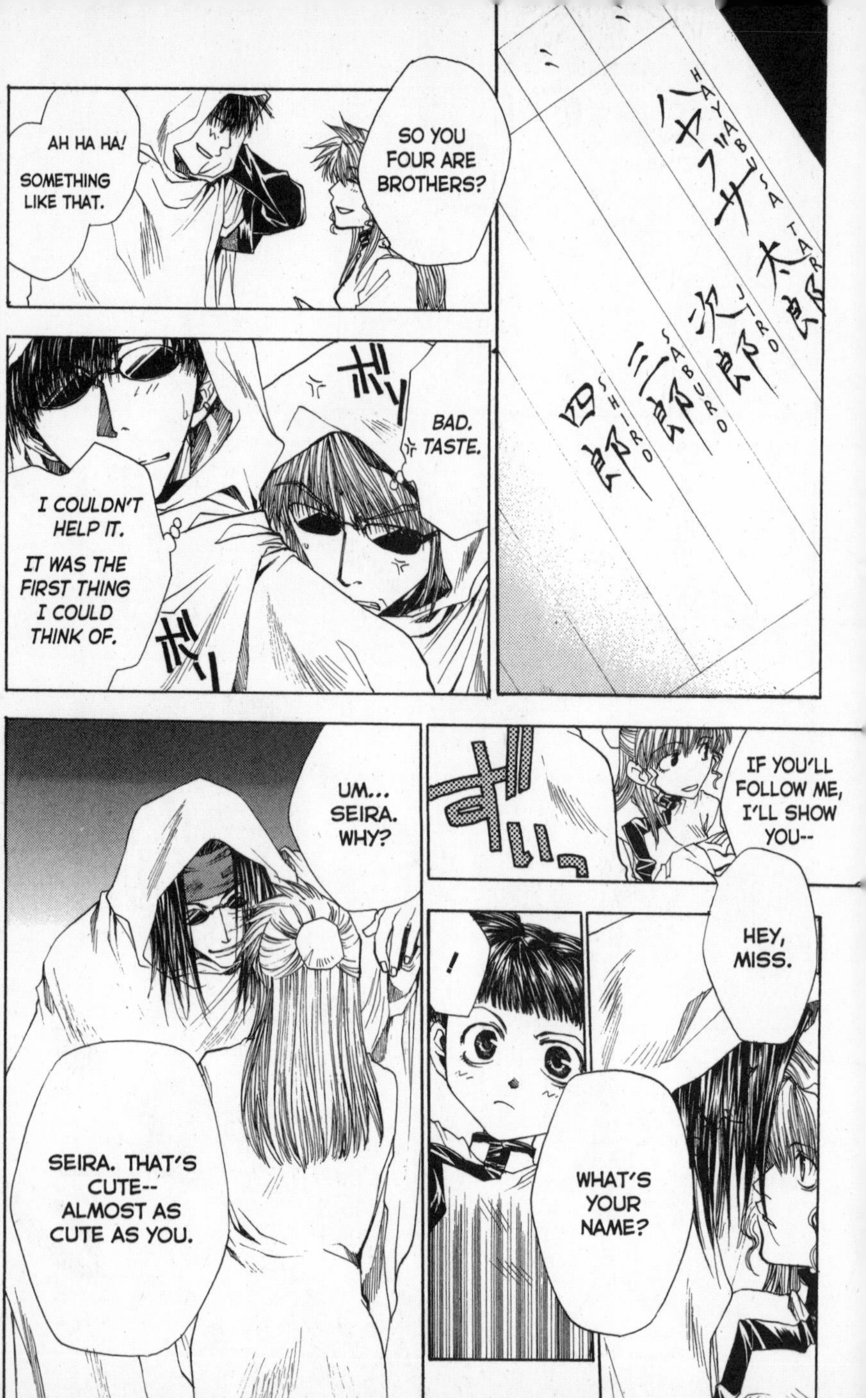
ハヤブサ HAYABUSA
太郎 TARO
次郎 JIRO
三郎 SABURO
四郎 SHIRO
SO YOU FOUR ARE BROTHERS?
AH HA HA! SOMETHING LIKE THAT.
ボソ
BAD. TASTE.
I COULDN'T HELP IT.
IT WAS THE FIRST THING I COULD THINK OF.
ボソ
IF YOU'LL FOLLOW ME, I'LL SHOW YOU--
すいっ
HEY, MISS.
WHAT'S YOUR NAME?
!
UM... SEIRA. WHY?
SEIRA. THAT'S CUTE-- ALMOST AS CUTE AS YOU.

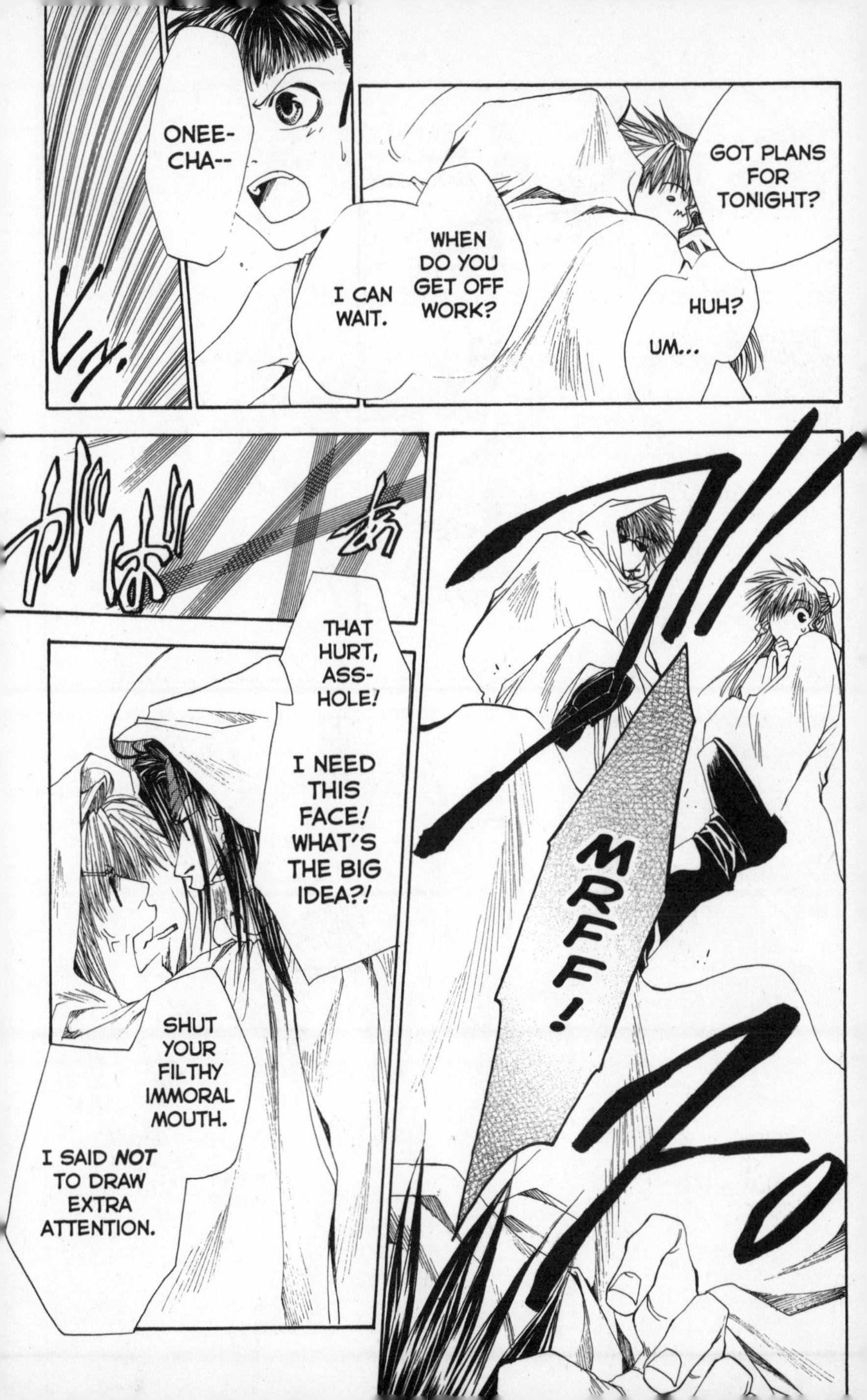
GOT PLANS FOR TONIGHT?
HUH? UM...
WHEN DO YOU GET OFF WORK?
I CAN WAIT.
ONEE-CHA--
MRFF!
THAT HURT, ASS-HOLE!
I NEED THIS FACE! WHAT'S THE BIG IDEA?!
SHUT YOUR FILTHY IMMORAL MOUTH.
I SAID *NOT* TO DRAW EXTRA ATTENTION.

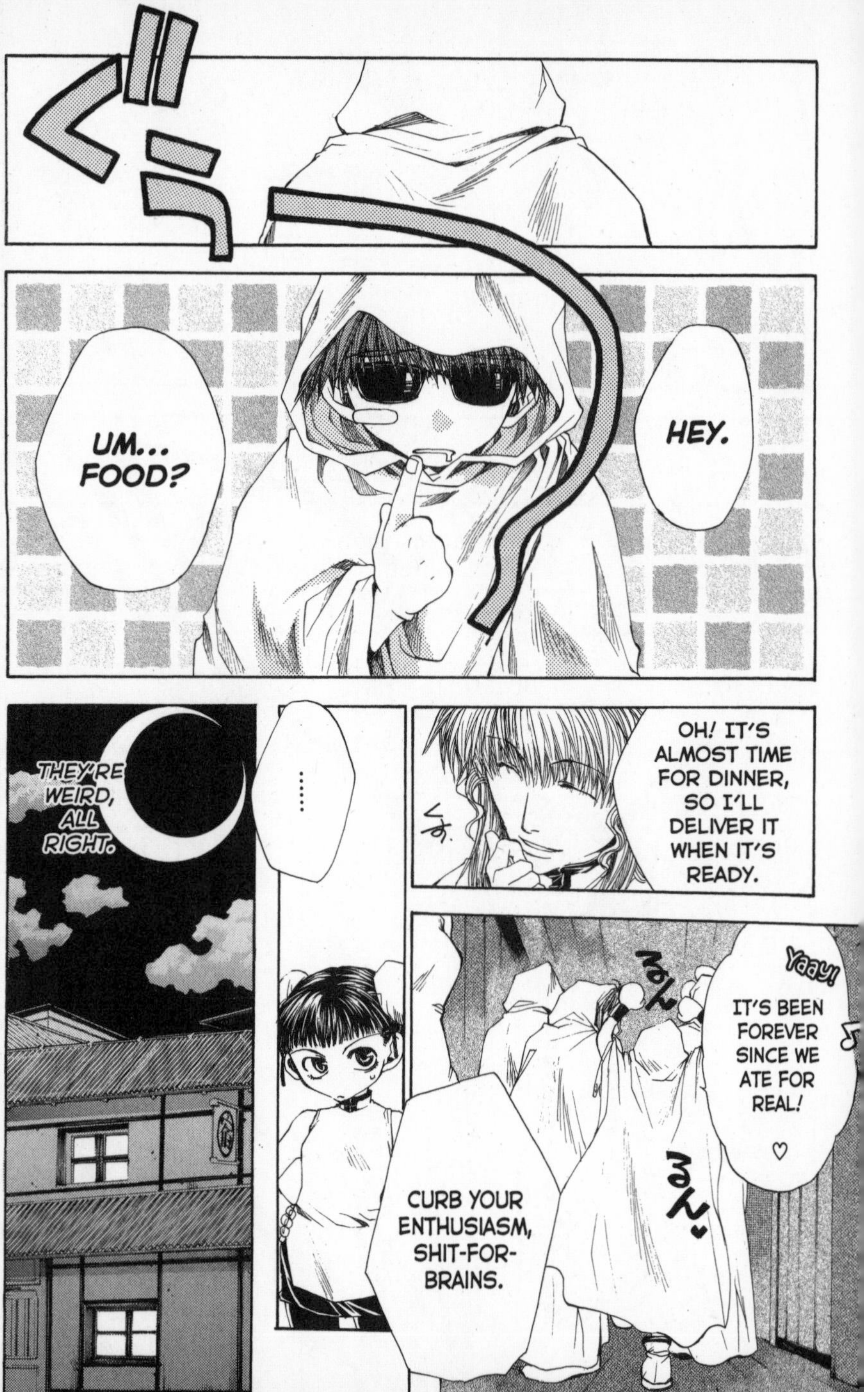
ぐぅ
HEY.
UM... FOOD?
OH! IT'S ALMOST TIME FOR DINNER, SO I'LL DELIVER IT WHEN IT'S READY.
くす
Yaay!
IT'S BEEN FOREVER SINCE WE ATE FOR REAL! ♡
るん
るん
......
CURB YOUR ENTHUSIASM, SHIT-FOR-BRAINS.
THEY'RE WEIRD, ALL RIGHT.

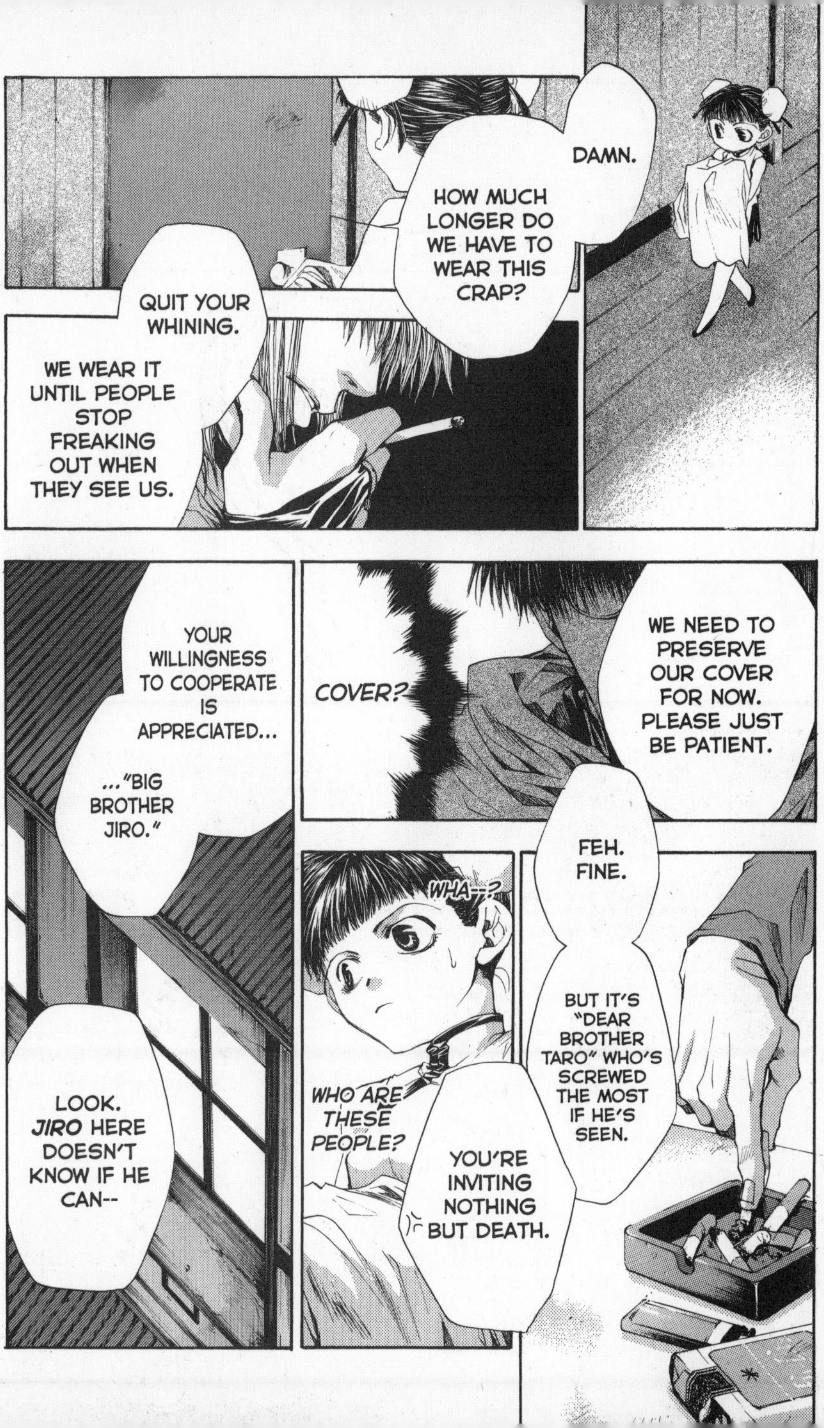
DAMN.
HOW MUCH LONGER DO WE HAVE TO WEAR THIS CRAP?
QUIT YOUR WHINING.
WE WEAR IT UNTIL PEOPLE STOP FREAKING OUT WHEN THEY SEE US.
WE NEED TO PRESERVE OUR COVER FOR NOW. PLEASE JUST BE PATIENT.
COVER?
FEH. FINE.
BUT IT'S "DEAR BROTHER TARO" WHO'S SCREWED THE MOST IF HE'S SEEN.
YOU'RE INVITING NOTHING BUT DEATH.
WHA--?
WHO ARE THESE PEOPLE?
YOUR WILLINGNESS TO COOPERATE IS APPRECIATED...
..."BIG BROTHER JIRO."
LOOK. JIRO HERE DOESN'T KNOW IF HE CAN--

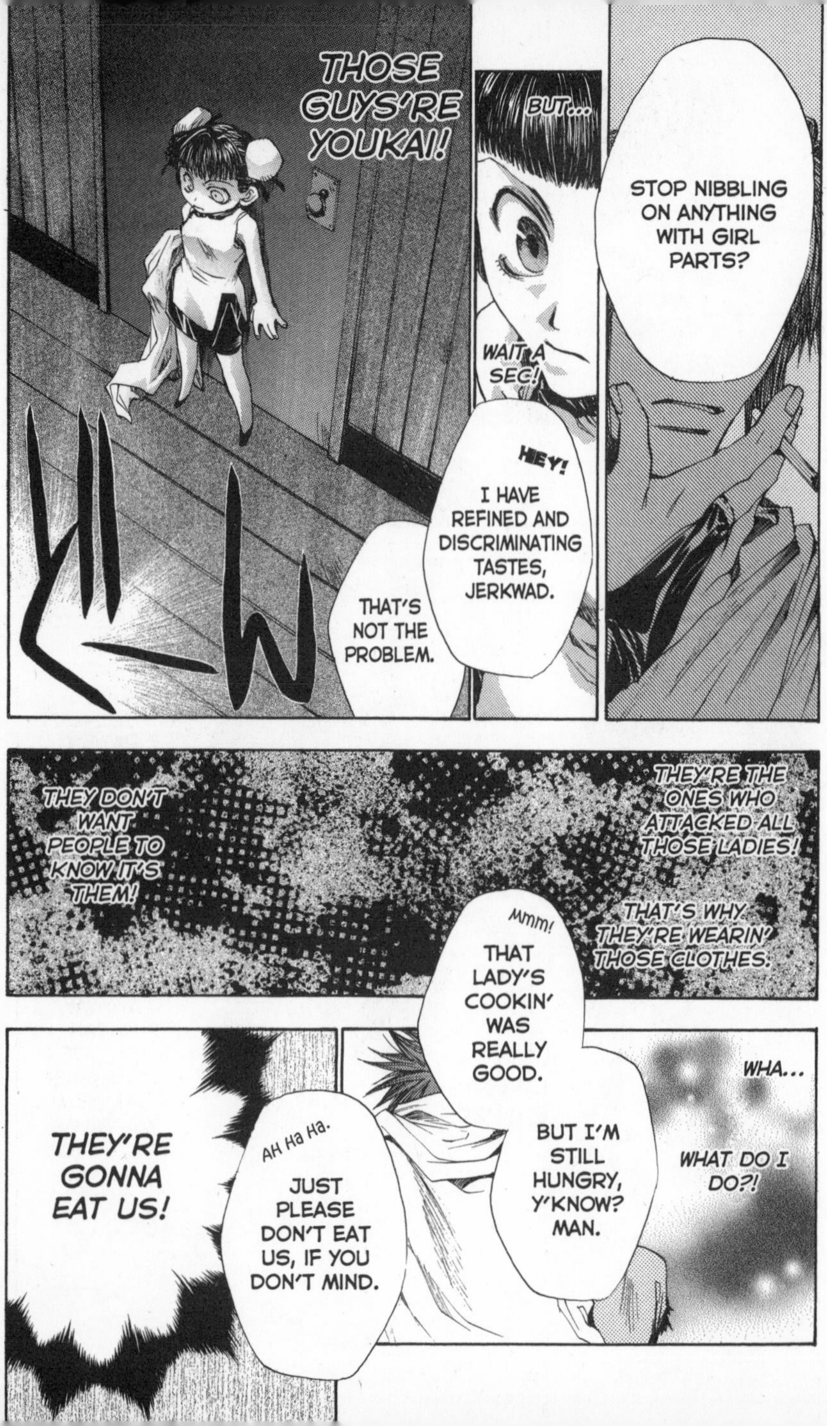
STOP NIBBLING ON ANYTHING WITH GIRL PARTS?
BUT...
WAIT A SEC!
HEY!
I HAVE REFINED AND DISCRIMINATING TASTES, JERKWAD.
THAT'S NOT THE PROBLEM.
THOSE GUYS'RE YOUKAI!
THEY'RE THE ONES WHO ATTACKED ALL THOSE LADIES!
THAT'S WHY THEY'RE WEARIN' THOSE CLOTHES.
THEY DON'T WANT PEOPLE TO KNOW IT'S THEM!
Mmm!
THAT LADY'S COOKIN' WAS REALLY GOOD.
WHA...
WHAT DO I DO?!
BUT I'M STILL HUNGRY, Y'KNOW? MAN.
AH Ha Ha.
JUST PLEASE DON'T EAT US, IF YOU DON'T MIND.
THEY'RE GONNA EAT US!

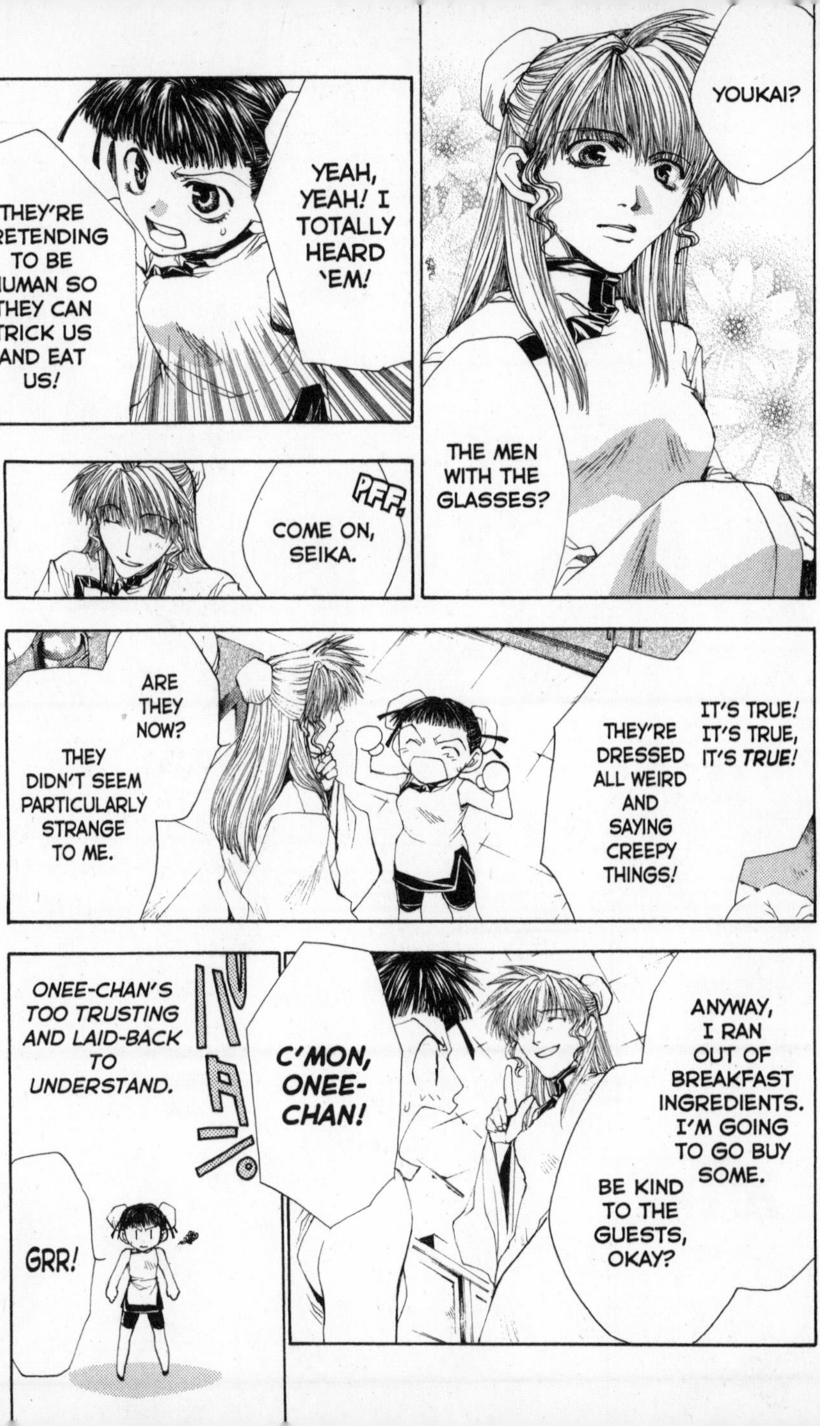
YOUKAI?
THE MEN WITH THE GLASSES?
YEAH, YEAH! I TOTALLY HEARD 'EM!
THEY'RE PRETENDING TO BE HUMAN SO THEY CAN TRICK US AND EAT US!
PFF,
COME ON, SEIKA.
IT'S TRUE! IT'S TRUE, IT'S TRUE!
THEY'RE DRESSED ALL WEIRD AND SAYING CREEPY THINGS!
ARE THEY NOW?
THEY DIDN'T SEEM PARTICULARLY STRANGE TO ME.
ANYWAY, I RAN OUT OF BREAKFAST INGREDIENTS. I'M GOING TO GO BUY SOME.
BE KIND TO THE GUESTS, OKAY?
C'MON, ONEE-CHAN!
ONEE-CHAN'S TOO TRUSTING AND LAID-BACK TO UNDERSTAND.
GRR!

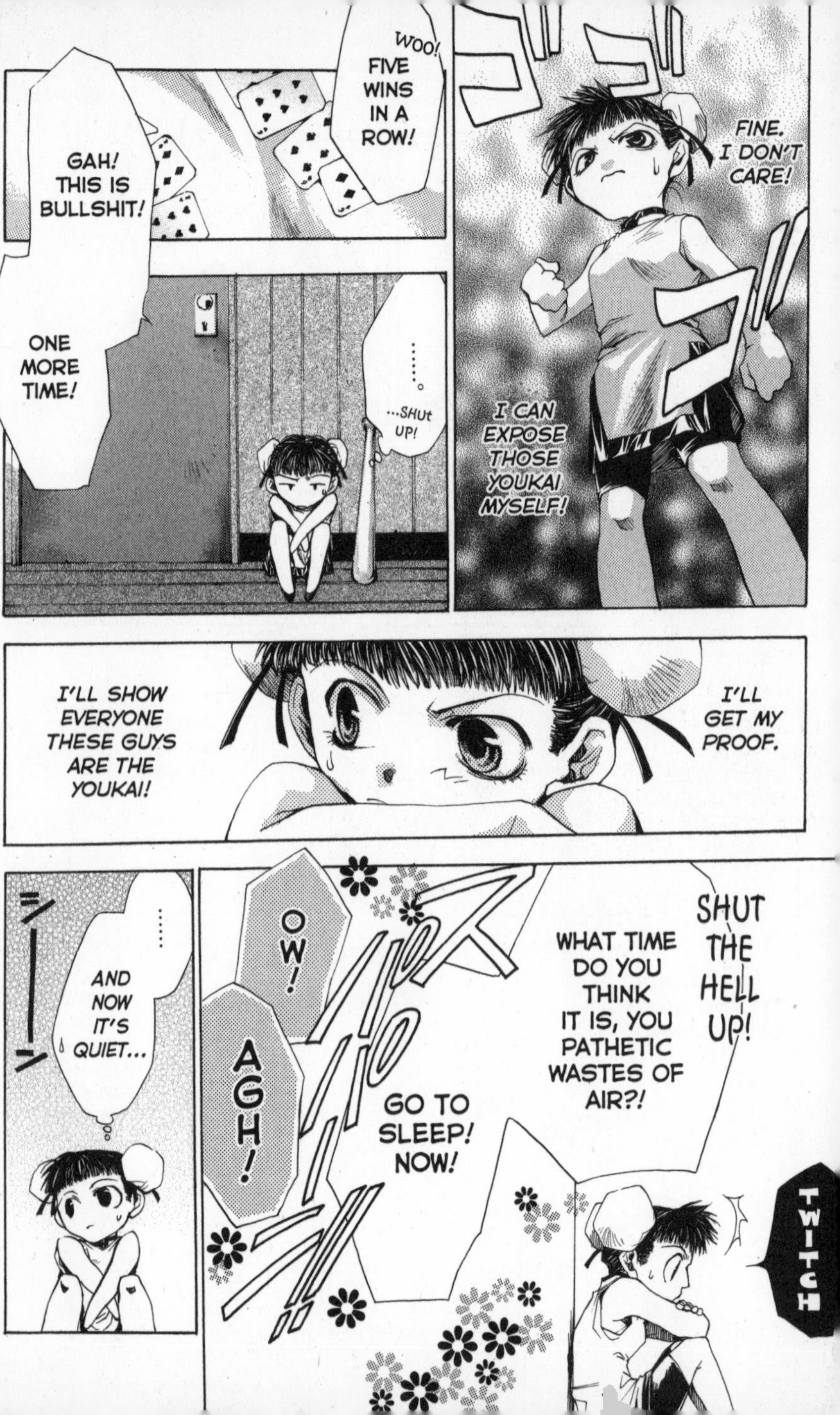
FINE. I DON'T CARE!
I CAN EXPOSE THOSE YOUKAI MYSELF!
WOO! FIVE WINS IN A ROW!
GAH! THIS IS BULLSHIT!
ONE MORE TIME!
......
...SHUt UP!
I'LL GET MY PROOF.
I'LL SHOW EVERYONE THESE GUYS ARE THE YOUKAI!
SHUT THE HELL UP!
WHAT TIME DO YOU THINK IT IS, YOU PATHETIC WASTES OF AIR?!
GO TO SLEEP! NOW!
OW!
AGH!
TWITCH
......
AND NOW IT'S QUIET...

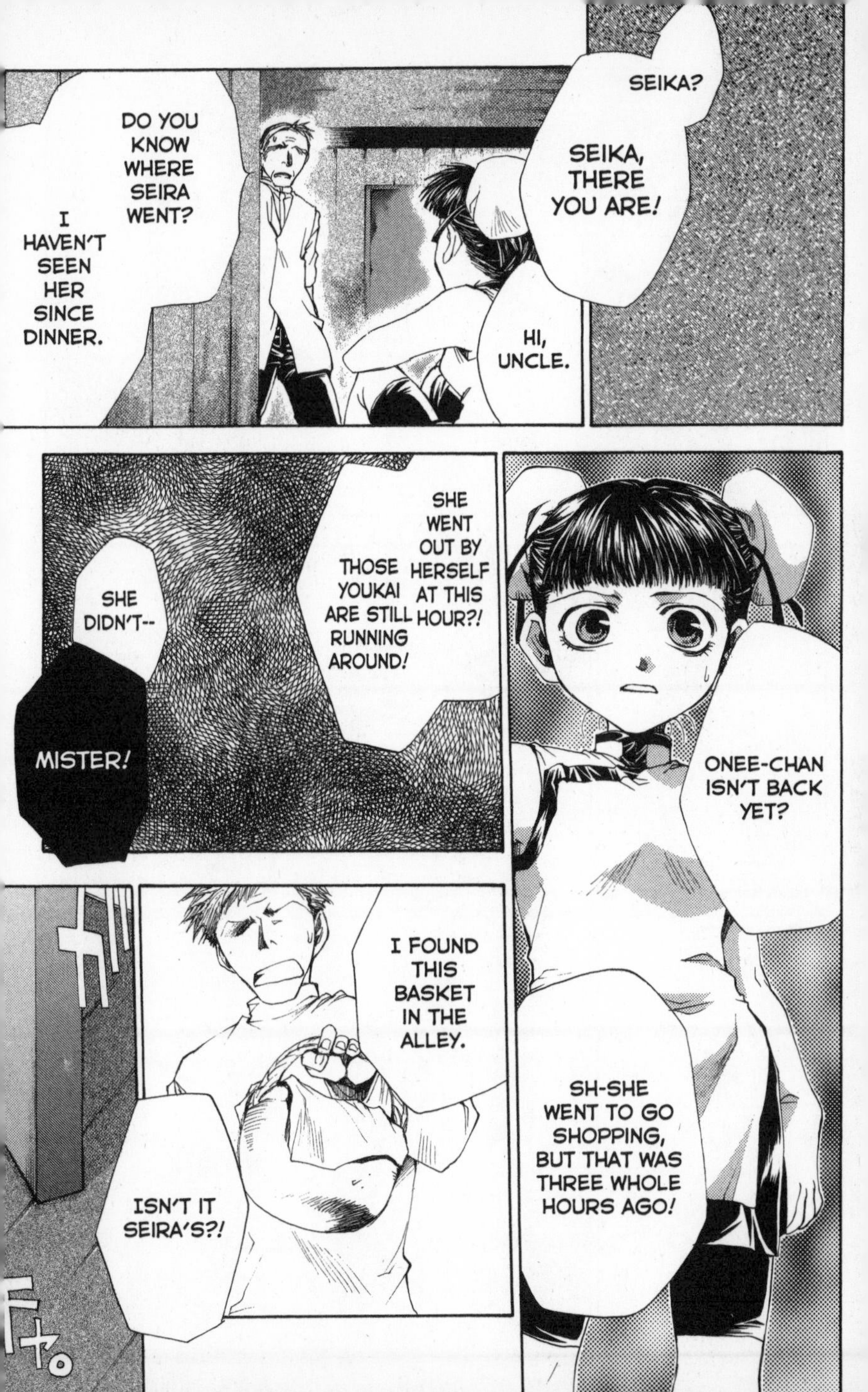
SEIKA?
SEIKA, THERE YOU ARE!
HI, UNCLE.
DO YOU KNOW WHERE SEIRA WENT?
I HAVEN'T SEEN HER SINCE DINNER.
ONEE-CHAN ISN'T BACK YET?
SH-SHE WENT TO GO SHOPPING, BUT THAT WAS THREE WHOLE HOURS AGO!
SHE WENT OUT BY HERSELF AT THIS HOUR?!
THOSE YOUKAI ARE STILL RUNNING AROUND!
SHE DIDN'T--
MISTER!
I FOUND THIS BASKET IN THE ALLEY.
ISN'T IT SEIRA'S?!

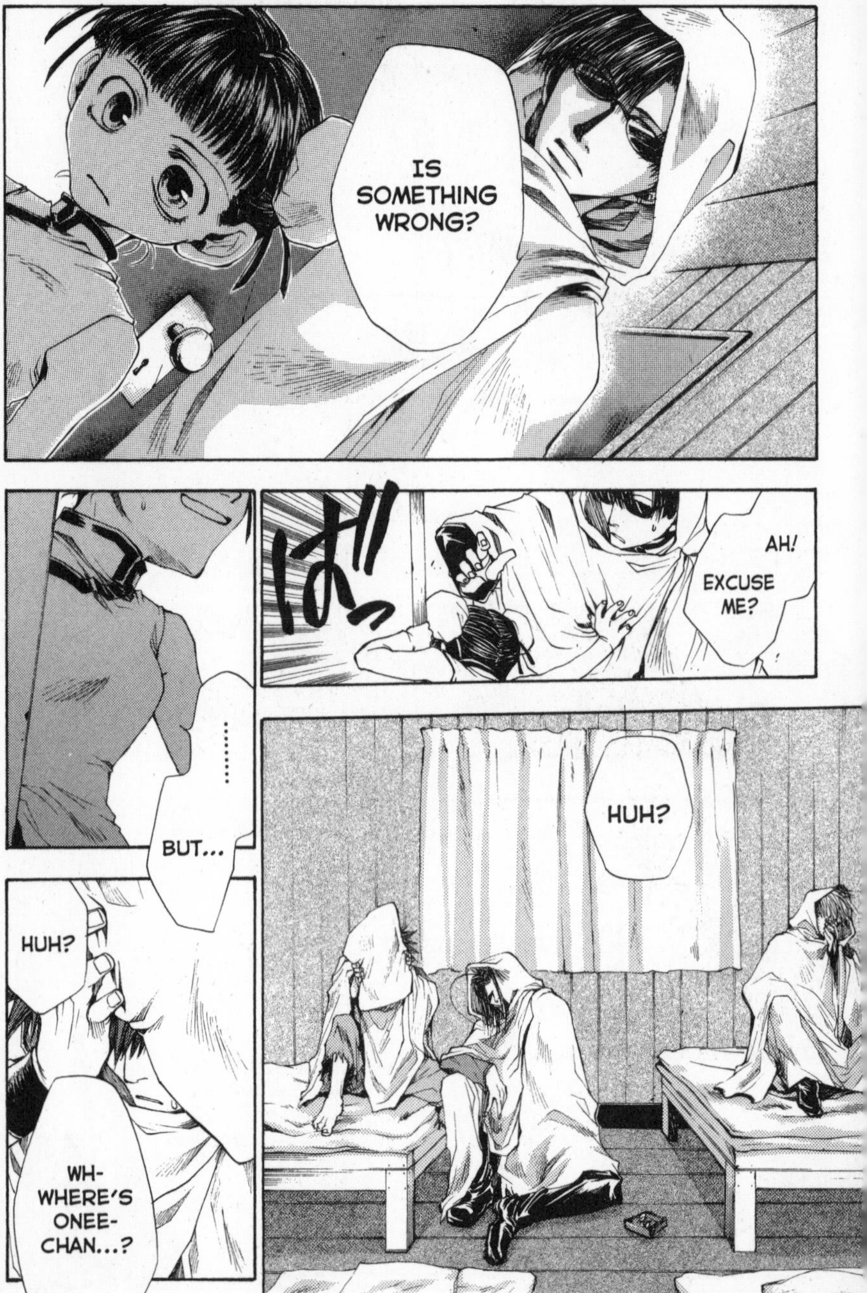
IS SOMETHING WRONG?
ばっ
AH!
EXCUSE ME?
HUH?
......
BUT...
HUH?
WH- WHERE'S ONEE- CHAN...?

I THOUGHT YOU GUYS WERE THE YOUKAI!

......

WHAT ARE YOU TALKING ABOUT?

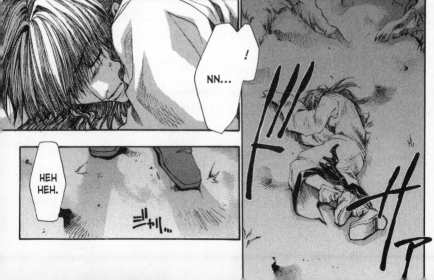

!

NN...

HEH HEH.

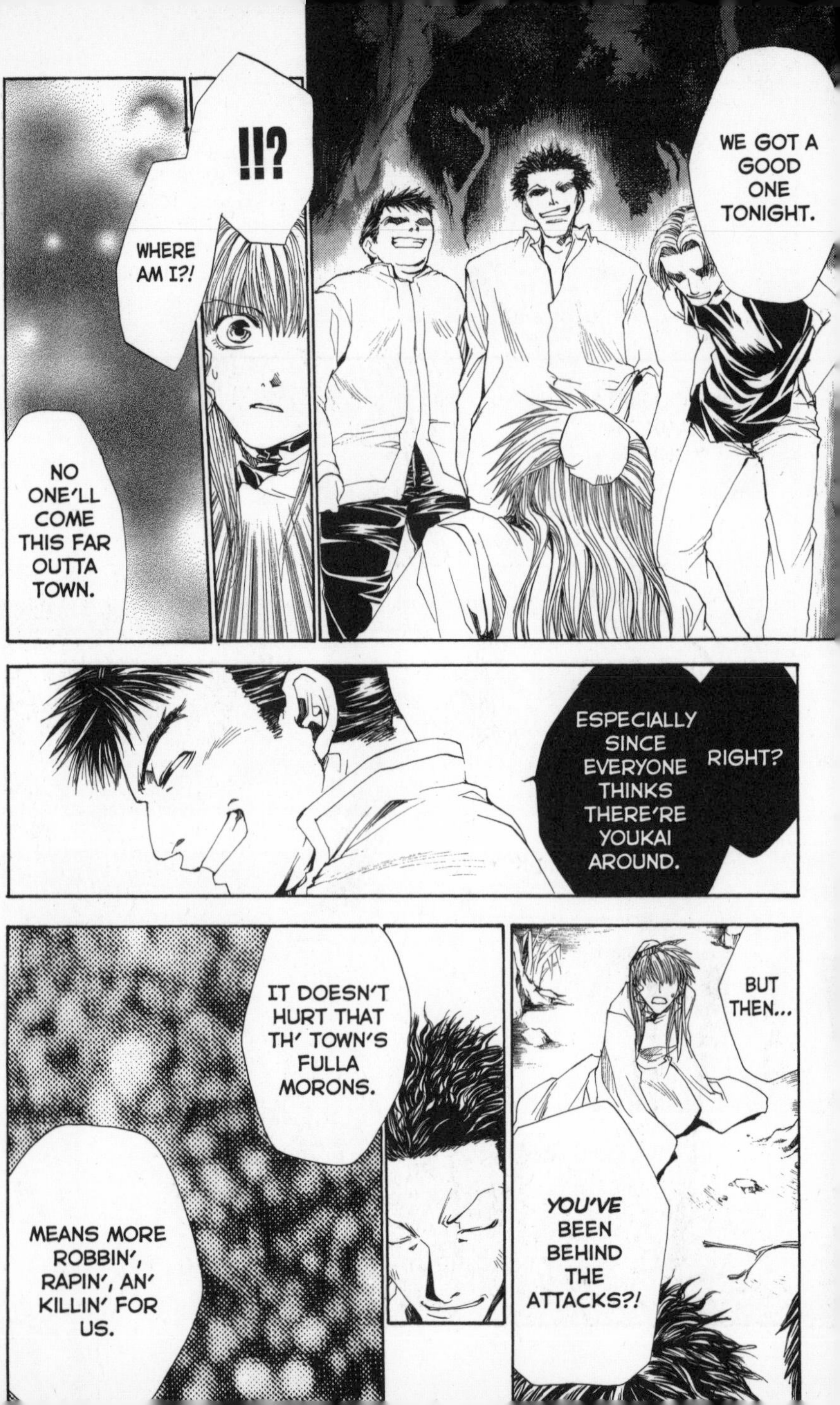
WE GOT A GOOD ONE TONIGHT.
!!?
WHERE AM I?!
NO ONE'LL COME THIS FAR OUTTA TOWN.
RIGHT?
ESPECIALLY SINCE EVERYONE THINKS THERE'RE YOUKAI AROUND.
BUT THEN...
YOU'VE BEEN BEHIND THE ATTACKS?!
IT DOESN'T HURT THAT TH' TOWN'S FULLA MORONS.
MEANS MORE ROBBIN', RAPIN', AN' KILLIN' FOR US.

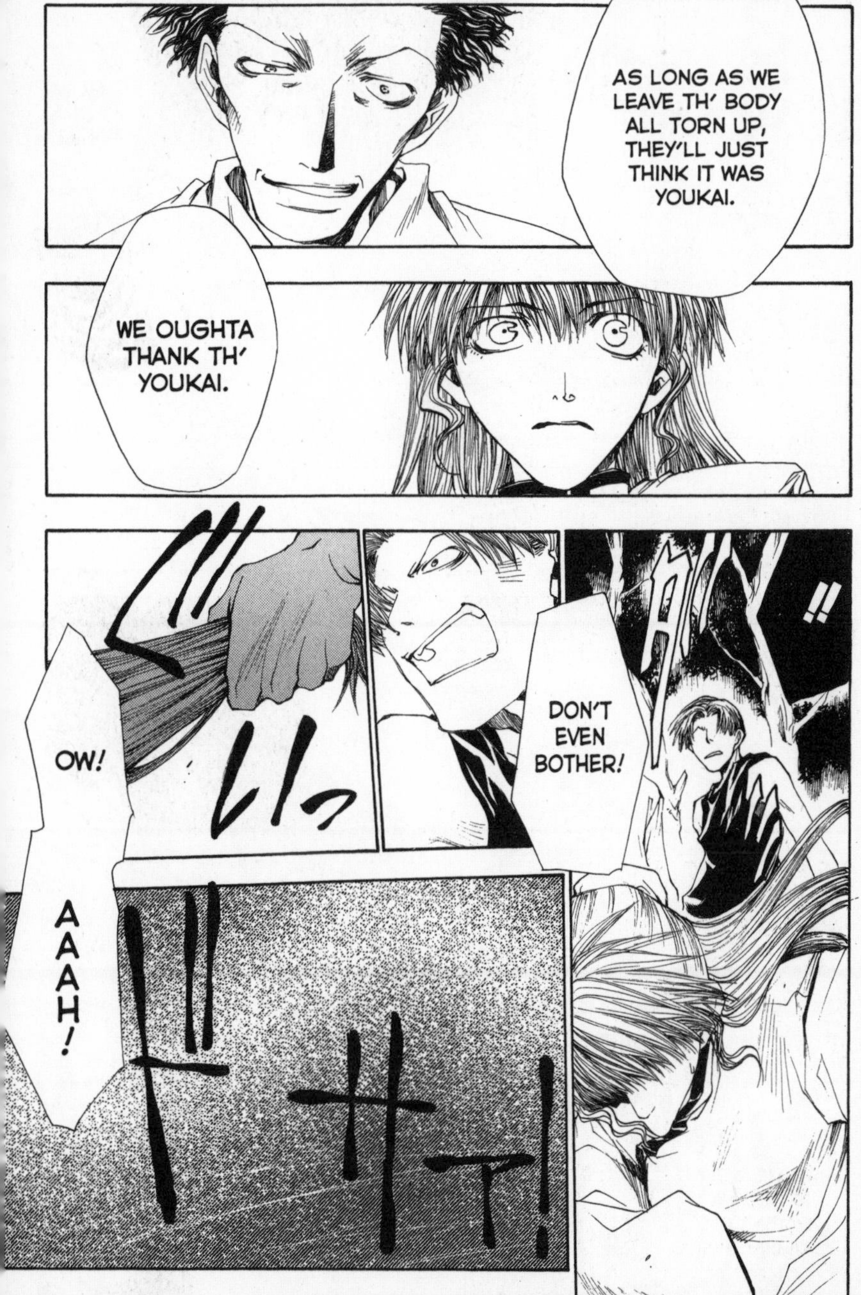
AS LONG AS WE LEAVE TH' BODY ALL TORN UP, THEY'LL JUST THINK IT WAS YOUKAI.
WE OUGHTA THANK TH' YOUKAI.
DON'T EVEN BOTHER!
OW!
AAAH!

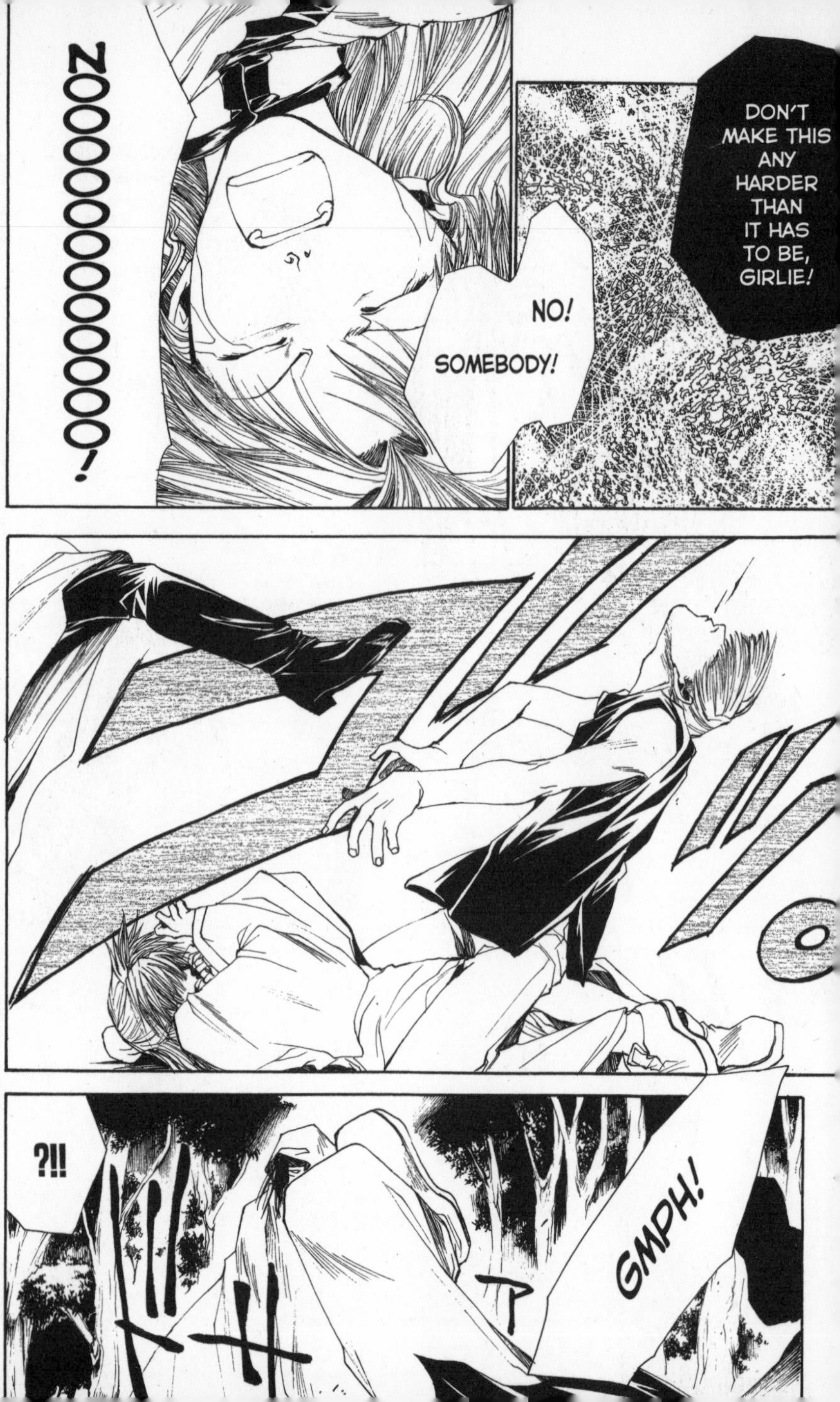
DON'T MAKE THIS ANY HARDER THAN IT HAS TO BE, GIRLIE!
NO!
SOMEBODY!
NOOOOOOOOOOOOO!
GMPH!
?!!

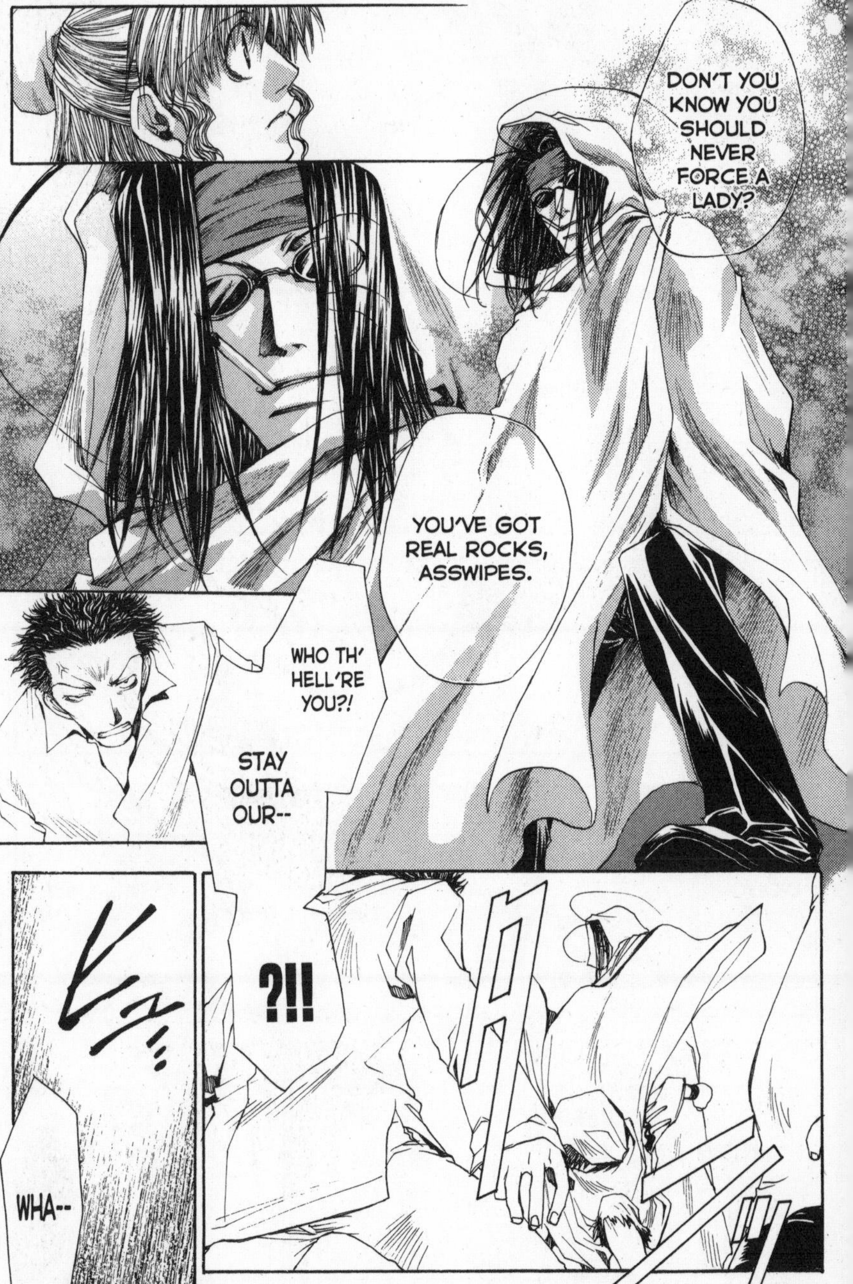
DON'T YOU KNOW YOU SHOULD NEVER FORCE A LADY?
YOU'VE GOT REAL ROCKS, ASSWIPES.
WHO TH' HELL'RE YOU?!
STAY OUTTA OUR--
?!!
WHA--

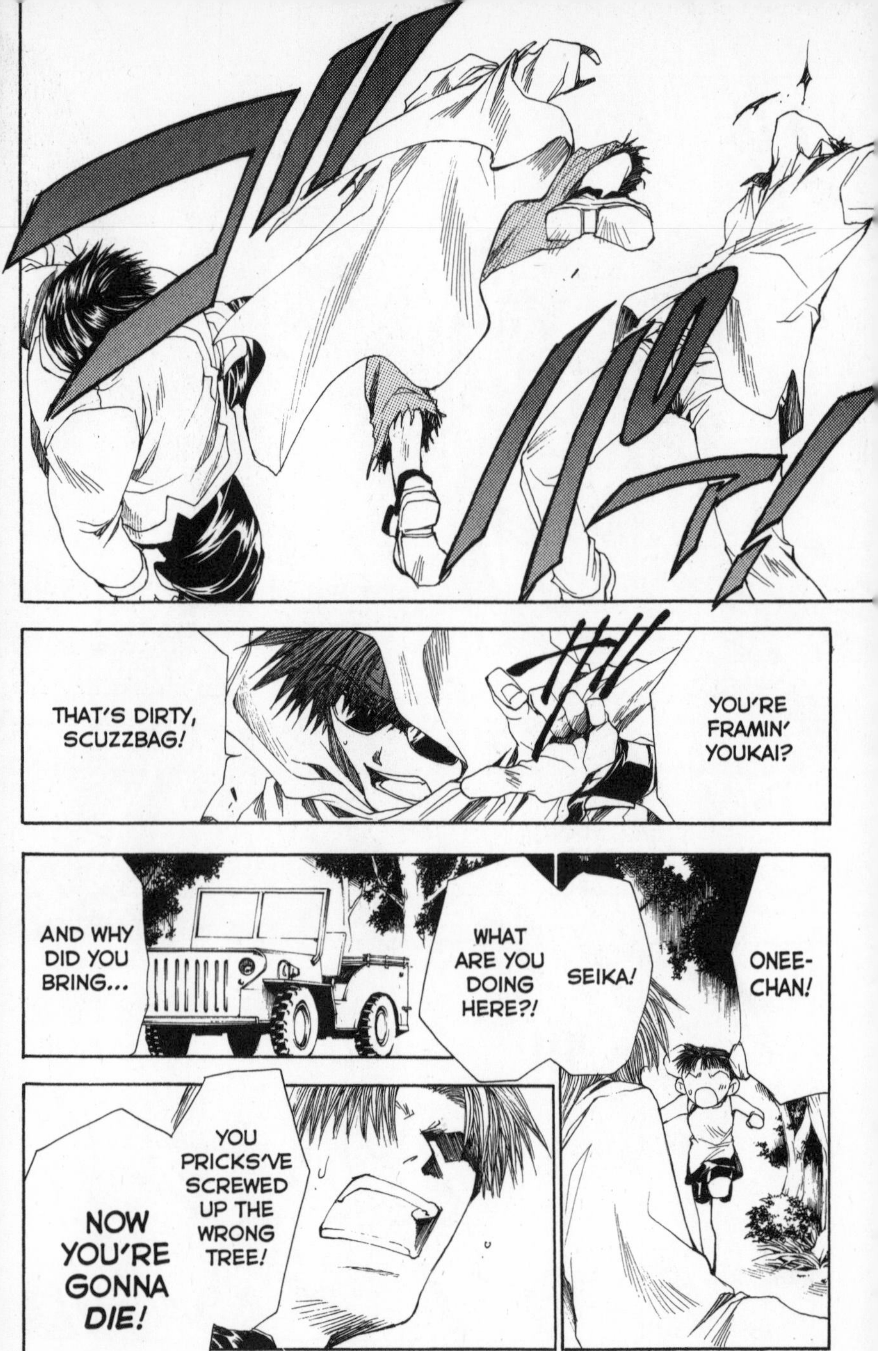
YOU'RE FRAMIN' YOUKAI?
THAT'S DIRTY, SCUZZBAG!
ONEE-CHAN!
SEIKA!
WHAT ARE YOU DOING HERE?!
AND WHY DID YOU BRING...
YOU PRICKS'VE SCREWED UP THE WRONG TREE!
NOW YOU'RE GONNA DIE!

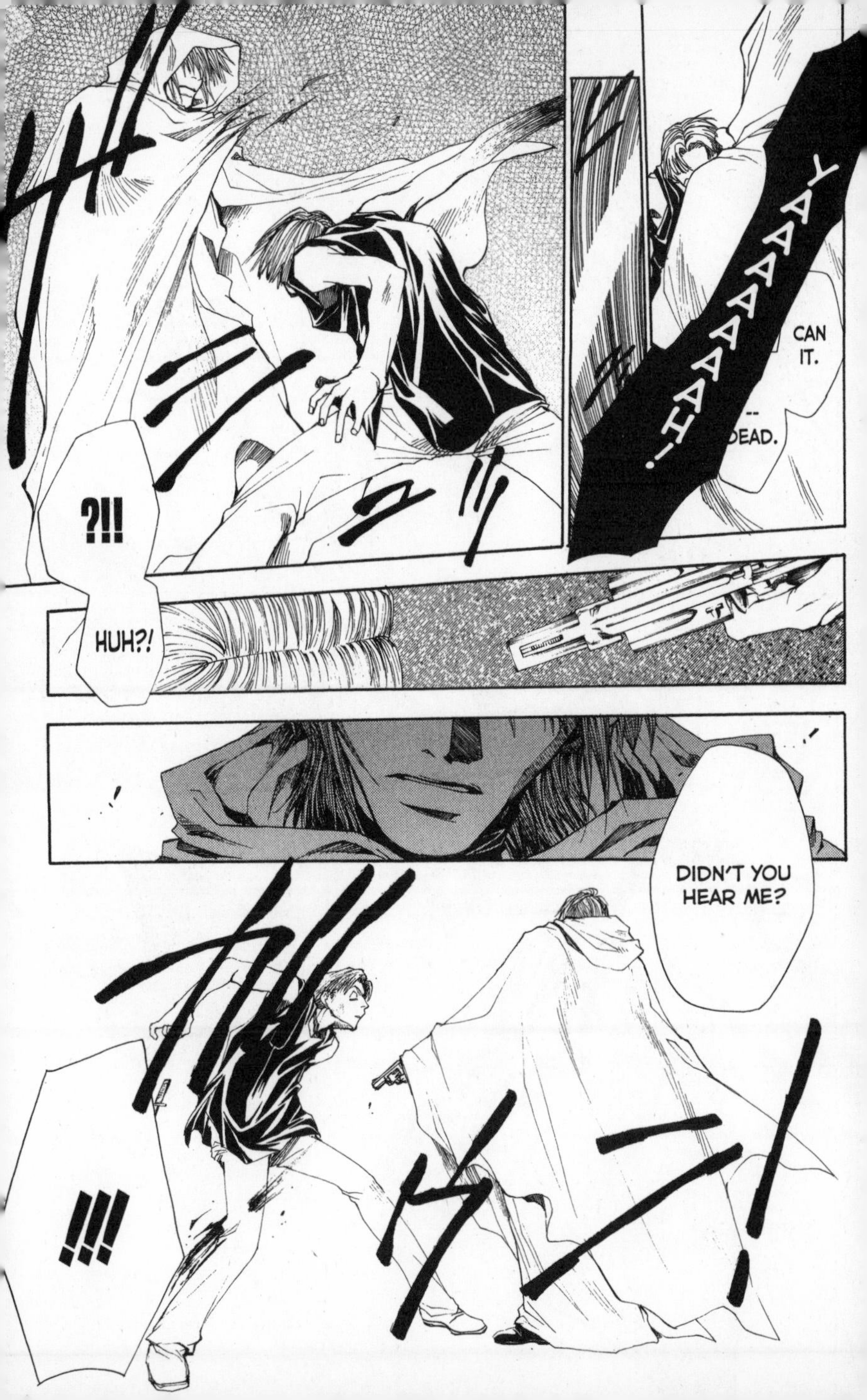
CAN IT.
YAAAAAAAAAH!
-- DEAD.
?!!
HUH?!
DIDN'T YOU HEAR ME?
!!!

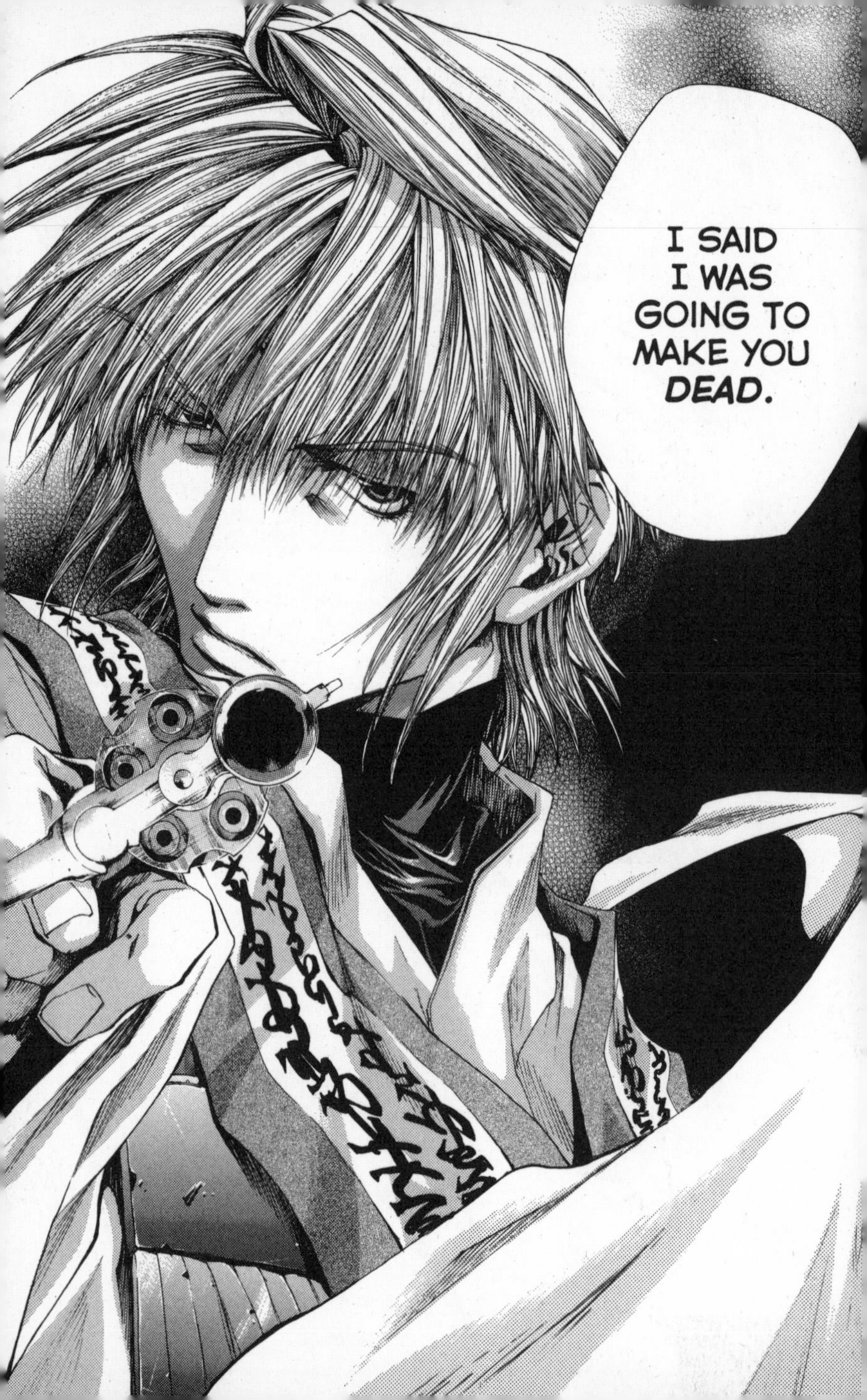
I SAID I WAS GOING TO MAKE YOU *DEAD*.

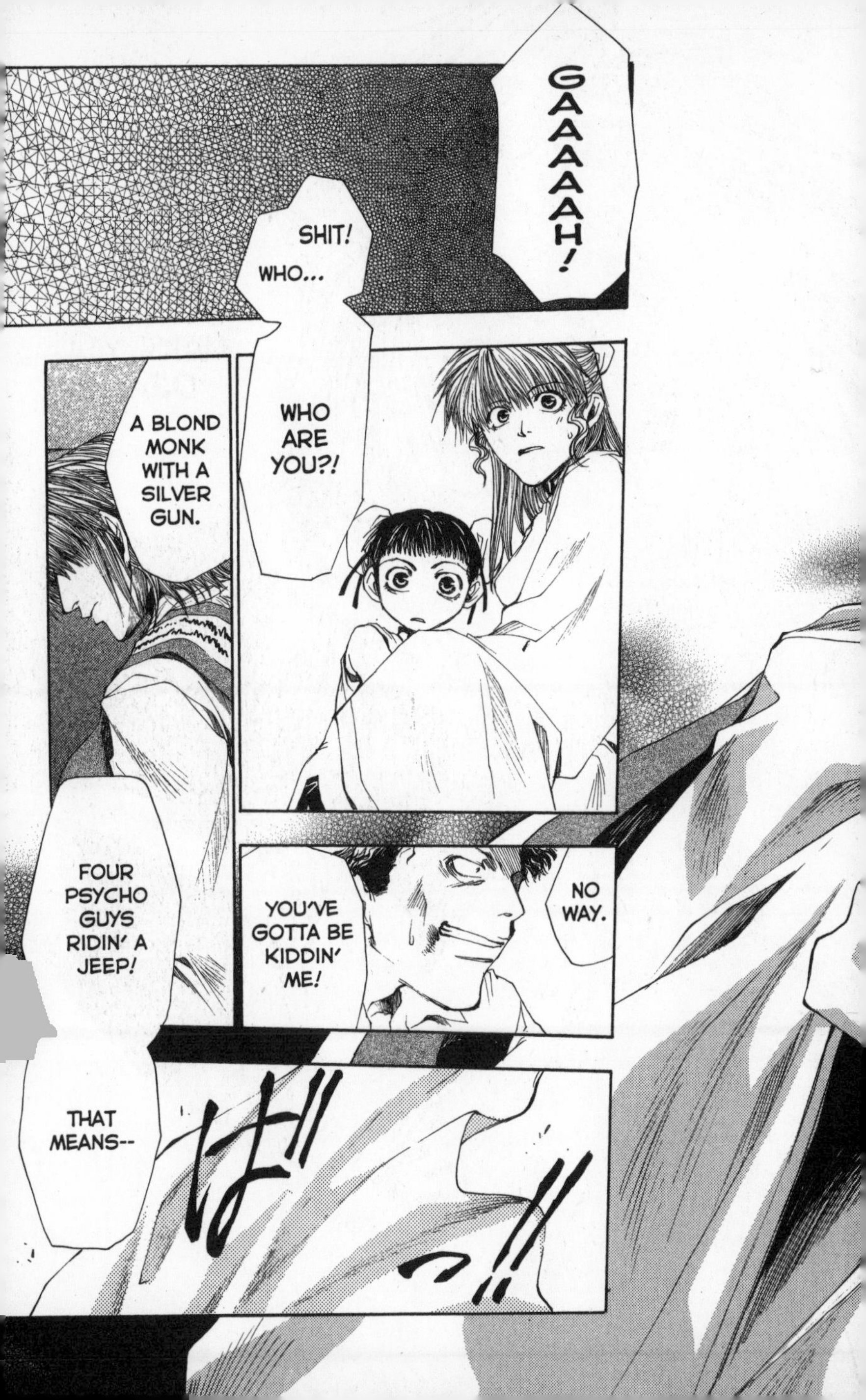
GAAAAAH!
SHIT! WHO...
WHO ARE YOU?!
NO WAY.
YOU'VE GOTTA BE KIDDIN' ME!
A BLOND MONK WITH A SILVER GUN.
FOUR PSYCHO GUYS RIDIN' A JEEP!
はっ!!
THAT MEANS--

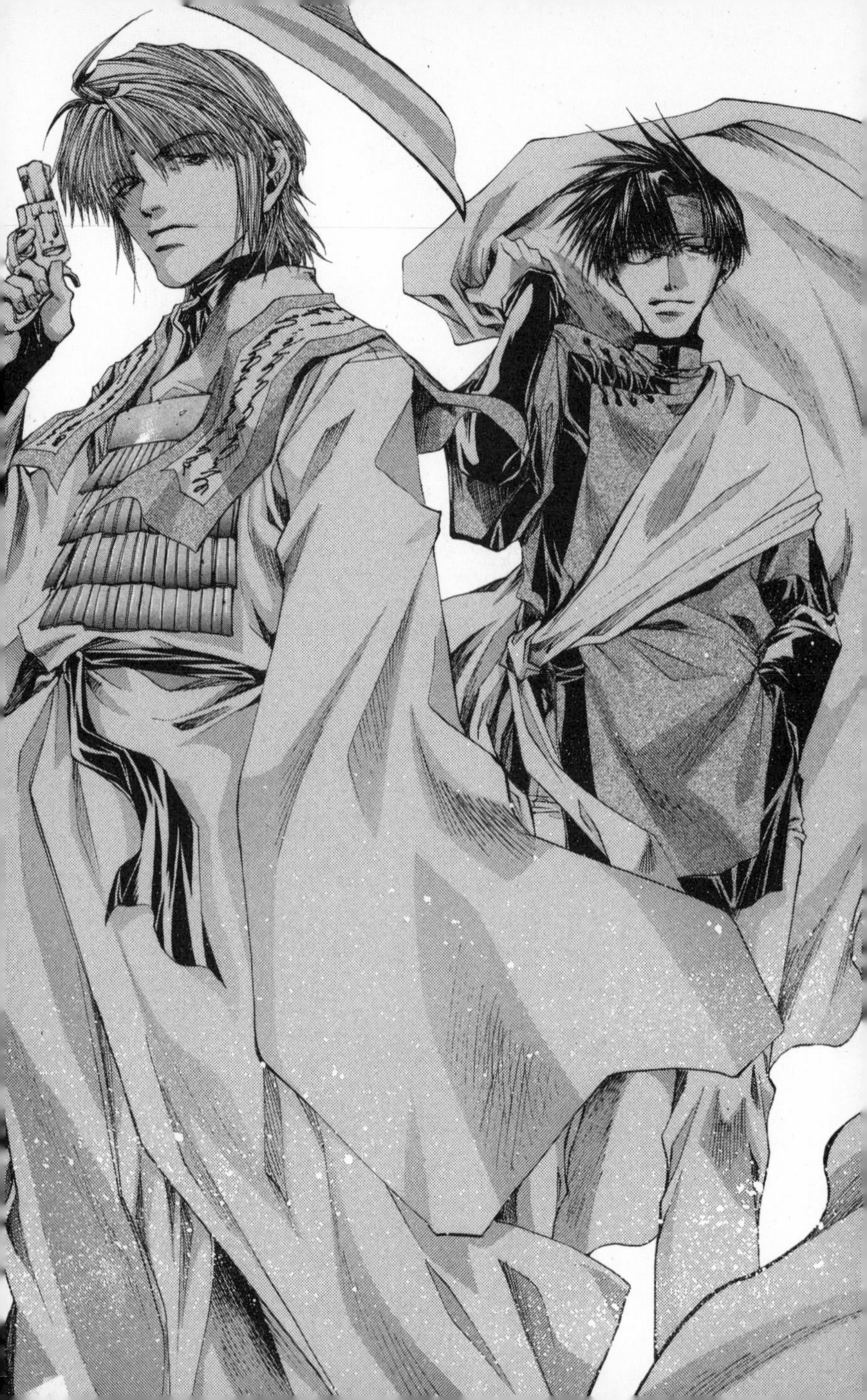

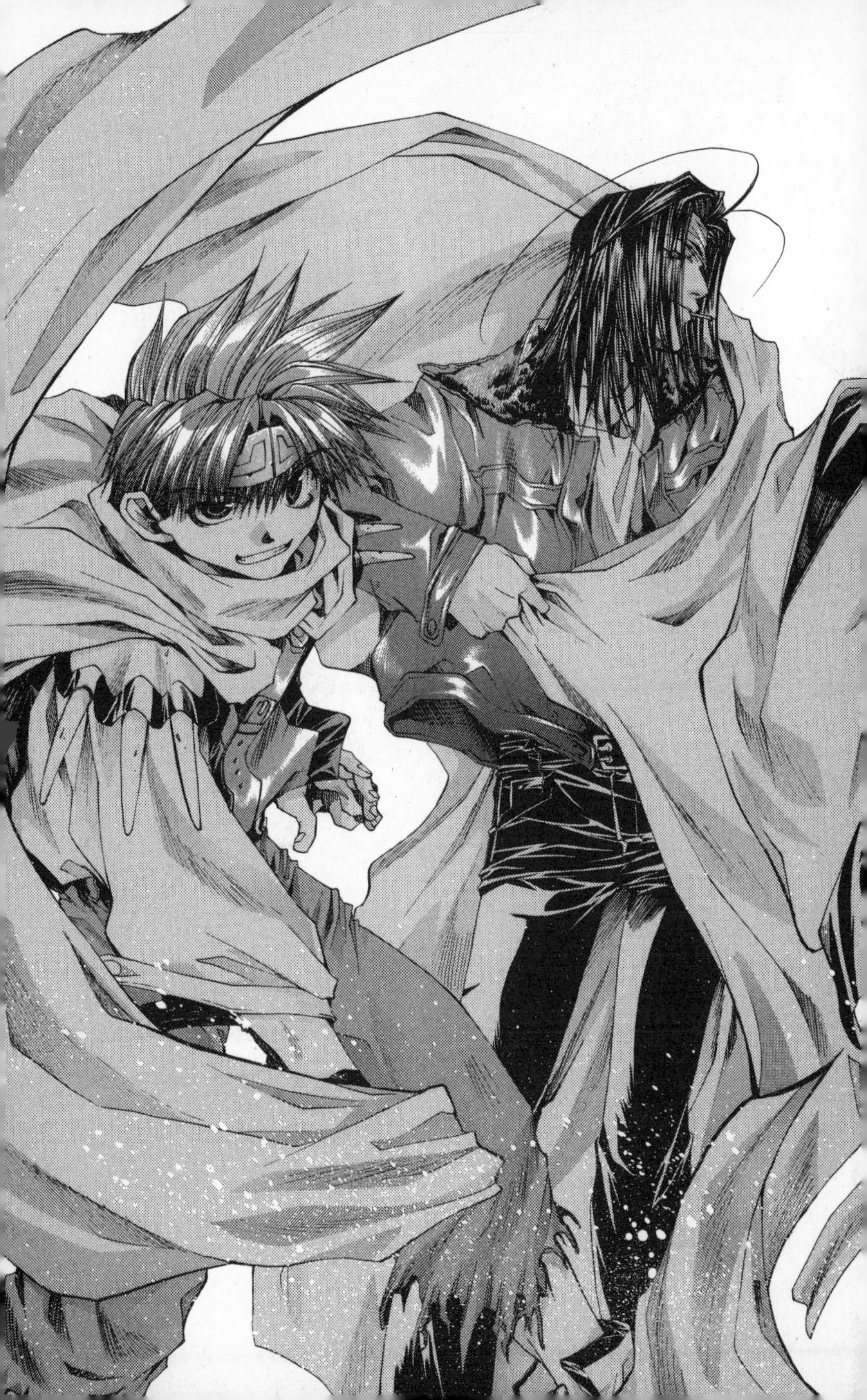

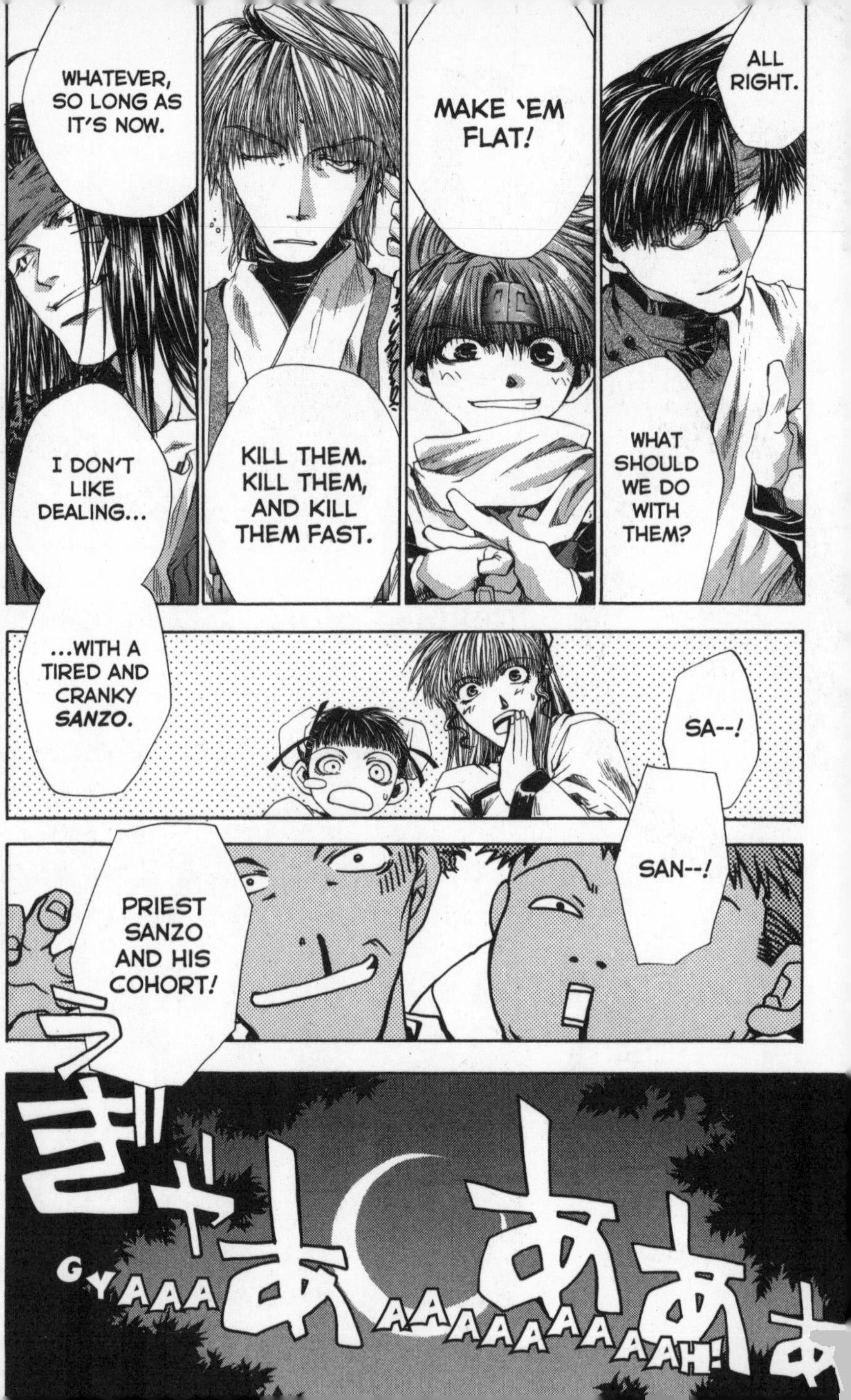
ALL RIGHT.
WHAT SHOULD WE DO WITH THEM?
MAKE 'EM FLAT!
KILL THEM. KILL THEM, AND KILL THEM FAST.
WHATEVER, SO LONG AS IT'S NOW.
I DON'T LIKE DEALING...
...WITH A TIRED AND CRANKY *SANZO.*
SA--!
SAN--!
PRIEST SANZO AND HIS COHORT!
GYAAAAAAAAAAAAAAAH!

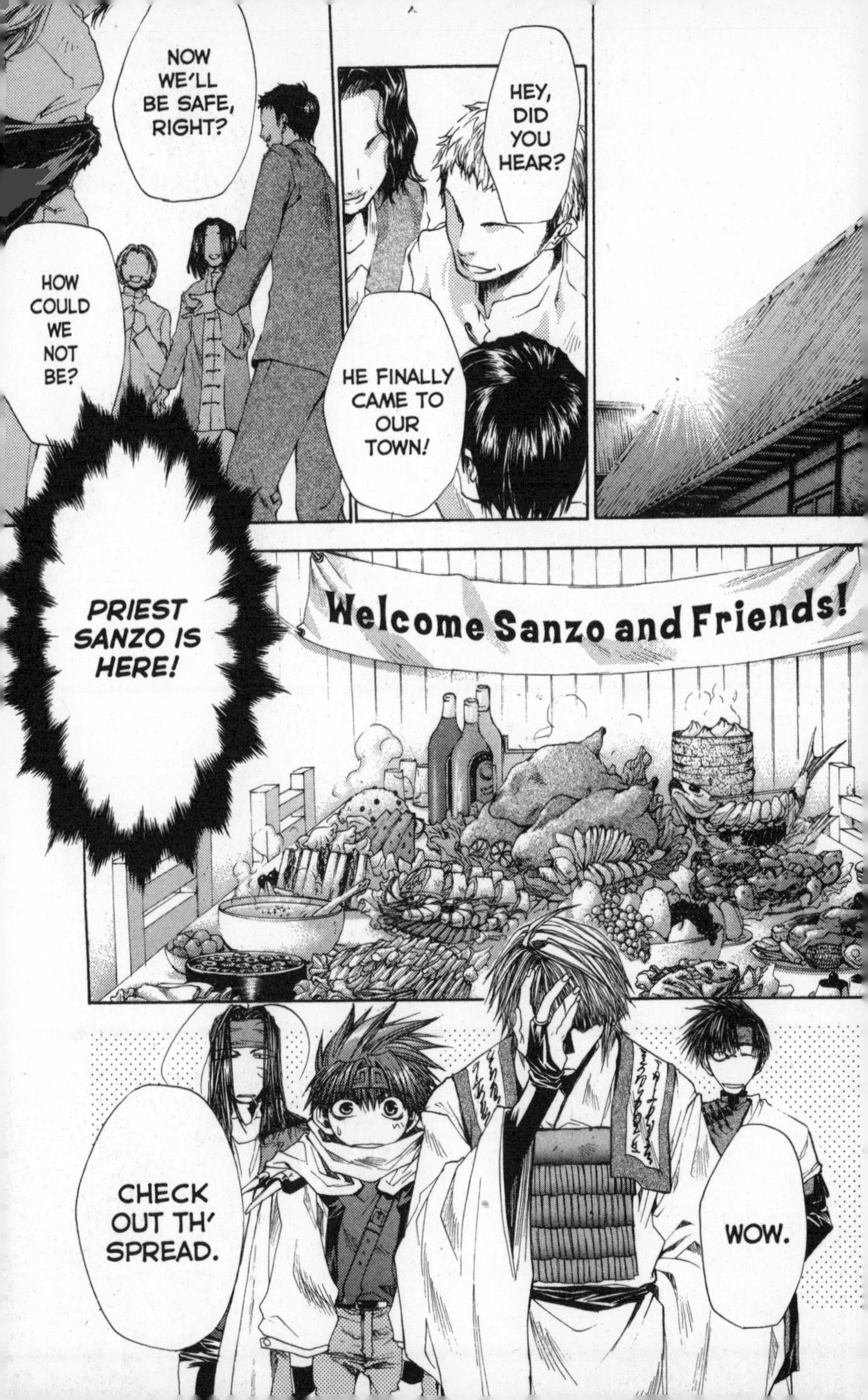
HEY, DID YOU HEAR?
HE FINALLY CAME TO OUR TOWN!
NOW WE'LL BE SAFE, RIGHT?
HOW COULD WE NOT BE?
PRIEST SANZO IS HERE!
Welcome Sanzo and Friends!
WOW.
CHECK OUT TH' SPREAD.

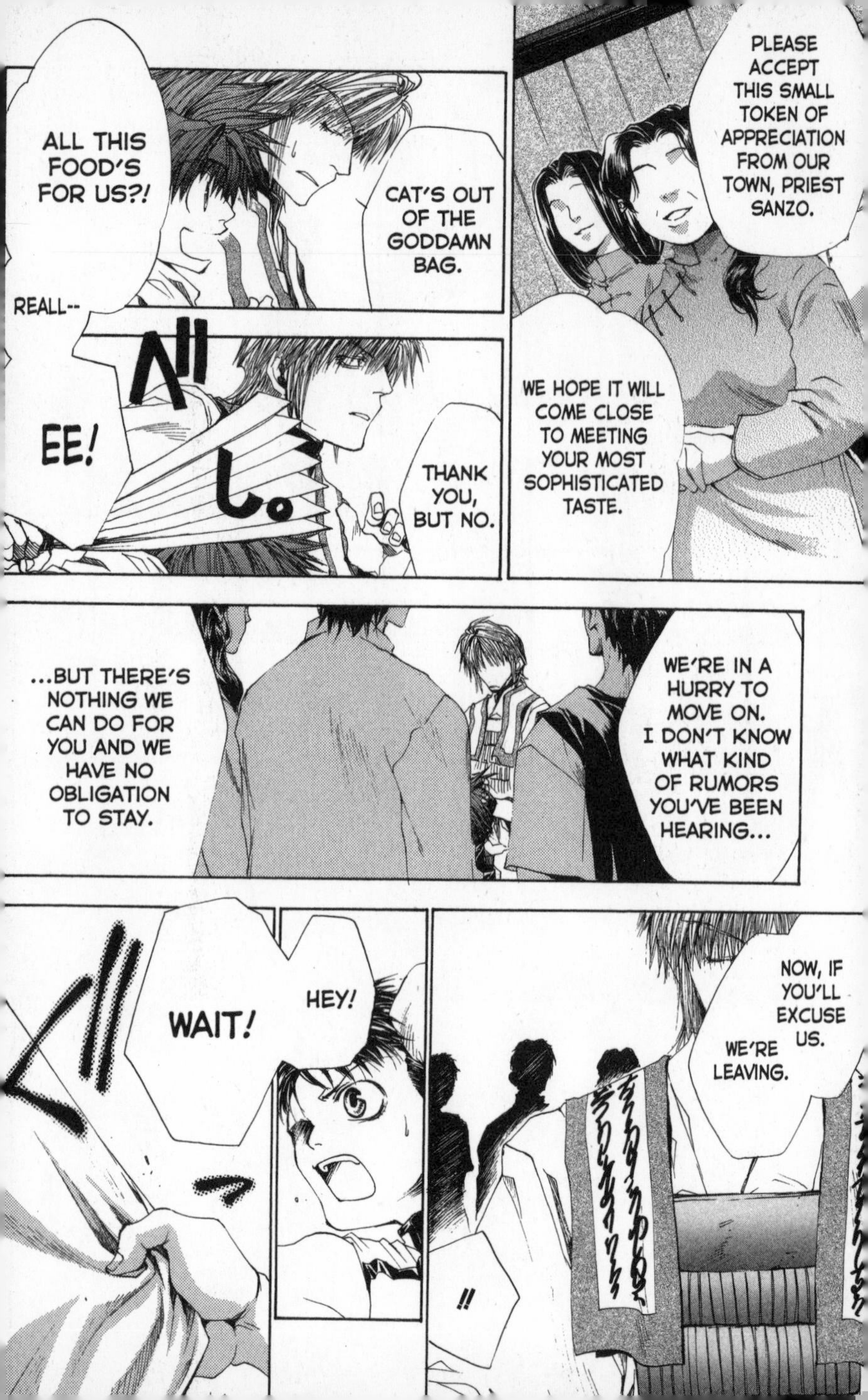
PLEASE ACCEPT THIS SMALL TOKEN OF APPRECIATION FROM OUR TOWN, PRIEST SANZO.
WE HOPE IT WILL COME CLOSE TO MEETING YOUR MOST SOPHISTICATED TASTE.
ALL THIS FOOD'S FOR US?!
CAT'S OUT OF THE GODDAMN BAG.
REALL--
EE!
THANK YOU, BUT NO.
WE'RE IN A HURRY TO MOVE ON. I DON'T KNOW WHAT KIND OF RUMORS YOU'VE BEEN HEARING...
...BUT THERE'S NOTHING WE CAN DO FOR YOU AND WE HAVE NO OBLIGATION TO STAY.
NOW, IF YOU'LL EXCUSE US.
WE'RE LEAVING.
HEY!
!!
WAIT!

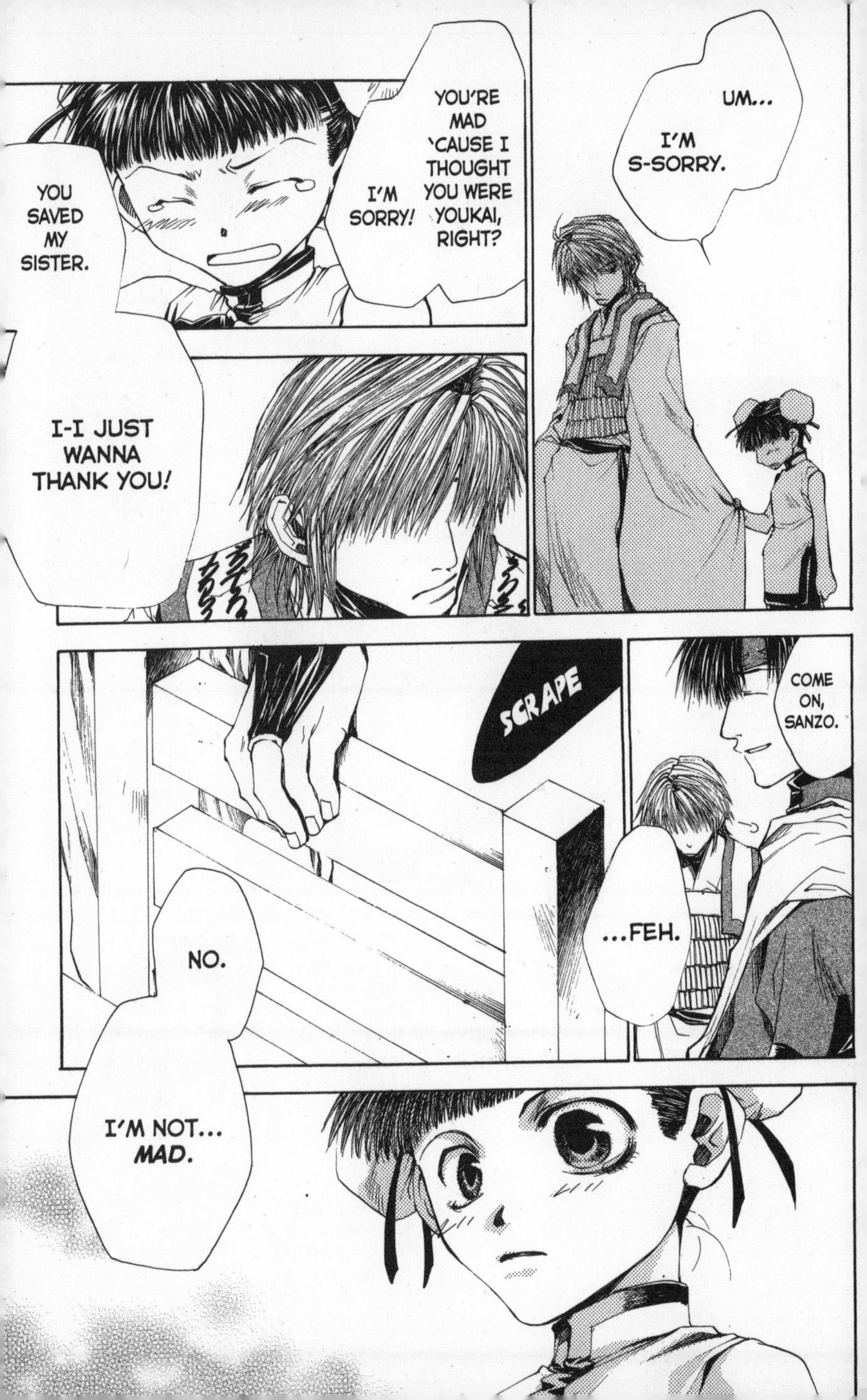
UM...
I'M S-SORRY.
YOU'RE MAD 'CAUSE I THOUGHT YOU WERE YOUKAI, RIGHT?
I'M SORRY!
YOU SAVED MY SISTER.
I-I JUST WANNA THANK YOU!
COME ON, SANZO.
...FEH.
SCRAPE
NO.
I'M NOT... *MAD*.

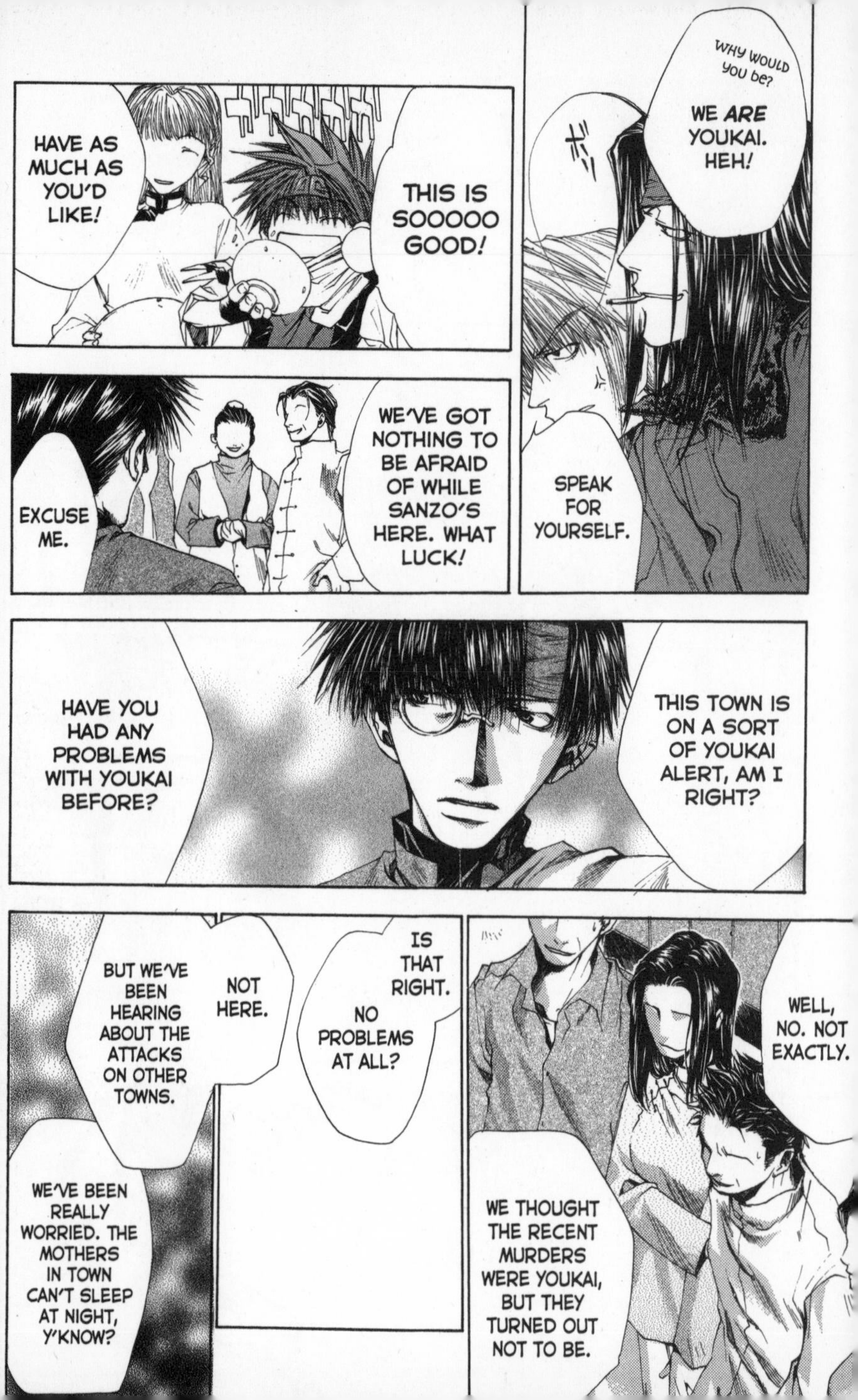
WHY WOULD YOU BE?
WE ARE YOUKAI. HEH!
SPEAK FOR YOURSELF.
THIS IS SOOOOO GOOD!
HAVE AS MUCH AS YOU'D LIKE!
WE'VE GOT NOTHING TO BE AFRAID OF WHILE SANZO'S HERE. WHAT LUCK!
EXCUSE ME.
THIS TOWN IS ON A SORT OF YOUKAI ALERT, AM I RIGHT?
HAVE YOU HAD ANY PROBLEMS WITH YOUKAI BEFORE?
WELL, NO. NOT EXACTLY.
WE THOUGHT THE RECENT MURDERS WERE YOUKAI, BUT THEY TURNED OUT NOT TO BE.
IS THAT RIGHT.
NO PROBLEMS AT ALL?
NOT HERE.
BUT WE'VE BEEN HEARING ABOUT THE ATTACKS ON OTHER TOWNS.
WE'VE BEEN REALLY WORRIED. THE MOTHERS IN TOWN CAN'T SLEEP AT NIGHT, Y'KNOW?

!

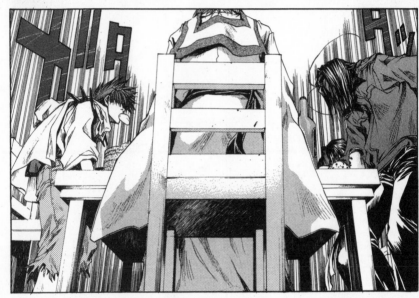

HUH?

THANK YOU FOR THE HOSPITALITY. *NOW* WE'RE LEAVING.

?

PRIEST SANZO?

SORRY FOR LEAVIN' LEFT-OVERS!

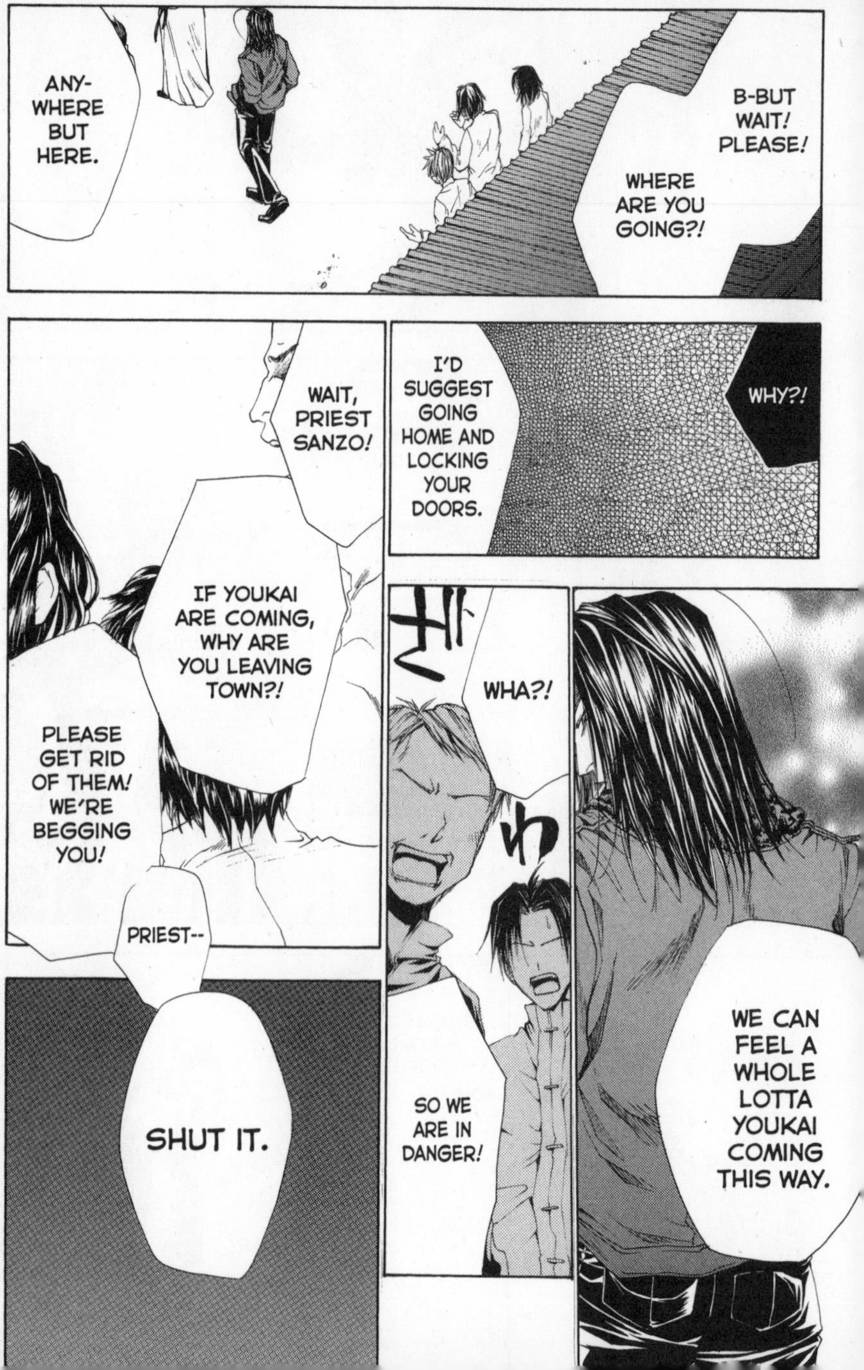
B-BUT WAIT! PLEASE!
WHERE ARE YOU GOING?!
ANY-WHERE BUT HERE.
WHY?!
I'D SUGGEST GOING HOME AND LOCKING YOUR DOORS.
WE CAN FEEL A WHOLE LOTTA YOUKAI COMING THIS WAY.
ざわ
WHA?!
SO WE ARE IN DANGER!
WAIT, PRIEST SANZO!
IF YOUKAI ARE COMING, WHY ARE YOU LEAVING TOWN?!
PLEASE GET RID OF THEM! WE'RE BEGGING YOU!
PRIEST--
SHUT IT.

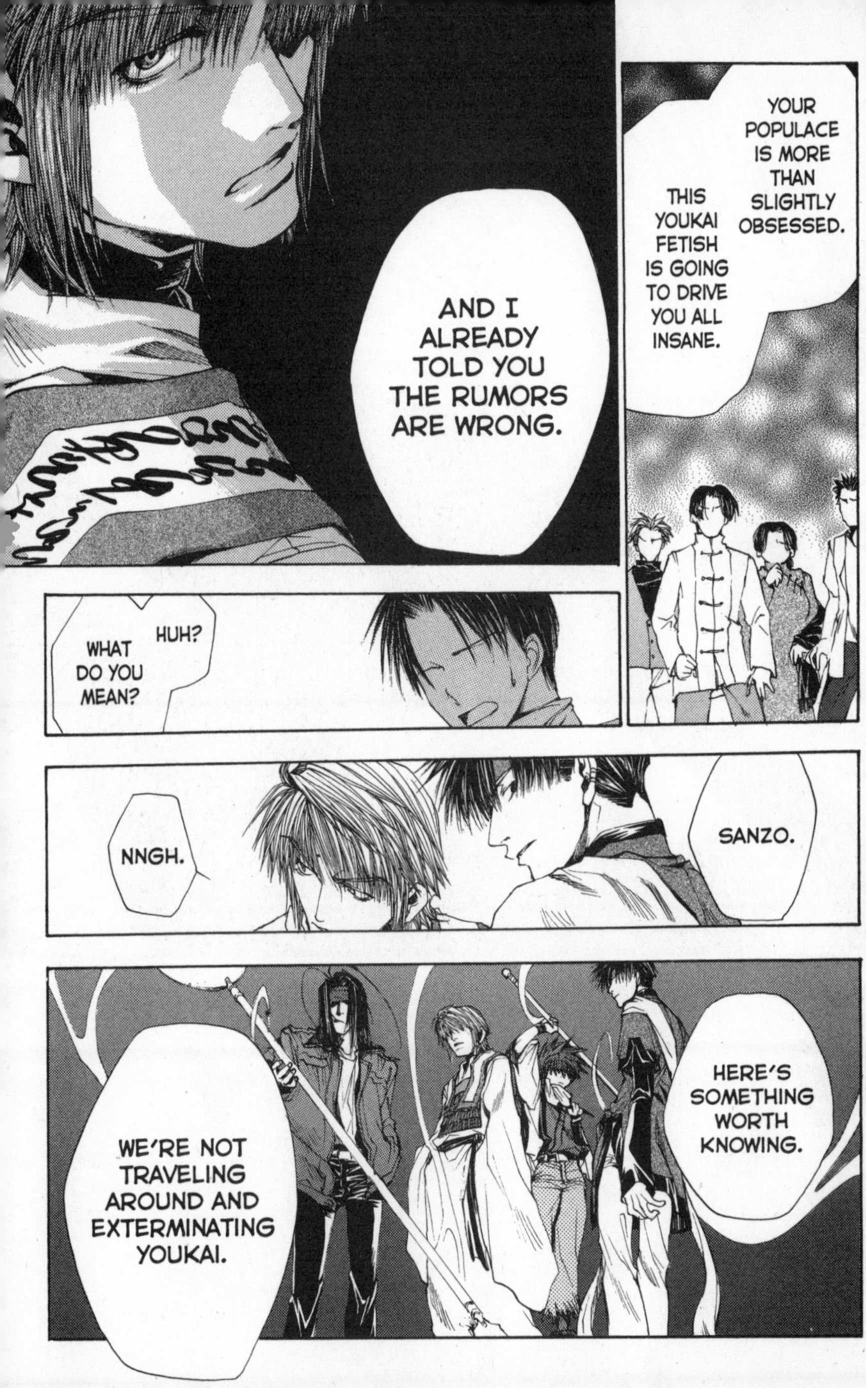
YOUR POPULACE IS MORE THAN SLIGHTLY OBSESSED.
THIS YOUKAI FETISH IS GOING TO DRIVE YOU ALL INSANE.
AND I ALREADY TOLD YOU THE RUMORS ARE WRONG.
HUH?
WHAT DO YOU MEAN?
SANZO.
NNGH.
HERE'S SOMETHING WORTH KNOWING.
WE'RE NOT TRAVELING AROUND AND EXTERMINATING YOUKAI.

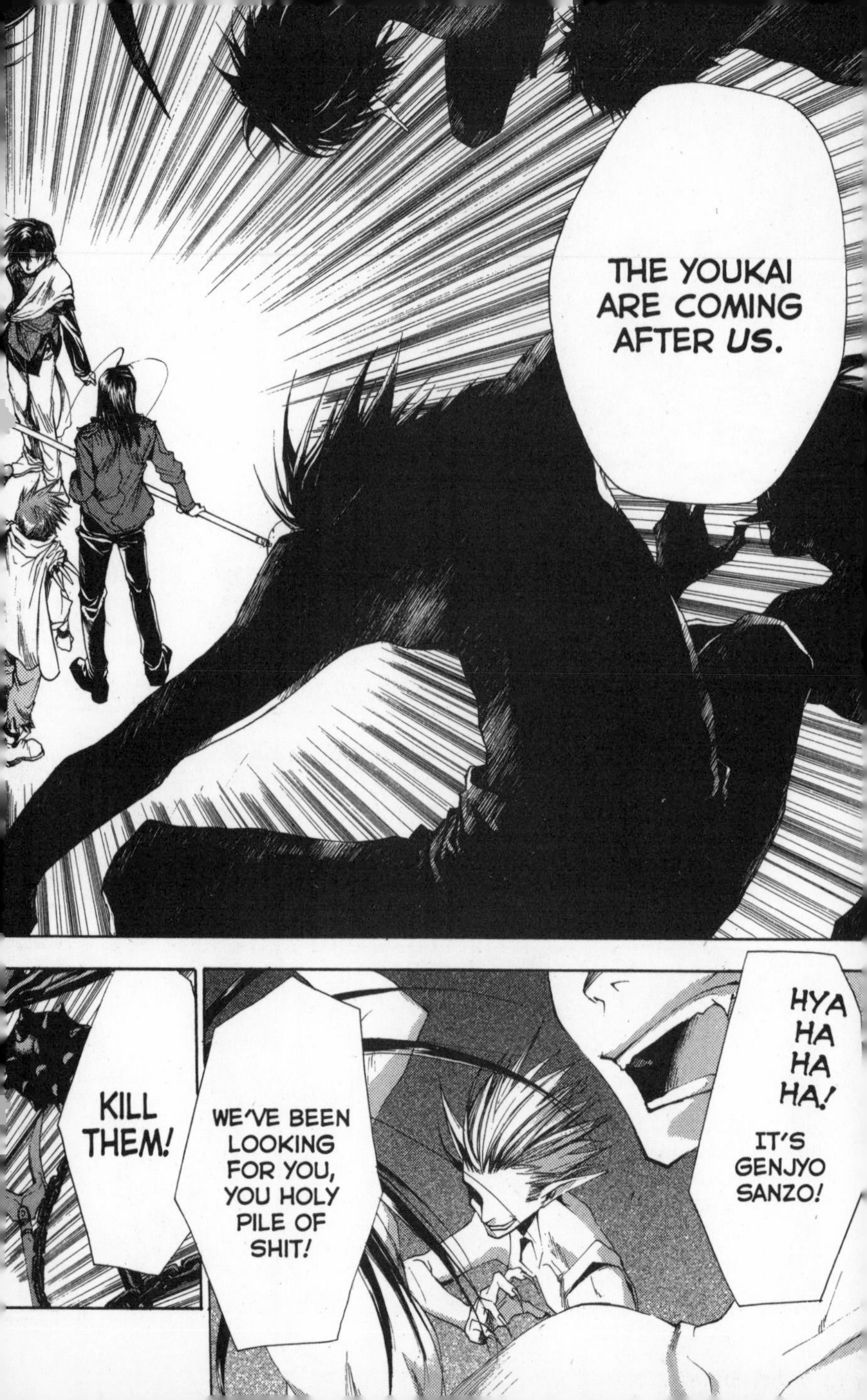
THE YOUKAI ARE COMING AFTER US.
HYA HA HA HA!
IT'S GENJYO SANZO!
WE'VE BEEN LOOKING FOR YOU, YOU HOLY PILE OF SHIT!
KILL THEM!

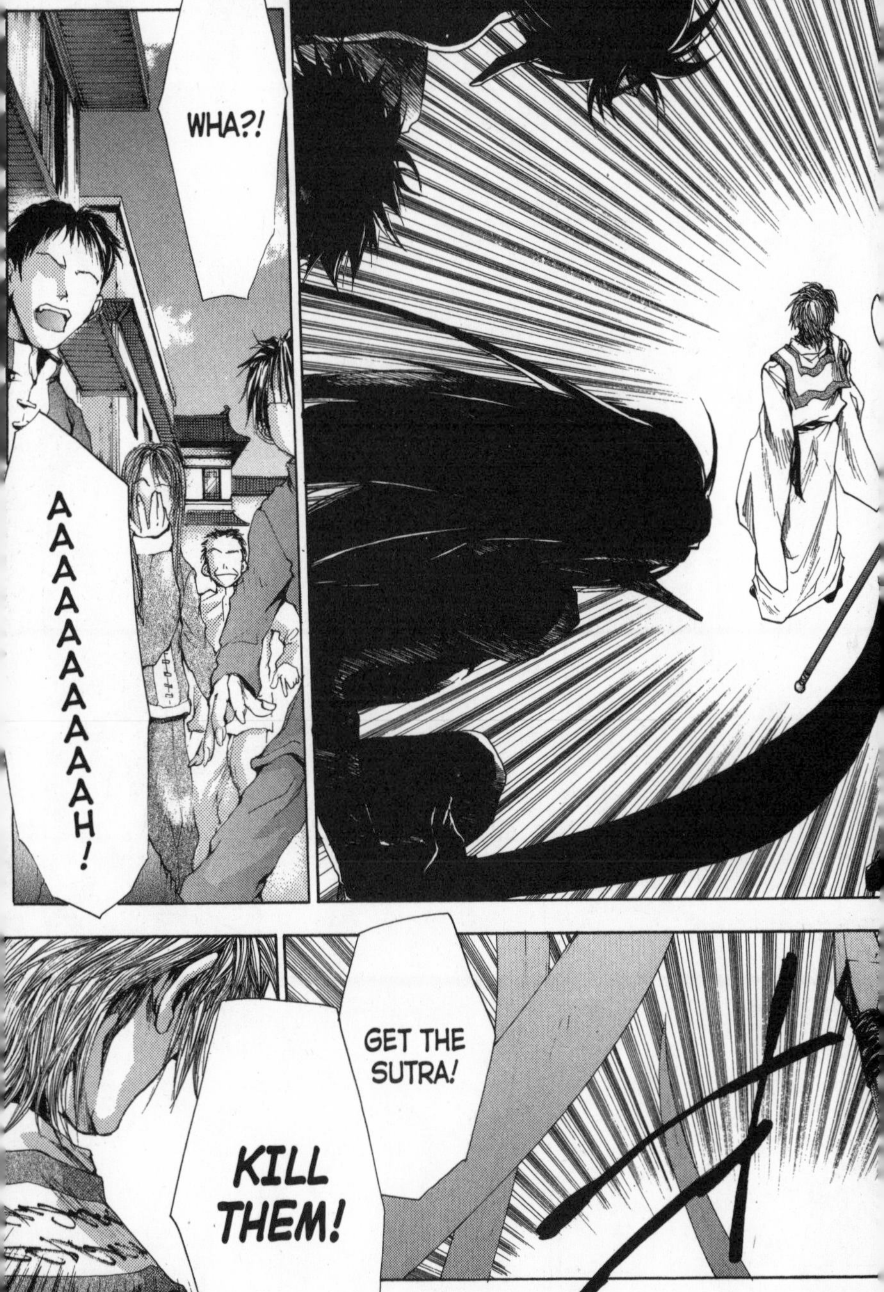
WHA?!
AAAAAAAAAAAAH!
GET THE SUTRA!
KILL THEM!

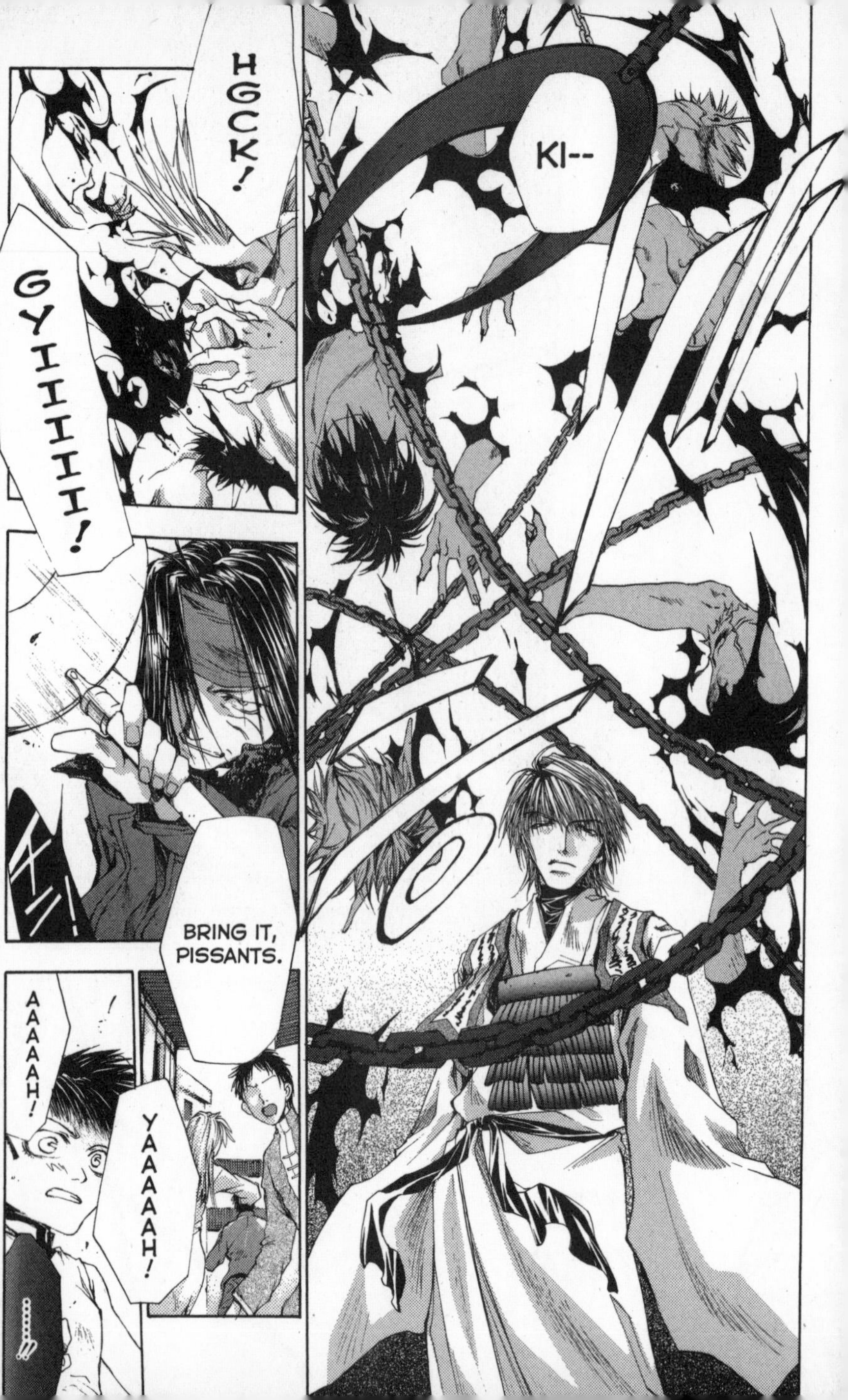
KI--
BRING IT, PISSANTS.
HGCK!
GYIIIIII!
YAAAAAAH!
AAAAAH!

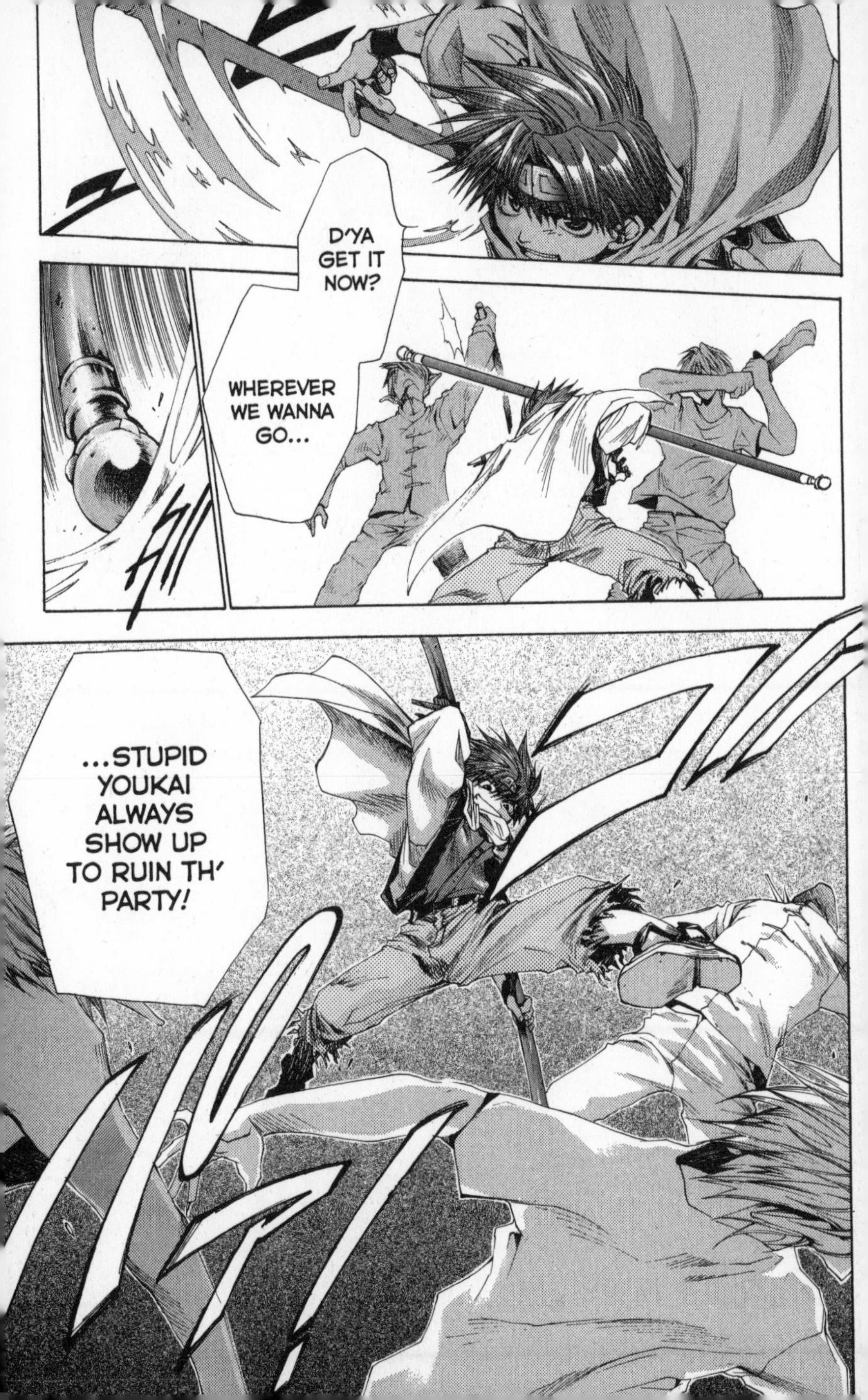
D'YA GET IT NOW?
WHEREVER WE WANNA GO...
...STUPID YOUKAI ALWAYS SHOW UP TO RUIN TH' PARTY!

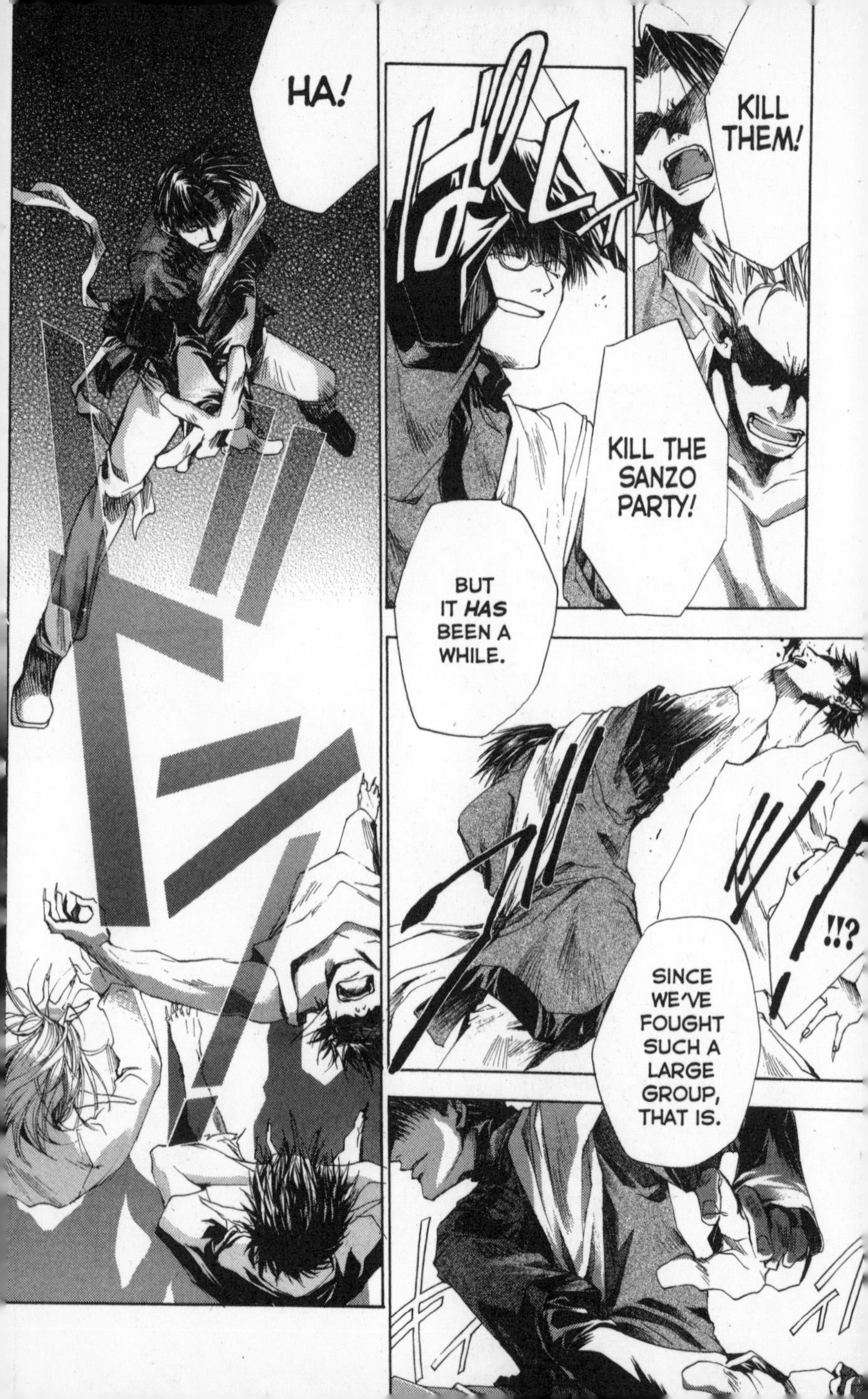
KILL THEM!
KILL THE SANZO PARTY!
BUT IT *HAS* BEEN A WHILE.
!!?
SINCE WE'VE FOUGHT SUCH A LARGE GROUP, THAT IS.
HA!

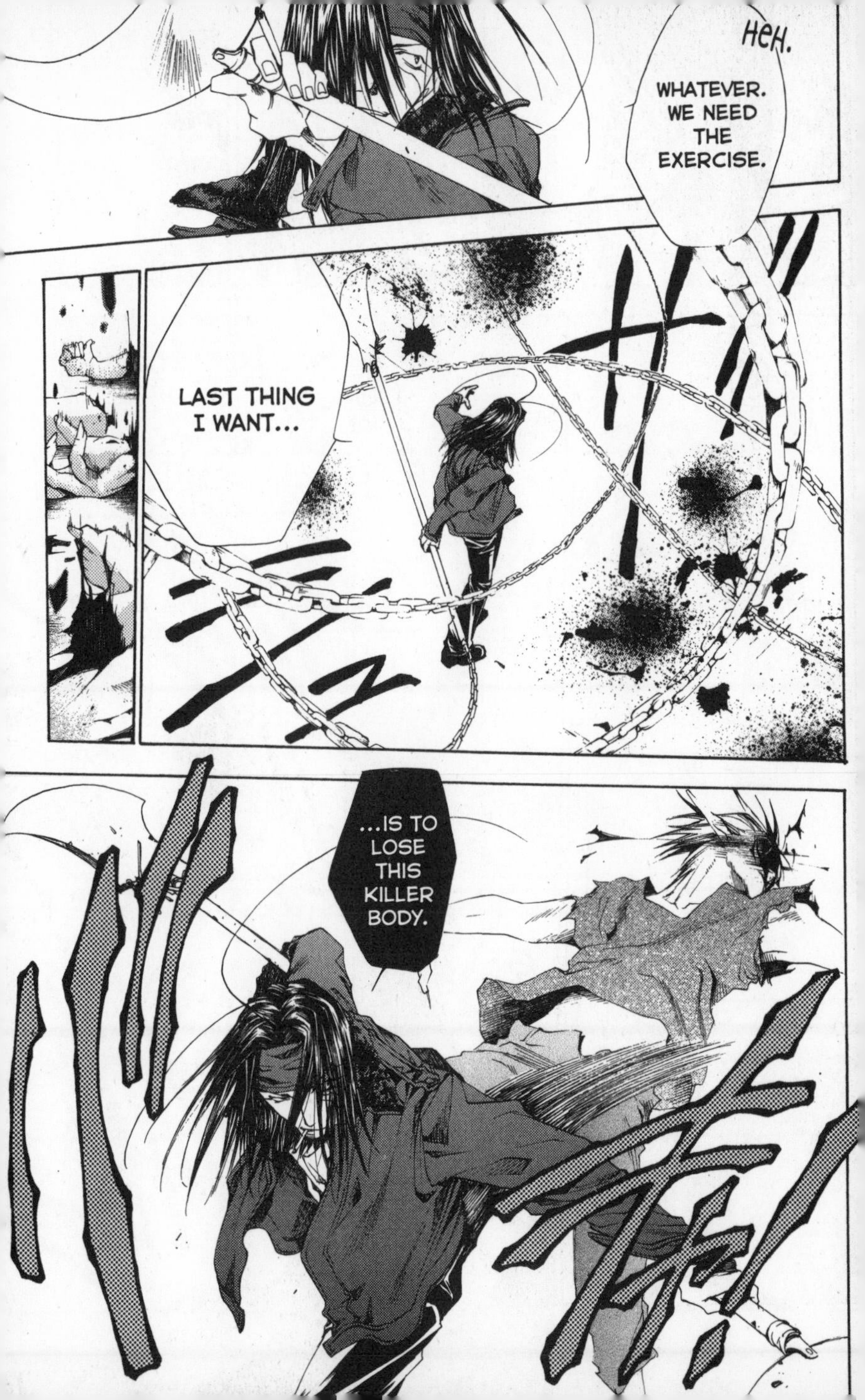
HeH.
WHATEVER. WE NEED THE EXERCISE.
LAST THING I WANT...
...IS TO LOSE THIS KILLER BODY.

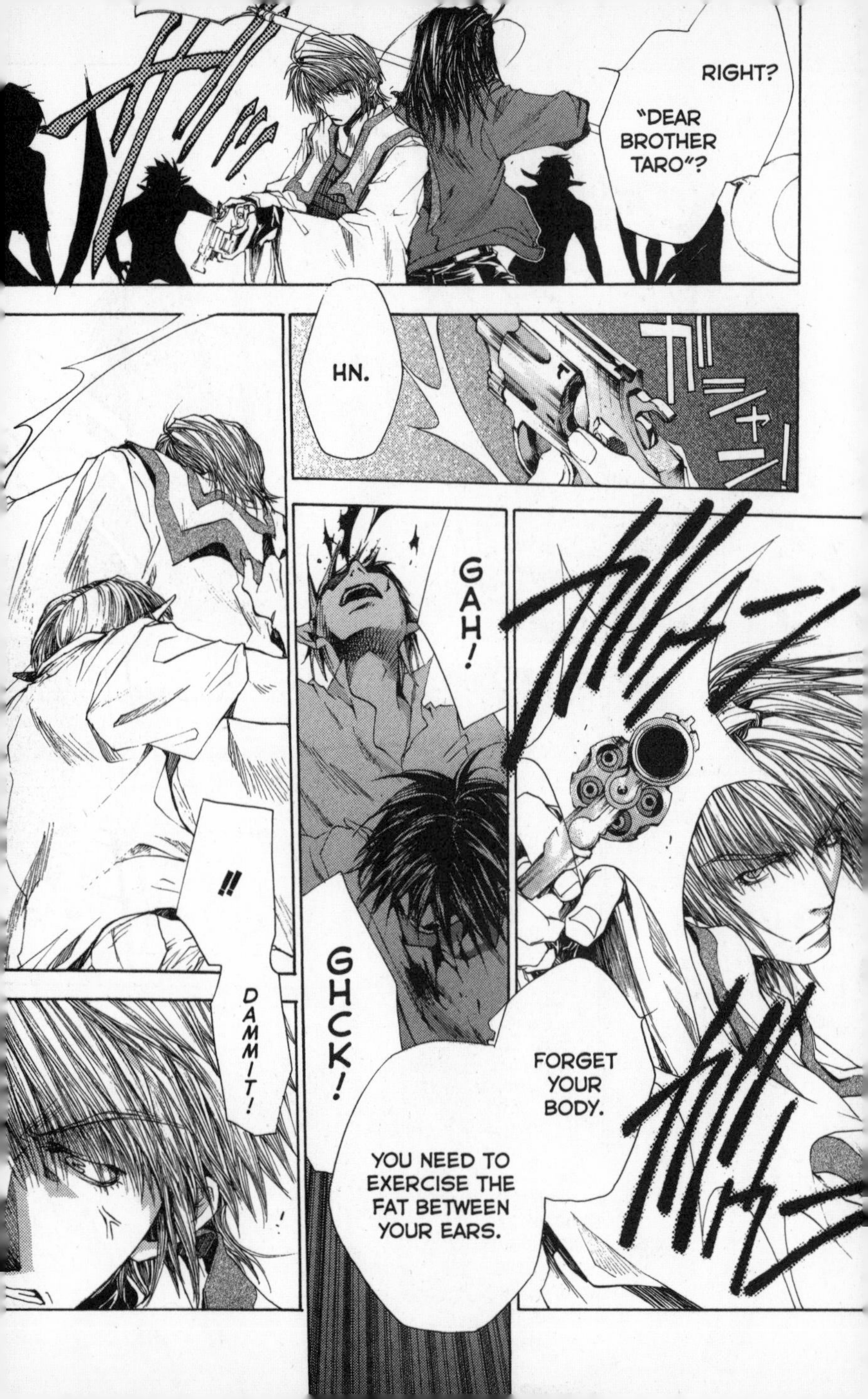
RIGHT?
"DEAR BROTHER TARO"?
HN.
FORGET YOUR BODY.
YOU NEED TO EXERCISE THE FAT BETWEEN YOUR EARS.
GAH!
GHCK!
!!
DAMMIT!

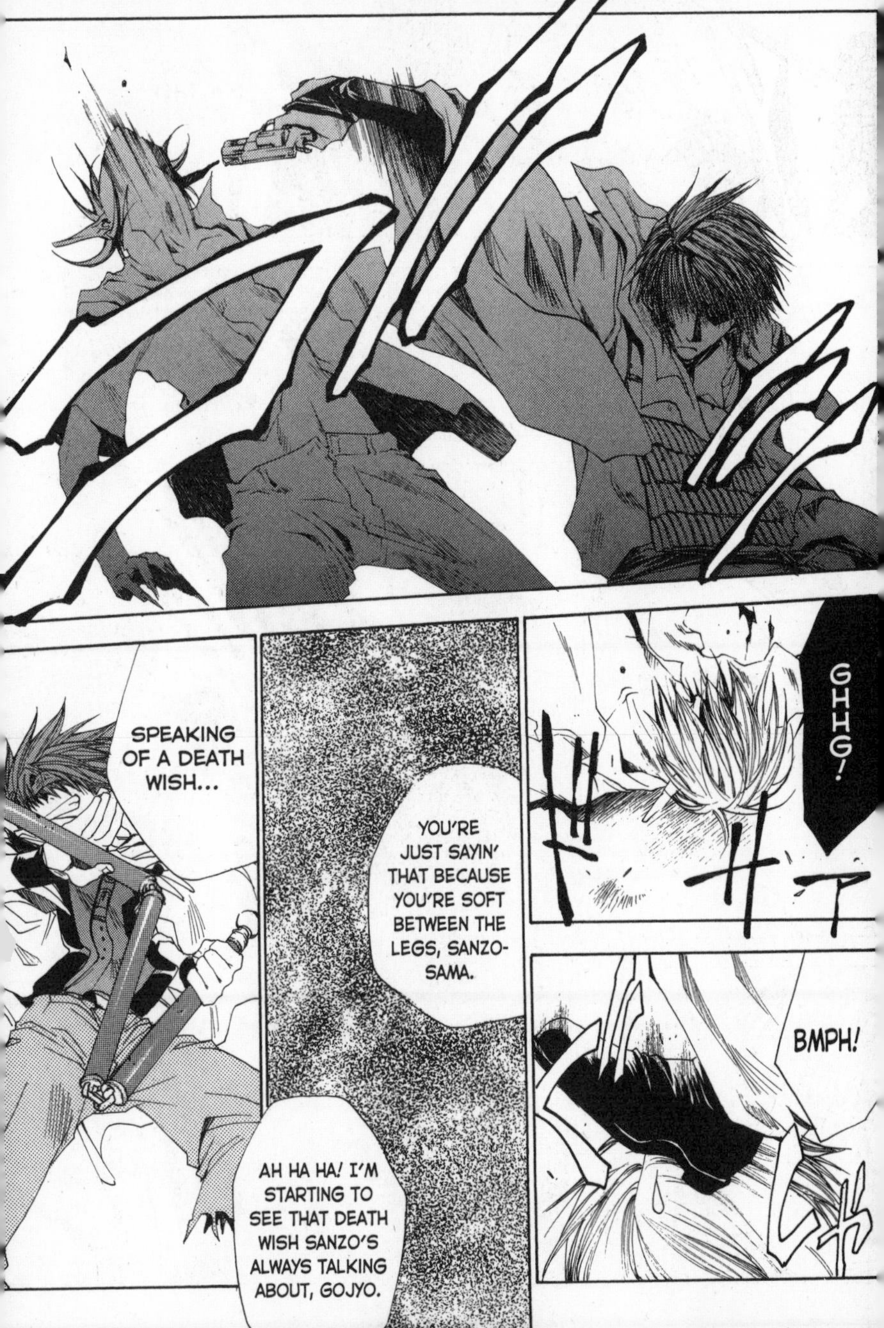
GHHG!
BMPH!
YOU'RE JUST SAYIN' THAT BECAUSE YOU'RE SOFT BETWEEN THE LEGS, SANZO-SAMA.
AH HA HA! I'M STARTING TO SEE THAT DEATH WISH SANZO'S ALWAYS TALKING ABOUT, GOJYO.
SPEAKING OF A DEATH WISH...

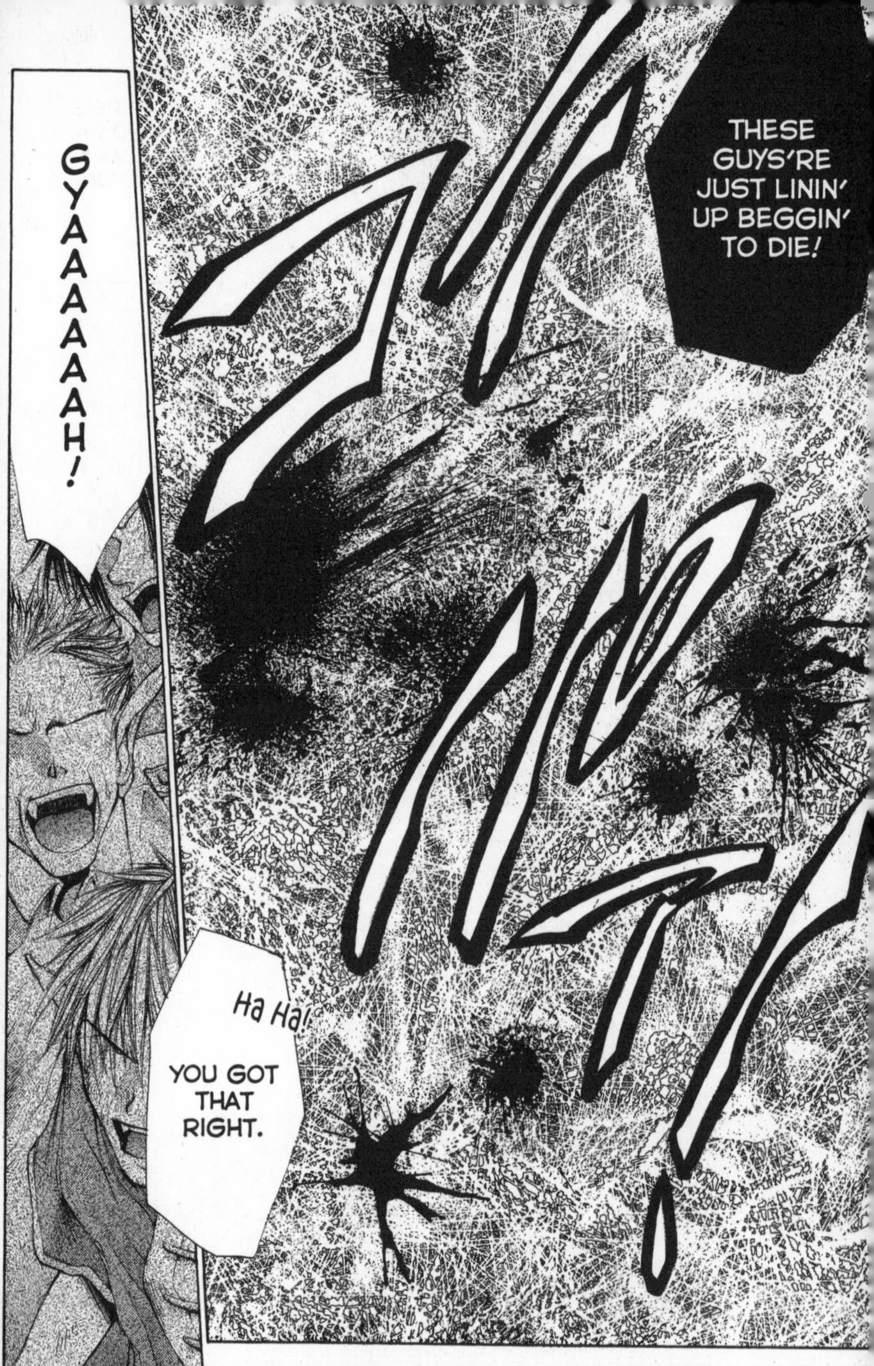
THESE GUYS'RE JUST LININ' UP BEGGIN' TO DIE!
GYAAAAAAAH!
Ha Ha!
YOU GOT THAT RIGHT.

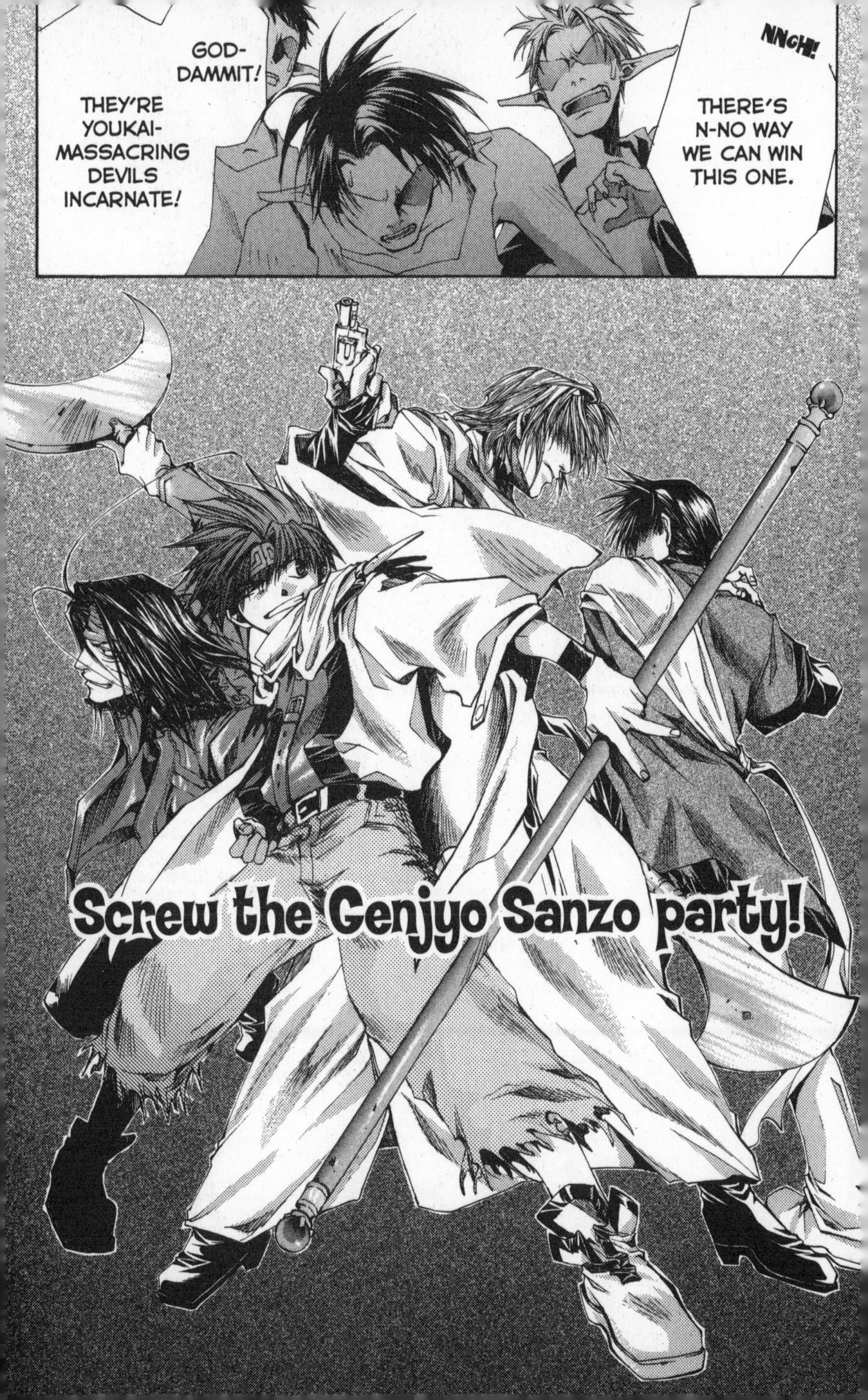
NNGH!
THERE'S N-NO WAY WE CAN WIN THIS ONE.
GOD-DAMMIT!
THEY'RE YOUKAI-MASSACRING DEVILS INCARNATE!
Screw the Genjyo Sanzo party!

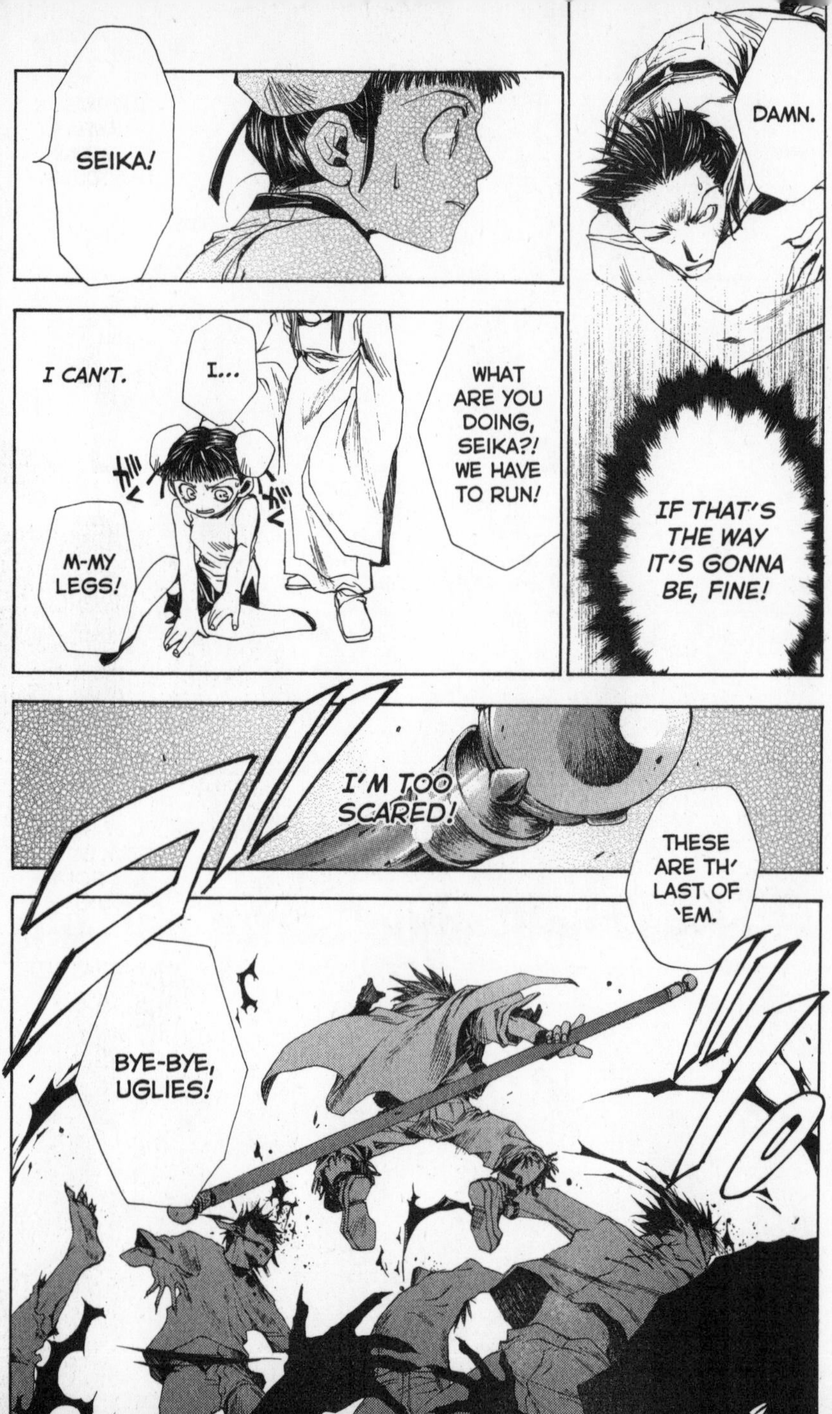
DAMN.
IF THAT'S THE WAY IT'S GONNA BE, FINE!
SEIKA!
WHAT ARE YOU DOING, SEIKA?! WE HAVE TO RUN!
I...
I CAN'T.
M-MY LEGS!
I'M TOO SCARED!
THESE ARE TH' LAST OF 'EM.
BYE-BYE, UGLIES!

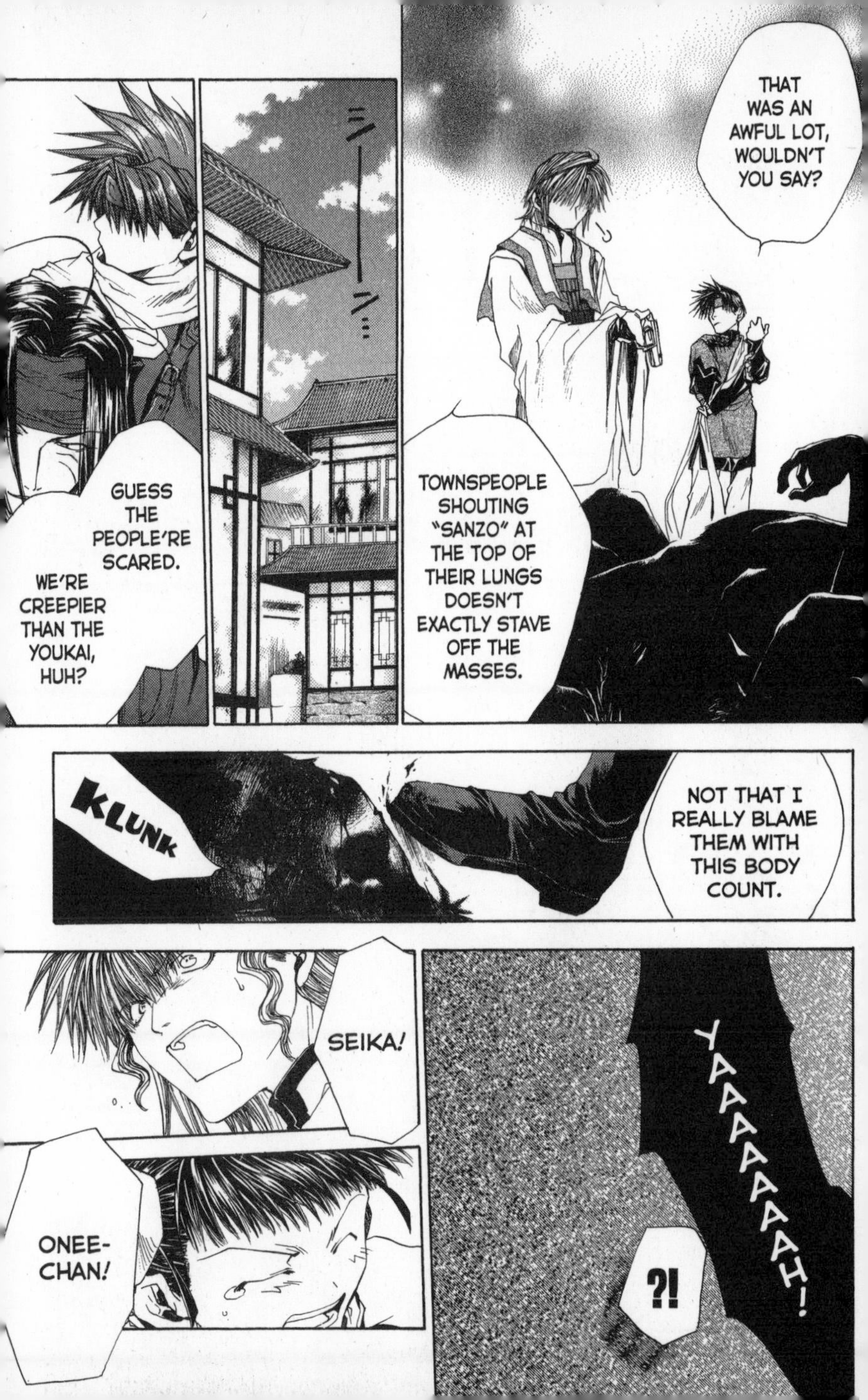
THAT WAS AN AWFUL LOT, WOULDN'T YOU SAY?
TOWNSPEOPLE SHOUTING "SANZO" AT THE TOP OF THEIR LUNGS DOESN'T EXACTLY STAVE OFF THE MASSES.
GUESS THE PEOPLE'RE SCARED.
WE'RE CREEPIER THAN THE YOUKAI, HUH?
NOT THAT I REALLY BLAME THEM WITH THIS BODY COUNT.
KLUNK
YAAAAAAAH!
?!
SEIKA!
ONEE-CHAN!

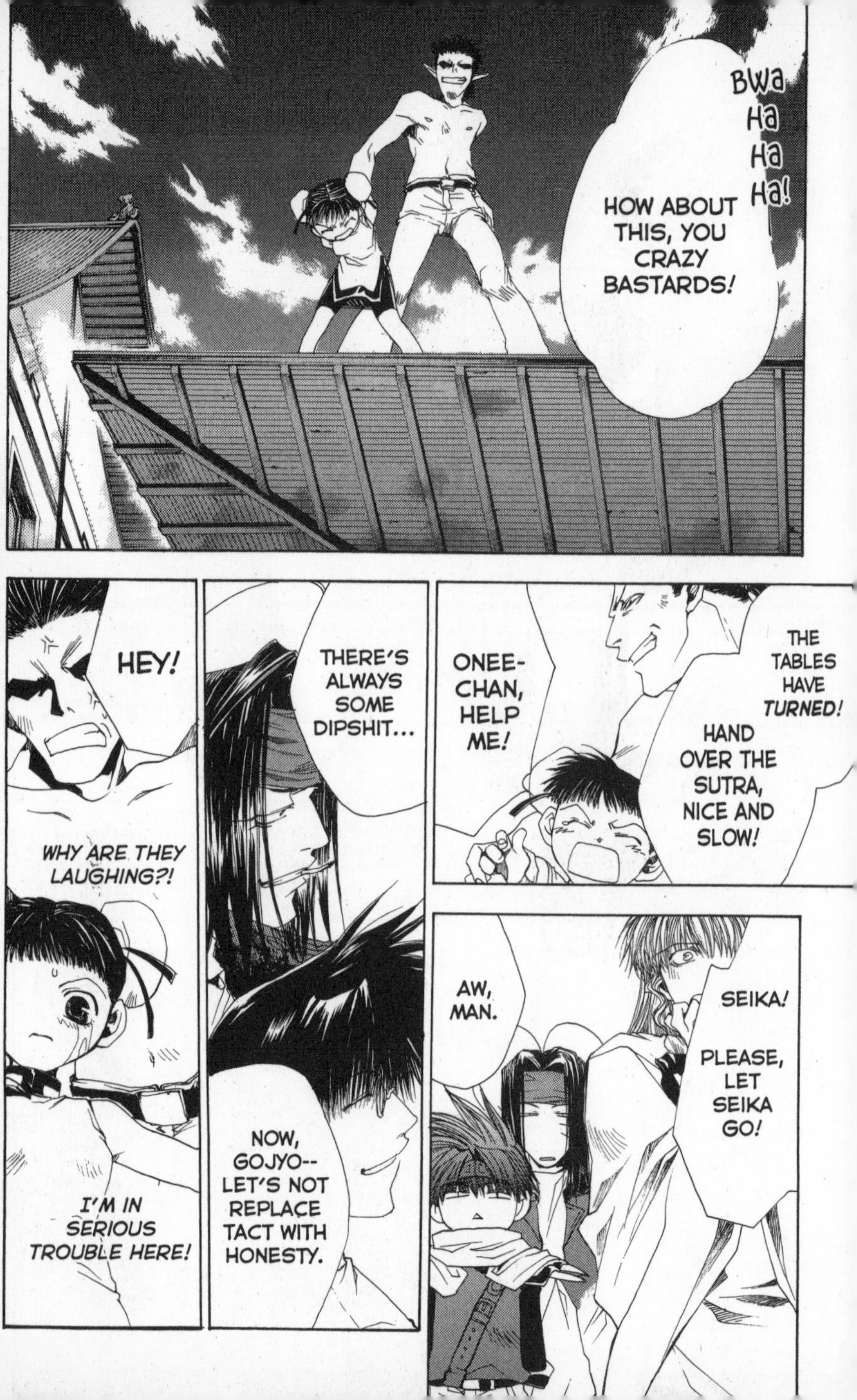
BWA HA HA HA!
HOW ABOUT THIS, YOU CRAZY BASTARDS!
THE TABLES HAVE *TURNED!*
HAND OVER THE SUTRA, NICE AND SLOW!
ONEE-CHAN, HELP ME!
SEIKA!
PLEASE, LET SEIKA GO!
AW, MAN.
THERE'S ALWAYS SOME DIPSHIT...
NOW, GOJYO-- LET'S NOT REPLACE TACT WITH HONESTY.
HEY!
WHY ARE THEY LAUGHING?!
I'M IN SERIOUS TROUBLE HERE!

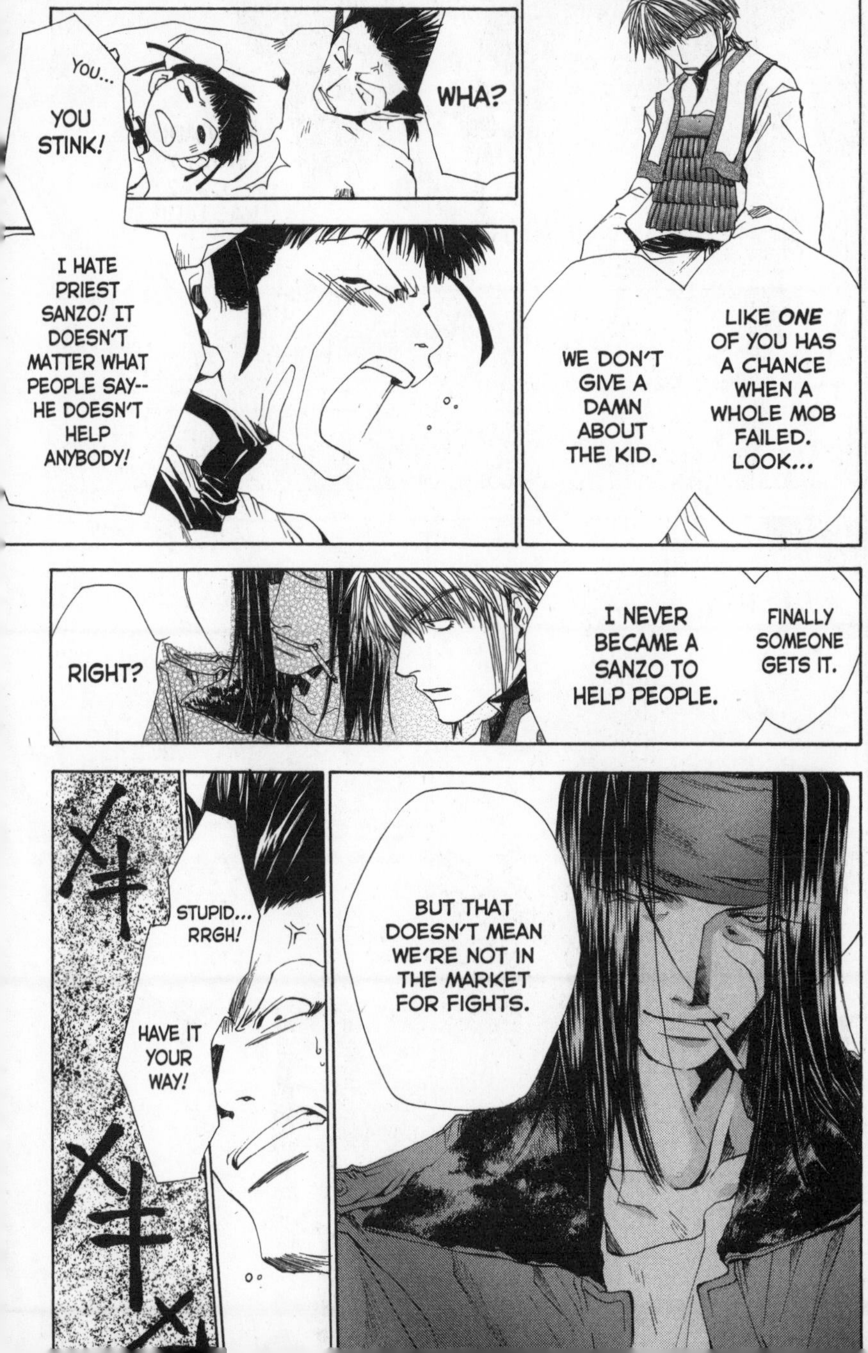
LIKE *ONE* OF YOU HAS A CHANCE WHEN A WHOLE MOB FAILED. LOOK...
WE DON'T GIVE A DAMN ABOUT THE KID.
YOU...
YOU STINK!
WHA?
I HATE PRIEST SANZO! IT DOESN'T MATTER WHAT PEOPLE SAY-- HE DOESN'T HELP ANYBODY!
FINALLY SOMEONE GETS IT.
I NEVER BECAME A SANZO TO HELP PEOPLE.
RIGHT?
BUT THAT DOESN'T MEAN WE'RE NOT IN THE MARKET FOR FIGHTS.
STUPID... RRGH!
HAVE IT YOUR WAY!

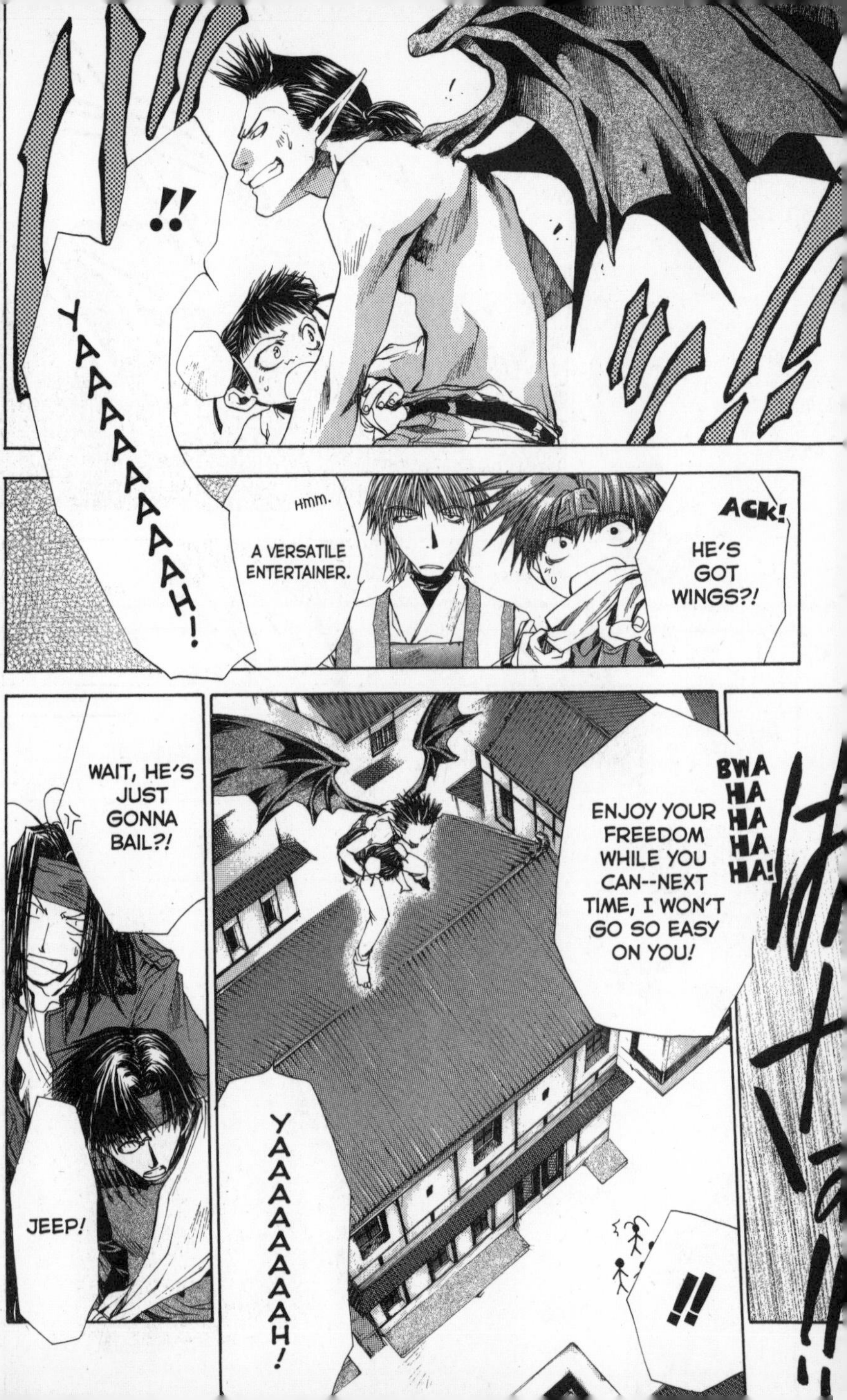
!!
YAAAAAAAAH!
ACK!
HE'S GOT WINGS?!
Hmm.
A VERSATILE ENTERTAINER.
BWA HA HA HA HA!
ENJOY YOUR FREEDOM WHILE YOU CAN--NEXT TIME, I WON'T GO SO EASY ON YOU!
!!
YAAAAAAAAH!
WAIT, HE'S JUST GONNA BAIL?!
JEEP!

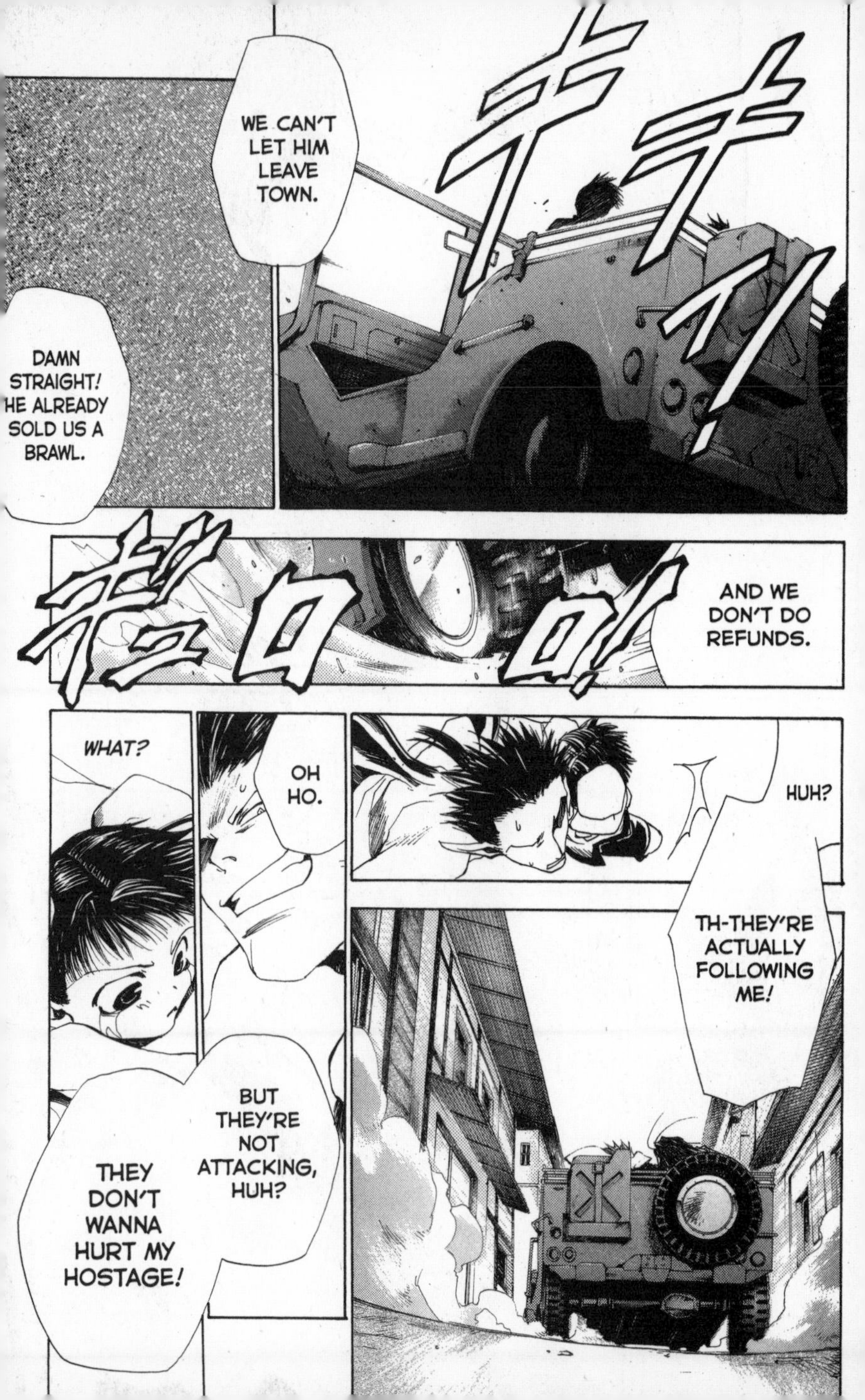

WE CAN'T LET HIM LEAVE TOWN.
DAMN STRAIGHT! HE ALREADY SOLD US A BRAWL.
AND WE DON'T DO REFUNDS.
HUH?
TH-THEY'RE ACTUALLY FOLLOWING ME!
OH HO.
WHAT?
BUT THEY'RE NOT ATTACKING, HUH?
THEY DON'T WANNA HURT MY HOSTAGE!

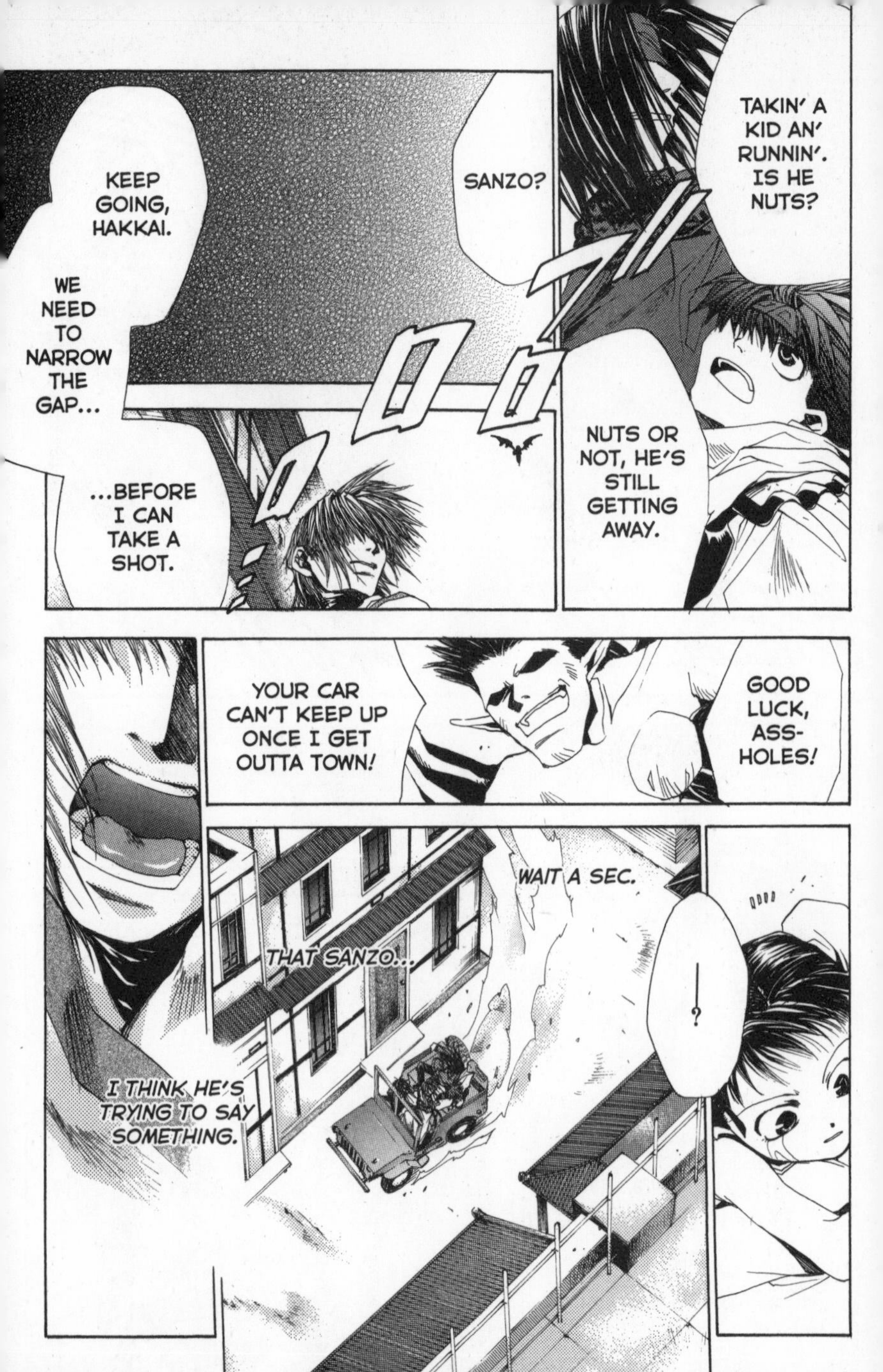
TAKIN' A KID AN' RUNNIN'. IS HE NUTS?
NUTS OR NOT, HE'S STILL GETTING AWAY.
SANZO?
KEEP GOING, HAKKAI.
WE NEED TO NARROW THE GAP...
...BEFORE I CAN TAKE A SHOT.
GOOD LUCK, ASS-HOLES!
YOUR CAR CAN'T KEEP UP ONCE I GET OUTTA TOWN!
!?
WAIT A SEC.
THAT SANZO...
I THINK HE'S TRYING TO SAY SOMETHING.

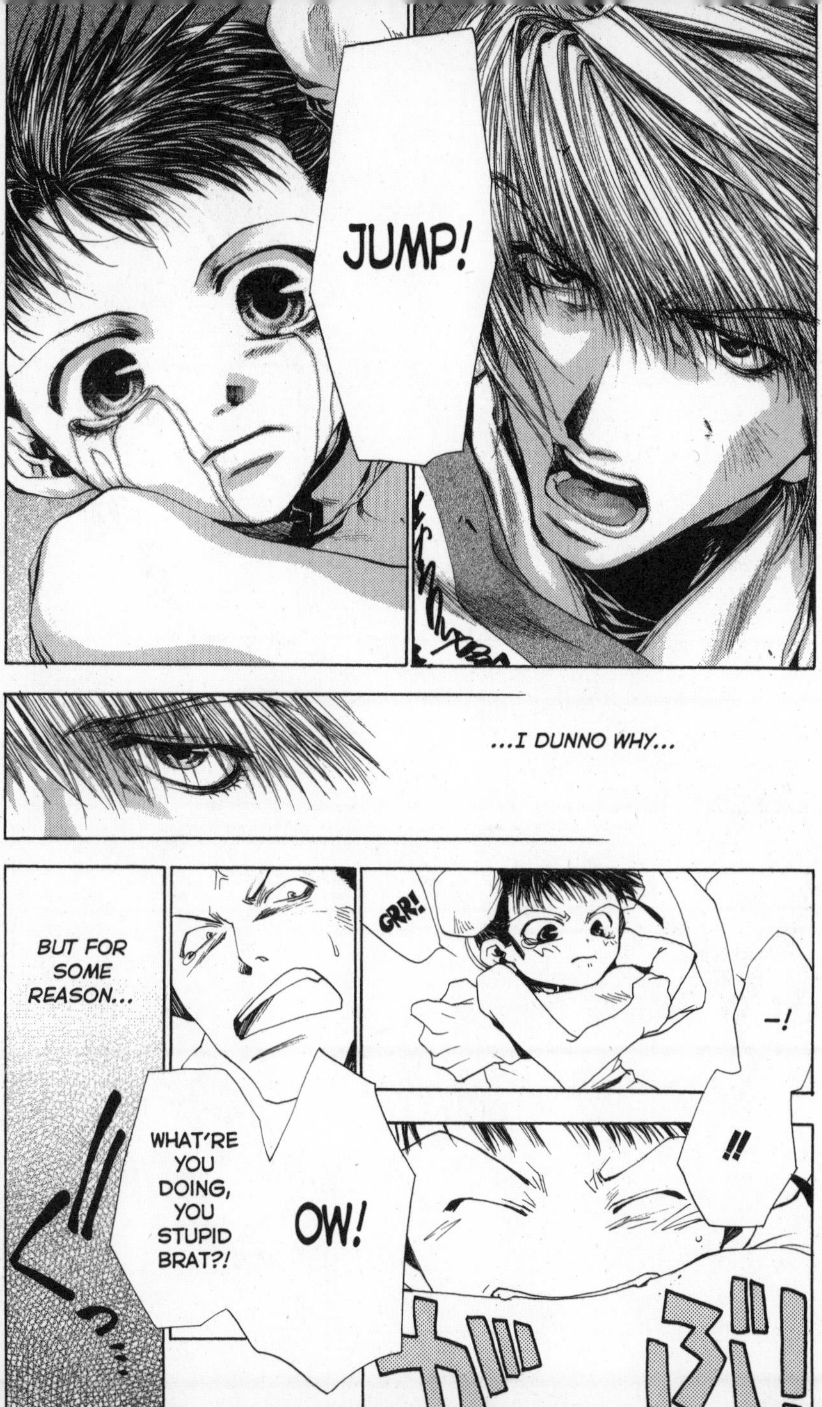

JUMP!
...I DUNNO WHY...
—!
GRR!
BUT FOR SOME REASON...
!!
ぶ!
OW!
WHAT'RE YOU DOING, YOU STUPID BRAT?!
ぐっ...

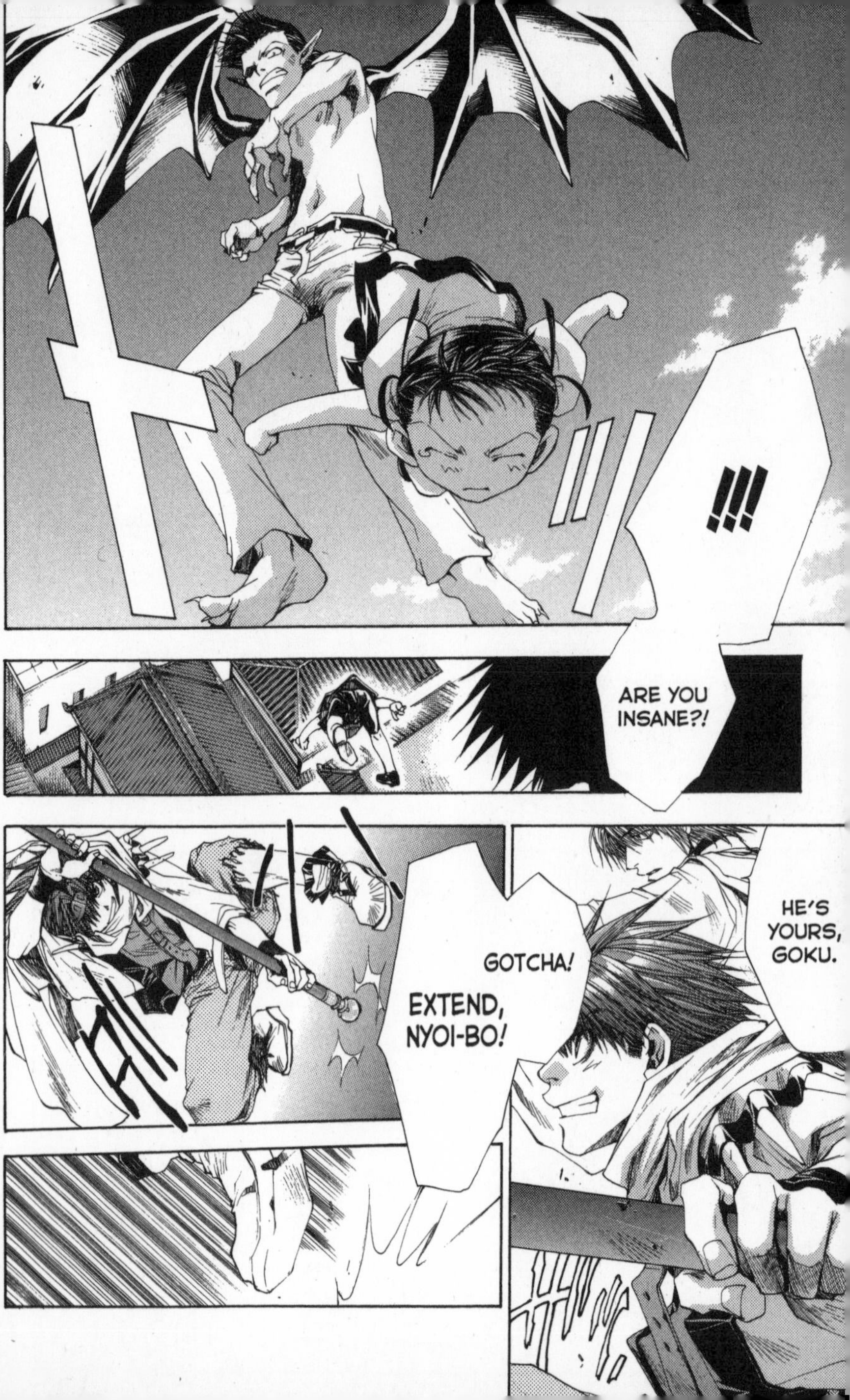
!!!!
ARE YOU INSANE?!
HE'S YOURS, GOKU.
GOTCHA!
EXTEND, NYOI-BO!

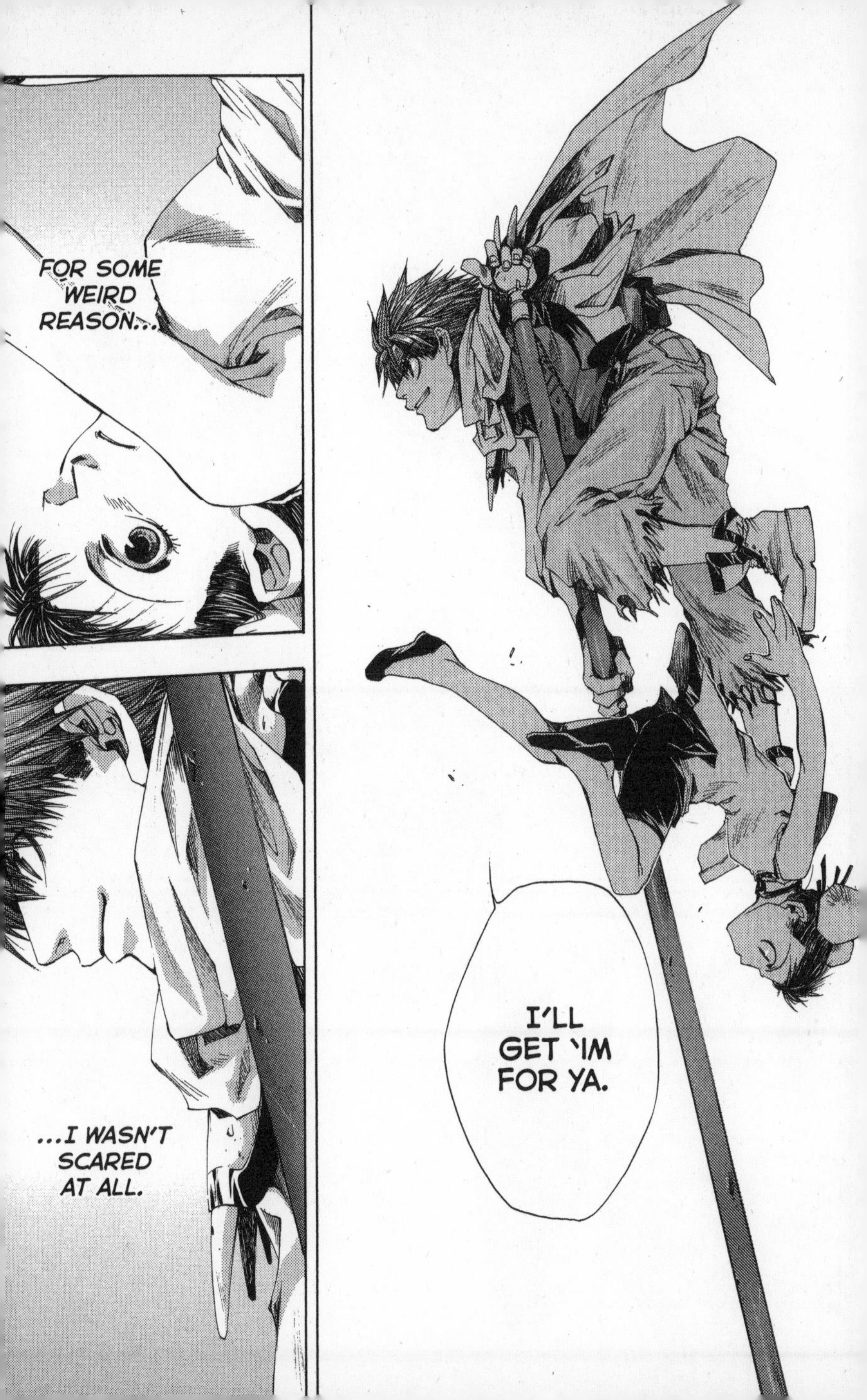
I'LL GET 'IM FOR YA.
FOR SOME WEIRD REASON...
...I WASN'T SCARED AT ALL.

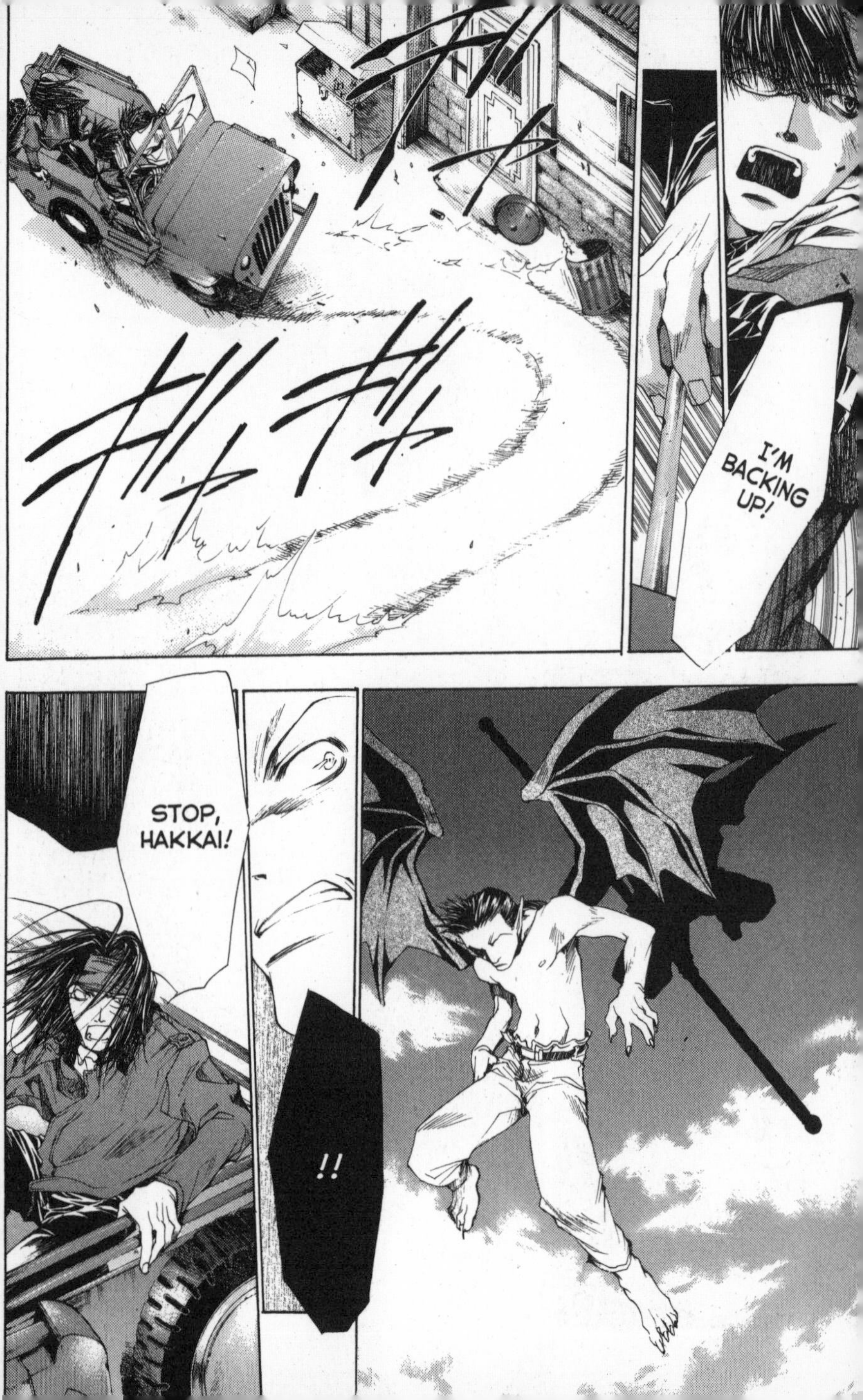
I'M BACKING UP!
STOP, HAKKAI!
!!

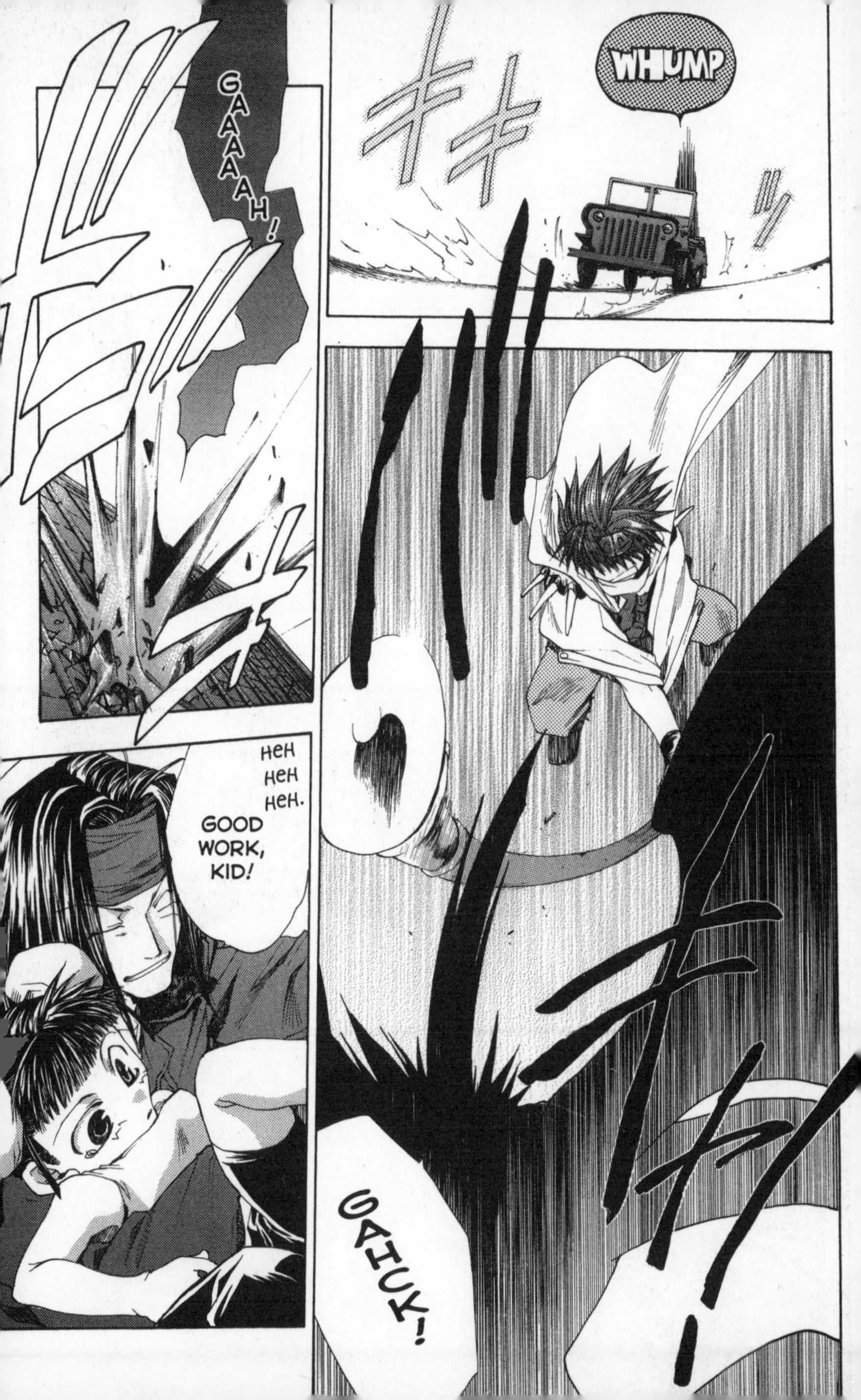
WHUMP
GAAAAAH!
GAHCK!
HEH HEH HEH.
GOOD WORK, KID!

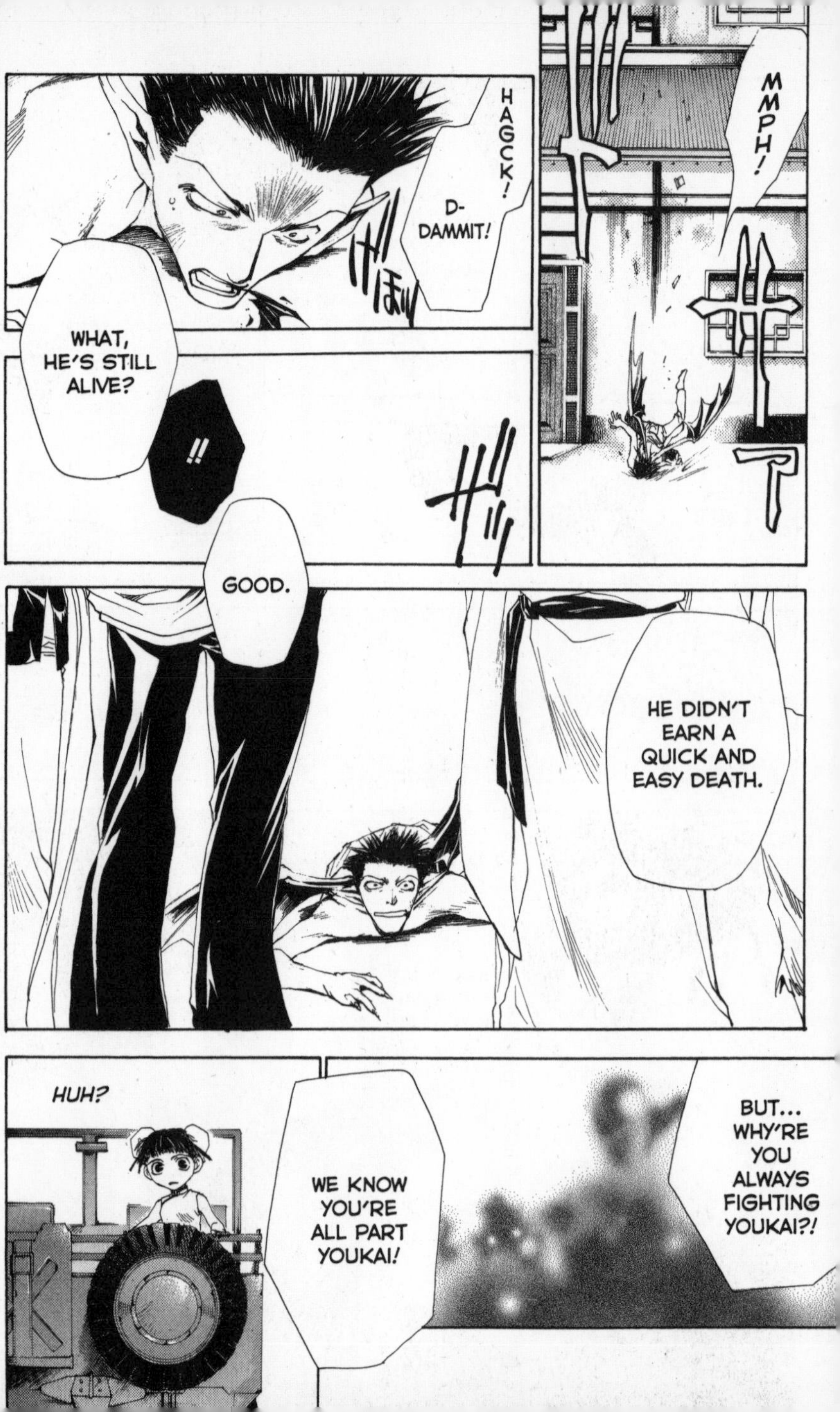
MMPH!
HAGCK!
D-DAMMIT!
WHAT, HE'S STILL ALIVE?
!!
GOOD.
HE DIDN'T EARN A QUICK AND EASY DEATH.
BUT... WHY'RE YOU ALWAYS FIGHTING YOUKAI?!
WE KNOW YOU'RE ALL PART YOUKAI!
HUH?

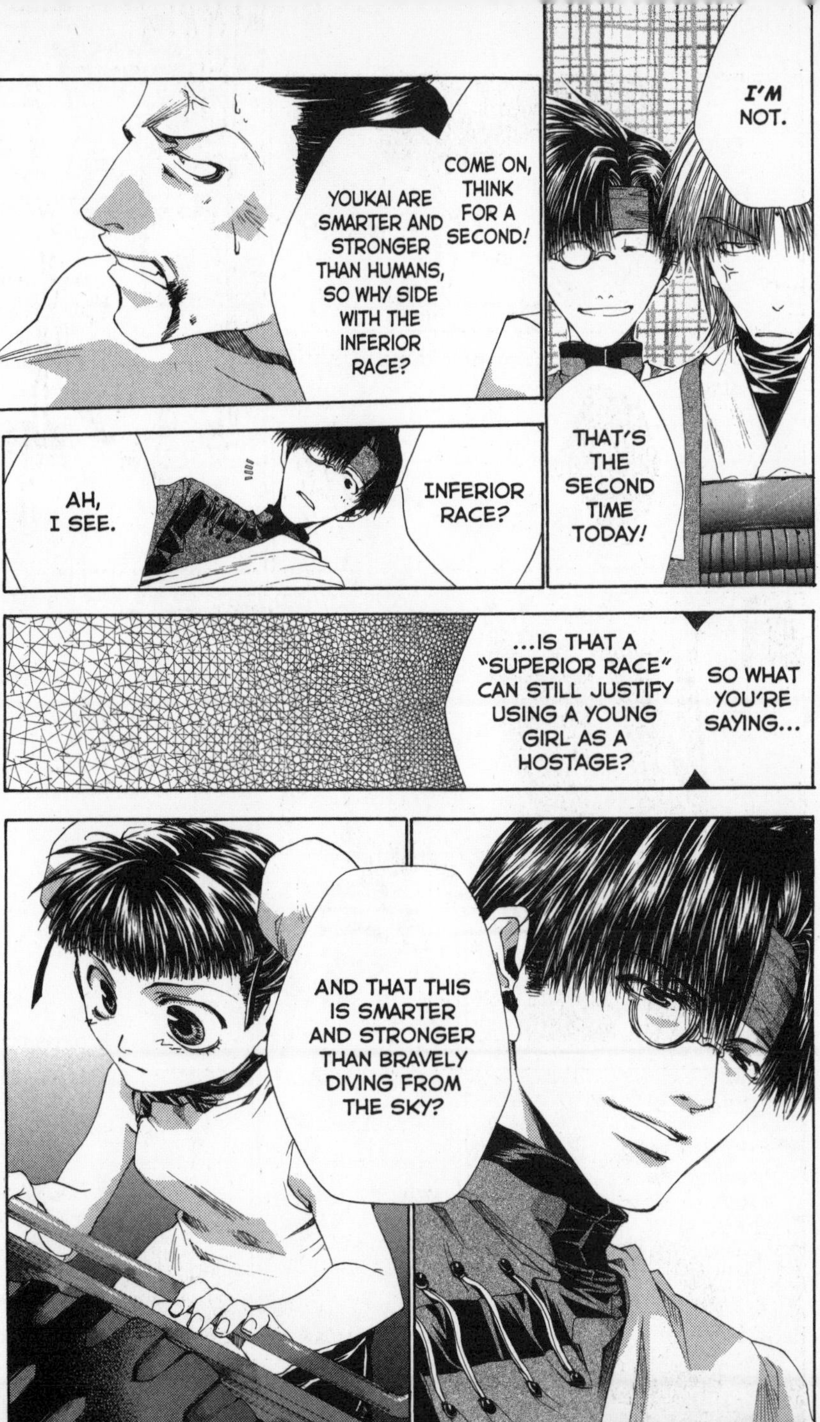
I'M NOT.
THAT'S THE SECOND TIME TODAY!
COME ON, THINK FOR A SECOND!
YOUKAI ARE SMARTER AND STRONGER THAN HUMANS, SO WHY SIDE WITH THE INFERIOR RACE?
INFERIOR RACE?
AH, I SEE.
SO WHAT YOU'RE SAYING...
..."IS THAT A "SUPERIOR RACE" CAN STILL JUSTIFY USING A YOUNG GIRL AS A HOSTAGE?
AND THAT THIS IS SMARTER AND STRONGER THAN BRAVELY DIVING FROM THE SKY?

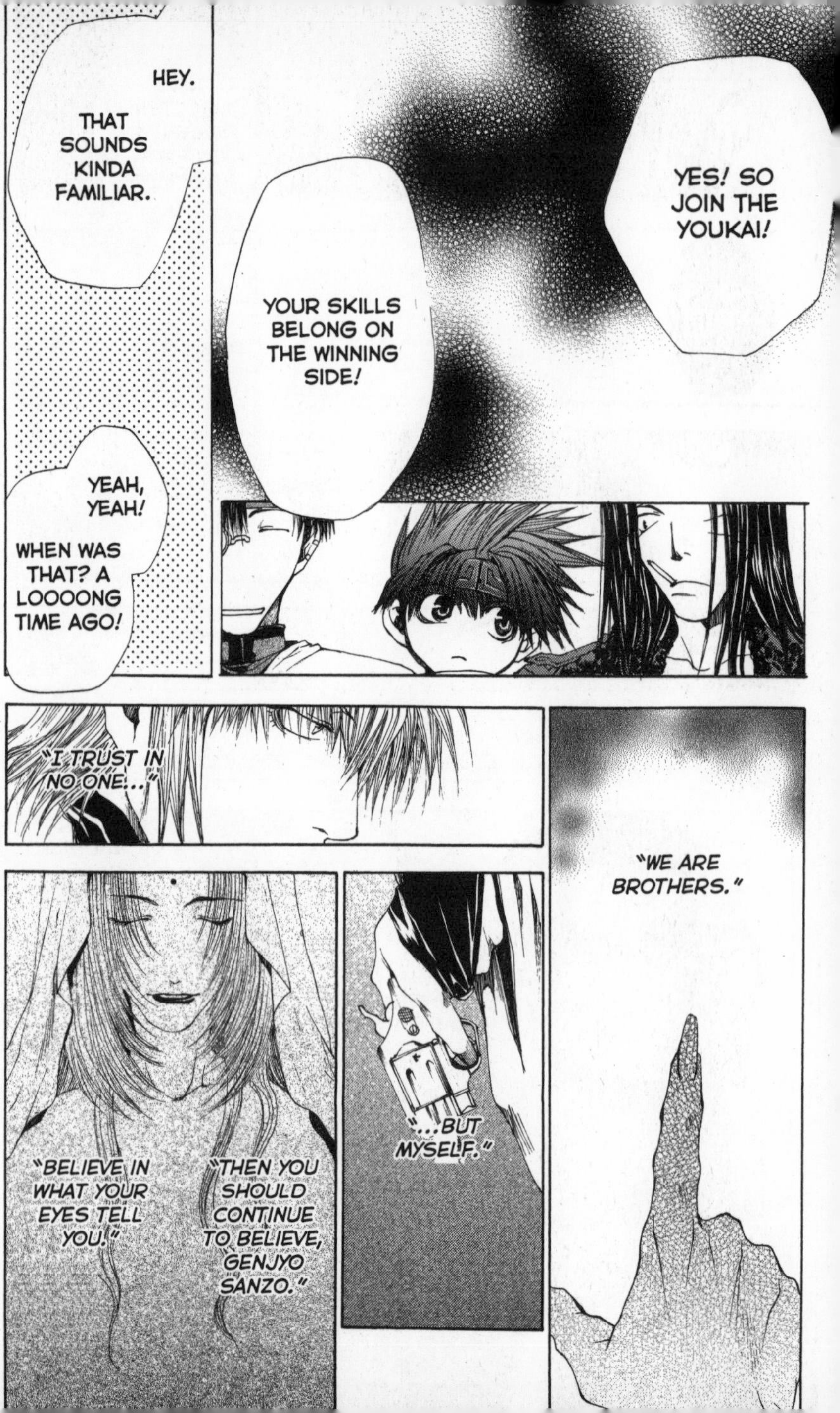
YES! SO JOIN THE YOUKAI!
YOUR SKILLS BELONG ON THE WINNING SIDE!
HEY.
THAT SOUNDS KINDA FAMILIAR.
YEAH, YEAH!
WHEN WAS THAT? A LOOOONG TIME AGO!
"WE ARE BROTHERS."
"I TRUST IN NO ONE..."
"...BUT MYSELF."
"THEN YOU SHOULD CONTINUE TO BELIEVE, GENJYO SANZO."
"BELIEVE IN WHAT YOUR EYES TELL YOU."

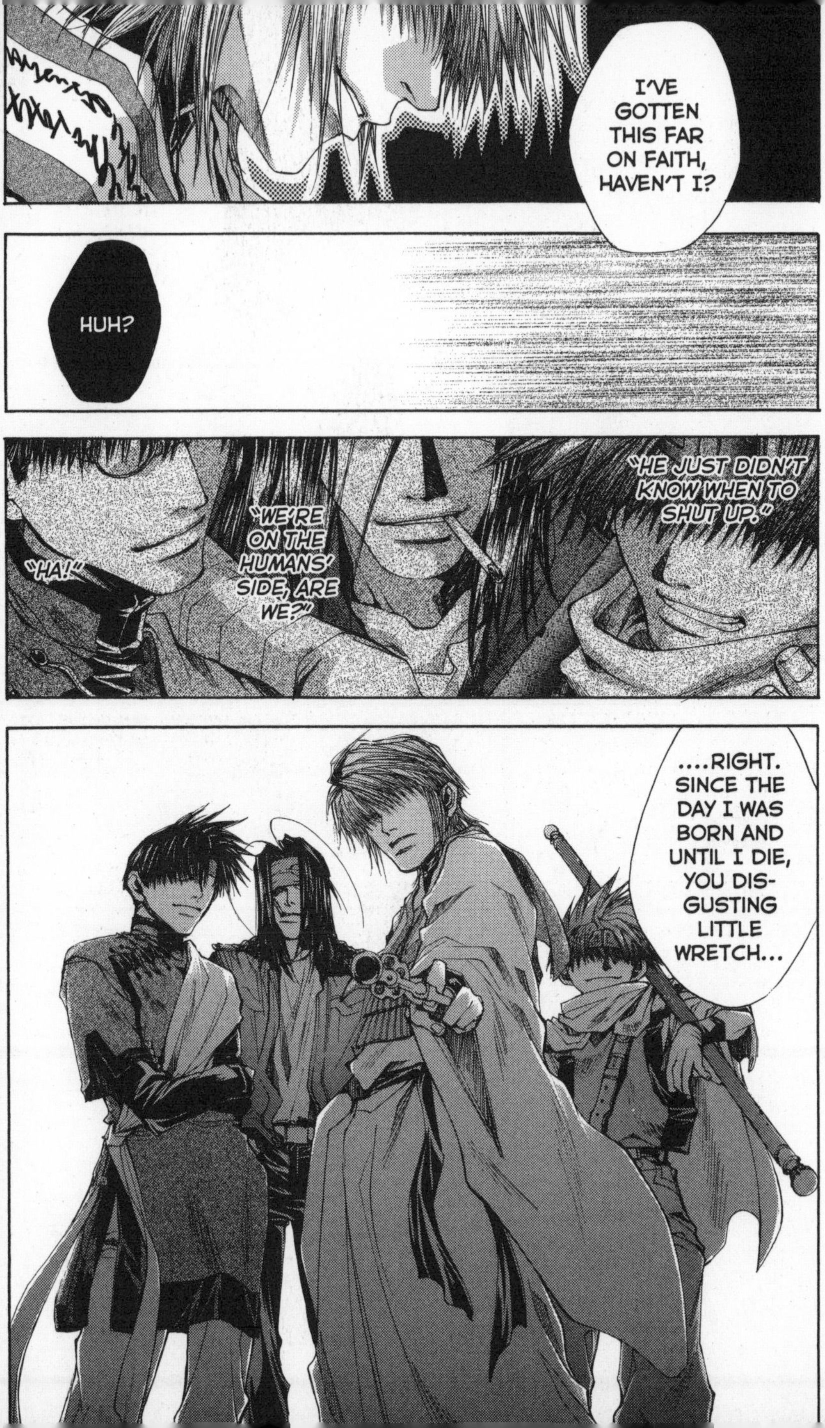
I'VE GOTTEN THIS FAR ON FAITH, HAVEN'T I?
HUH?
"HE JUST DIDN'T KNOW WHEN TO SHUT UP."
"WE'RE ON THE HUMANS' SIDE, ARE WE?"
"HA!"
....RIGHT. SINCE THE DAY I WAS BORN AND UNTIL I DIE, YOU DIS-GUSTING LITTLE WRETCH...

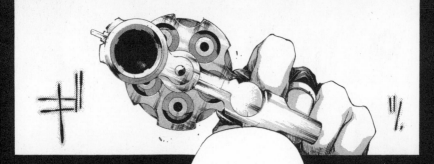

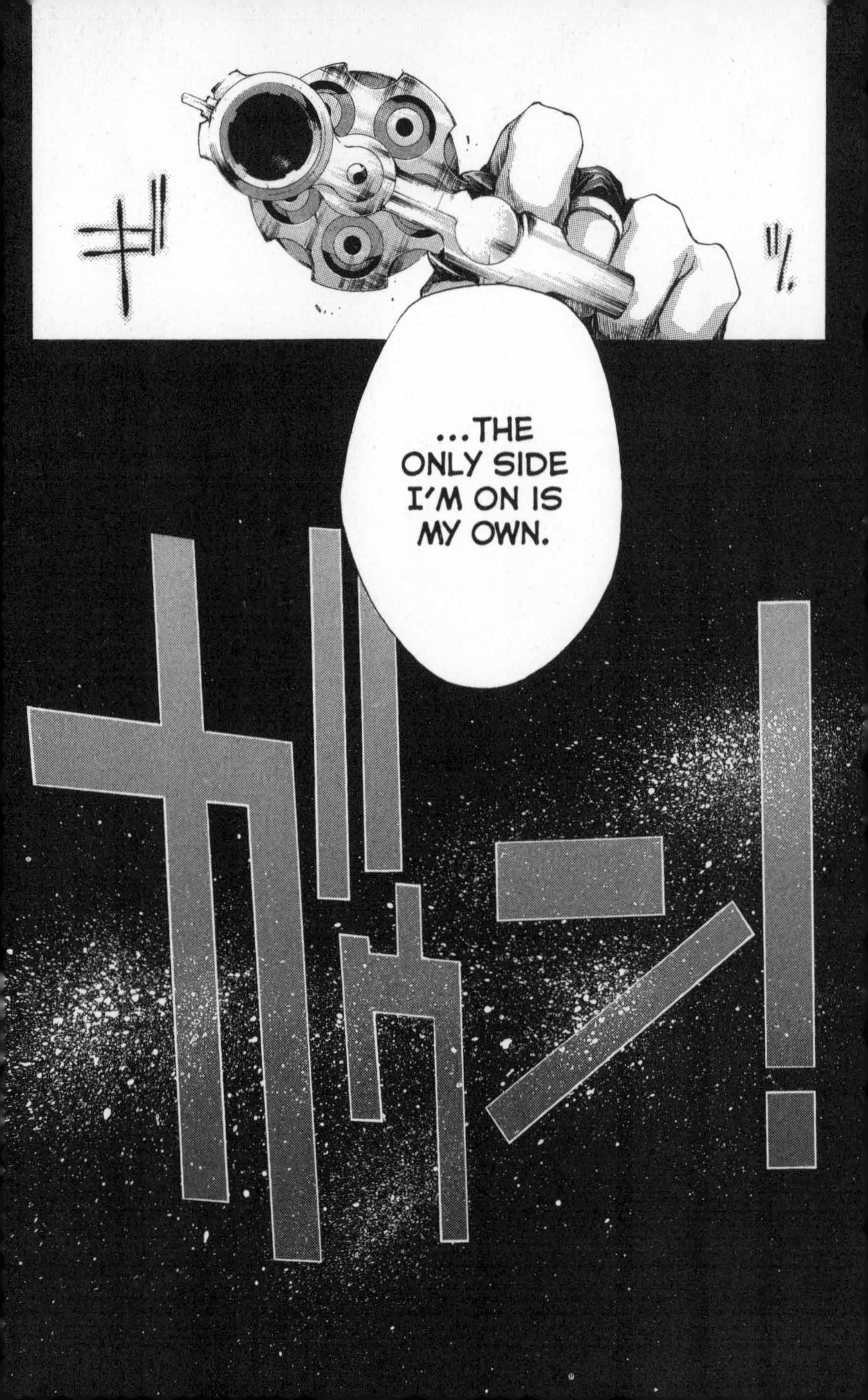

...THE ONLY SIDE I'M ON IS MY OWN.

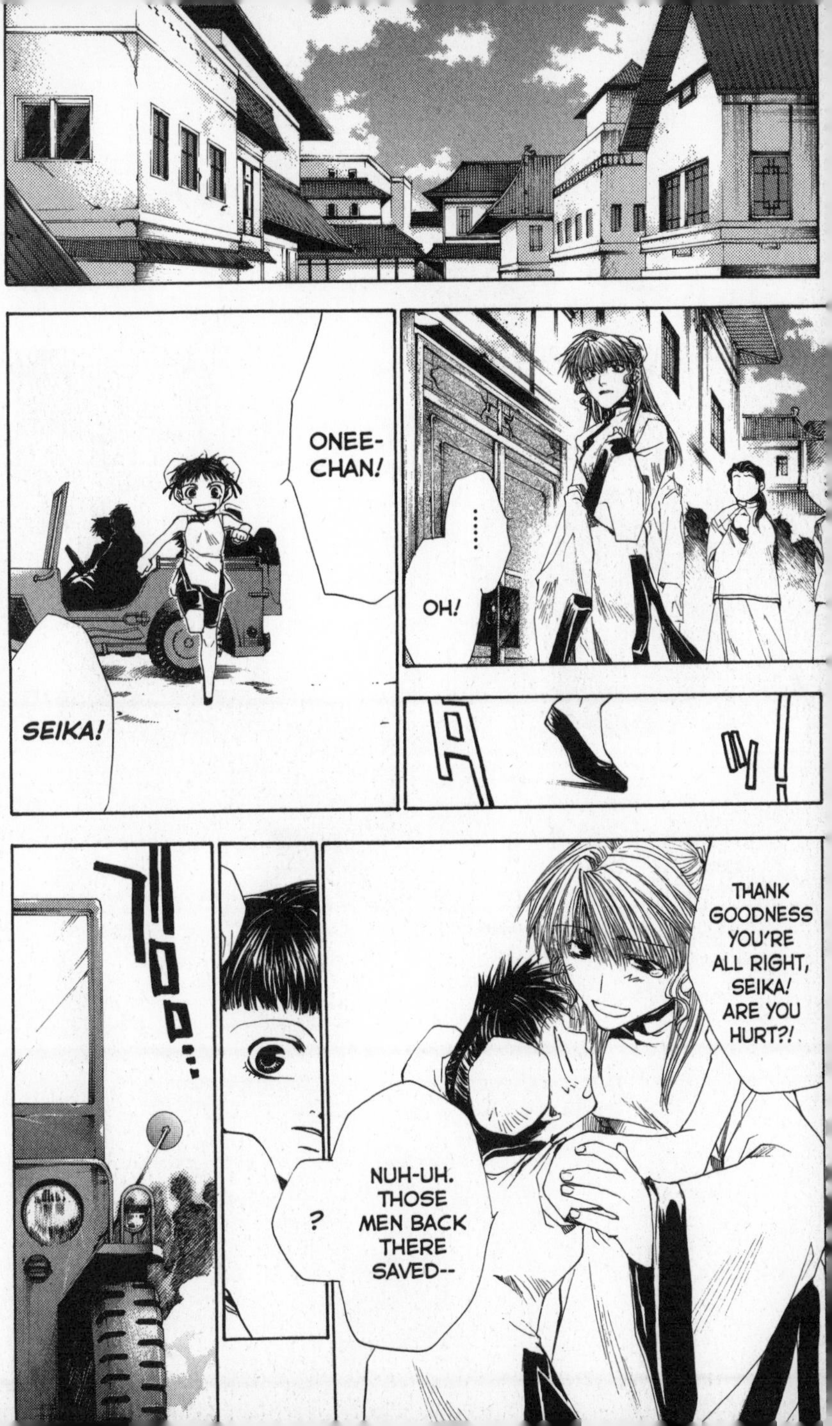
......
OH!
ONEE-CHAN!
SEIKA!
THANK GOODNESS YOU'RE ALL RIGHT, SEIKA! ARE YOU HURT?!
NUH-UH. THOSE MEN BACK THERE SAVED--
?

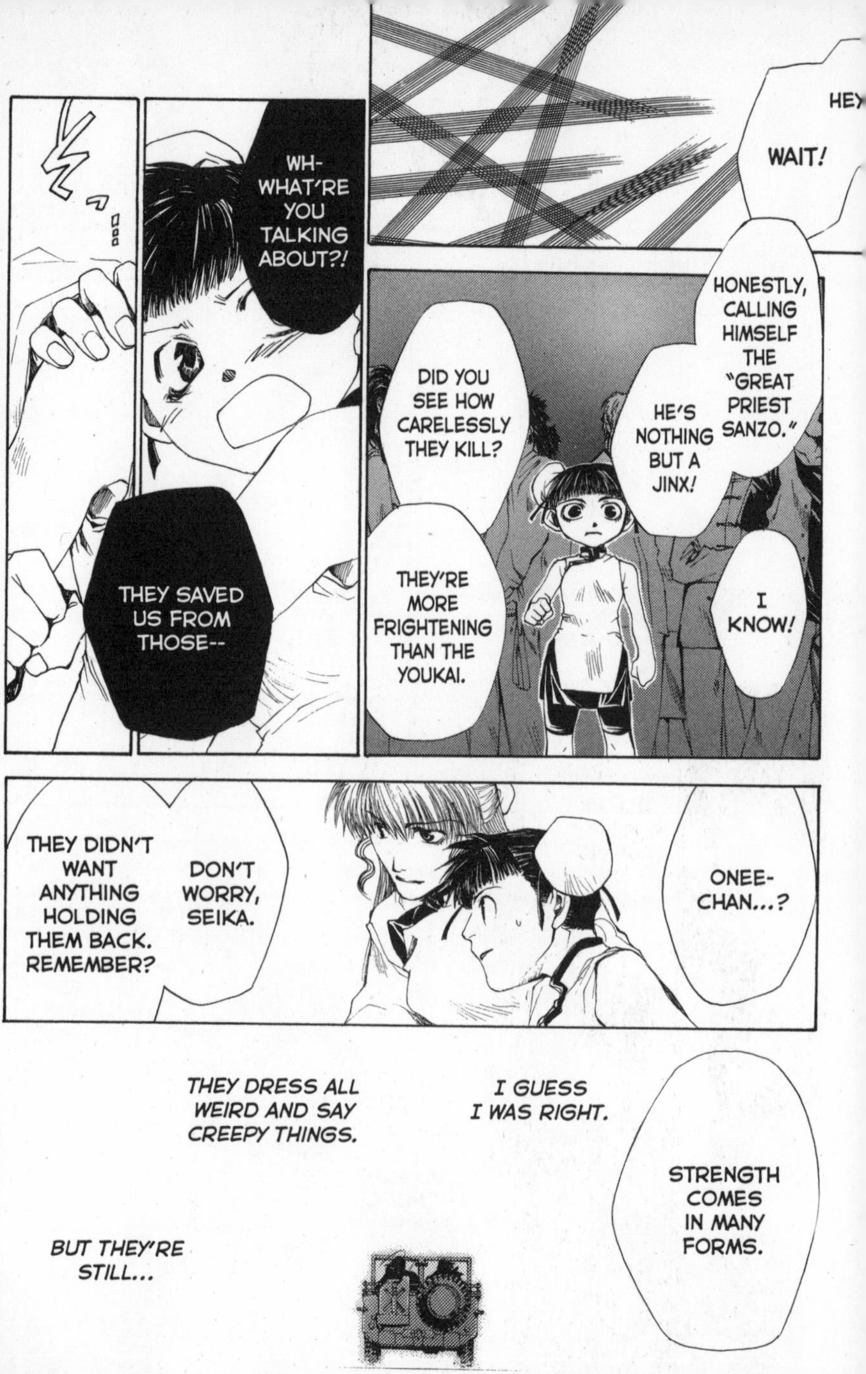
HEY
WAIT!
HONESTLY, CALLING HIMSELF THE "GREAT PRIEST SANZO."
HE'S NOTHING BUT A JINX!
DID YOU SEE HOW CARELESSLY THEY KILL?
I KNOW!
THEY'RE MORE FRIGHTENING THAN THE YOUKAI.
WH- WHAT'RE YOU TALKING ABOUT?!
THEY SAVED US FROM THOSE--
ONEE-CHAN...?
DON'T WORRY, SEIKA.
THEY DIDN'T WANT ANYTHING HOLDING THEM BACK. REMEMBER?
STRENGTH COMES IN MANY FORMS.
I GUESS I WAS RIGHT.
THEY DRESS ALL WEIRD AND SAY CREEPY THINGS.
BUT THEY'RE STILL...

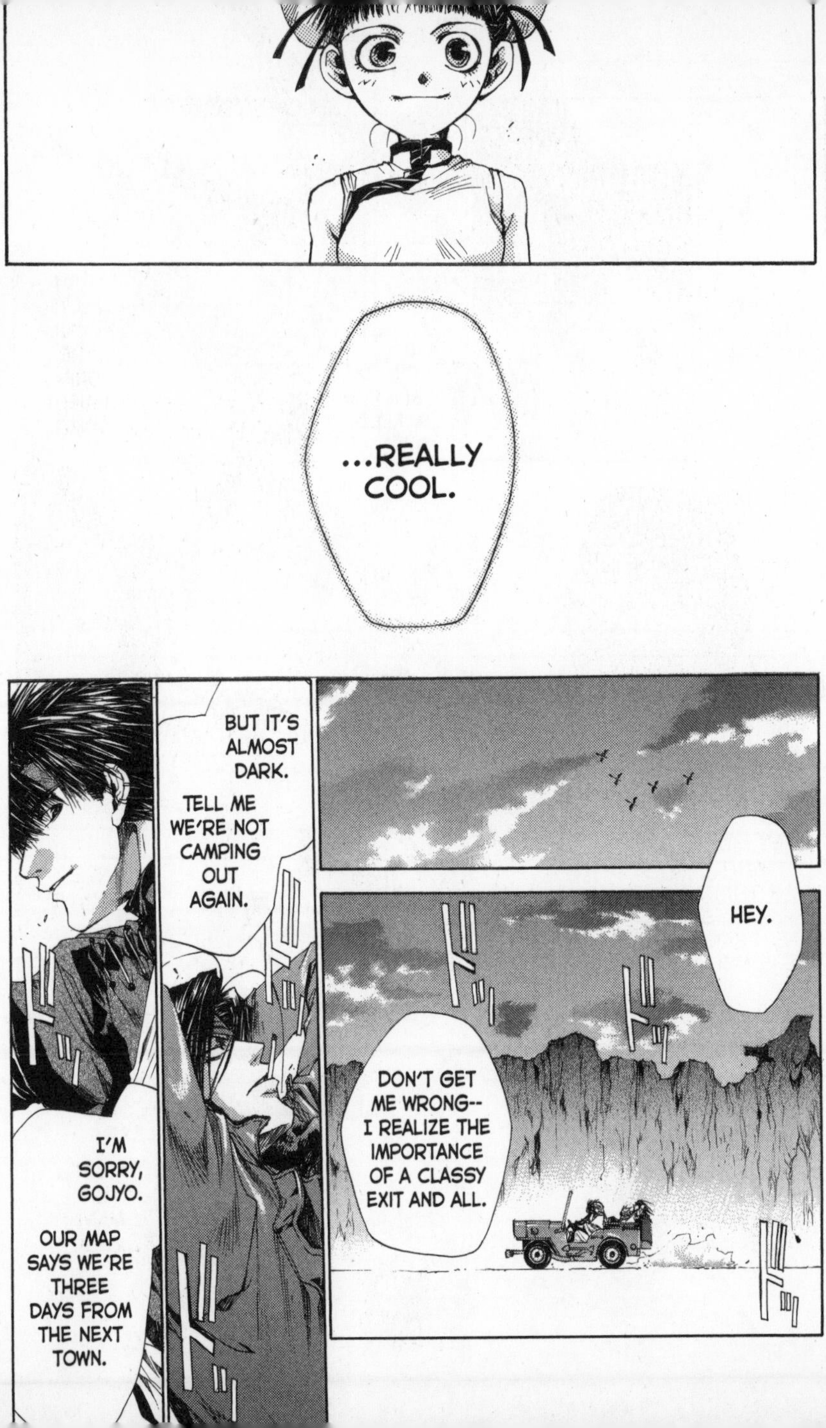
...REALLY COOL.
HEY.
DON'T GET ME WRONG-- I REALIZE THE IMPORTANCE OF A CLASSY EXIT AND ALL.
BUT IT'S ALMOST DARK.
TELL ME WE'RE NOT CAMPING OUT AGAIN.
I'M SORRY, GOJYO.
OUR MAP SAYS WE'RE THREE DAYS FROM THE NEXT TOWN.

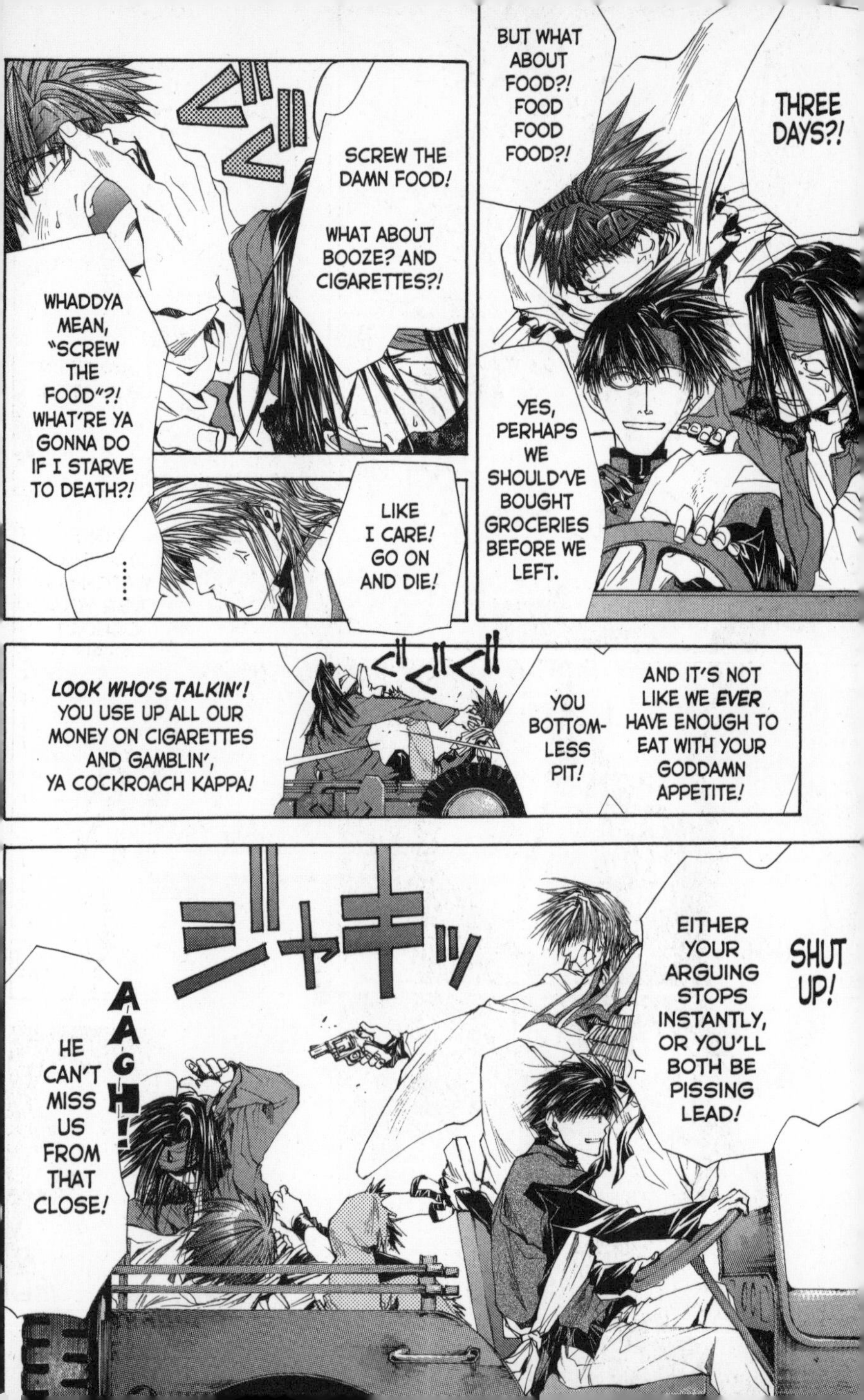
THREE DAYS?!
BUT WHAT ABOUT FOOD?! FOOD FOOD FOOD?!
YES, PERHAPS WE SHOULD'VE BOUGHT GROCERIES BEFORE WE LEFT.
SCREW THE DAMN FOOD!
WHAT ABOUT BOOZE? AND CIGARETTES?!
WHADDYA MEAN, "SCREW THE FOOD"?! WHAT'RE YA GONNA DO IF I STARVE TO DEATH?!
LIKE I CARE! GO ON AND DIE!
......
AND IT'S NOT LIKE WE *EVER* HAVE ENOUGH TO EAT WITH YOUR GODDAMN APPETITE!
YOU BOTTOMLESS PIT!
LOOK WHO'S TALKIN'! YOU USE UP ALL OUR MONEY ON CIGARETTES AND GAMBLIN', YA COCKROACH KAPPA!
SHUT UP!
EITHER YOUR ARGUING STOPS INSTANTLY, OR YOU'LL BOTH BE PISSING LEAD!
AAAGH!!
HE CAN'T MISS US FROM THAT CLOSE!

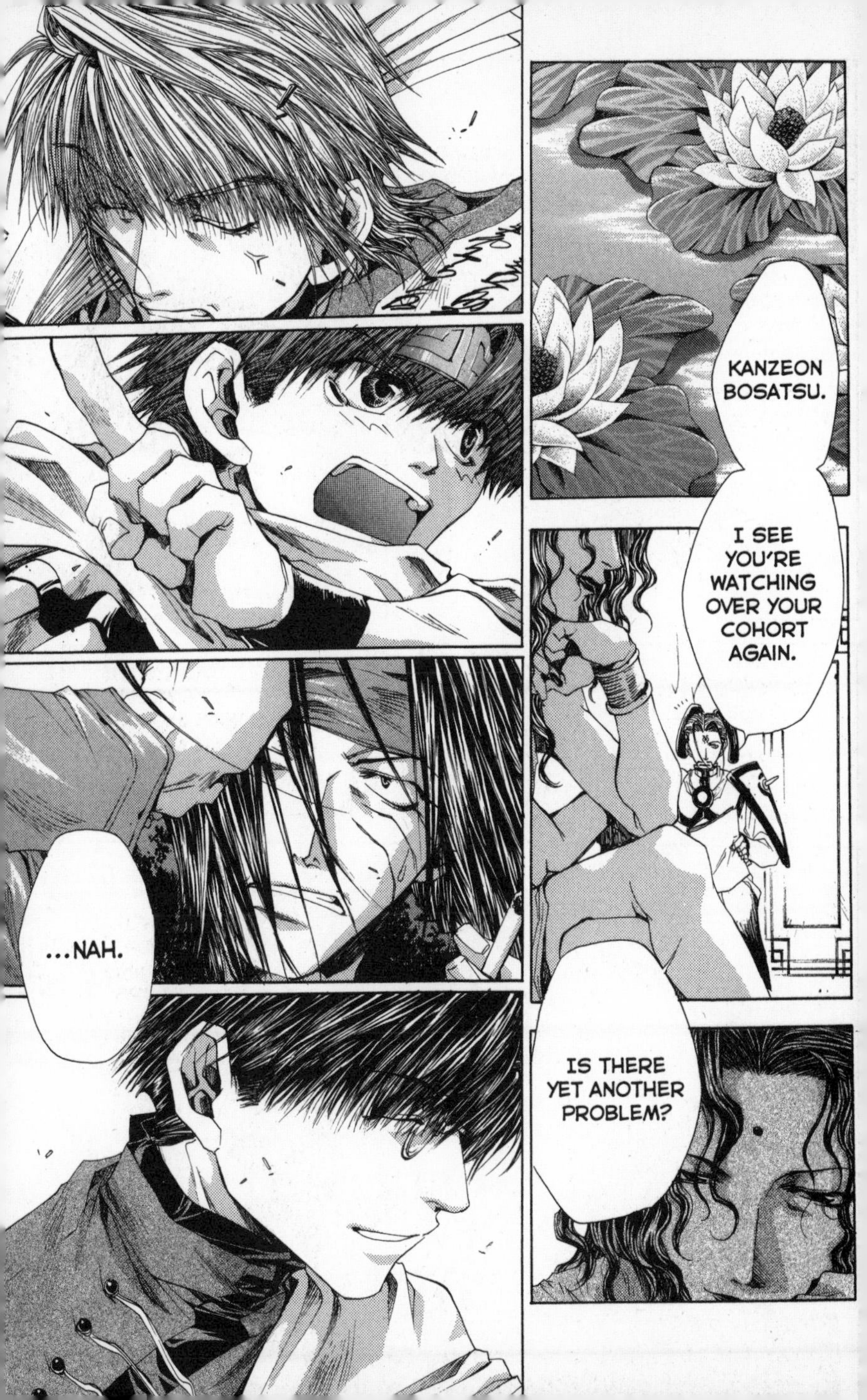
KANZEON BOSATSU.
I SEE YOU'RE WATCHING OVER YOUR COHORT AGAIN.
IS THERE YET ANOTHER PROBLEM?
...NAH.

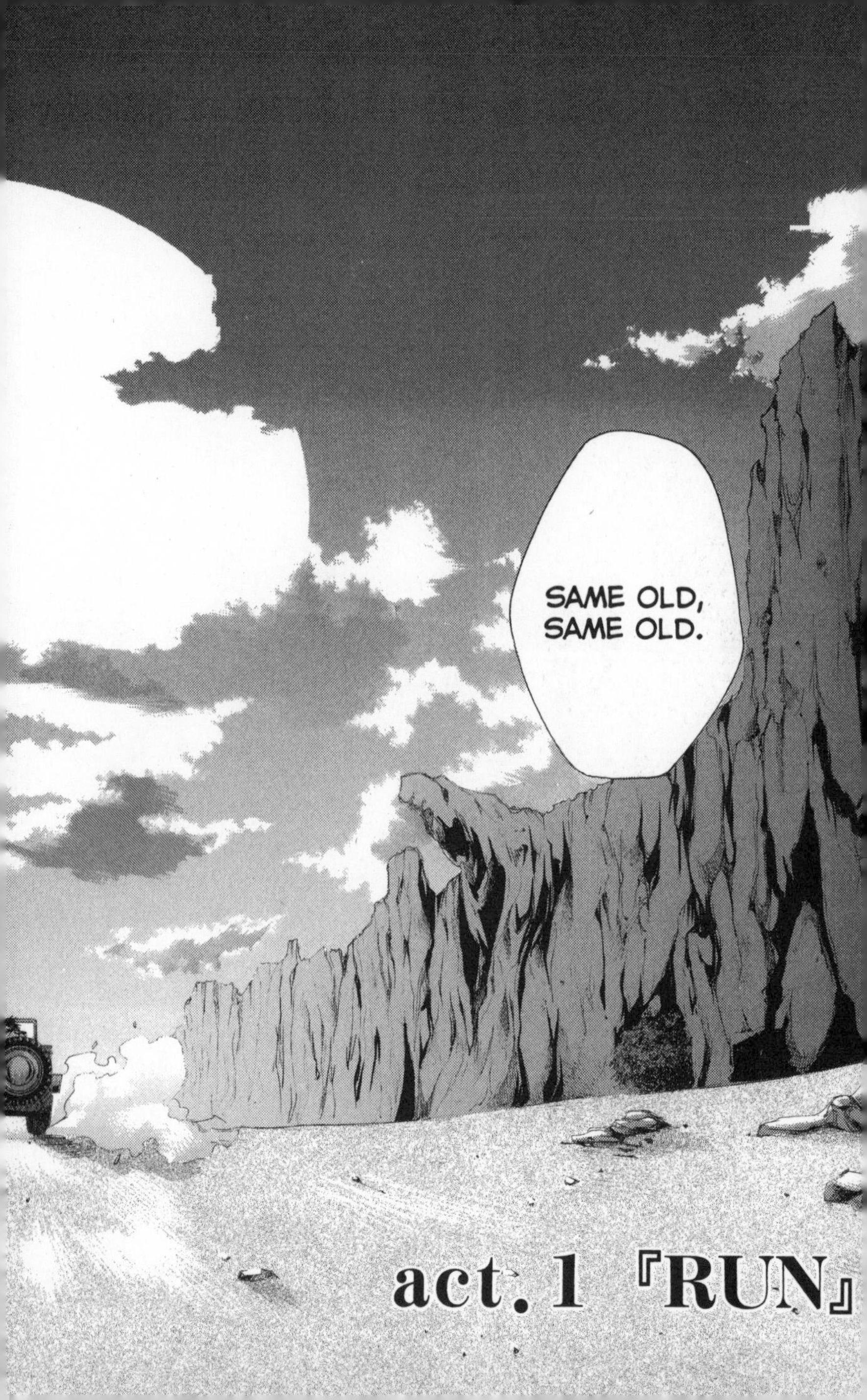
SAME OLD,
SAME OLD.
act. 1 『RUN』

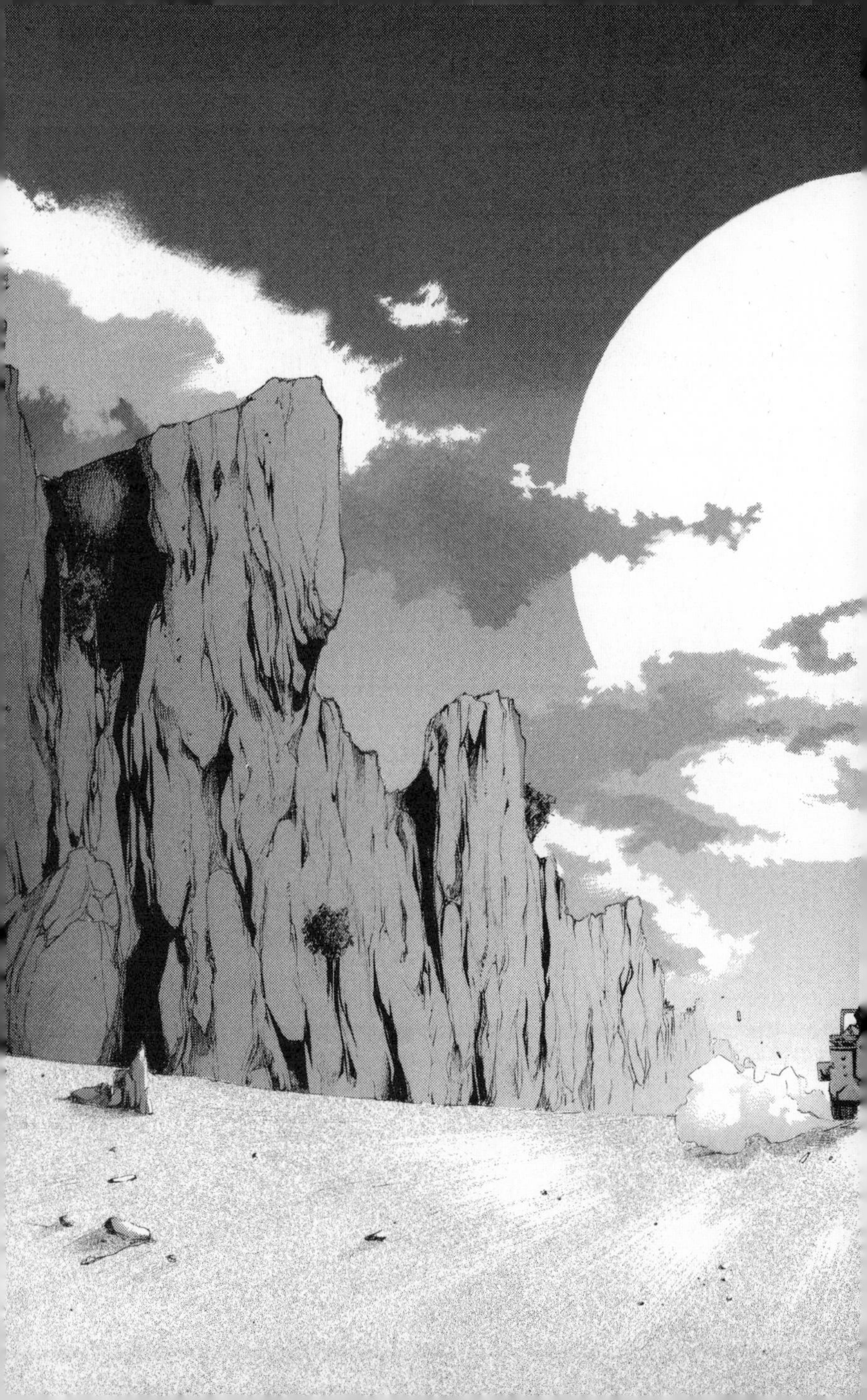

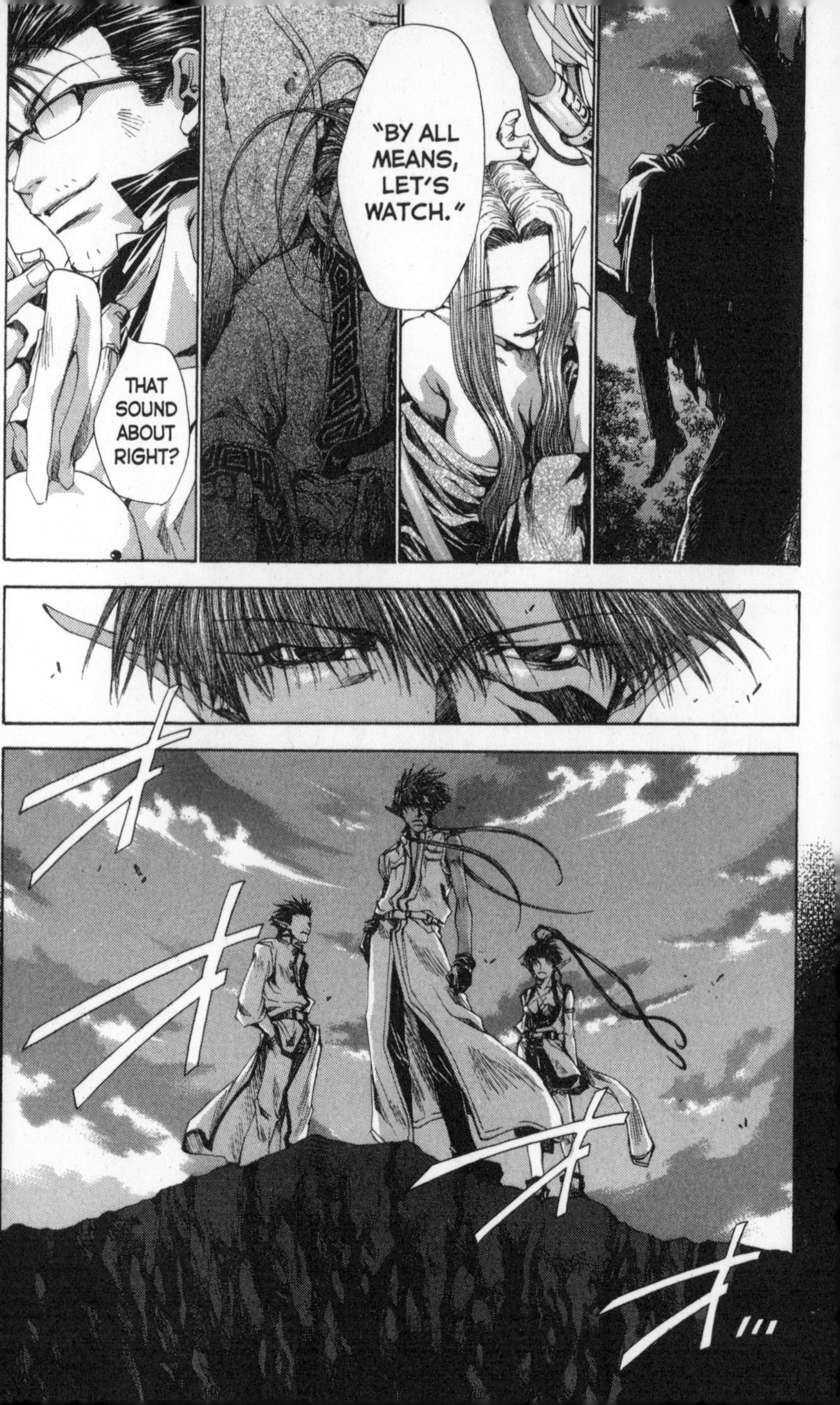
"BY ALL MEANS, LET'S WATCH."
THAT SOUND ABOUT RIGHT?

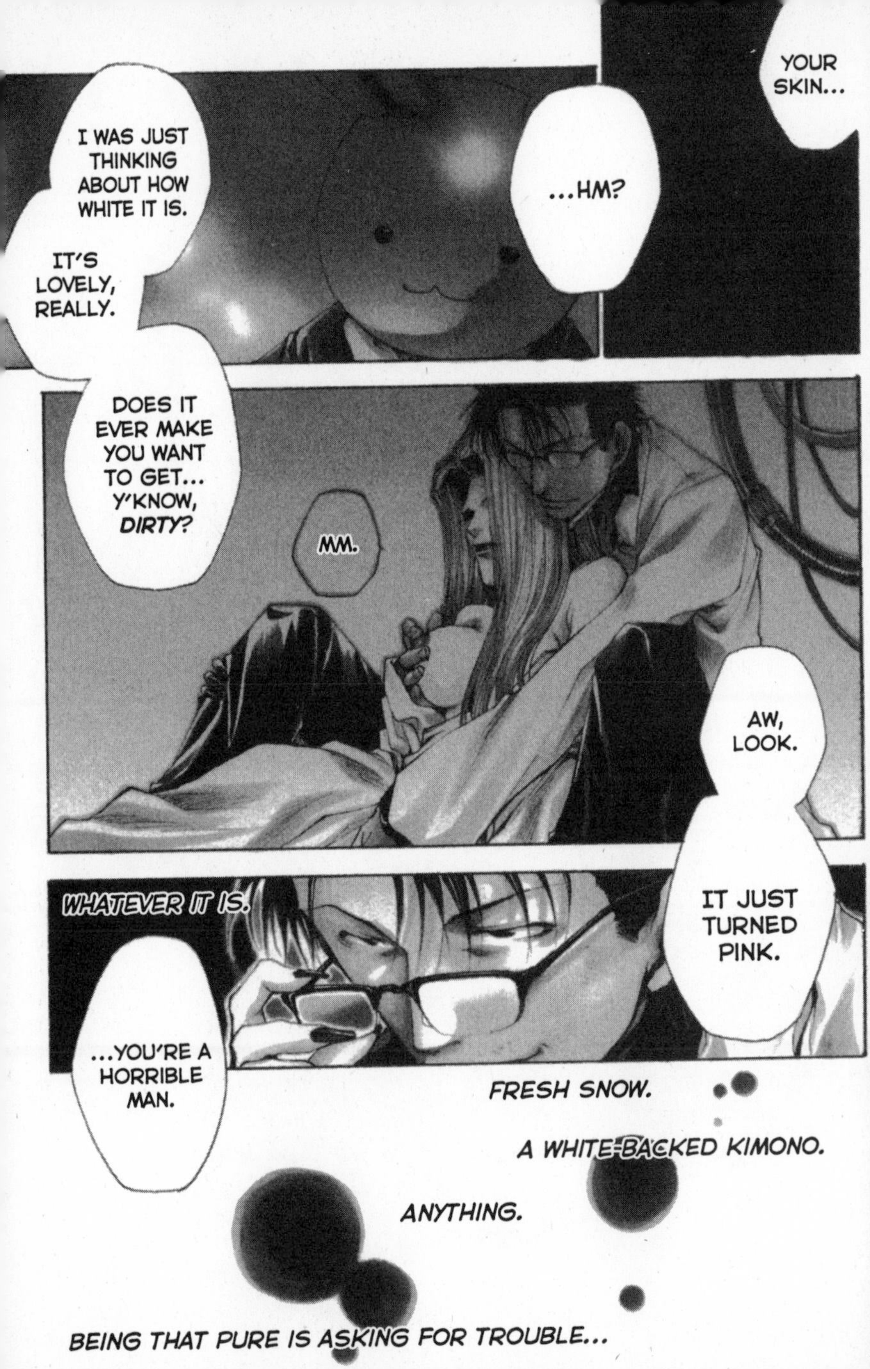
YOUR SKIN...
...HM?
I WAS JUST THINKING ABOUT HOW WHITE IT IS.
IT'S LOVELY, REALLY.
DOES IT EVER MAKE YOU WANT TO GET... Y'KNOW, *DIRTY?*
MM.
AW, LOOK.
IT JUST TURNED PINK.
WHATEVER IT IS.
...YOU'RE A HORRIBLE MAN.
FRESH SNOW.
A WHITE-BACKED KIMONO.
ANYTHING.
BEING THAT PURE IS ASKING FOR TROUBLE...

act.2『snow drop 1』

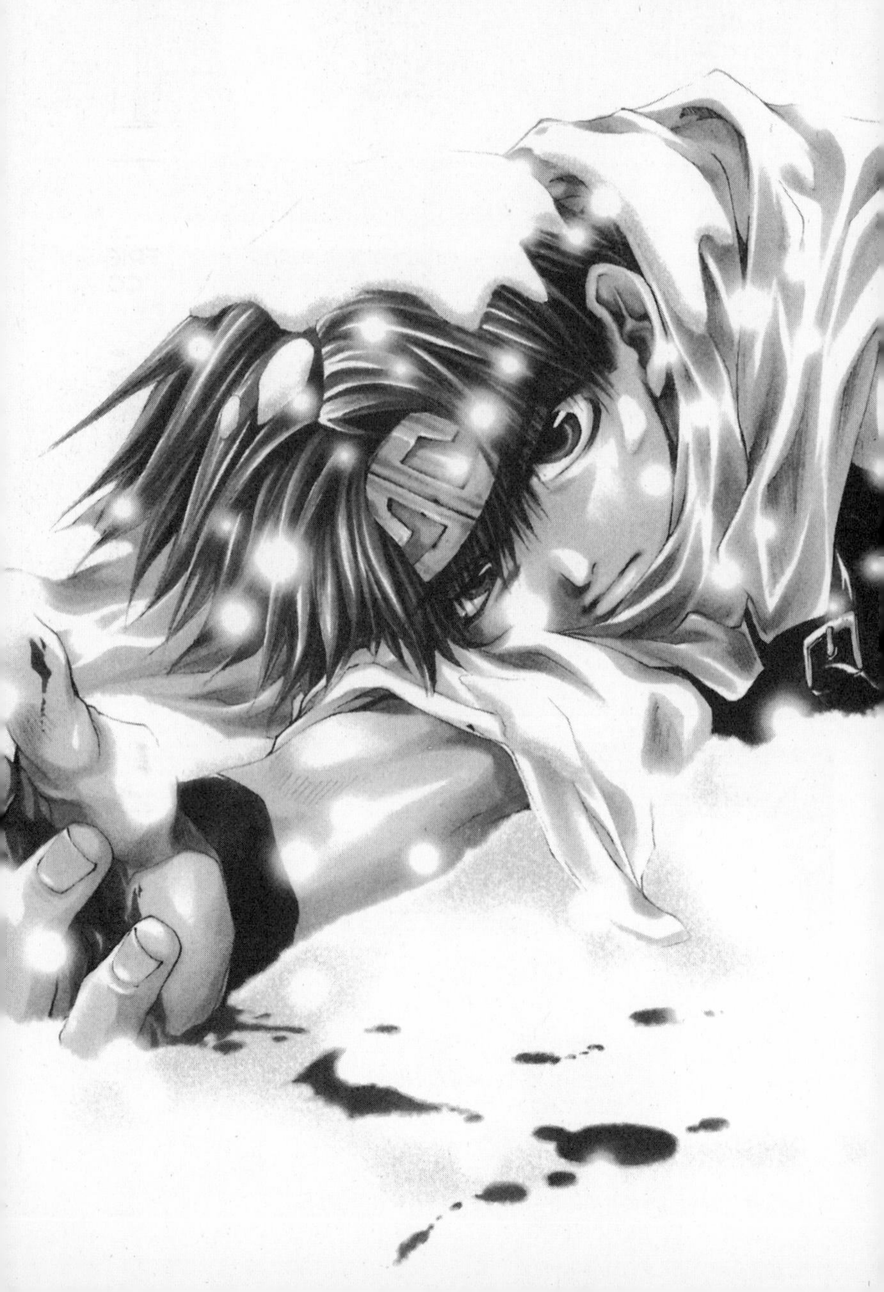

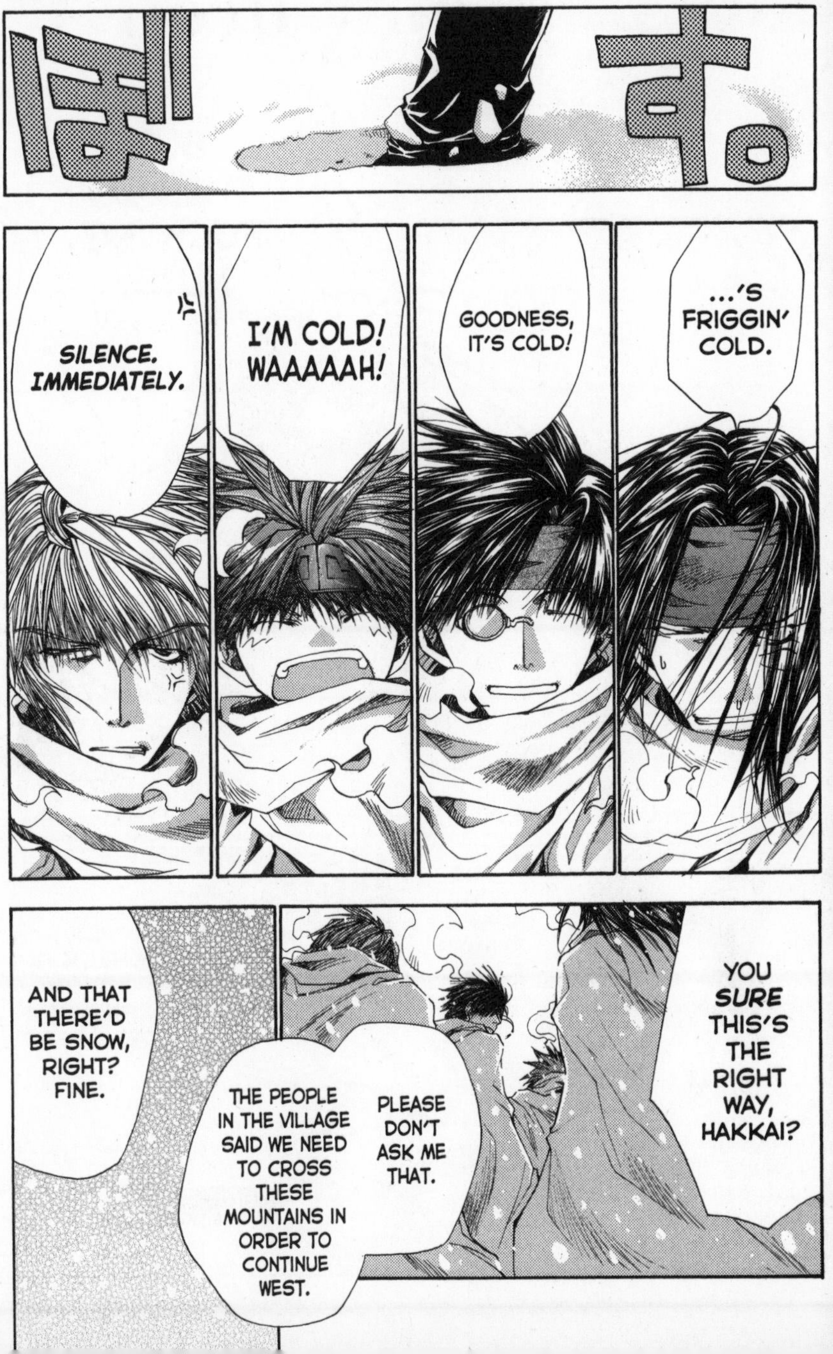
ぼ す。
...'S FRIGGIN' COLD.
GOODNESS, IT'S COLD!
I'M COLD! WAAAAAH!
SILENCE. IMMEDIATELY.
YOU *SURE* THIS'S THE RIGHT WAY, HAKKAI?
PLEASE DON'T ASK ME THAT.
THE PEOPLE IN THE VILLAGE SAID WE NEED TO CROSS THESE MOUNTAINS IN ORDER TO CONTINUE WEST.
AND THAT THERE'D BE SNOW, RIGHT? FINE.

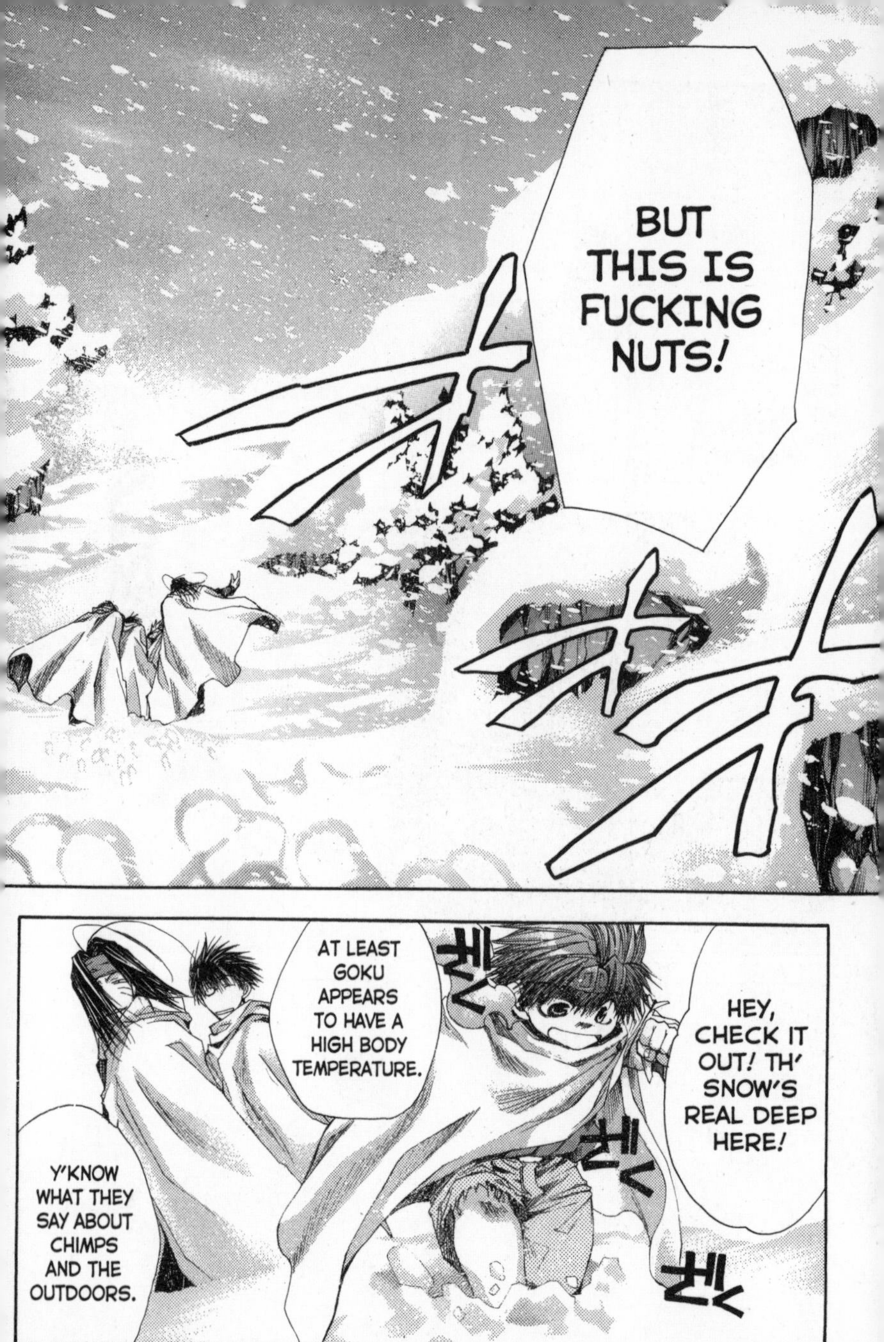
BUT THIS IS FUCKING NUTS!
HEY, CHECK IT OUT! TH' SNOW'S REAL DEEP HERE!
AT LEAST GOKU APPEARS TO HAVE A HIGH BODY TEMPERATURE.
Y'KNOW WHAT THEY SAY ABOUT CHIMPS AND THE OUTDOORS.

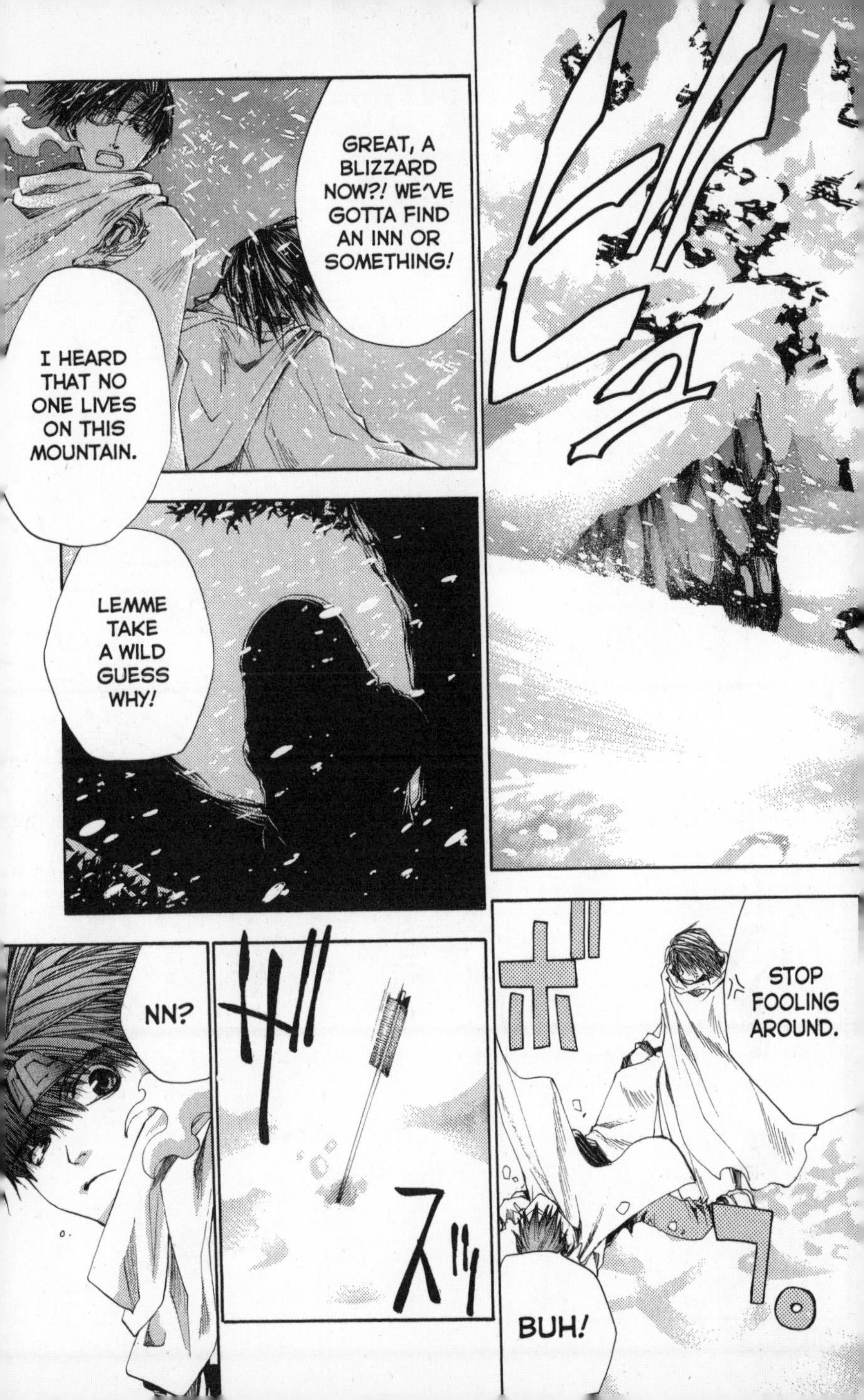
GREAT, A BLIZZARD NOW?! WE'VE GOTTA FIND AN INN OR SOMETHING!
I HEARD THAT NO ONE LIVES ON THIS MOUNTAIN.
LEMME TAKE A WILD GUESS WHY!
STOP FOOLING AROUND.
BUH!
NN?

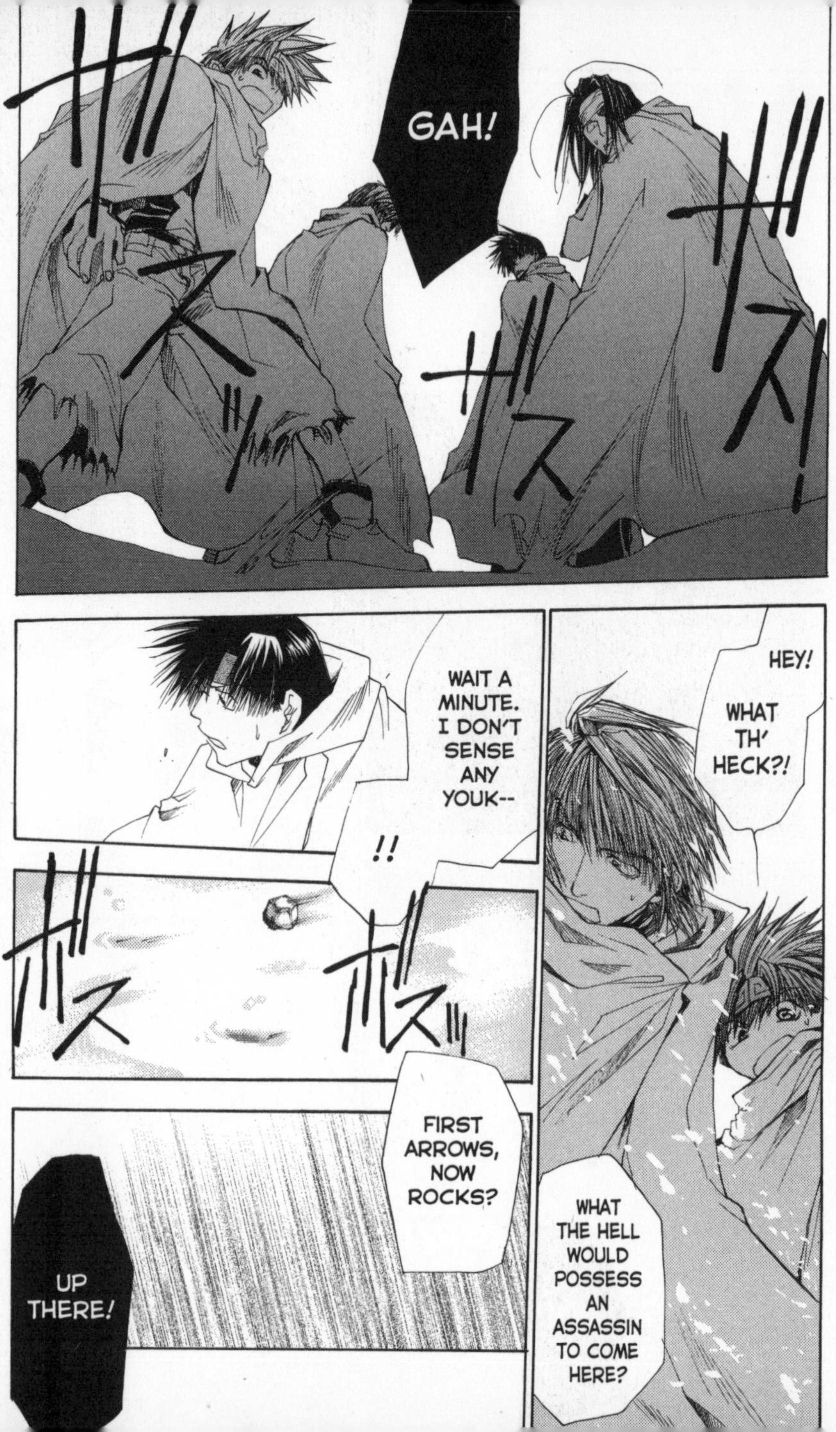
GAH!
HEY!
WHAT TH' HECK?!
WAIT A MINUTE. I DON'T SENSE ANY YOUK--
!!
FIRST ARROWS, NOW ROCKS?
WHAT THE HELL WOULD POSSESS AN ASSASSIN TO COME HERE?
UP THERE!

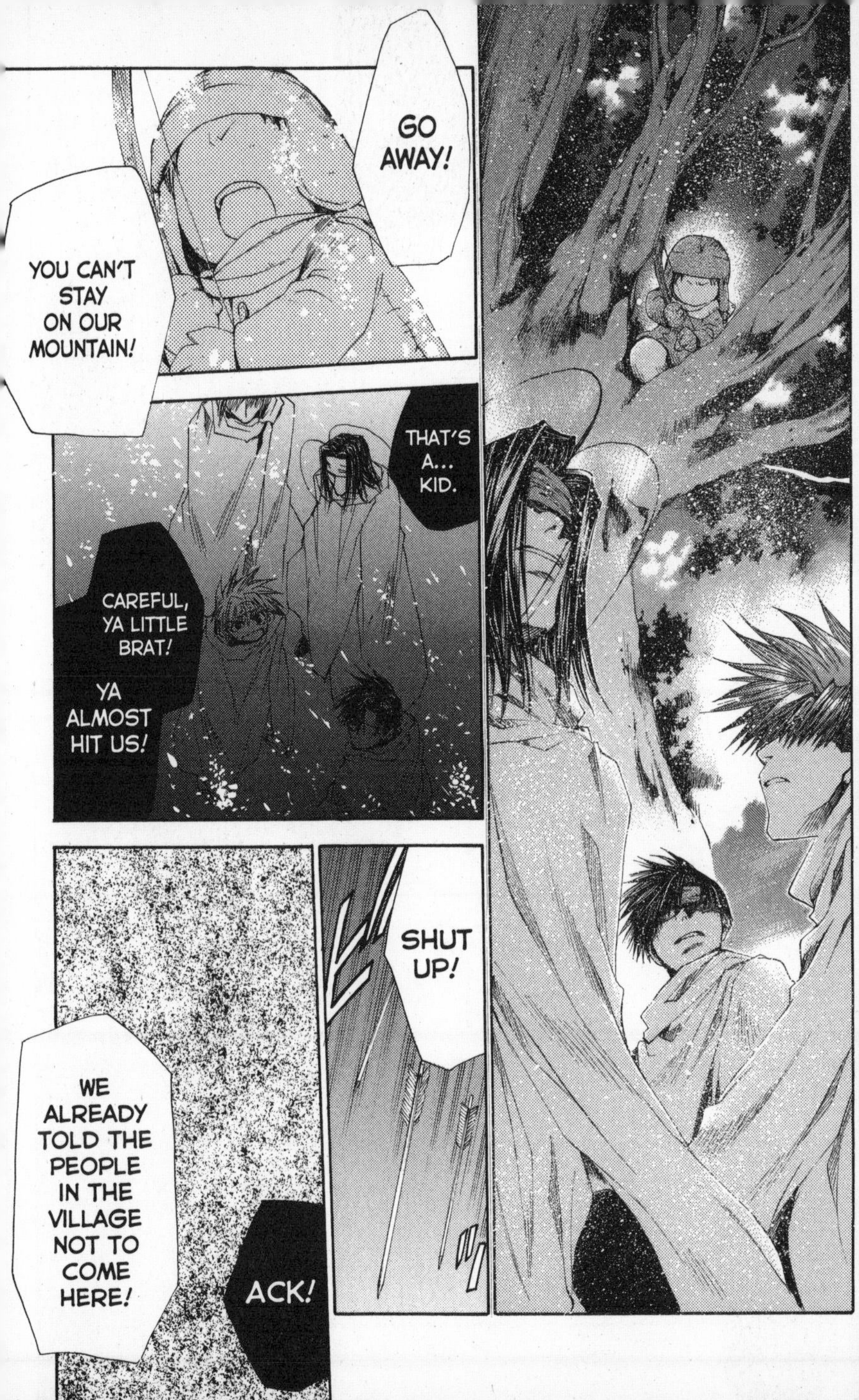
GO AWAY!
YOU CAN'T STAY ON OUR MOUNTAIN!
THAT'S A... KID.
CAREFUL, YA LITTLE BRAT!
YA ALMOST HIT US!
SHUT UP!
ACK!
WE ALREADY TOLD THE PEOPLE IN THE VILLAGE NOT TO COME HERE!

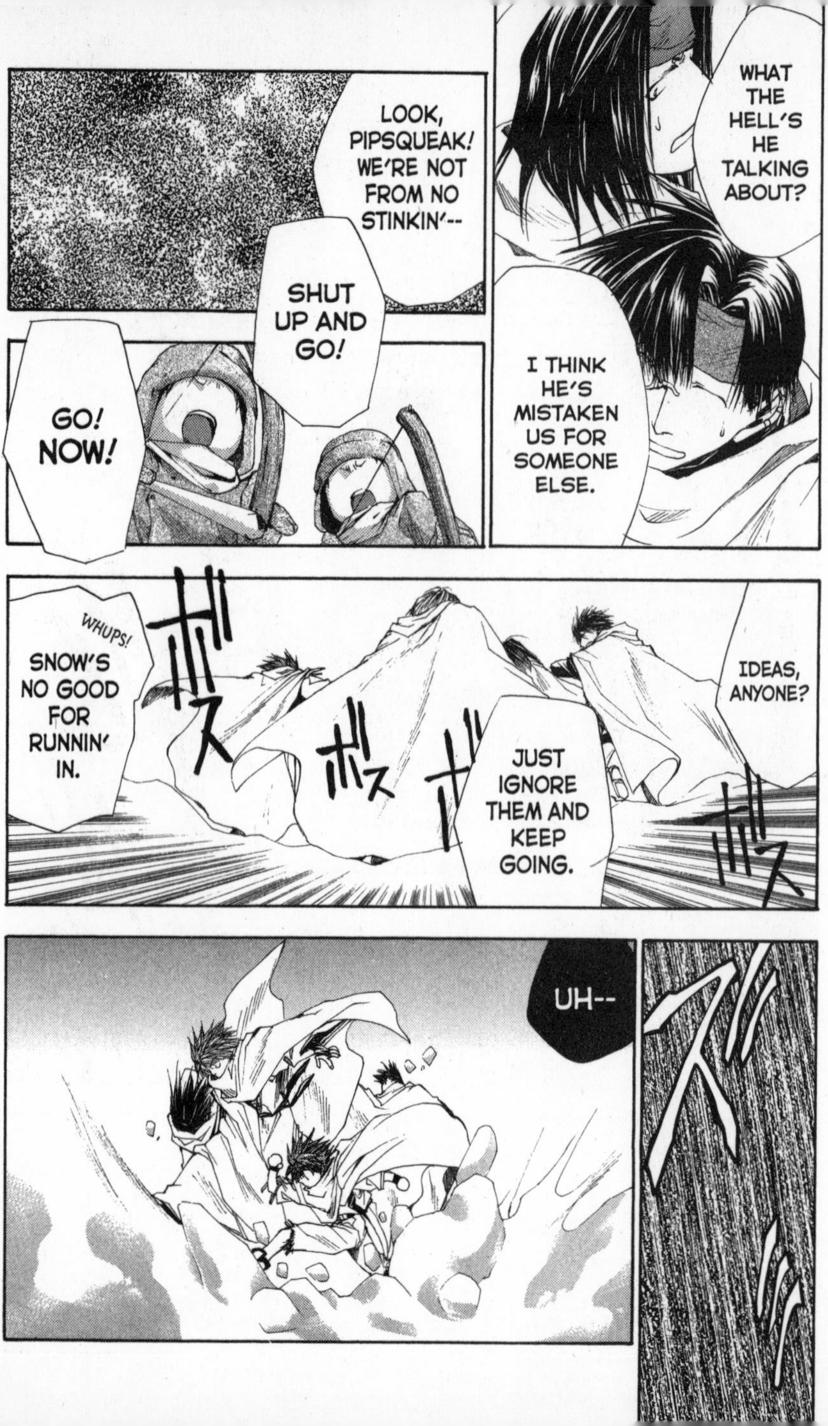
WHAT THE HELL'S HE TALKING ABOUT?
I THINK HE'S MISTAKEN US FOR SOMEONE ELSE.
LOOK, PIPSQUEAK! WE'RE NOT FROM NO STINKIN'--
SHUT UP AND GO!
GO! NOW!
IDEAS, ANYONE?
JUST IGNORE THEM AND KEEP GOING.
WHUPS!
SNOW'S NO GOOD FOR RUNNIN' IN.
UH--

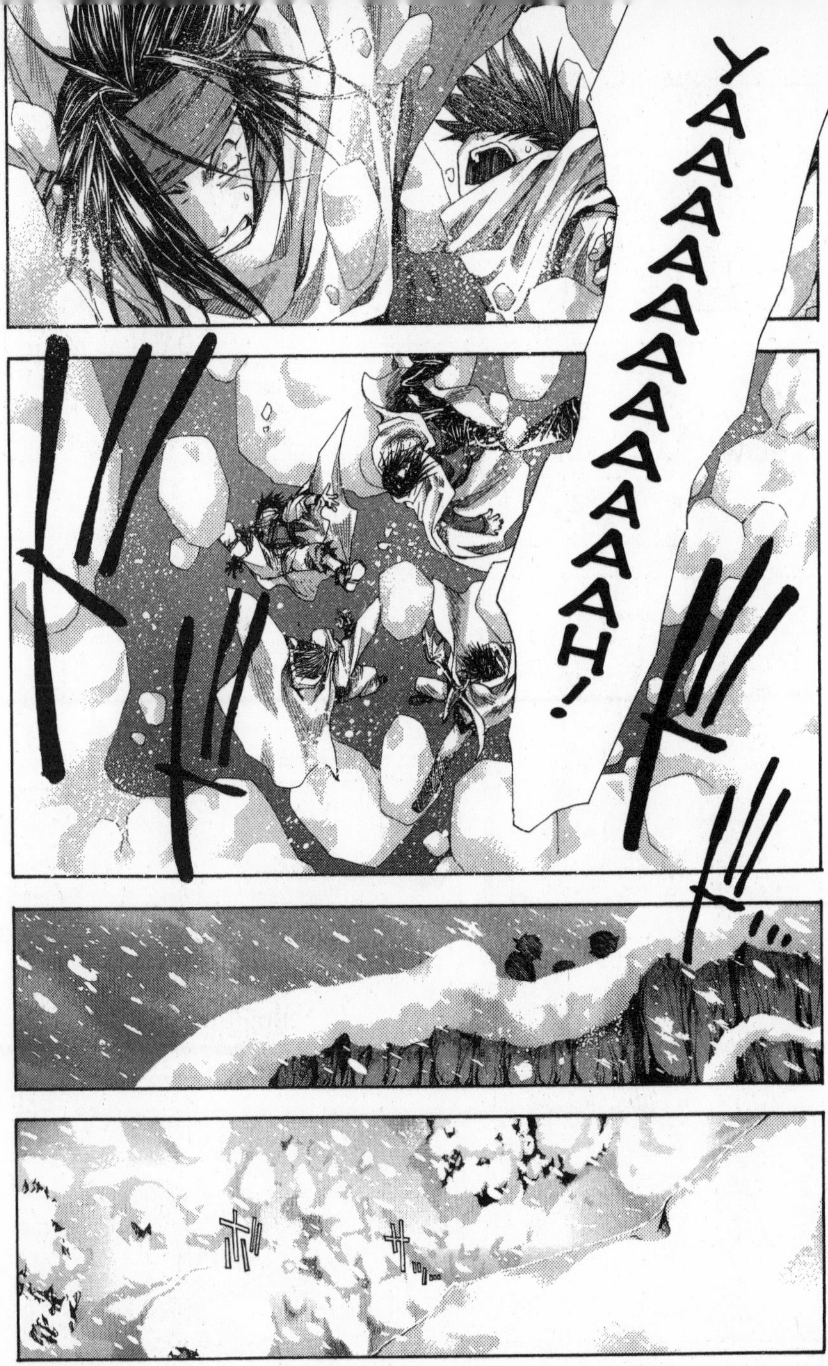
YAAAAAAAAAAAH!

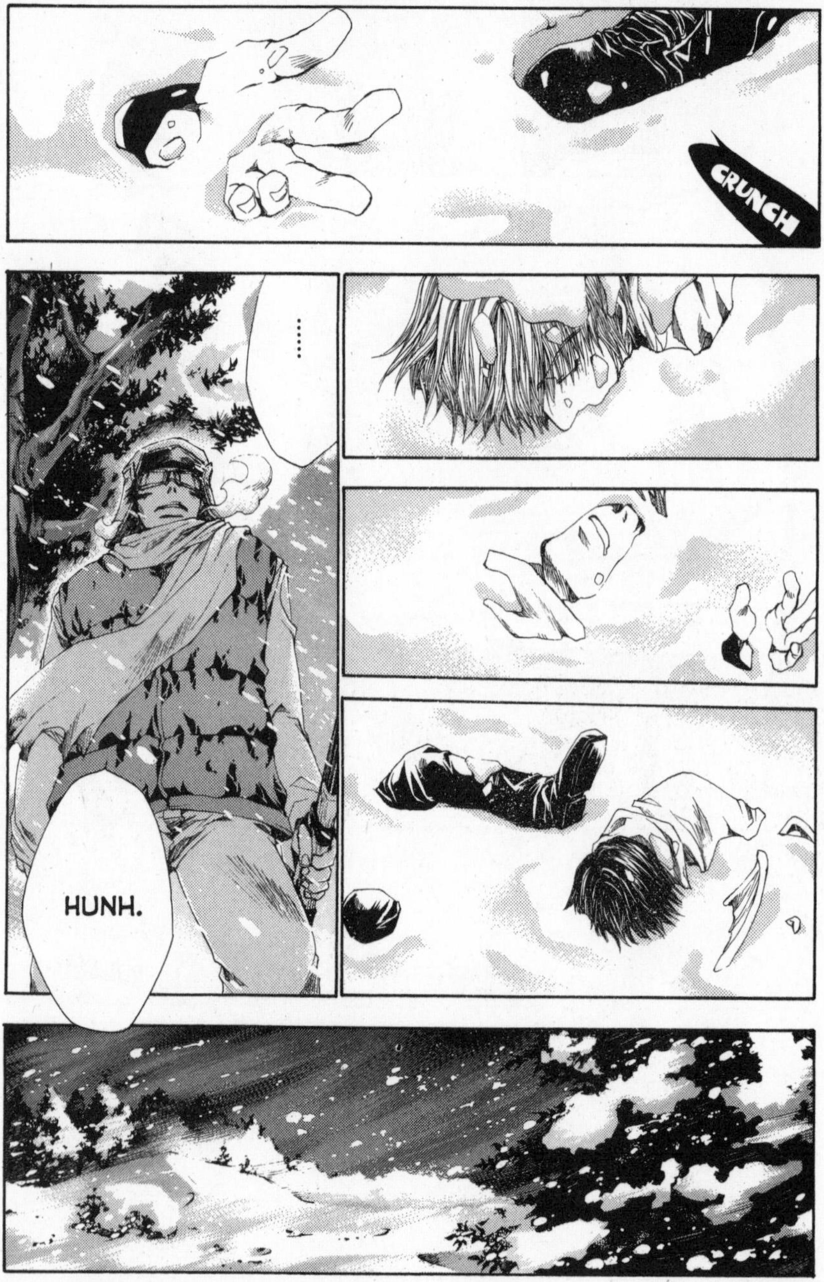
CRUNCH
......
HUNH.

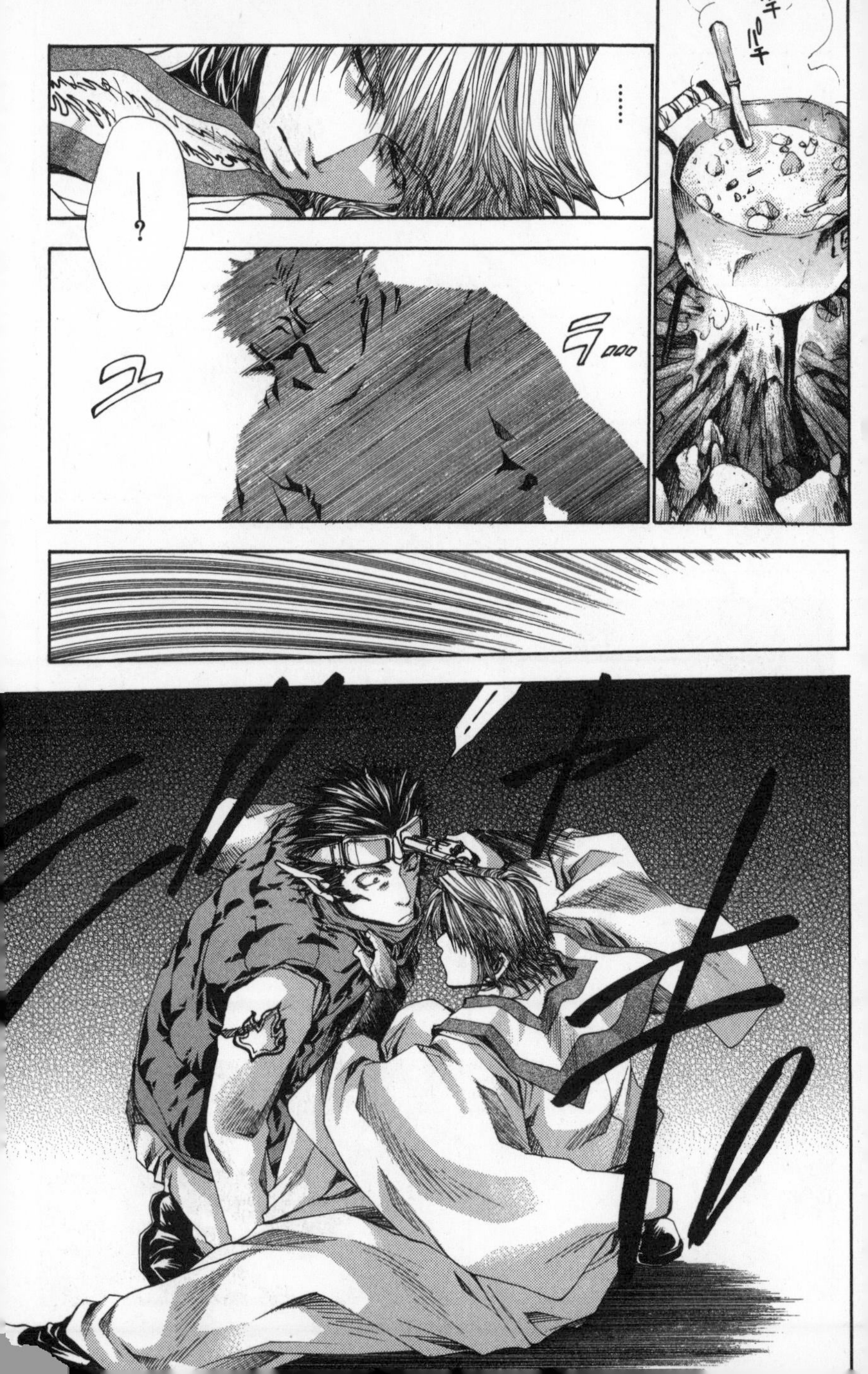
パチ
パチ
……
―!?
ユ
ラ...

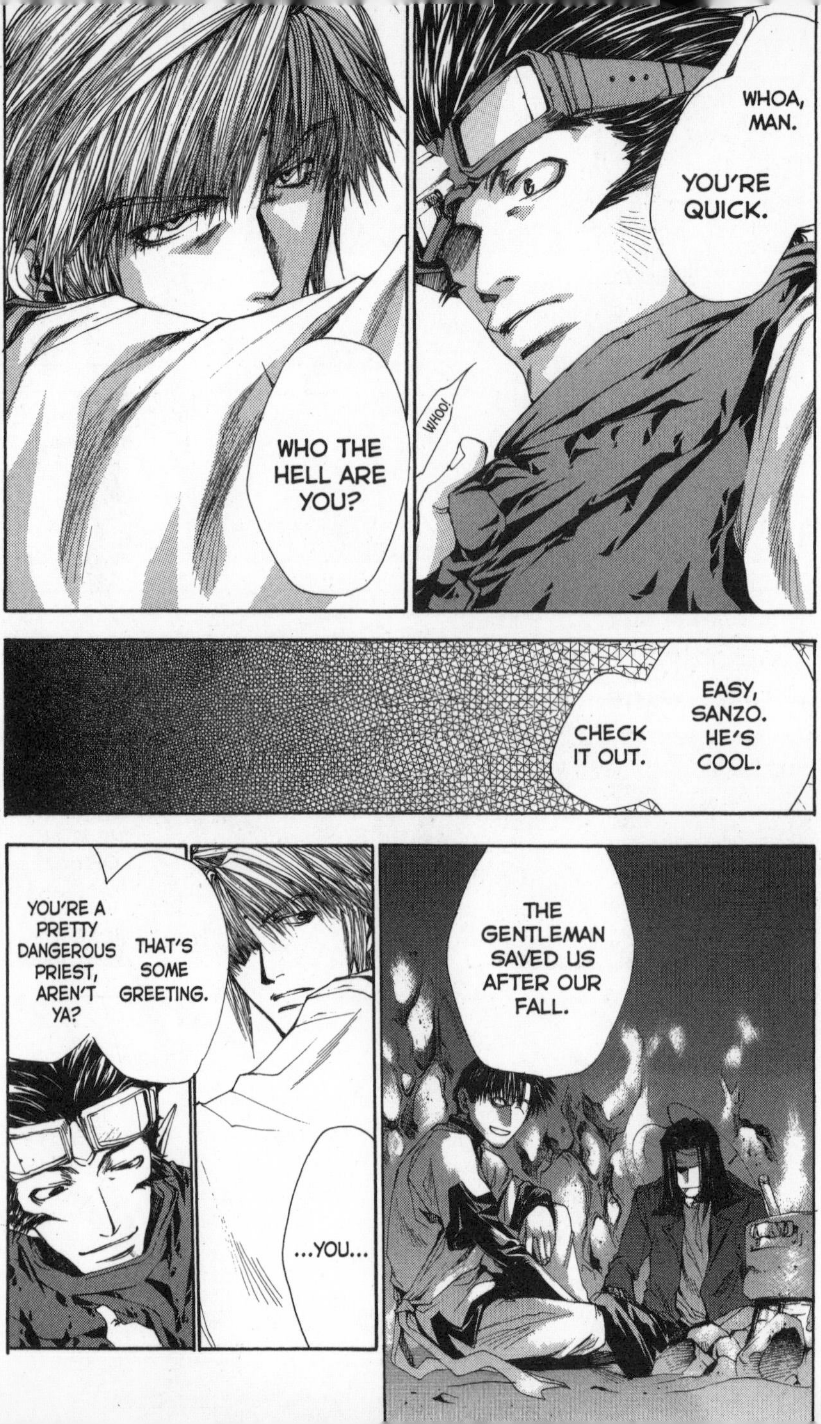
WHOA, MAN.
YOU'RE QUICK.
WHOO!
WHO THE HELL ARE YOU?
EASY, SANZO. HE'S COOL.
CHECK IT OUT.
THE GENTLEMAN SAVED US AFTER OUR FALL.
THAT'S SOME GREETING.
YOU'RE A PRETTY DANGEROUS PRIEST, AREN'T YA?
...YOU...

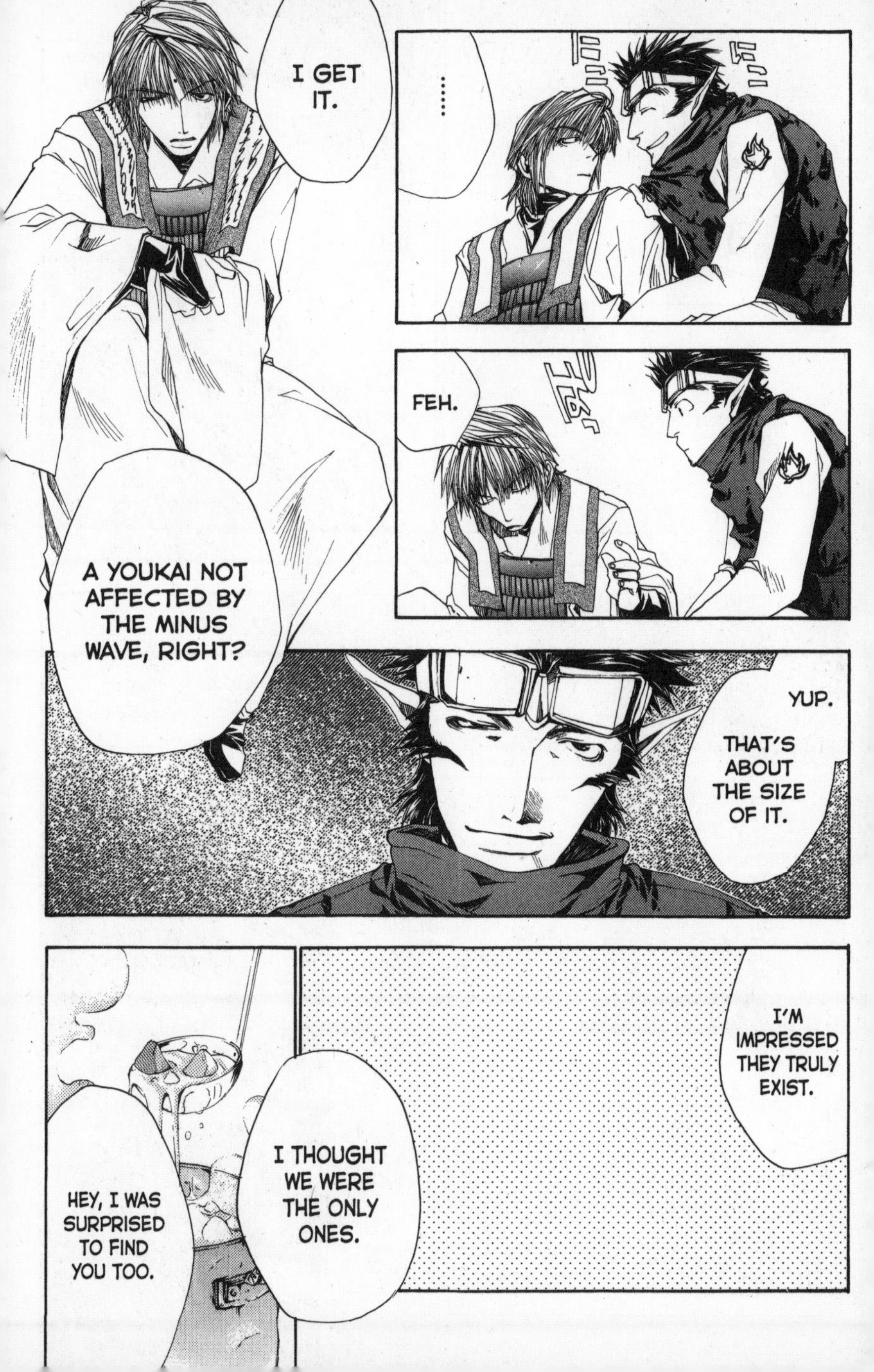
......
FEH.
I GET IT.
A YOUKAI NOT AFFECTED BY THE MINUS WAVE, RIGHT?
YUP.
THAT'S ABOUT THE SIZE OF IT.
I'M IMPRESSED THEY TRULY EXIST.
I THOUGHT WE WERE THE ONLY ONES.
HEY, I WAS SURPRISED TO FIND YOU TOO.

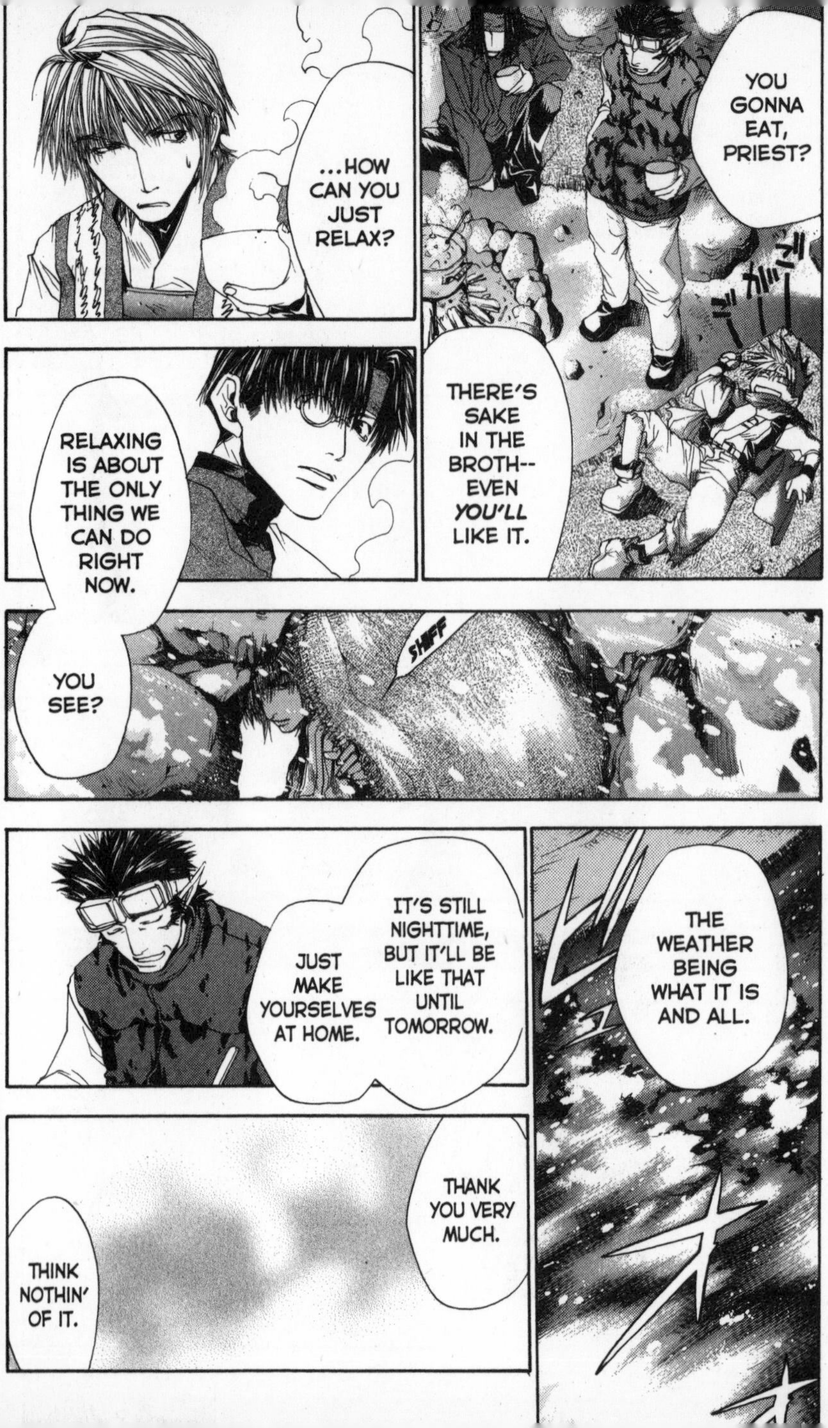
YOU GONNA EAT, PRIEST?
THERE'S SAKE IN THE BROTH-- EVEN *YOU'LL* LIKE IT.
...HOW CAN YOU JUST RELAX?
RELAXING IS ABOUT THE ONLY THING WE CAN DO RIGHT NOW.
YOU SEE?
SHFF
THE WEATHER BEING WHAT IT IS AND ALL.
IT'S STILL NIGHTTIME, BUT IT'LL BE LIKE THAT UNTIL TOMORROW.
JUST MAKE YOURSELVES AT HOME.
THANK YOU VERY MUCH.
THINK NOTHIN' OF IT.

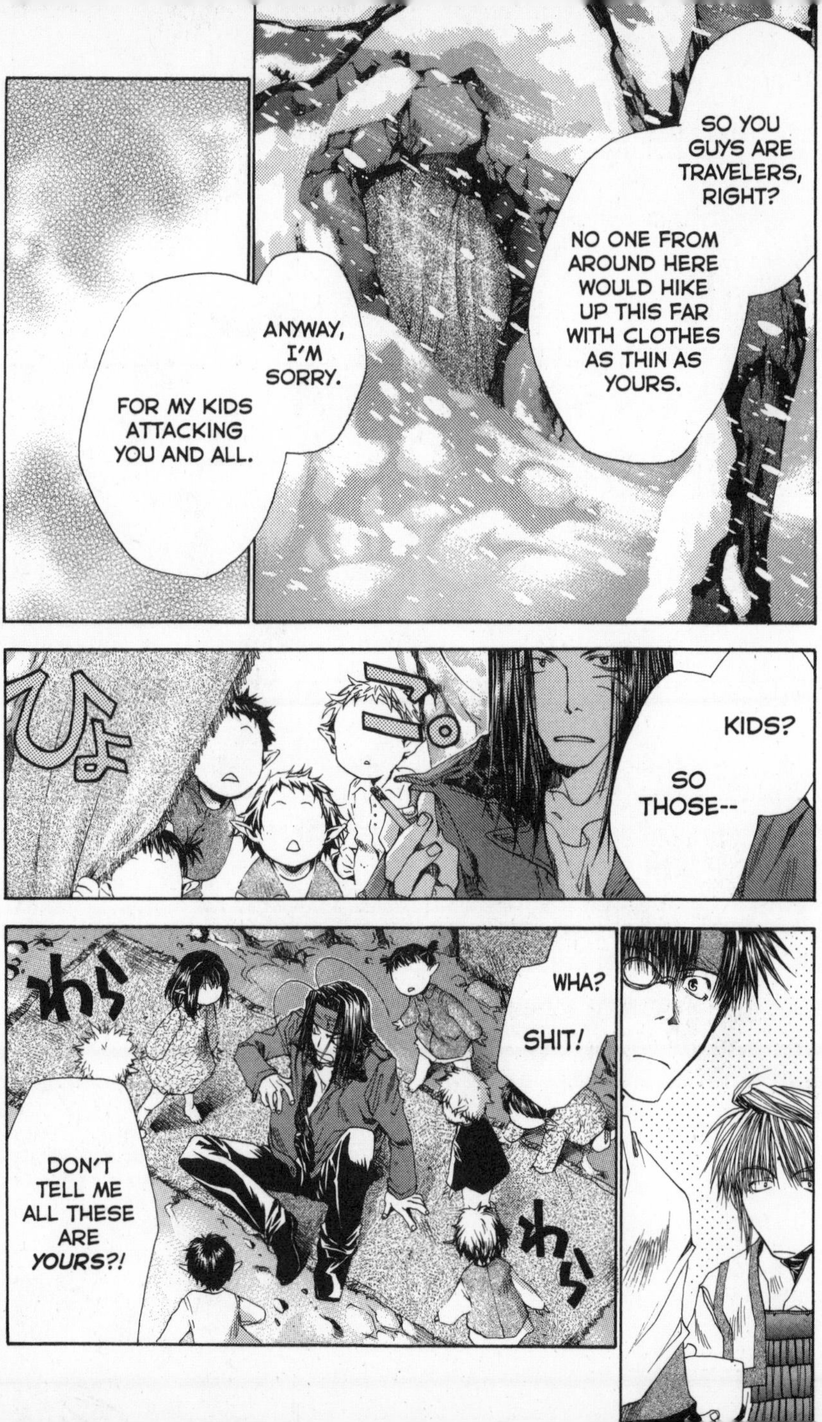
SO YOU GUYS ARE TRAVELERS, RIGHT?
NO ONE FROM AROUND HERE WOULD HIKE UP THIS FAR WITH CLOTHES AS THIN AS YOURS.
ANYWAY, I'M SORRY.
FOR MY KIDS ATTACKING YOU AND ALL.
KIDS?
SO THOSE--
WHA?
SHIT!
わら
わら
DON'T TELL ME ALL THESE ARE *YOURS*?!

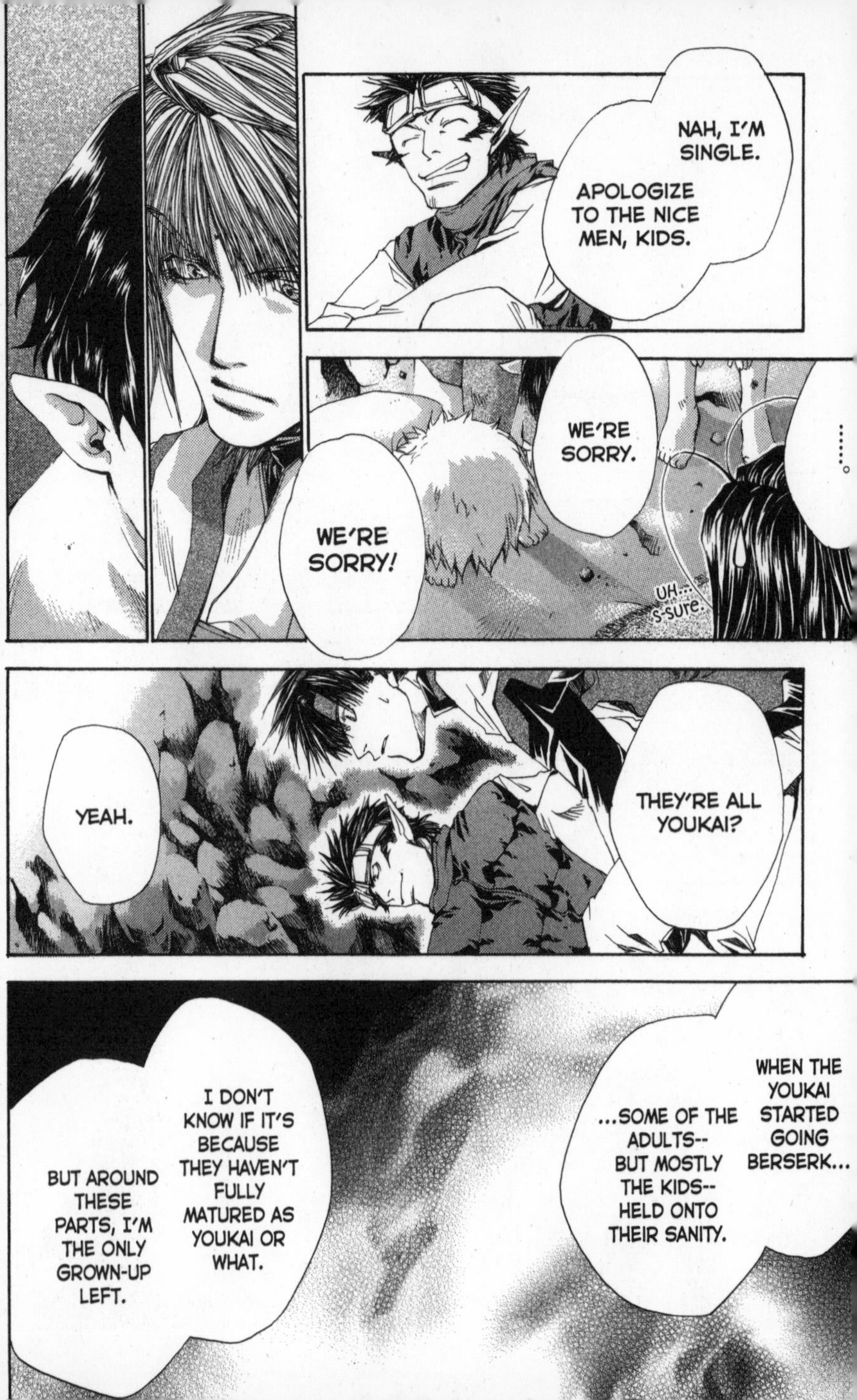
NAH, I'M SINGLE.
APOLOGIZE TO THE NICE MEN, KIDS.
......
WE'RE SORRY.
WE'RE SORRY!
UH... S-SURE.
THEY'RE ALL YOUKAI?
YEAH.
WHEN THE YOUKAI STARTED GOING BERSERK...
...SOME OF THE ADULTS-- BUT MOSTLY THE KIDS-- HELD ONTO THEIR SANITY.
I DON'T KNOW IF IT'S BECAUSE THEY HAVEN'T FULLY MATURED AS YOUKAI OR WHAT.
BUT AROUND THESE PARTS, I'M THE ONLY GROWN-UP LEFT.

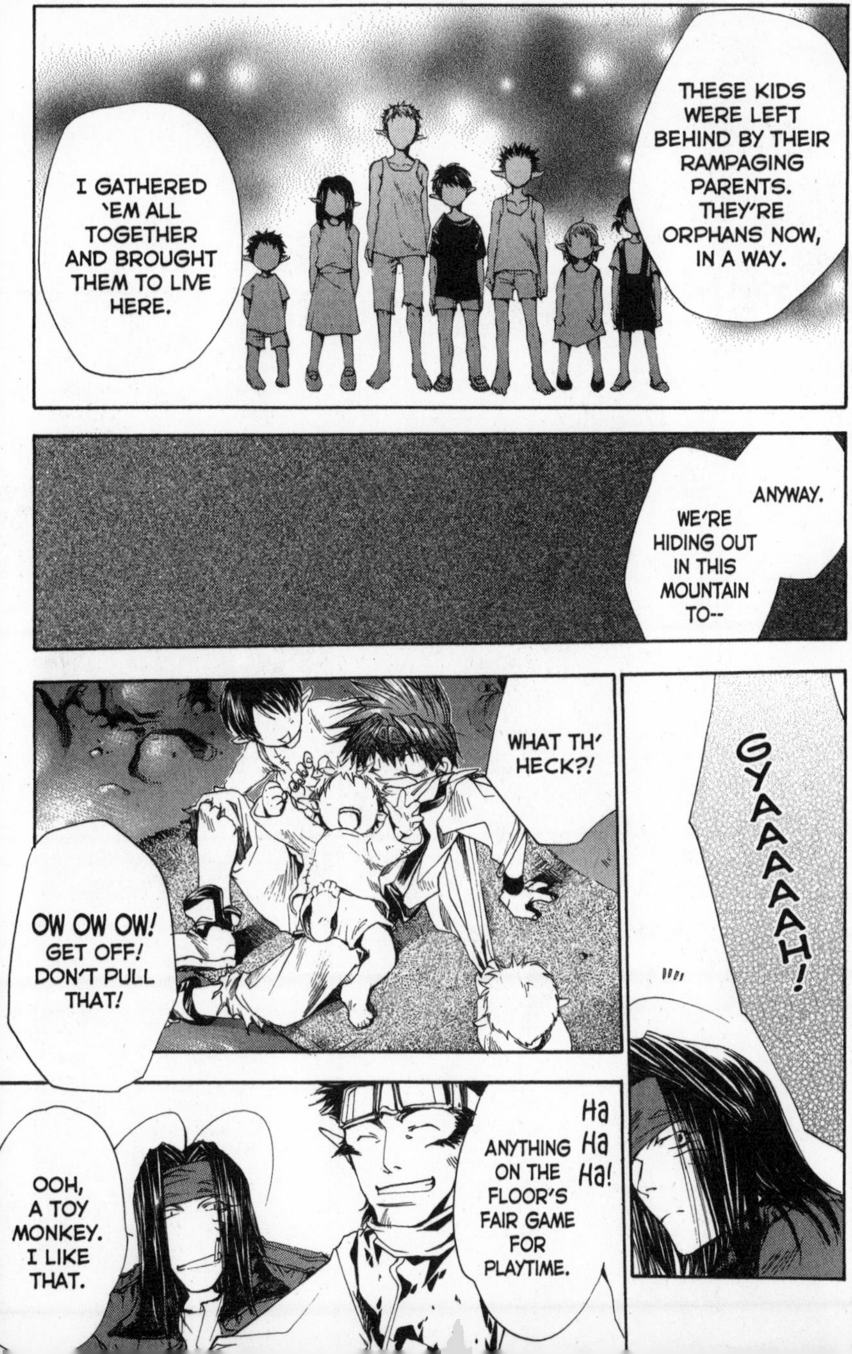
THESE KIDS WERE LEFT BEHIND BY THEIR RAMPAGING PARENTS. THEY'RE ORPHANS NOW, IN A WAY.
I GATHERED 'EM ALL TOGETHER AND BROUGHT THEM TO LIVE HERE.
ANYWAY.
WE'RE HIDING OUT IN THIS MOUNTAIN TO--
GYAAAAAH!
WHAT TH' HECK?!
OW OW OW! GET OFF! DON'T PULL THAT!
Ha Ha Ha!
ANYTHING ON THE FLOOR'S FAIR GAME FOR PLAYTIME.
OOH, A TOY MONKEY. I LIKE THAT.

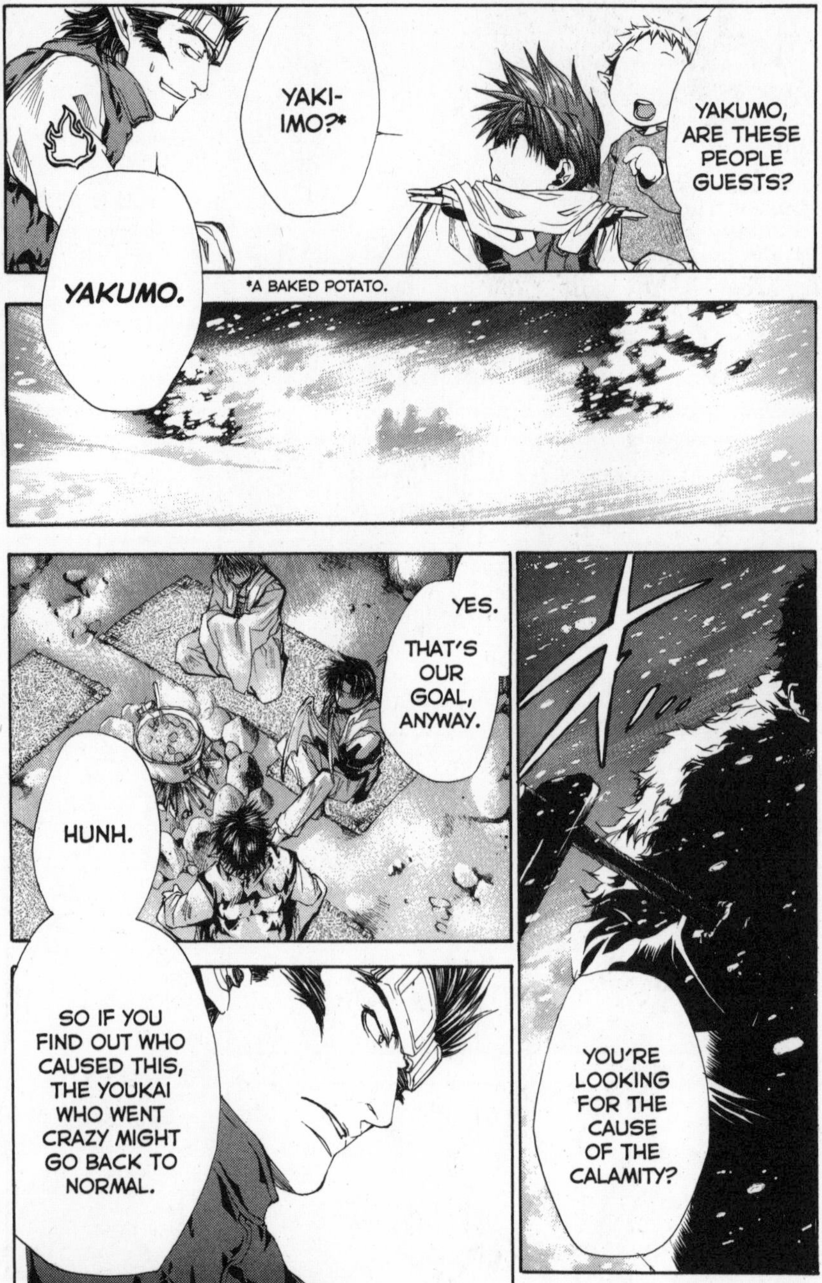
YAKUMO, ARE THESE PEOPLE GUESTS?
YAKI-IMO?*
YAKUMO.
*A BAKED POTATO.
YOU'RE LOOKING FOR THE CAUSE OF THE CALAMITY?
YES.
THAT'S OUR GOAL, ANYWAY.
HUNH.
SO IF YOU FIND OUT WHO CAUSED THIS, THE YOUKAI WHO WENT CRAZY MIGHT GO BACK TO NORMAL.

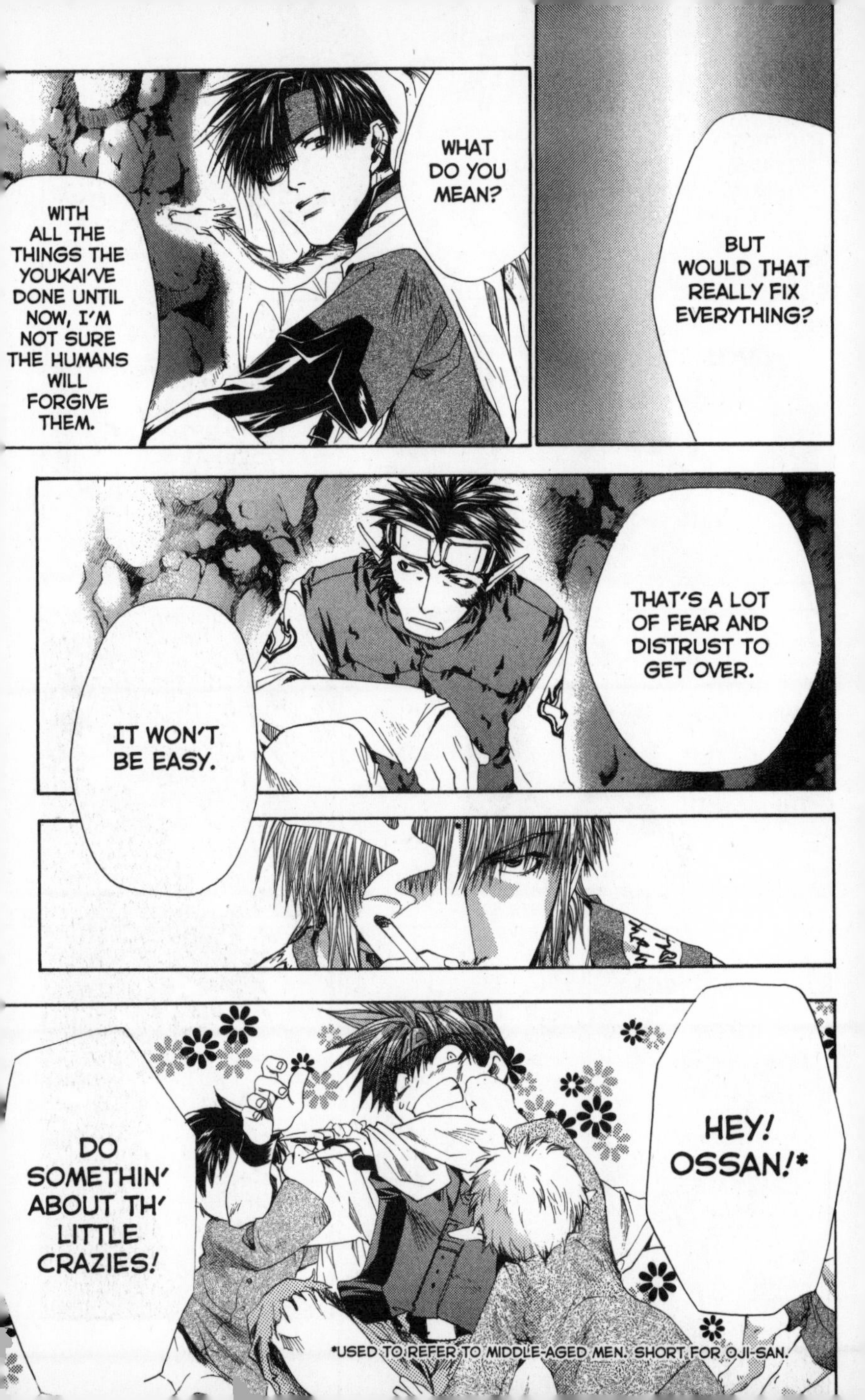
BUT WOULD THAT REALLY FIX EVERYTHING?
WHAT DO YOU MEAN?
WITH ALL THE THINGS THE YOUKAI'VE DONE UNTIL NOW, I'M NOT SURE THE HUMANS WILL FORGIVE THEM.
THAT'S A LOT OF FEAR AND DISTRUST TO GET OVER.
IT WON'T BE EASY.
HEY! OSSAN!*
DO SOMETHIN' ABOUT TH' LITTLE CRAZIES!

*USED TO REFER TO MIDDLE-AGED MEN. SHORT FOR OJI-SAN.

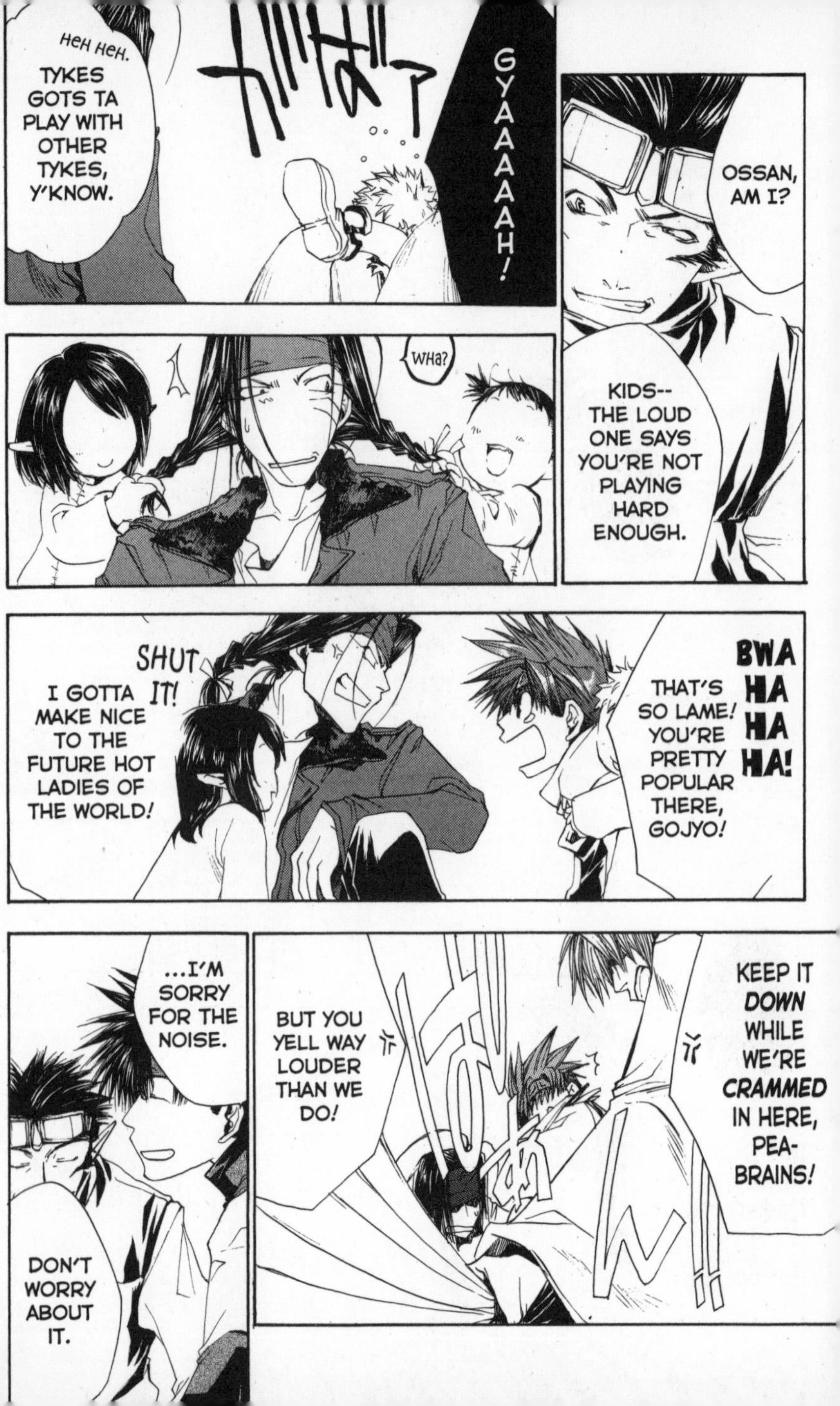
HEH HEH.
TYKES GOTS TA PLAY WITH OTHER TYKES, Y'KNOW.
GYAAAAAAH!
OSSAN, AM I?
KIDS-- THE LOUD ONE SAYS YOU'RE NOT PLAYING HARD ENOUGH.
WHA?
BWA HA HA HA!
THAT'S SO LAME! YOU'RE PRETTY POPULAR THERE, GOJYO!
SHUT IT!
I GOTTA MAKE NICE TO THE FUTURE HOT LADIES OF THE WORLD!
KEEP IT DOWN WHILE WE'RE CRAMMED IN HERE, PEA-BRAINS!
BUT YOU YELL WAY LOUDER THAN WE DO!
...I'M SORRY FOR THE NOISE.
DON'T WORRY ABOUT IT.

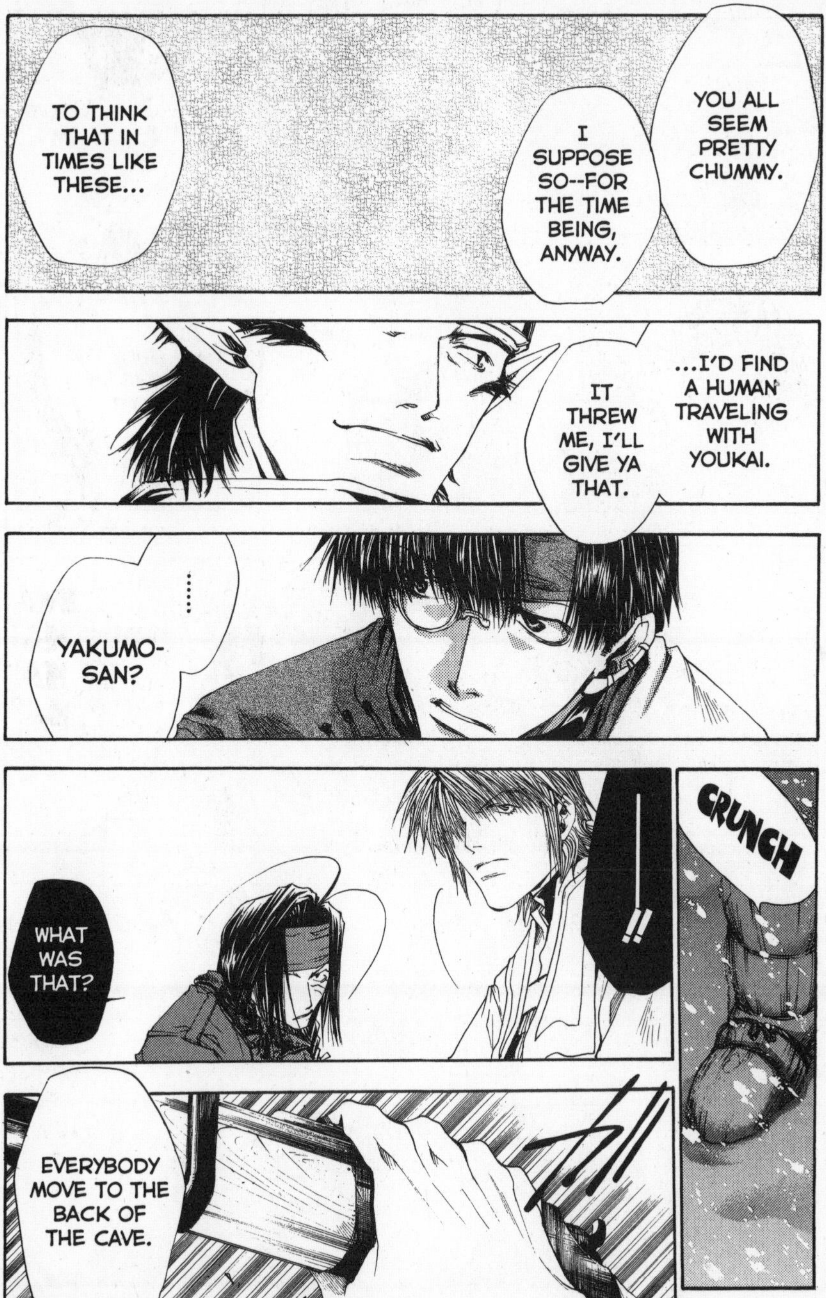
YOU ALL SEEM PRETTY CHUMMY.
I SUPPOSE SO--FOR THE TIME BEING, ANYWAY.
TO THINK THAT IN TIMES LIKE THESE...
...I'D FIND A HUMAN TRAVELING WITH YOUKAI.
IT THREW ME, I'LL GIVE YA THAT.
......
YAKUMO-SAN?
CRUNCH
!!
WHAT WAS THAT?
EVERYBODY MOVE TO THE BACK OF THE CAVE.

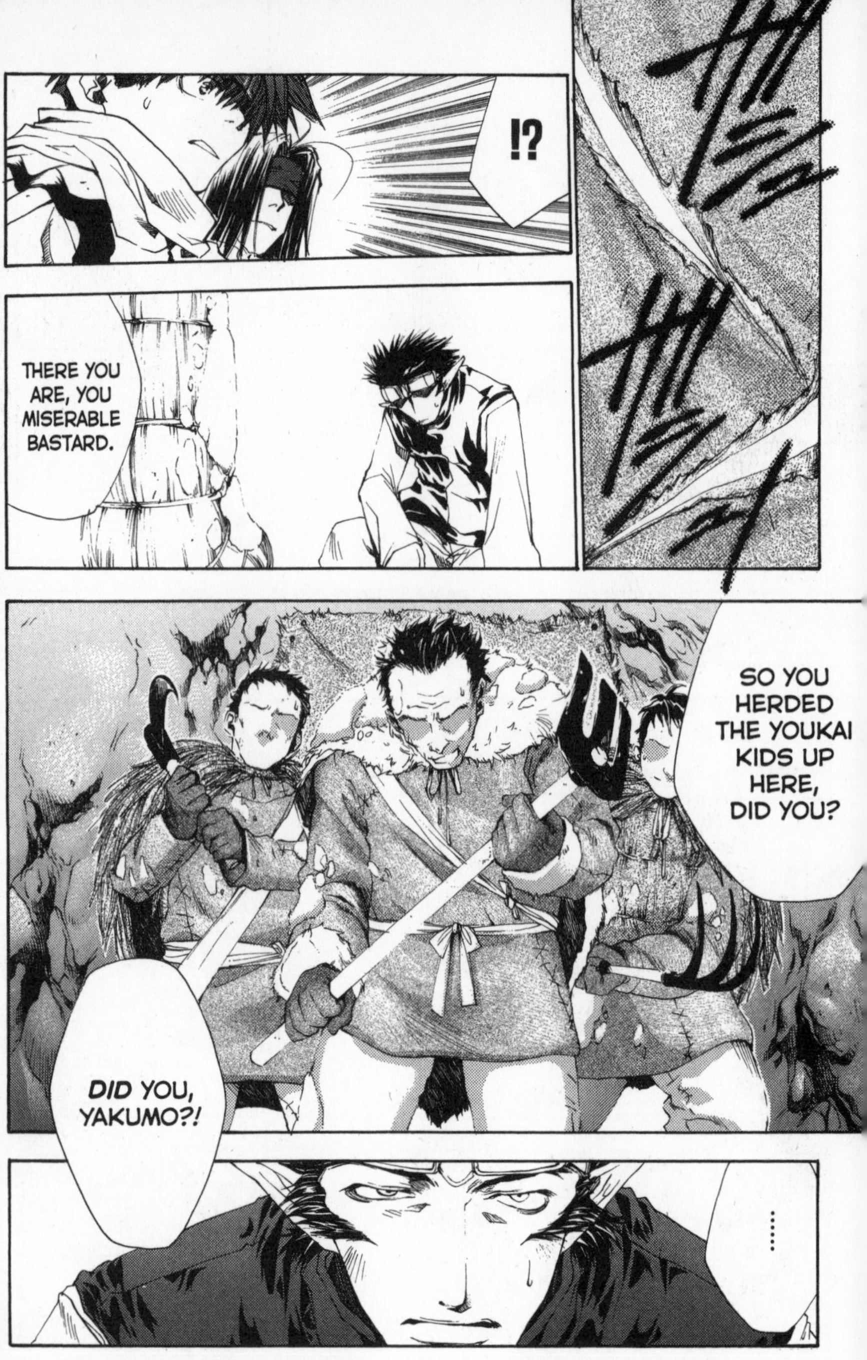
!?
THERE YOU ARE, YOU MISERABLE BASTARD.
SO YOU HERDED THE YOUKAI KIDS UP HERE, DID YOU?
DID YOU, YAKUMO?!
......

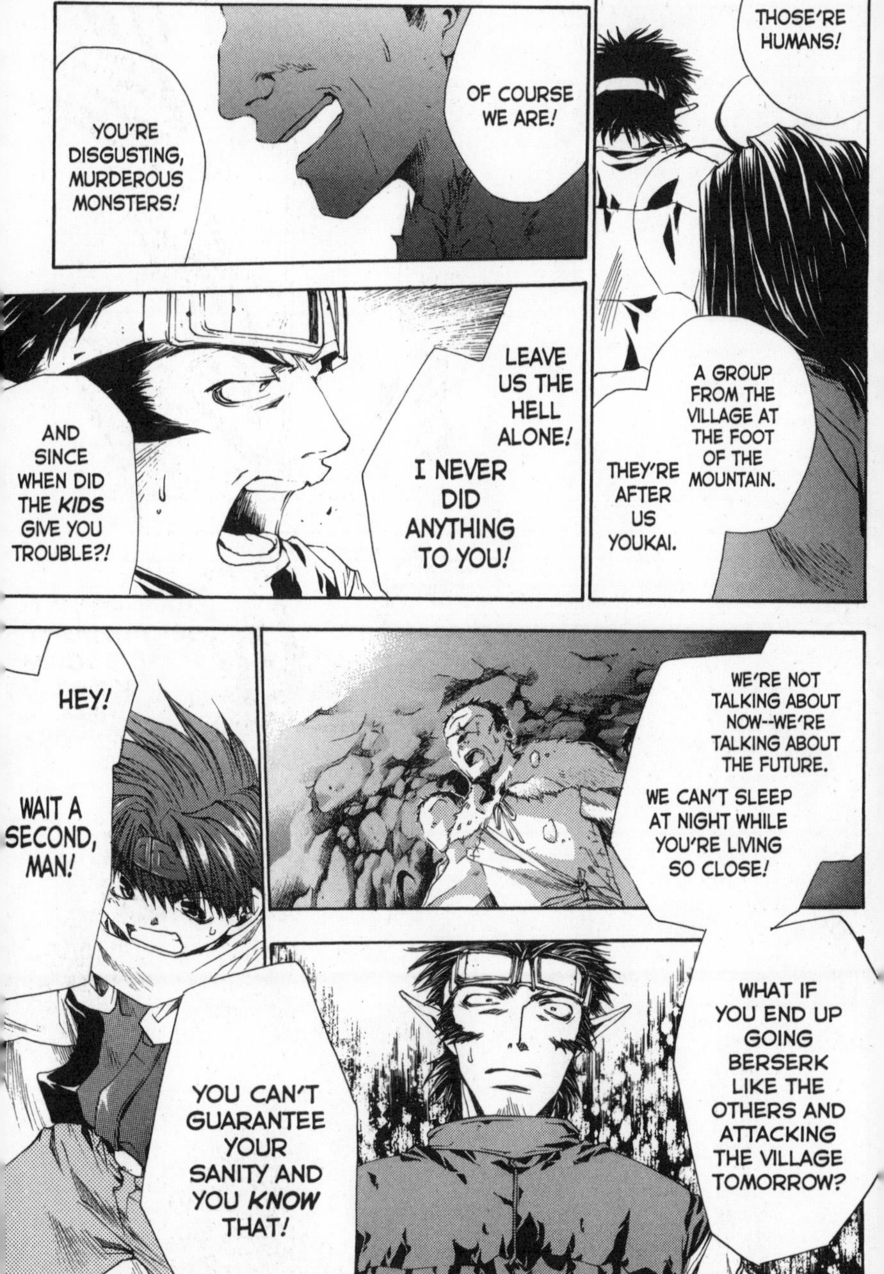
THOSE'RE HUMANS!
A GROUP FROM THE VILLAGE AT THE FOOT OF THE MOUNTAIN.
THEY'RE AFTER US YOUKAI.
OF COURSE WE ARE!
YOU'RE DISGUSTING, MURDEROUS MONSTERS!
LEAVE US THE HELL ALONE!
I NEVER DID ANYTHING TO YOU!
AND SINCE WHEN DID THE *KIDS* GIVE YOU TROUBLE?!
WE'RE NOT TALKING ABOUT NOW--WE'RE TALKING ABOUT THE FUTURE.
WE CAN'T SLEEP AT NIGHT WHILE YOU'RE LIVING SO CLOSE!
WHAT IF YOU END UP GOING BERSERK LIKE THE OTHERS AND ATTACKING THE VILLAGE TOMORROW?
YOU CAN'T GUARANTEE YOUR SANITY AND YOU *KNOW* THAT!
HEY!
WAIT A SECOND, MAN!

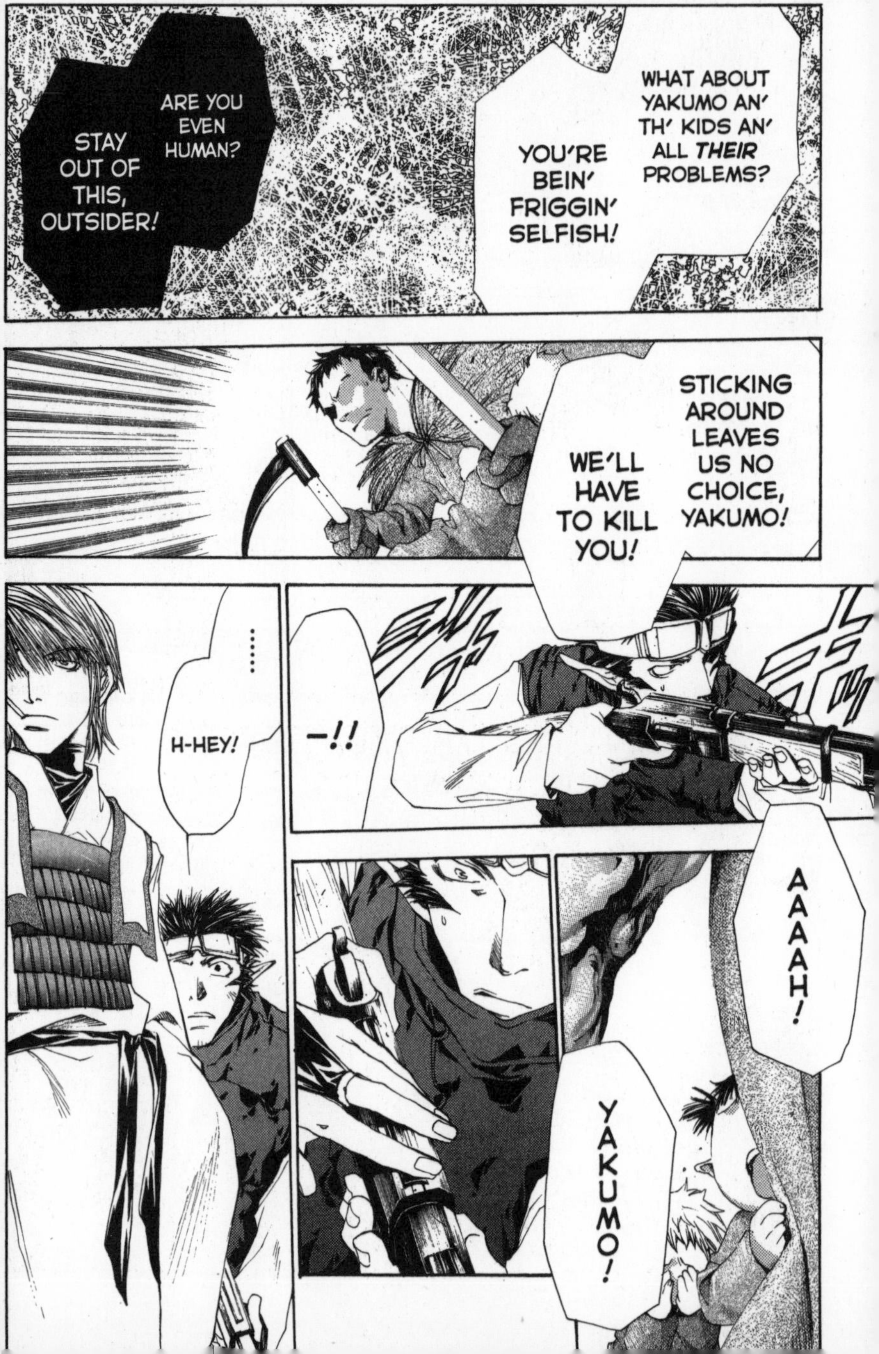
WHAT ABOUT YAKUMO AN' TH' KIDS AN' ALL *THEIR* PROBLEMS?
YOU'RE BEIN' FRIGGIN' SELFISH!
ARE YOU EVEN HUMAN?
STAY OUT OF THIS, OUTSIDER!
STICKING AROUND LEAVES US NO CHOICE, YAKUMO!
WE'LL HAVE TO KILL YOU!
—!!
AAAAH!
YAKUMO!
......
H-HEY!

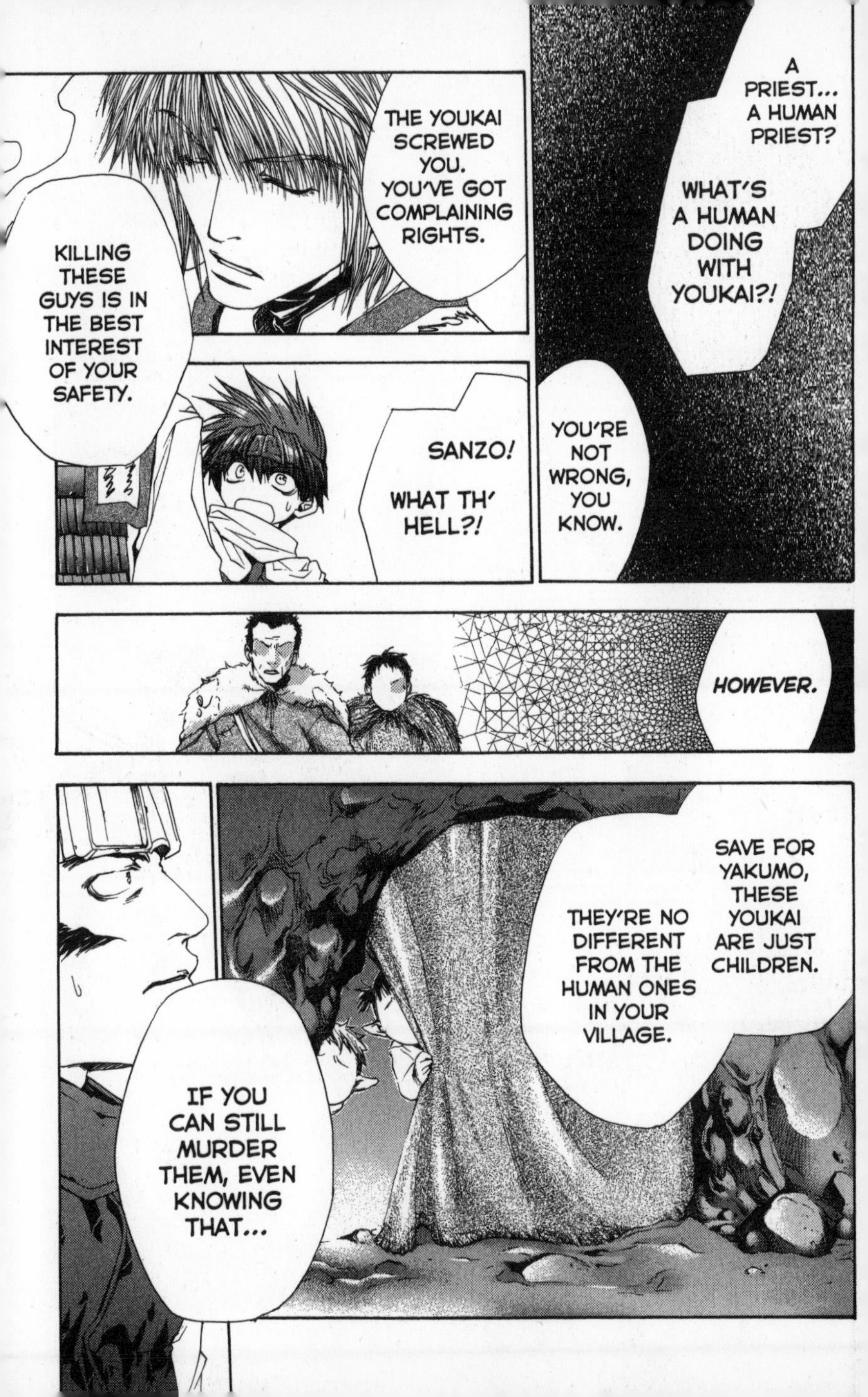
A PRIEST... A HUMAN PRIEST?
WHAT'S A HUMAN DOING WITH YOUKAI?!
YOU'RE NOT WRONG, YOU KNOW.
THE YOUKAI SCREWED YOU. YOU'VE GOT COMPLAINING RIGHTS.
KILLING THESE GUYS IS IN THE BEST INTEREST OF YOUR SAFETY.
SANZO!
WHAT TH' HELL?!
HOWEVER.
SAVE FOR YAKUMO, THESE YOUKAI ARE JUST CHILDREN.
THEY'RE NO DIFFERENT FROM THE HUMAN ONES IN YOUR VILLAGE.
IF YOU CAN STILL MURDER THEM, EVEN KNOWING THAT...

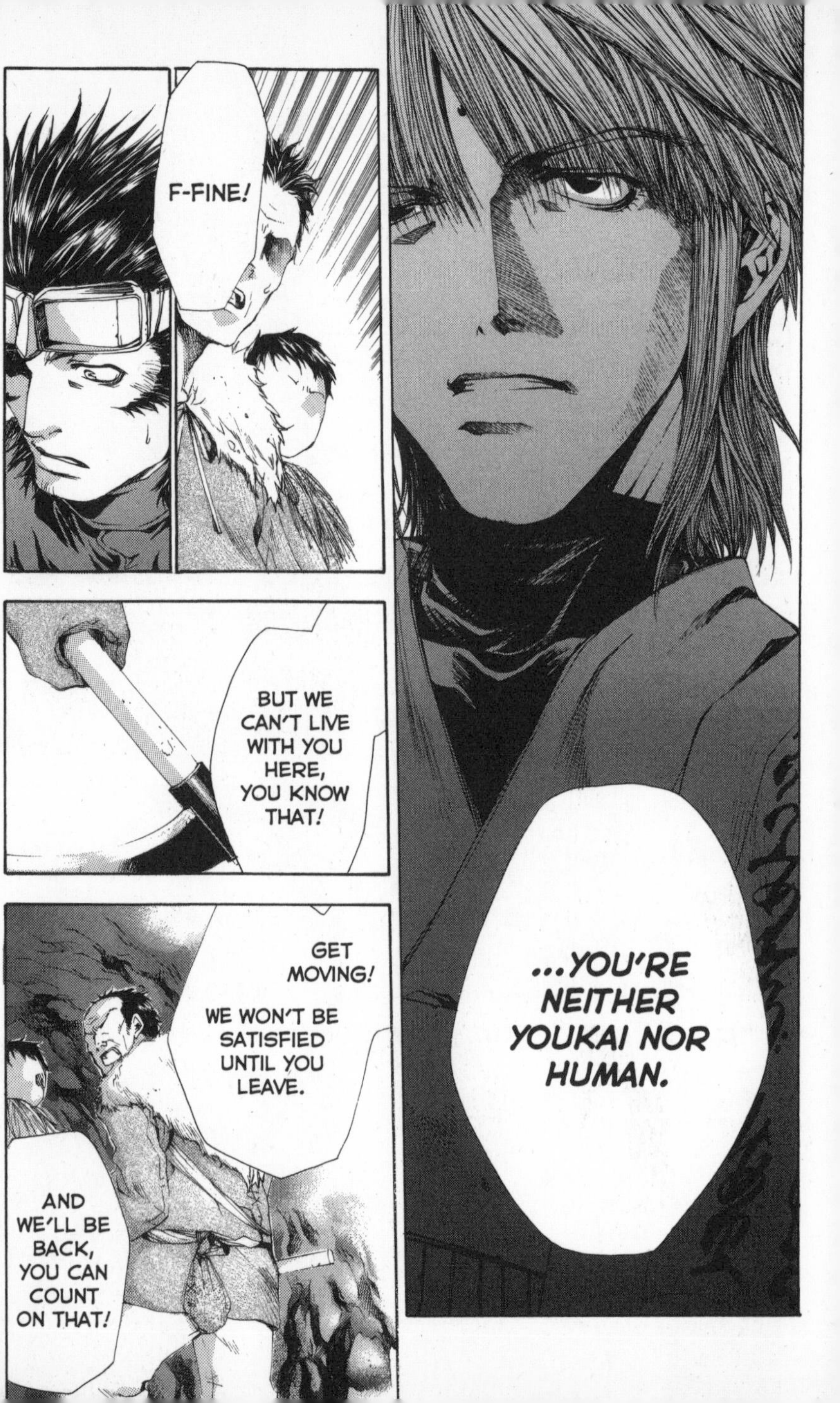
...YOU'RE NEITHER YOUKAI NOR HUMAN.
F-FINE!
BUT WE CAN'T LIVE WITH YOU HERE, YOU KNOW THAT!
GET MOVING!
WE WON'T BE SATISFIED UNTIL YOU LEAVE.
AND WE'LL BE BACK, YOU CAN COUNT ON THAT!

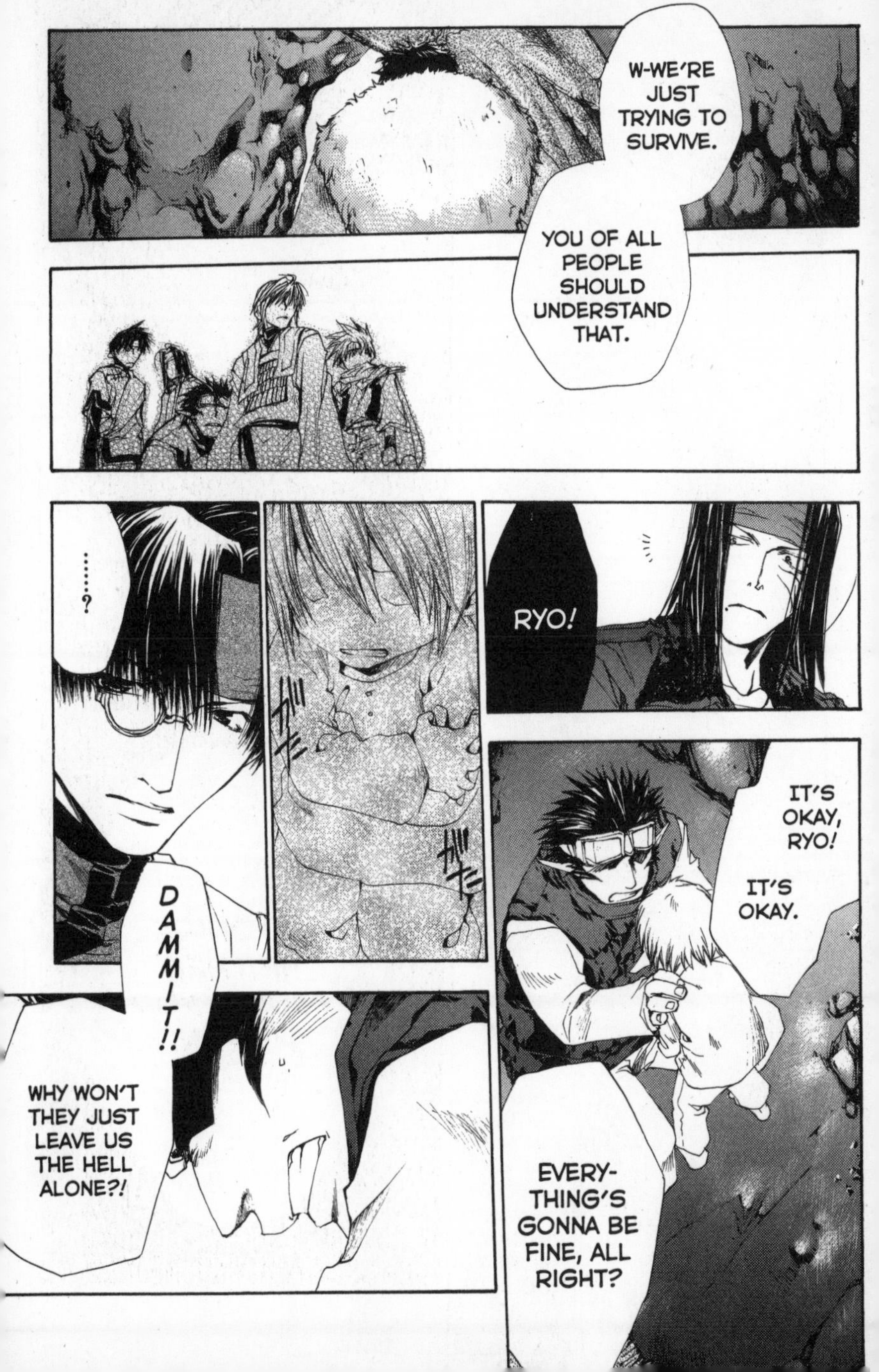
W-WE'RE JUST TRYING TO SURVIVE.
YOU OF ALL PEOPLE SHOULD UNDERSTAND THAT.
RYO!
IT'S OKAY, RYO!
IT'S OKAY.
EVERY-THING'S GONNA BE FINE, ALL RIGHT?
ガタ
ガタ
......?
DAMMIT!!
WHY WON'T THEY JUST LEAVE US THE HELL ALONE?!

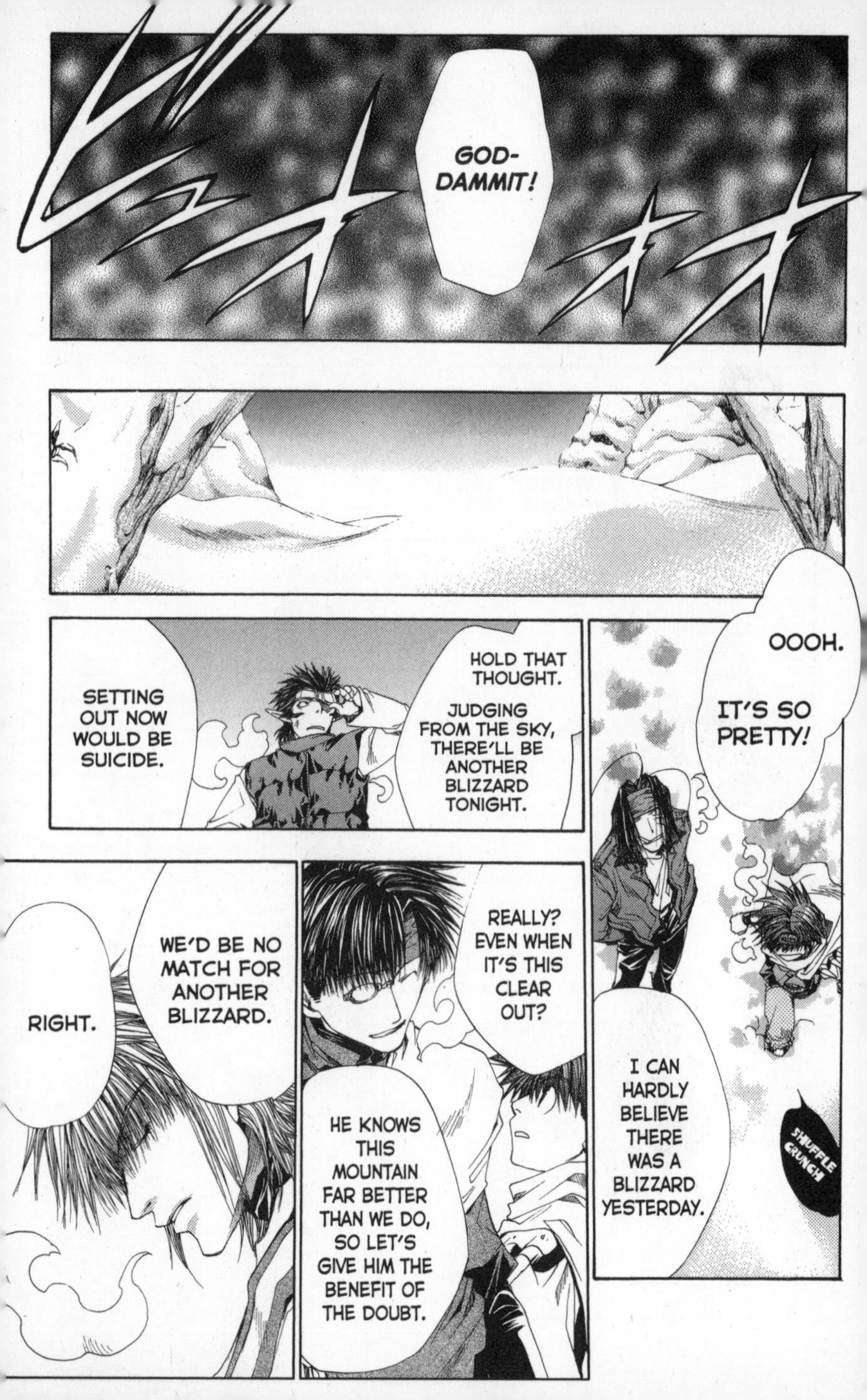
GOD-DAMMIT!
OOOH.
IT'S SO PRETTY!
I CAN HARDLY BELIEVE THERE WAS A BLIZZARD YESTERDAY.
SHUFFLE CRUNCH
HOLD THAT THOUGHT.
JUDGING FROM THE SKY, THERE'LL BE ANOTHER BLIZZARD TONIGHT.
SETTING OUT NOW WOULD BE SUICIDE.
REALLY? EVEN WHEN IT'S THIS CLEAR OUT?
HE KNOWS THIS MOUNTAIN FAR BETTER THAN WE DO, SO LET'S GIVE HIM THE BENEFIT OF THE DOUBT.
WE'D BE NO MATCH FOR ANOTHER BLIZZARD.
RIGHT.

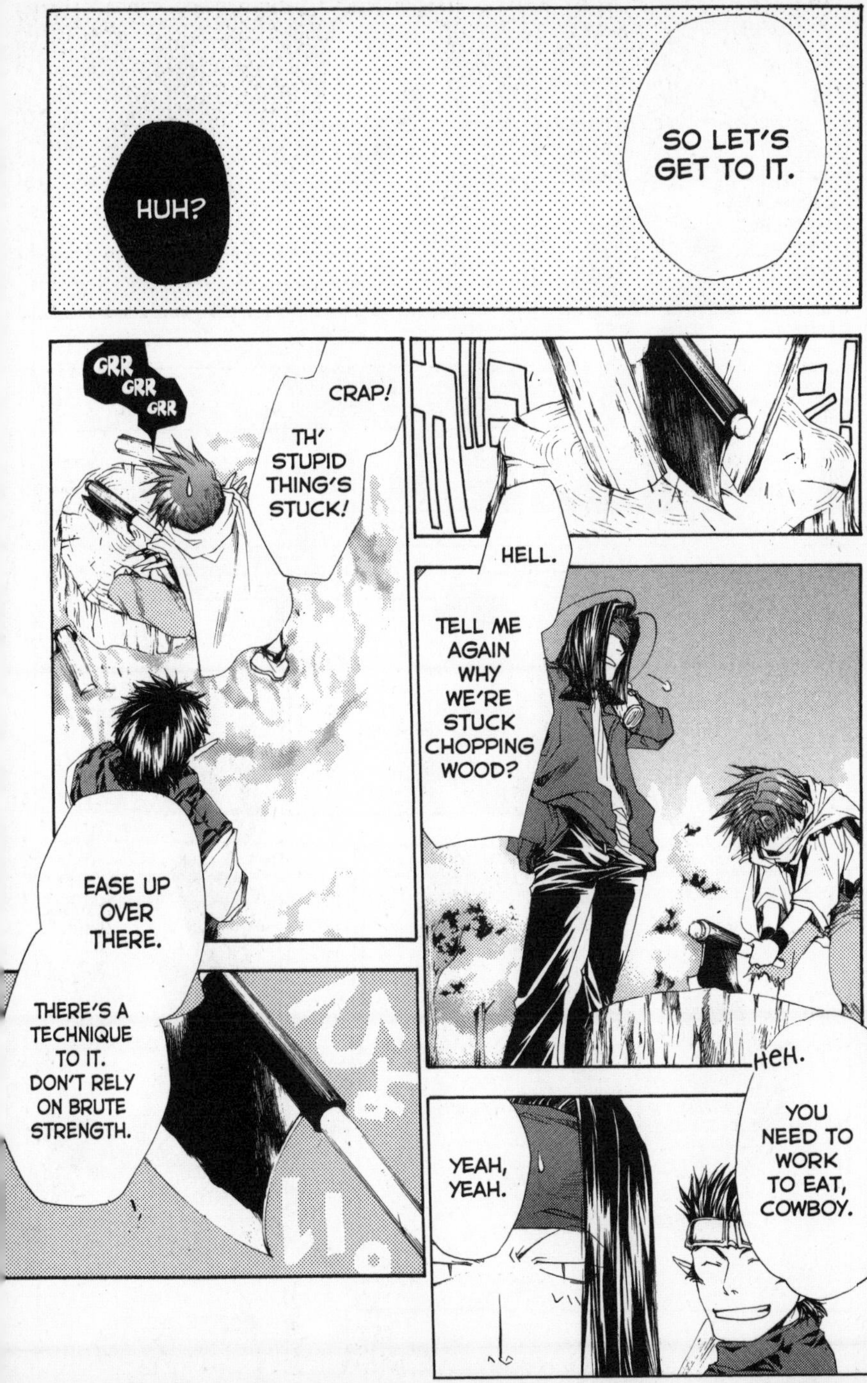
SO LET'S GET TO IT.
HUH?
GRR GRR GRR
CRAP!
TH' STUPID THING'S STUCK!
EASE UP OVER THERE.
THERE'S A TECHNIQUE TO IT. DON'T RELY ON BRUTE STRENGTH.
HELL.
TELL ME AGAIN WHY WE'RE STUCK CHOPPING WOOD?
HEH.
YOU NEED TO WORK TO EAT, COWBOY.
YEAH, YEAH.

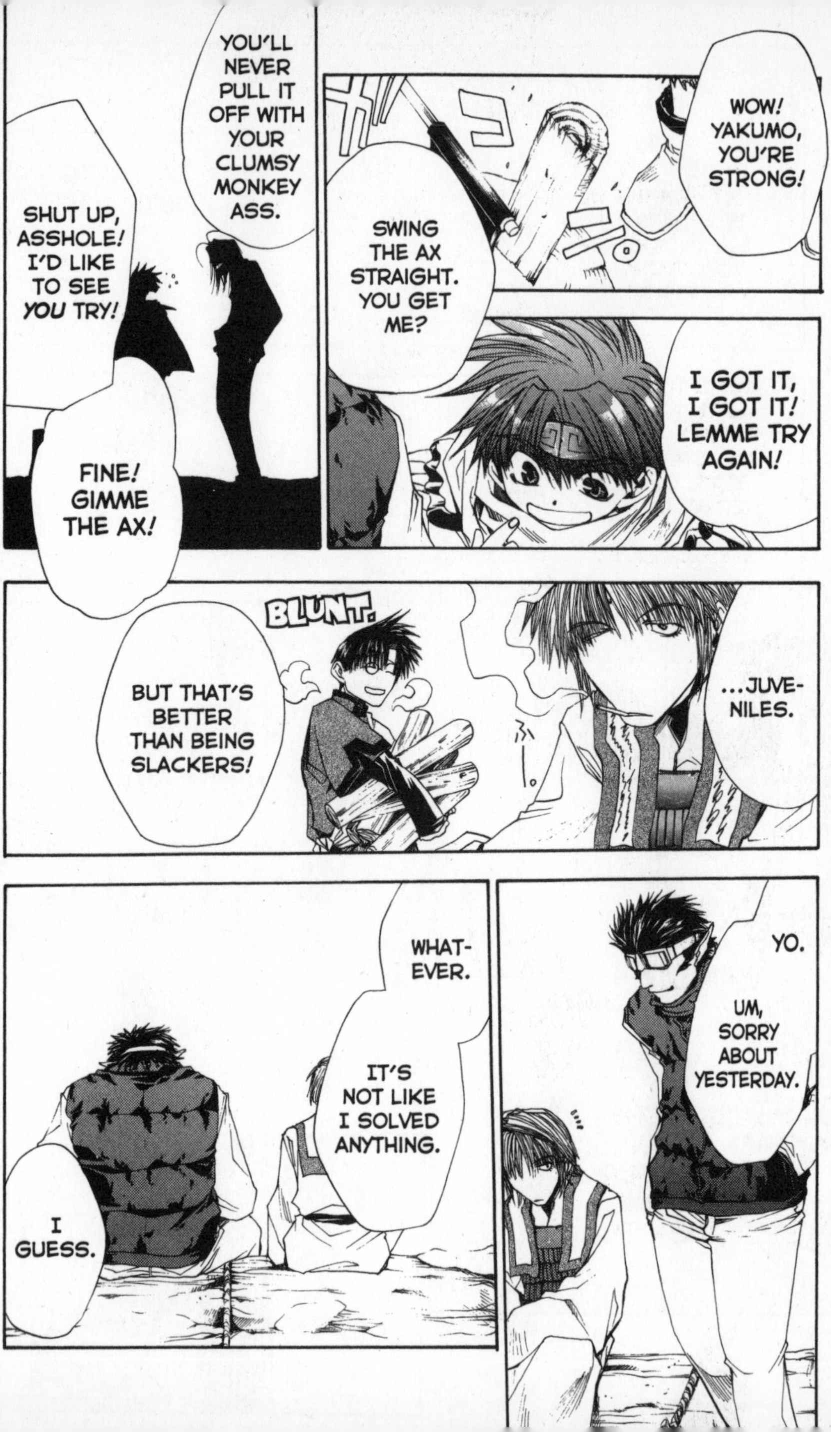
WOW! YAKUMO, YOU'RE STRONG!
SWING THE AX STRAIGHT. YOU GET ME?
I GOT IT, I GOT IT! LEMME TRY AGAIN!
YOU'LL NEVER PULL IT OFF WITH YOUR CLUMSY MONKEY ASS.
SHUT UP, ASSHOLE! I'D LIKE TO SEE *YOU* TRY!
FINE! GIMME THE AX!
...JUVE-NILES.
BLUNT.
BUT THAT'S BETTER THAN BEING SLACKERS!
YO.
UM, SORRY ABOUT YESTERDAY.
WHAT-EVER.
IT'S NOT LIKE I SOLVED ANYTHING.
I GUESS.

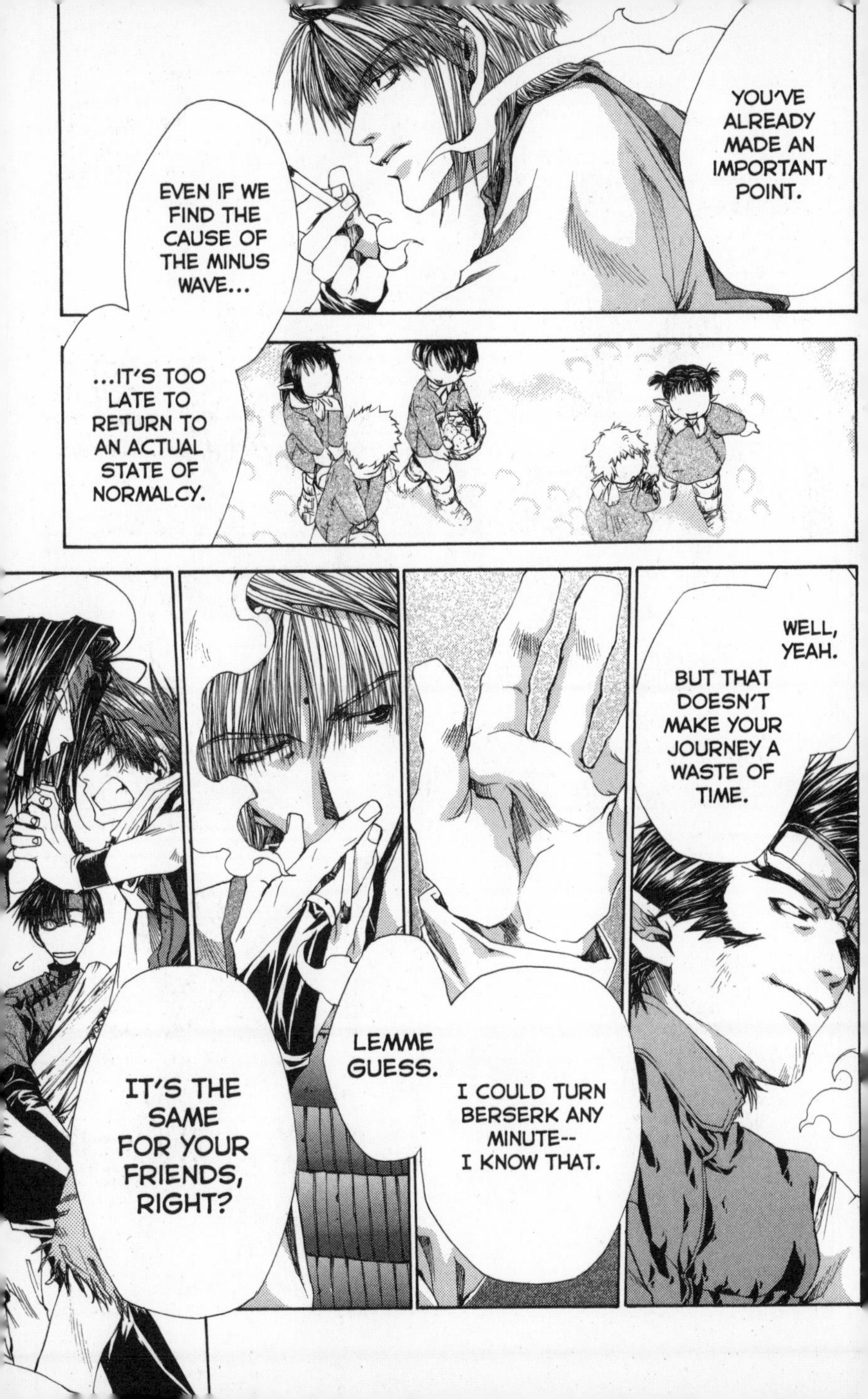
YOU'VE ALREADY MADE AN IMPORTANT POINT.
EVEN IF WE FIND THE CAUSE OF THE MINUS WAVE...
...IT'S TOO LATE TO RETURN TO AN ACTUAL STATE OF NORMALCY.
WELL, YEAH.
BUT THAT DOESN'T MAKE YOUR JOURNEY A WASTE OF TIME.
LEMME GUESS.
I COULD TURN BERSERK ANY MINUTE-- I KNOW THAT.
IT'S THE SAME FOR YOUR FRIENDS, RIGHT?

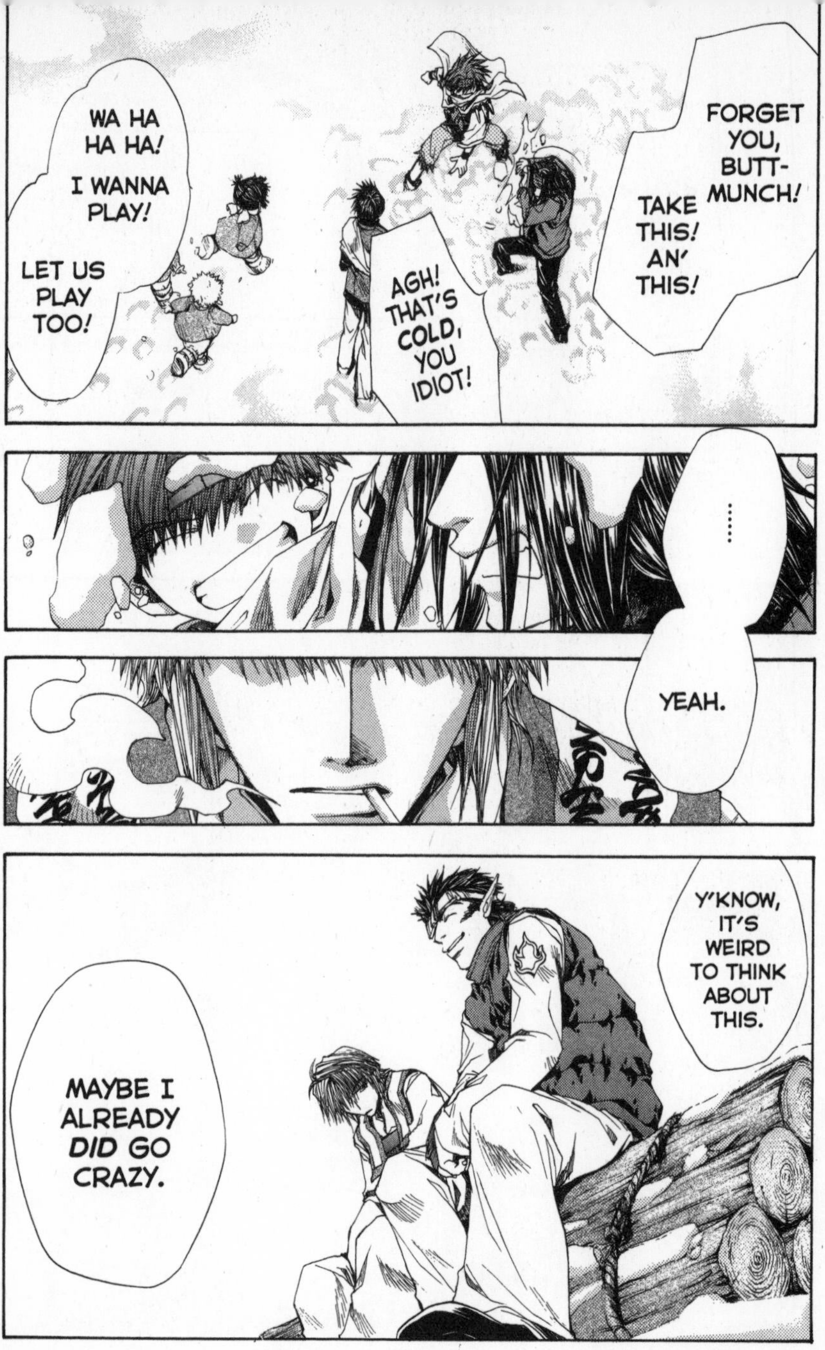
FORGET YOU, BUTT-MUNCH!
TAKE THIS! AN' THIS!
AGH! THAT'S COLD, YOU IDIOT!
WA HA HA HA!
I WANNA PLAY!
LET US PLAY TOO!
......
YEAH.
Y'KNOW, IT'S WEIRD TO THINK ABOUT THIS.
MAYBE I ALREADY *DID* GO CRAZY.

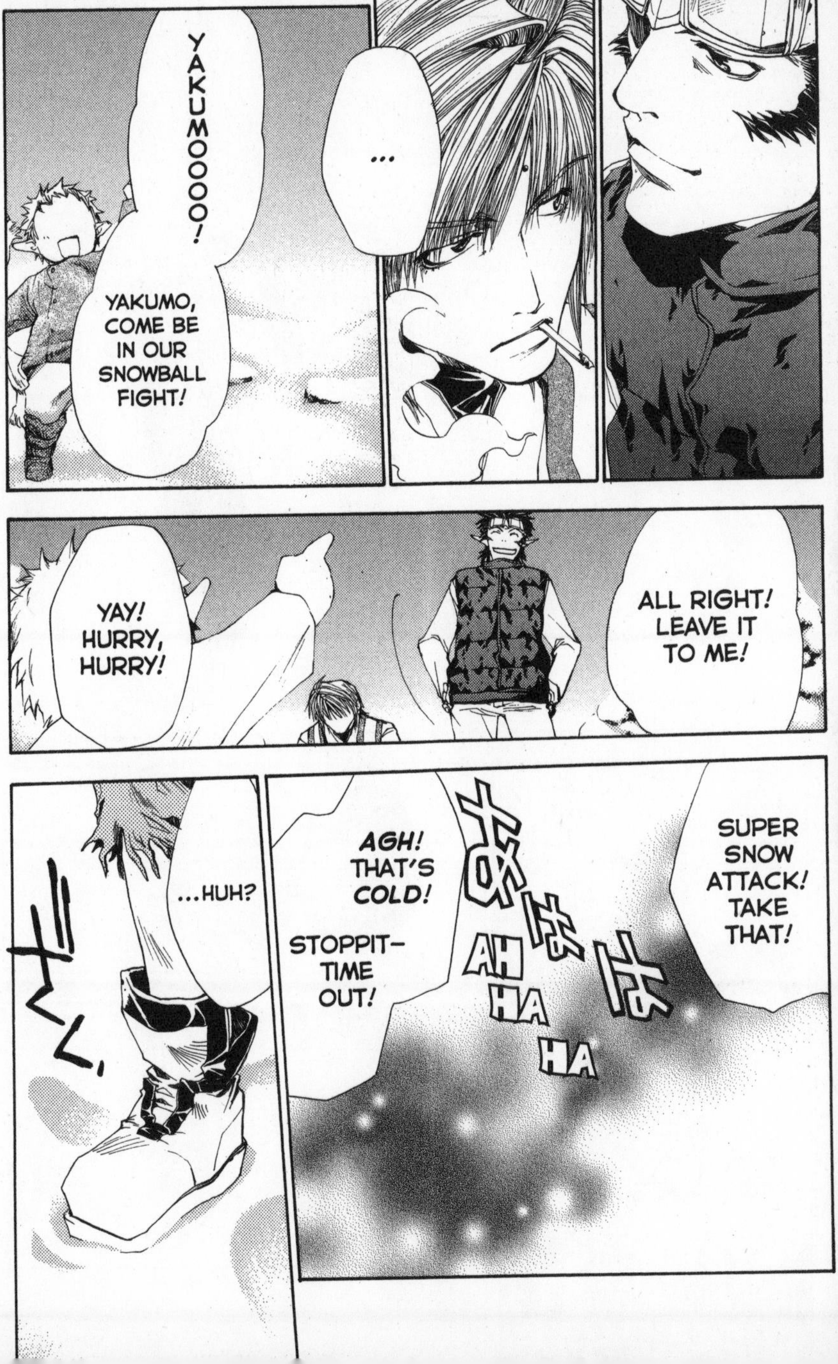
...
YAKUMOOOOO!
YAKUMO, COME BE IN OUR SNOWBALL FIGHT!
ALL RIGHT! LEAVE IT TO ME!
YAY! HURRY, HURRY!
SUPER SNOW ATTACK! TAKE THAT!
AH HA HA
AGH! THAT'S COLD!
STOPPIT— TIME OUT!
...HUH?

WHAT ARE...

THEY'RE GRAVES.

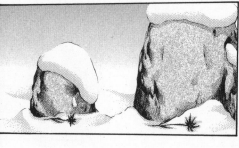

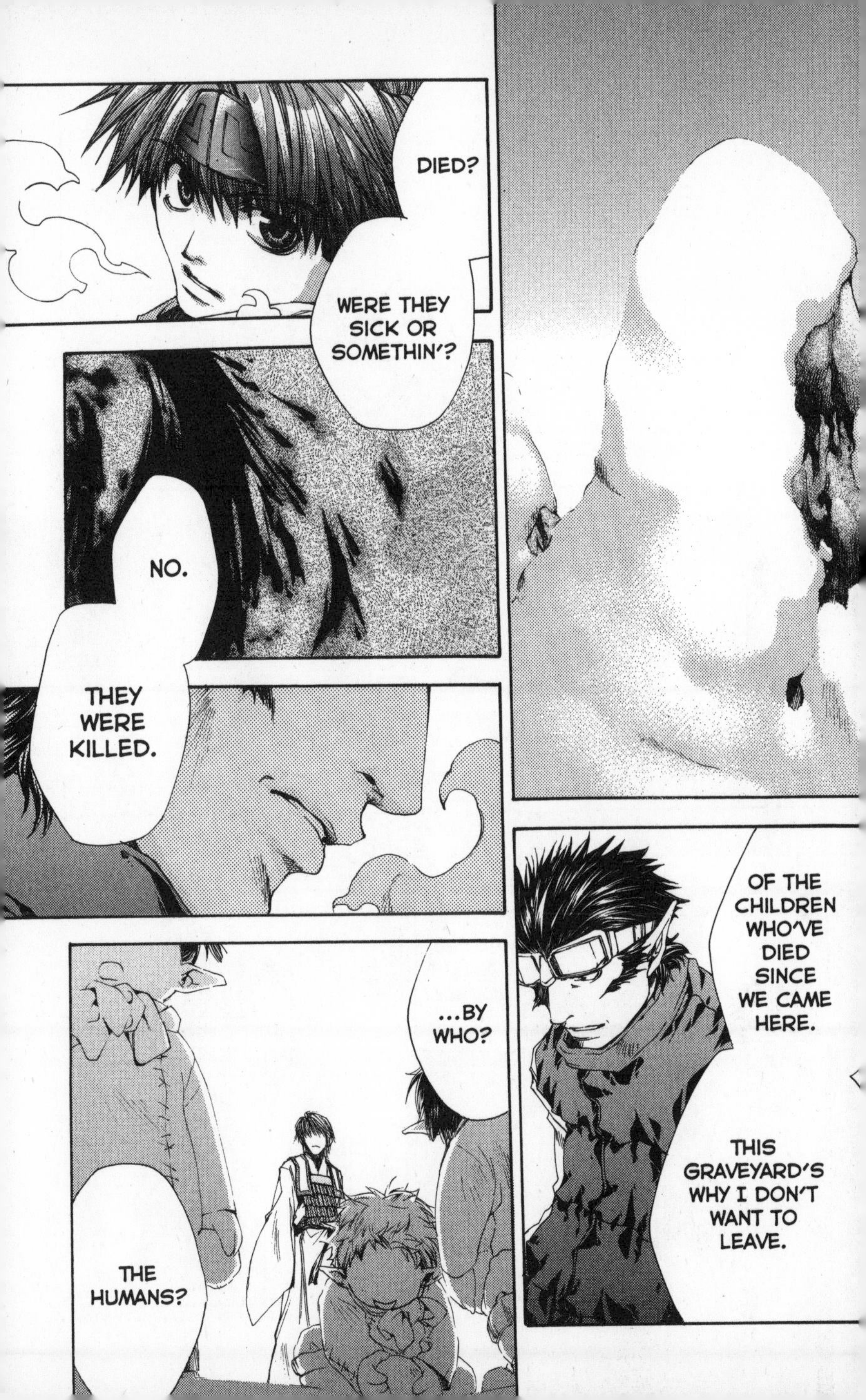
OF THE CHILDREN WHO'VE DIED SINCE WE CAME HERE.
THIS GRAVEYARD'S WHY I DON'T WANT TO LEAVE.
DIED?
WERE THEY SICK OR SOMETHIN'?
NO.
THEY WERE KILLED.
...BY WHO?
THE HUMANS?

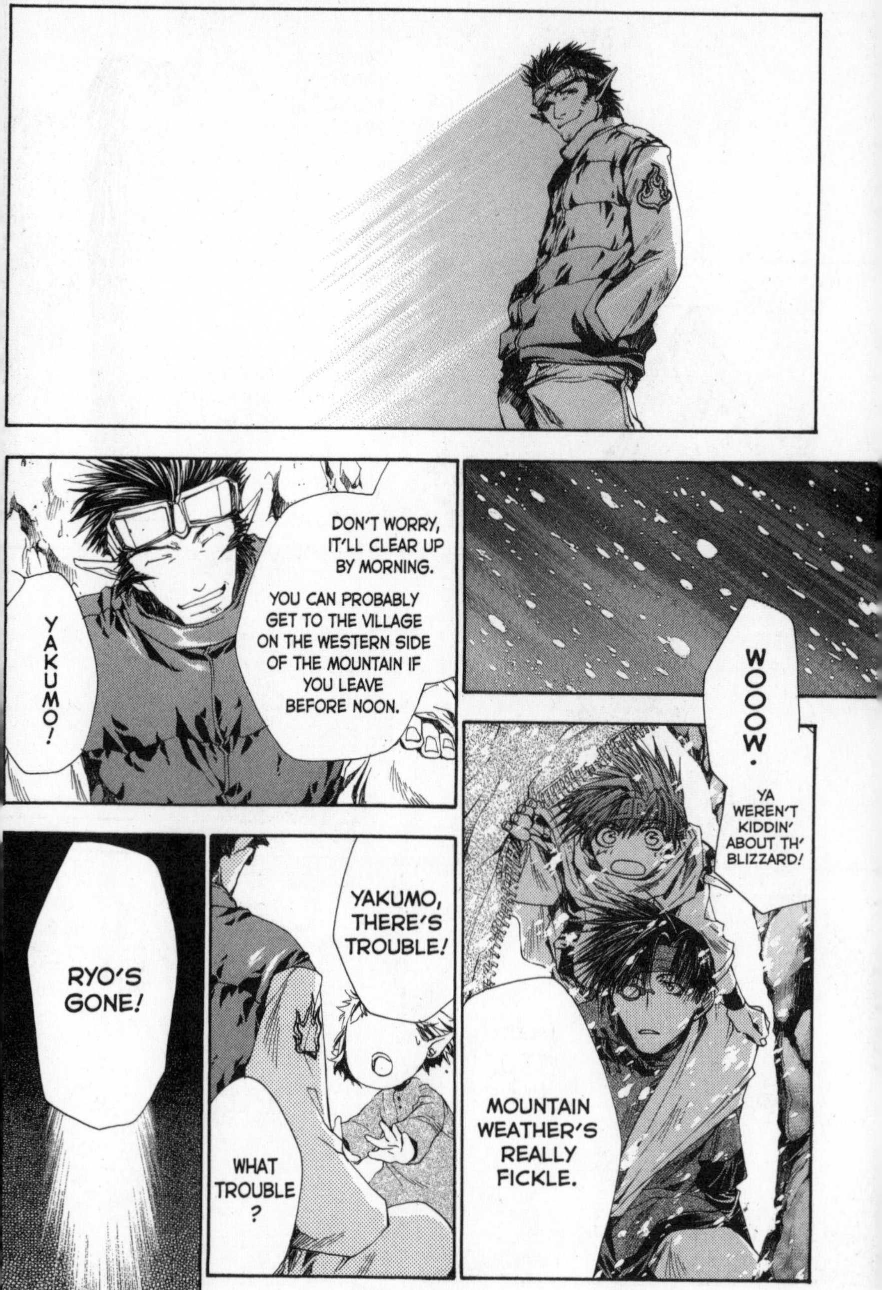
WOOOW.
YA WEREN'T KIDDIN' ABOUT TH' BLIZZARD!
MOUNTAIN WEATHER'S REALLY FICKLE.
DON'T WORRY, IT'LL CLEAR UP BY MORNING.
YOU CAN PROBABLY GET TO THE VILLAGE ON THE WESTERN SIDE OF THE MOUNTAIN IF YOU LEAVE BEFORE NOON.
YAKUMO!
YAKUMO, THERE'S TROUBLE!
WHAT TROUBLE?
RYO'S GONE!

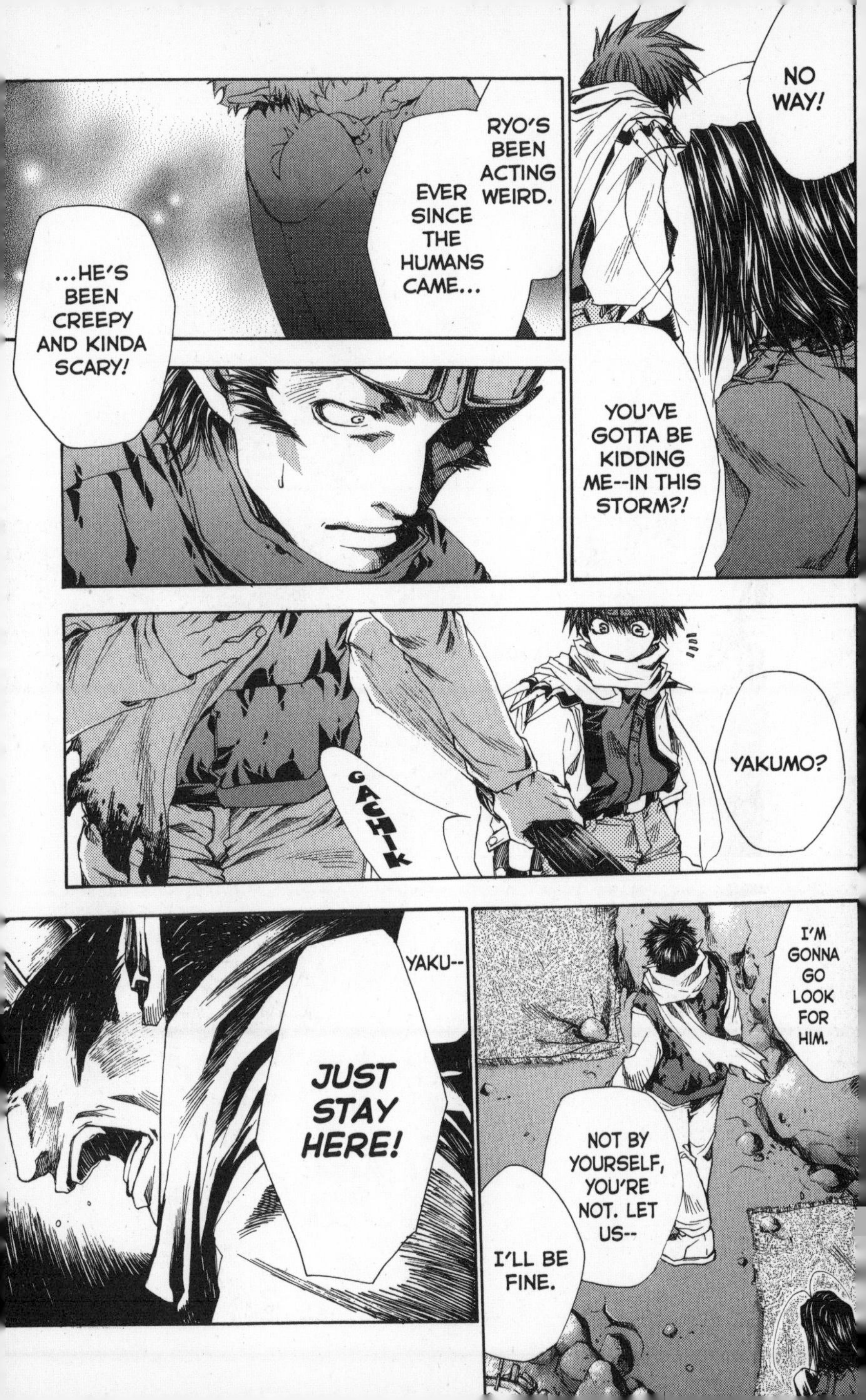
NO WAY!
YOU'VE GOTTA BE KIDDING ME--IN THIS STORM?!
RYO'S BEEN ACTING WEIRD.
EVER SINCE THE HUMANS CAME...
...HE'S BEEN CREEPY AND KINDA SCARY!
YAKUMO?
GACHIK
I'M GONNA GO LOOK FOR HIM.
NOT BY YOURSELF, YOU'RE NOT. LET US--
I'LL BE FINE.
YAKU--
JUST STAY HERE!

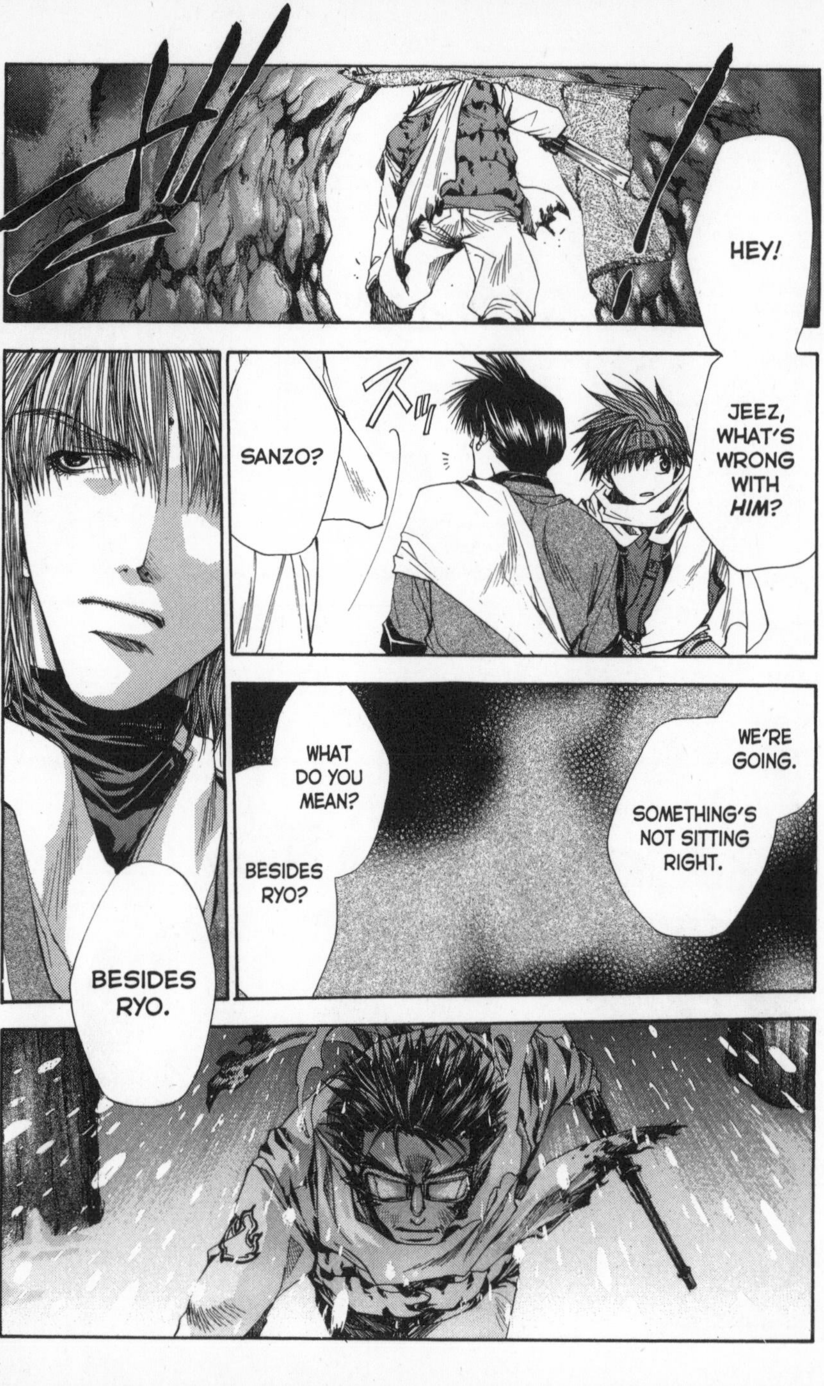
HEY!
JEEZ, WHAT'S WRONG WITH *HIM*?
スッ
SANZO?
WE'RE GOING.
SOMETHING'S NOT SITTING RIGHT.
WHAT DO YOU MEAN?
BESIDES RYO?
BESIDES RYO.

...IT'S A DREAM.

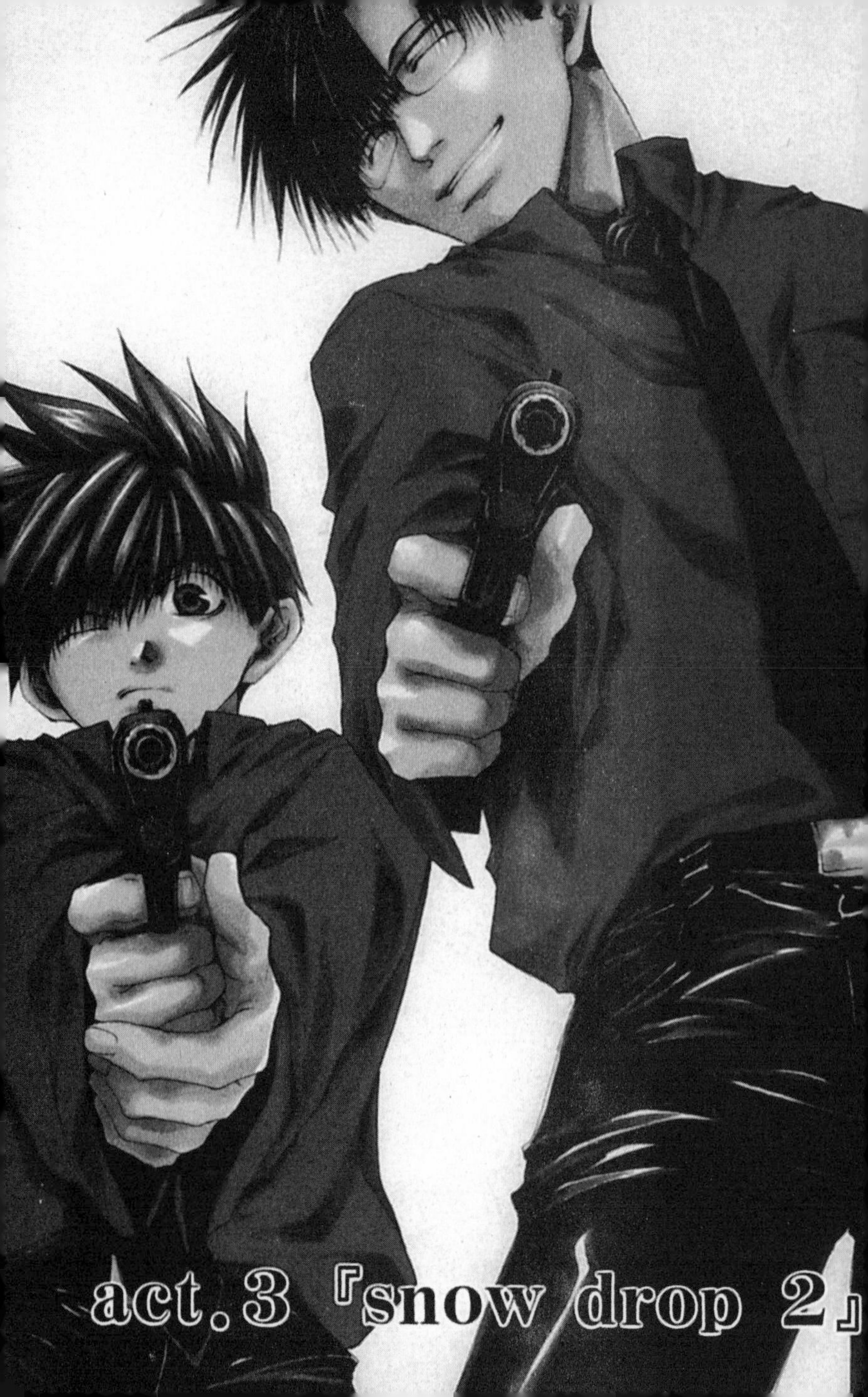
act.3 「snow drop 2」

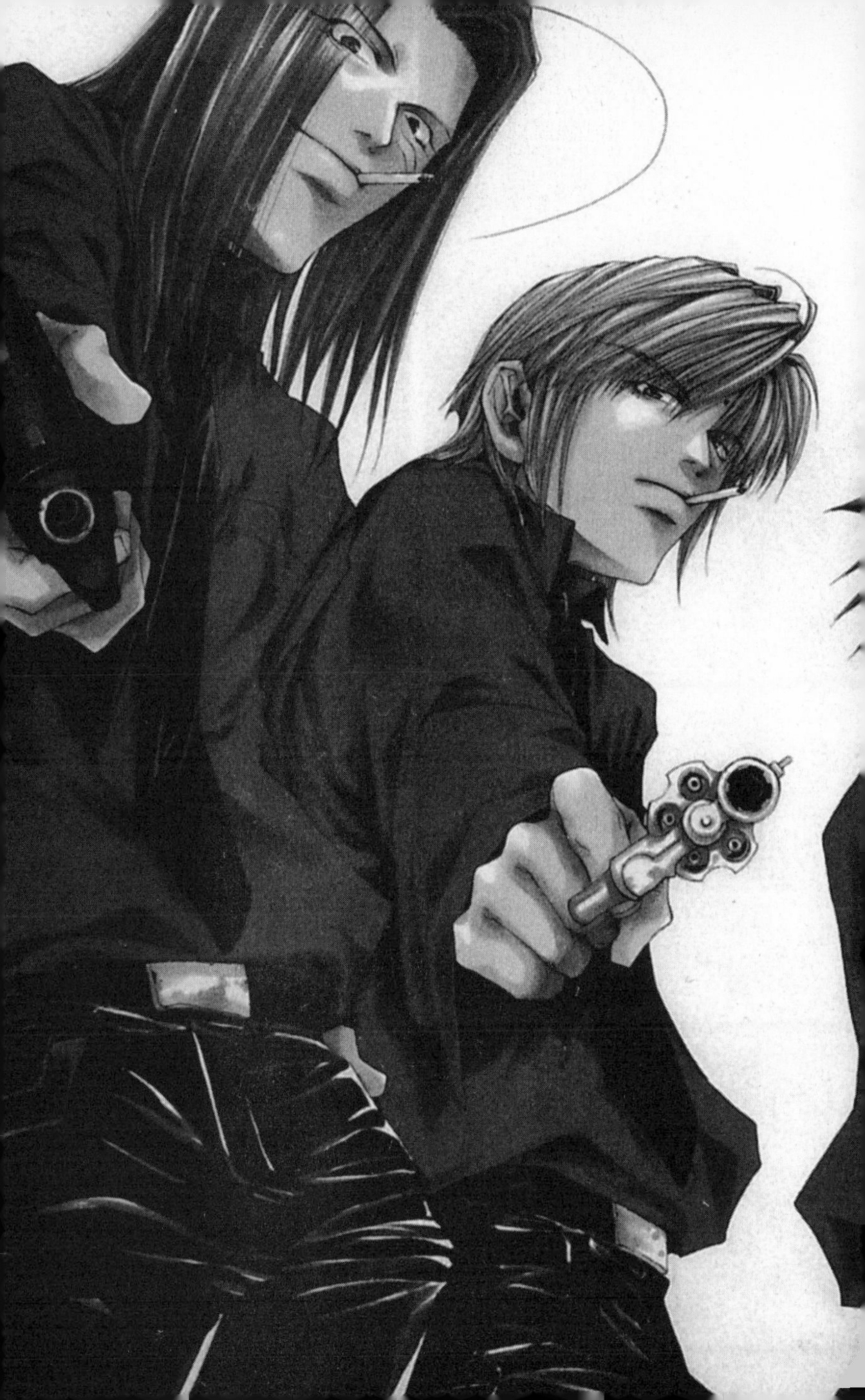

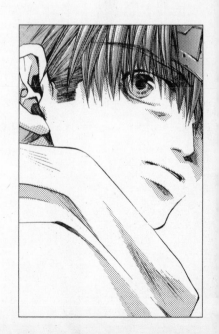

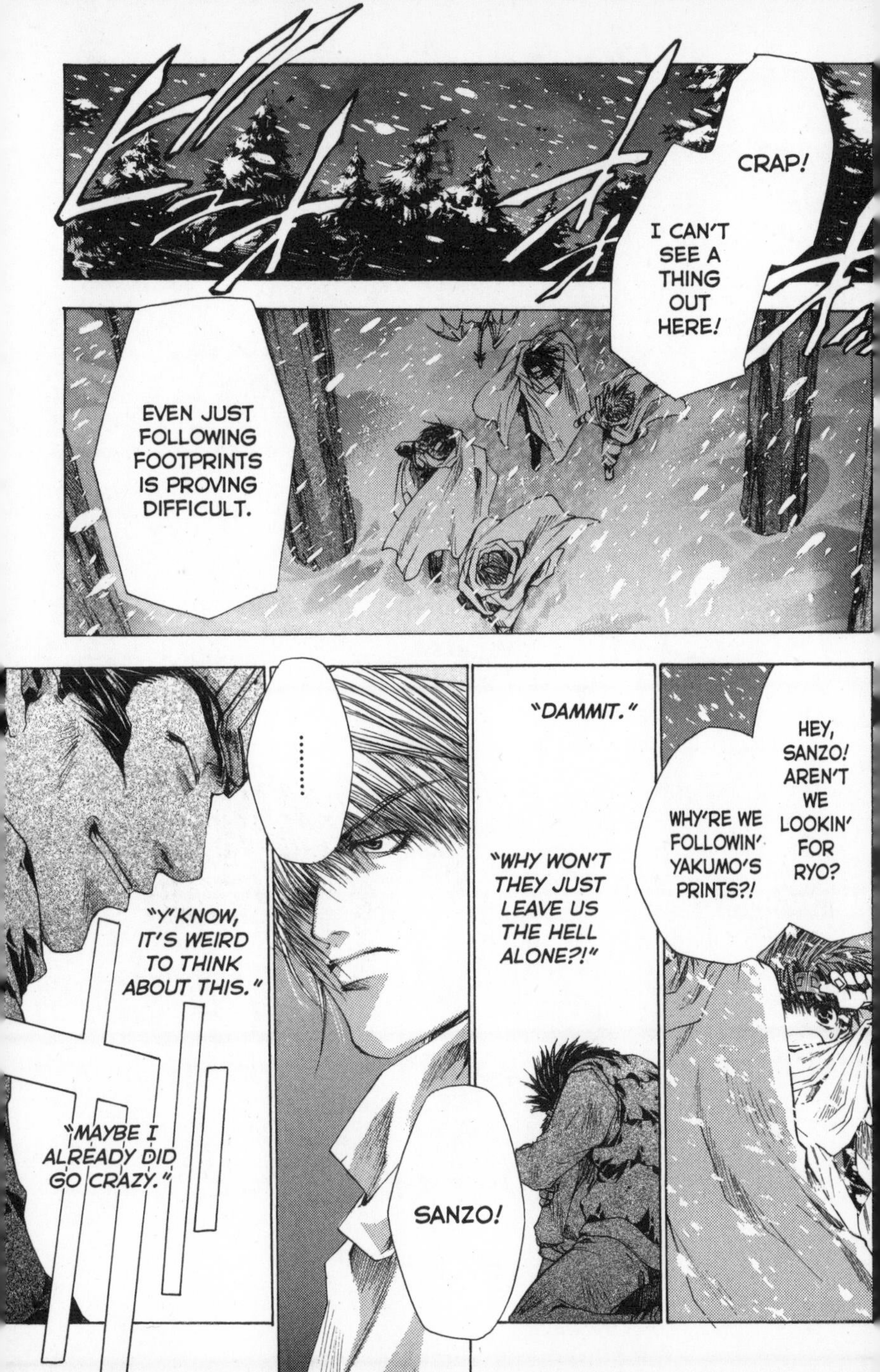
CRAP!
I CAN'T SEE A THING OUT HERE!
EVEN JUST FOLLOWING FOOTPRINTS IS PROVING DIFFICULT.
HEY, SANZO! AREN'T WE LOOKIN' FOR RYO?
WHY'RE WE FOLLOWIN' YAKUMO'S PRINTS?!
"DAMMIT."
"WHY WON'T THEY JUST LEAVE US THE HELL ALONE?!"
......
SANZO!
"Y'KNOW, IT'S WEIRD TO THINK ABOUT THIS."
"MAYBE I ALREADY DID GO CRAZY."

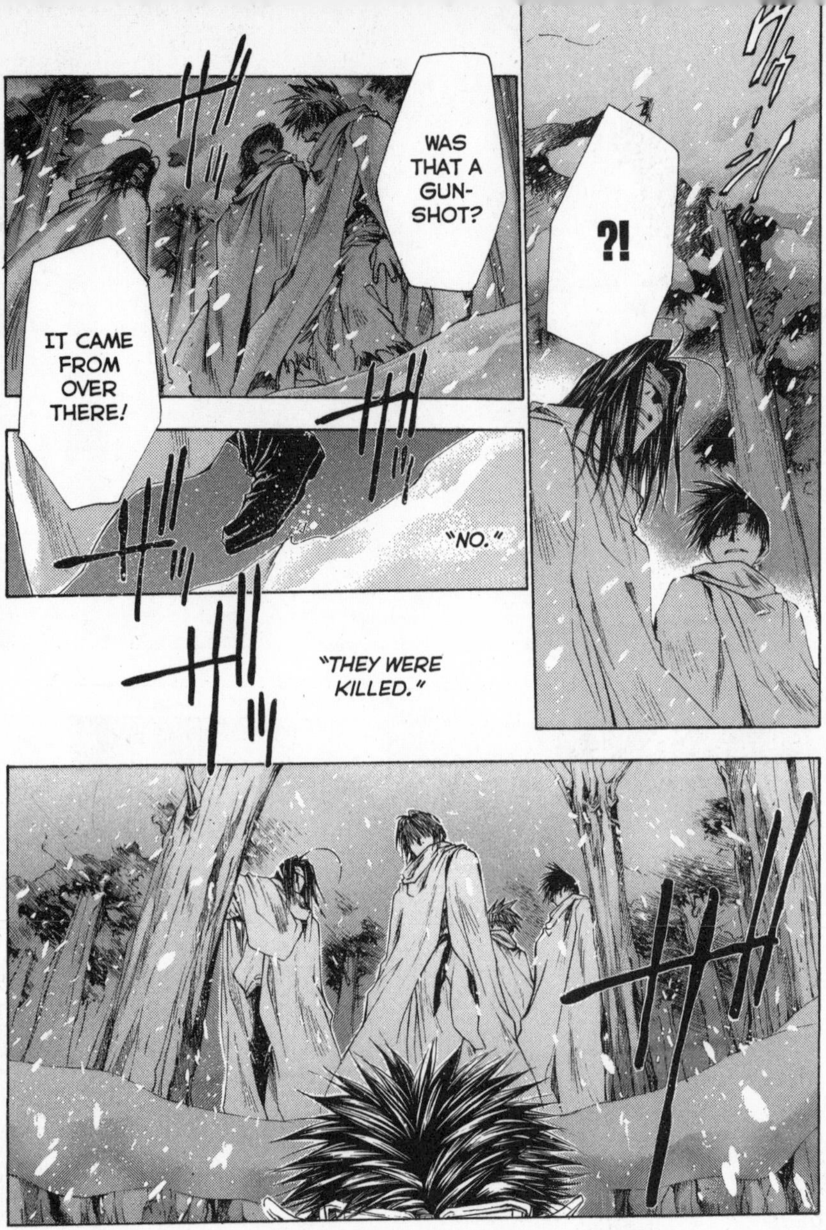
?!
WAS THAT A GUN-SHOT?
IT CAME FROM OVER THERE!
"NO."
"THEY WERE KILLED."

...BY WHO?

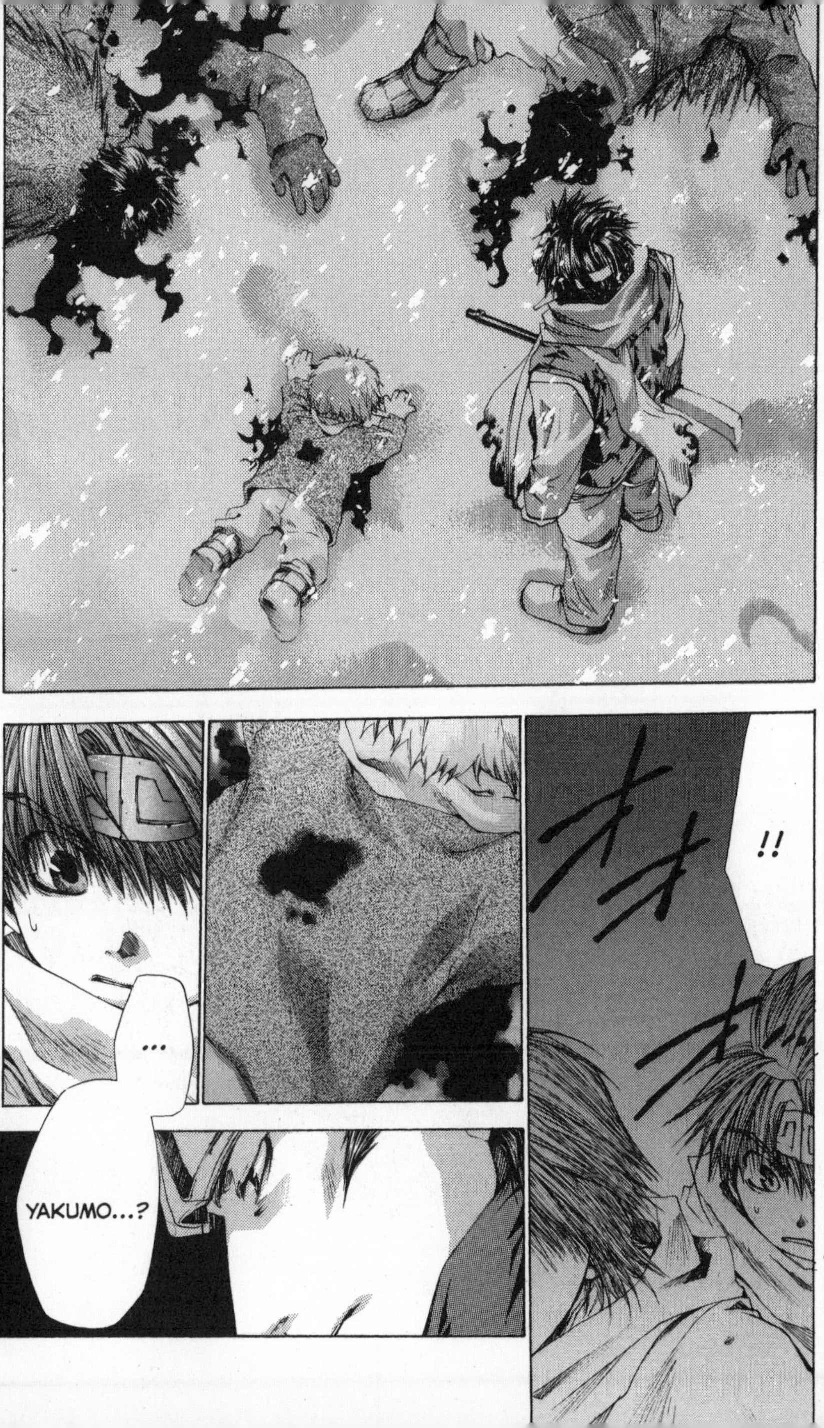
!!
...
YAKUMO...?

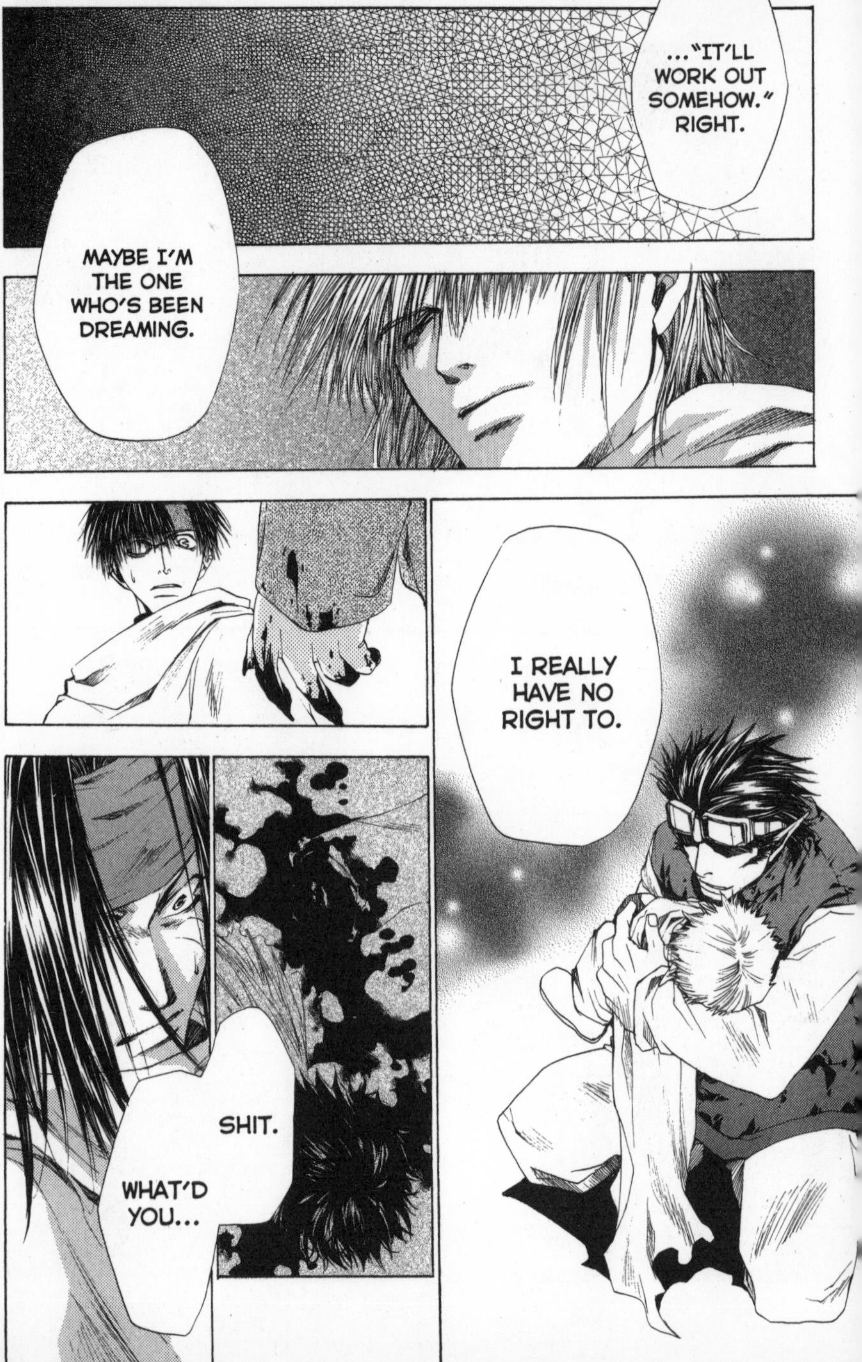
..."IT'LL WORK OUT SOMEHOW." RIGHT.
MAYBE I'M THE ONE WHO'S BEEN DREAMING.
I REALLY HAVE NO RIGHT TO.
SHIT.
WHAT'D YOU...

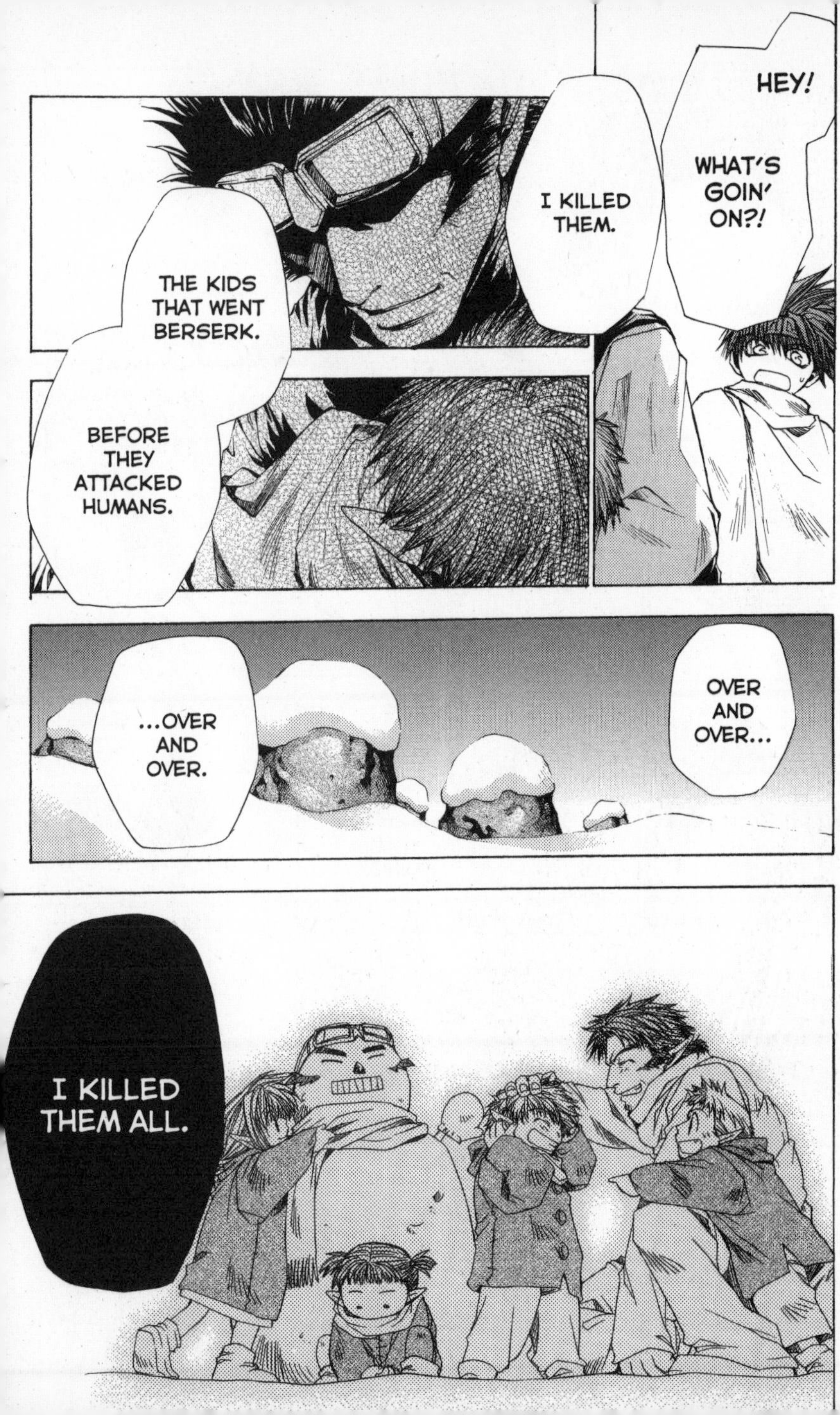
HEY!
WHAT'S GOIN' ON?!
I KILLED THEM.
THE KIDS THAT WENT BERSERK.
BEFORE THEY ATTACKED HUMANS.
OVER AND OVER...
...OVER AND OVER.
I KILLED THEM ALL.

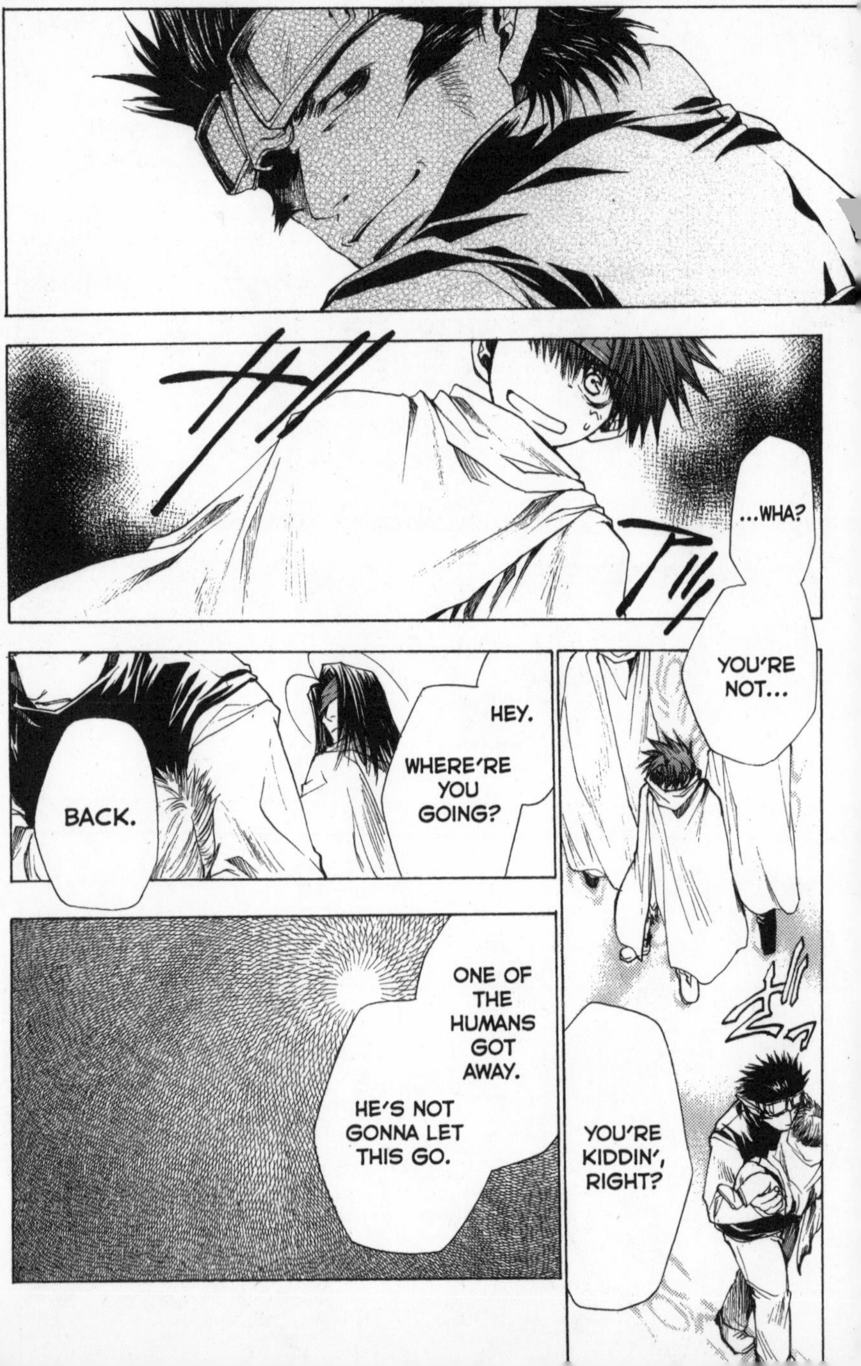
...WHA?
YOU'RE NOT...
YOU'RE KIDDIN', RIGHT?
HEY.
WHERE'RE YOU GOING?
BACK.
ONE OF THE HUMANS GOT AWAY.
HE'S NOT GONNA LET THIS GO.

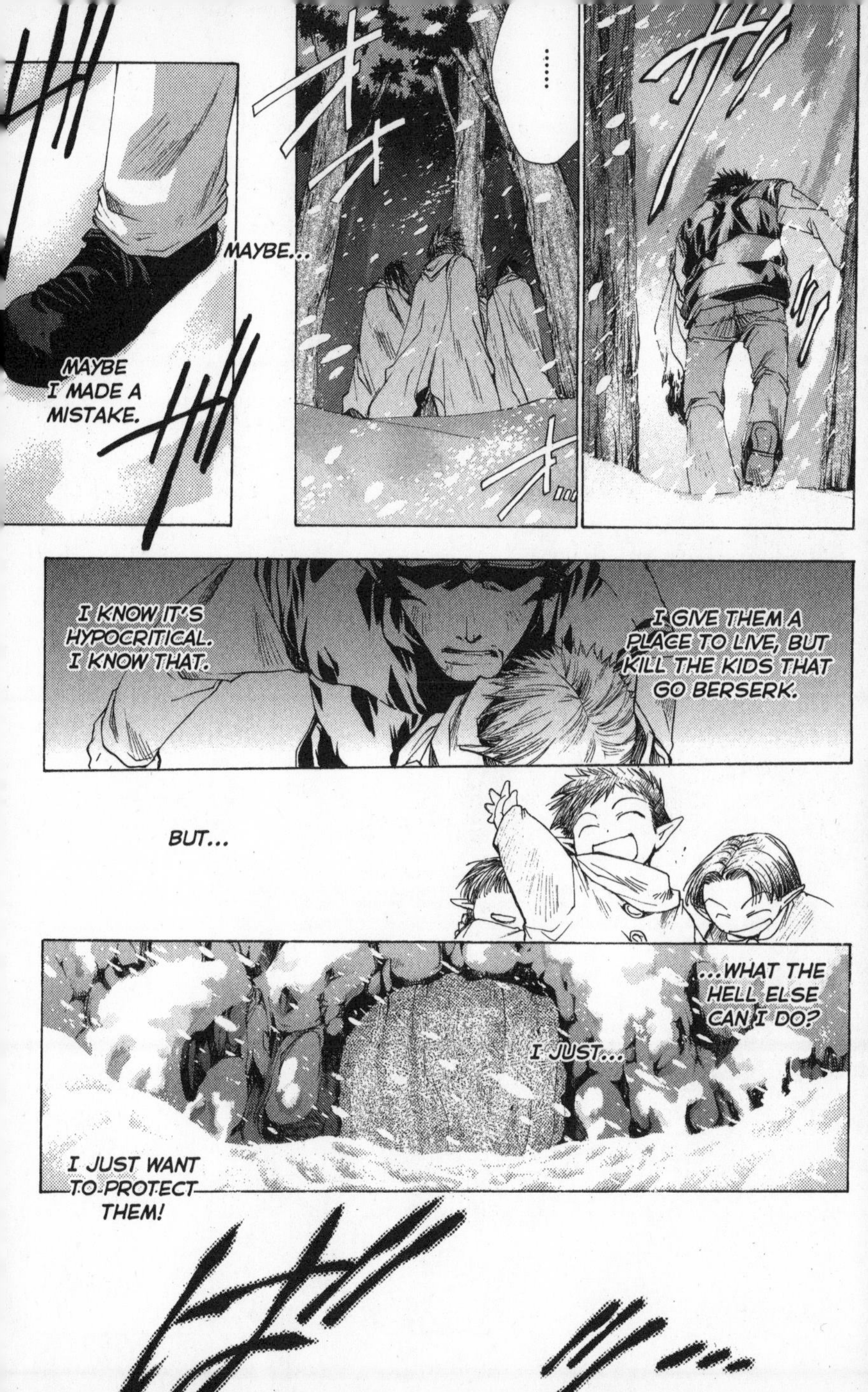
......
MAYBE...
MAYBE I MADE A MISTAKE.
I GIVE THEM A PLACE TO LIVE, BUT KILL THE KIDS THAT GO BERSERK.
I KNOW IT'S HYPOCRITICAL. I KNOW THAT.
BUT...
...WHAT THE HELL ELSE CAN I DO?
I JUST...
I JUST WANT TO PROTECT THEM!

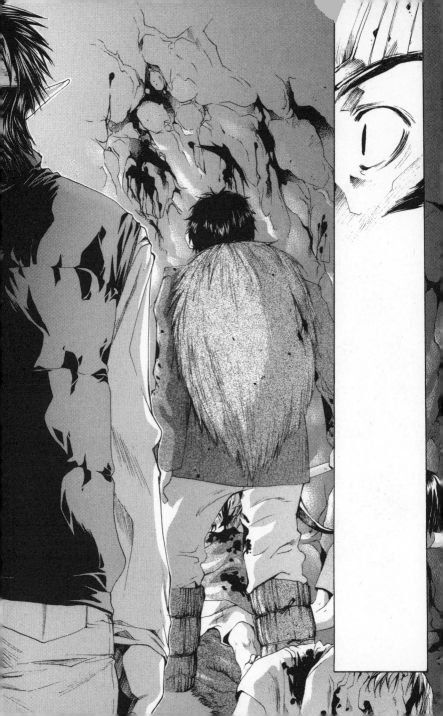

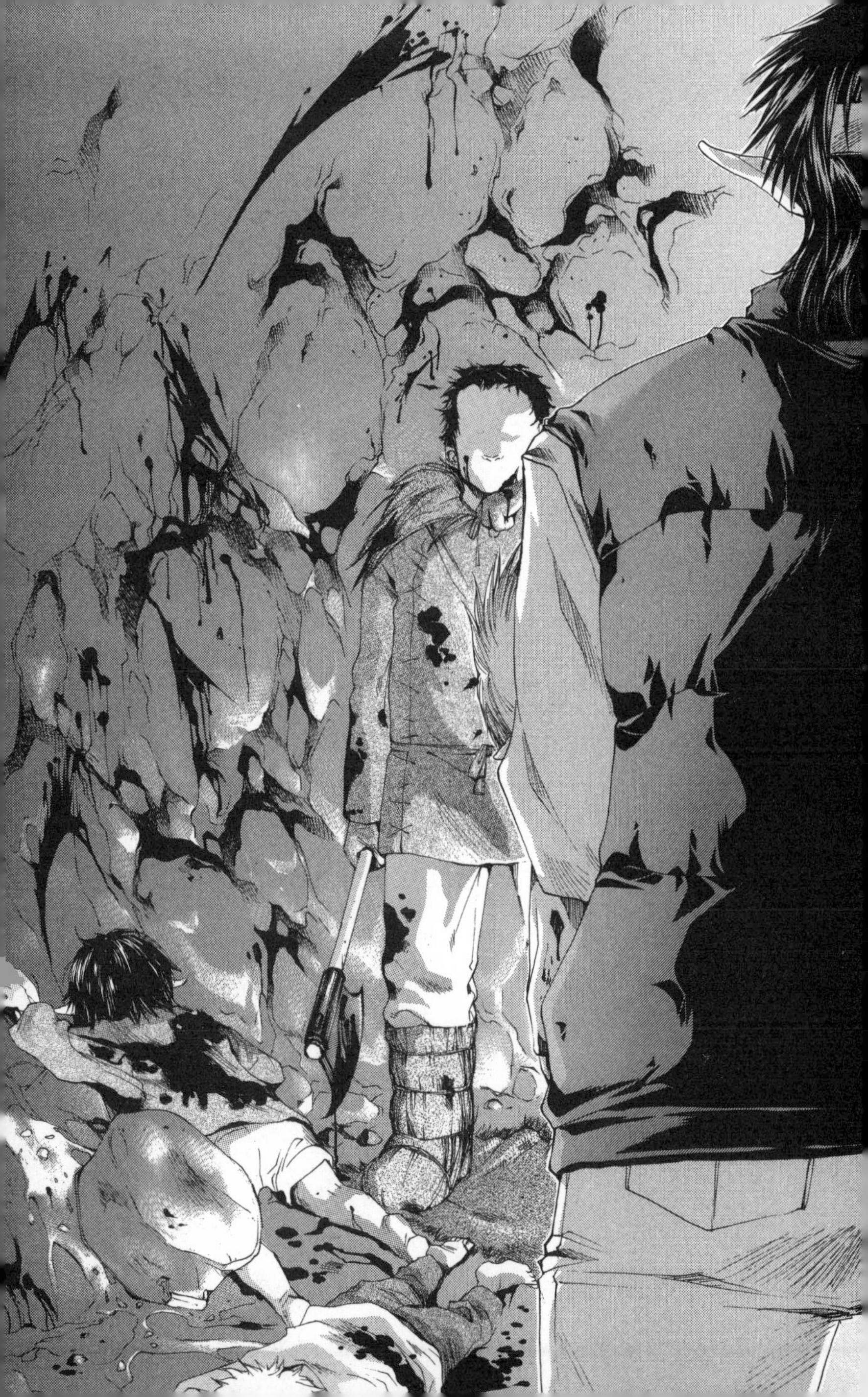

I JUST...

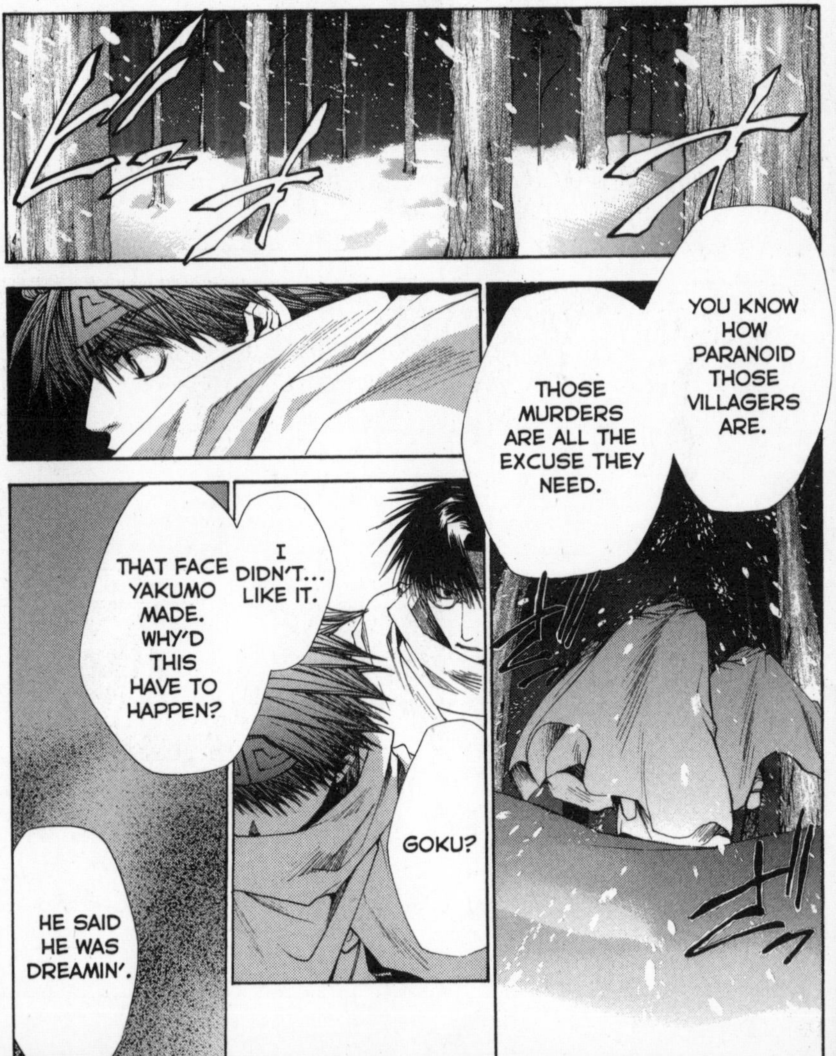
YOU KNOW HOW PARANOID THOSE VILLAGERS ARE.
THOSE MURDERS ARE ALL THE EXCUSE THEY NEED.
I DIDN'T... LIKE IT.
THAT FACE YAKUMO MADE. WHY'D THIS HAVE TO HAPPEN?
GOKU?
HE SAID HE WAS DREAMIN'.

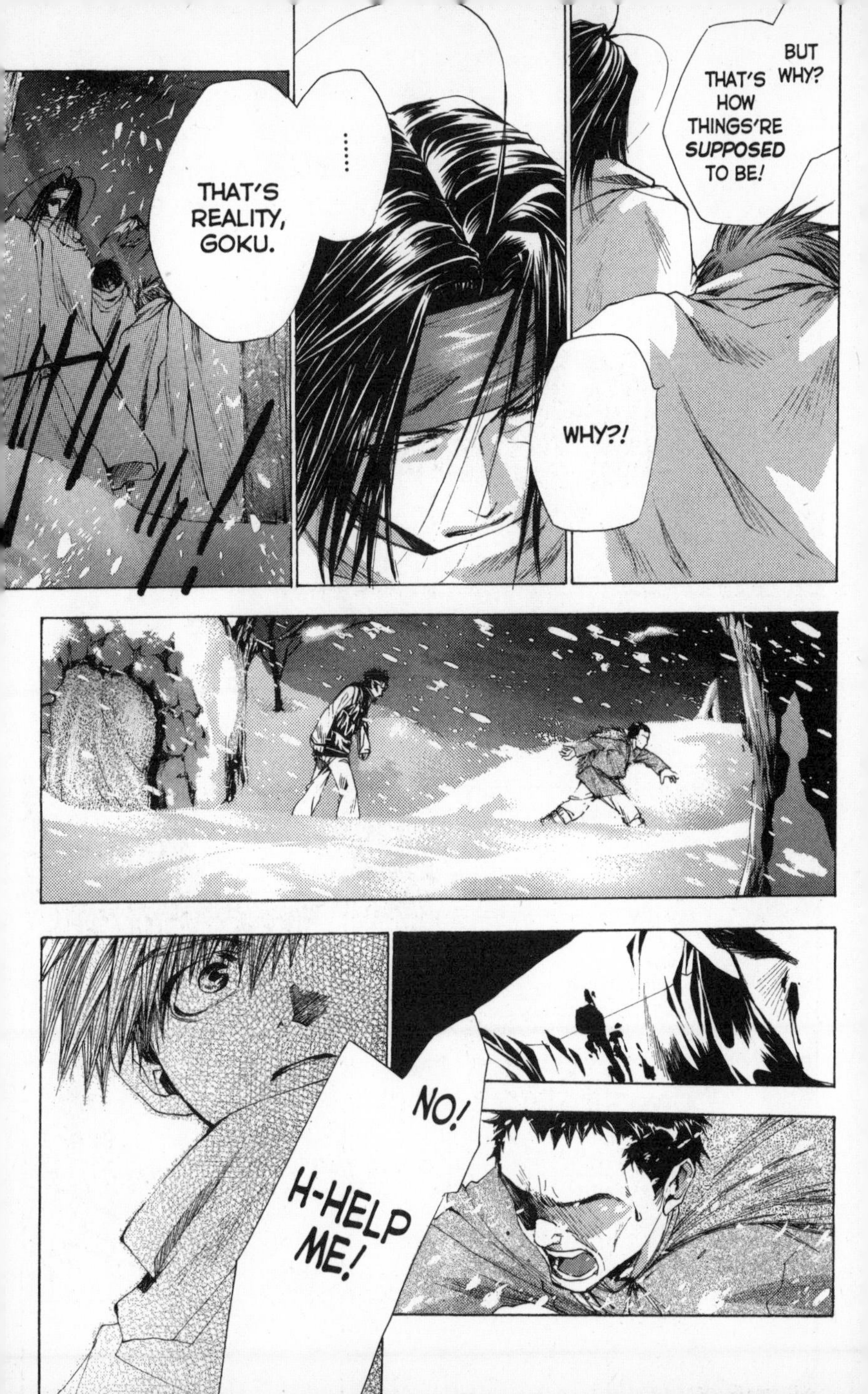
BUT WHY? THAT'S HOW THINGS'RE SUPPOSED TO BE!
WHY?!
......
THAT'S REALITY, GOKU.
NO!
H-HELP ME!

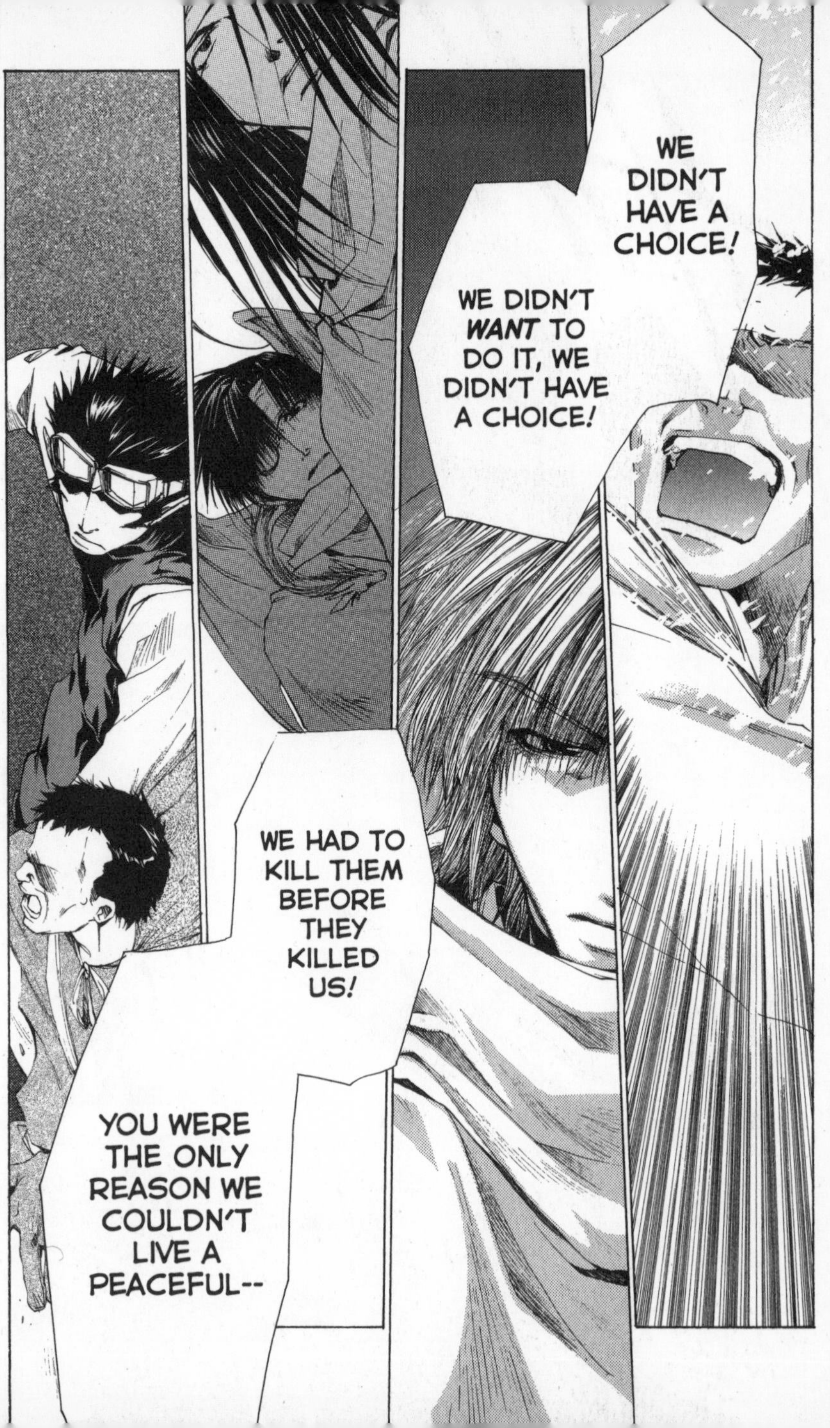
WE DIDN'T HAVE A CHOICE!
WE DIDN'T *WANT* TO DO IT, WE DIDN'T HAVE A CHOICE!
WE HAD TO KILL THEM BEFORE THEY KILLED US!
YOU WERE THE ONLY REASON WE COULDN'T LIVE A PEACEFUL--

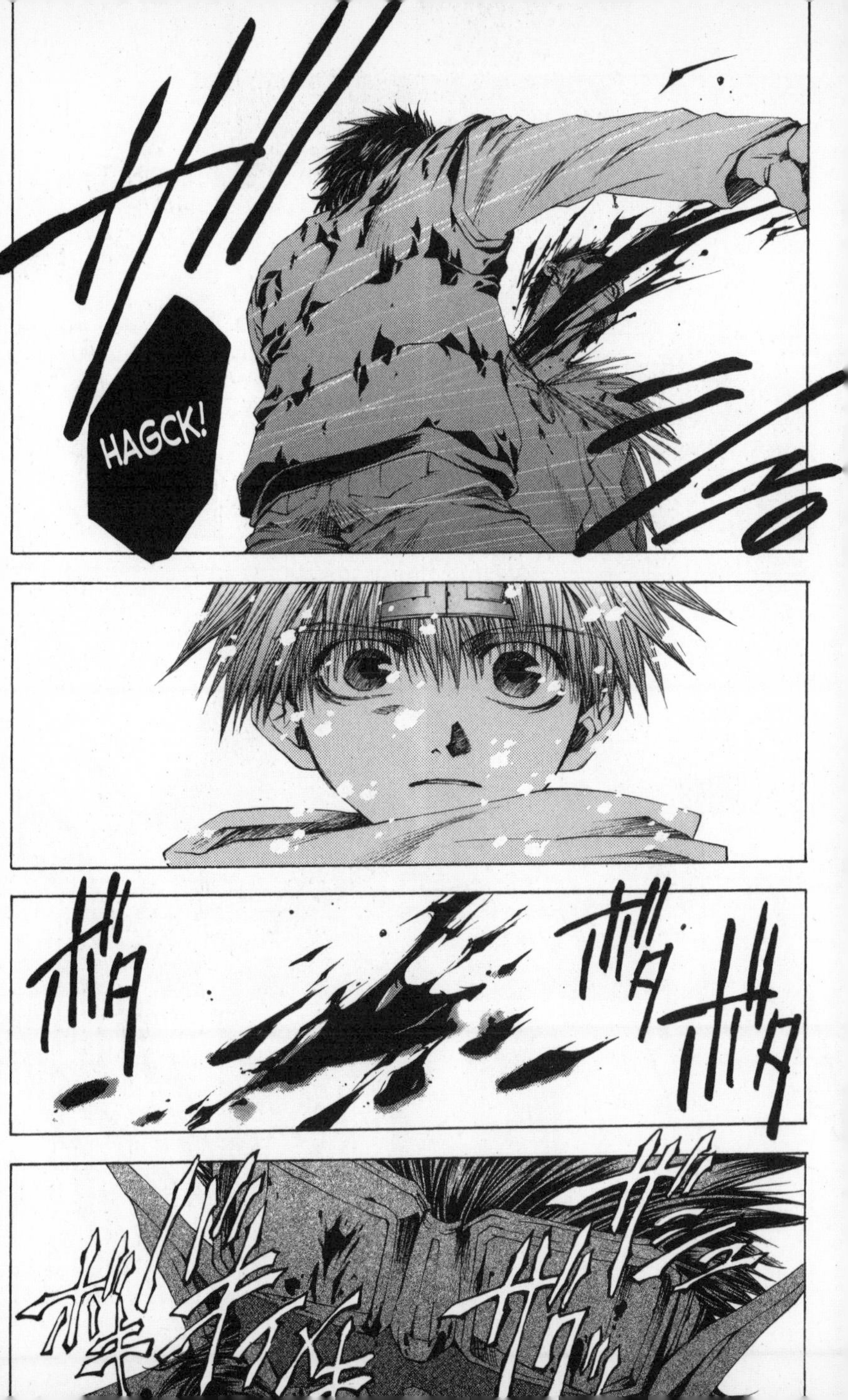
HAGCK!
ボタ
ボタ
ボタ

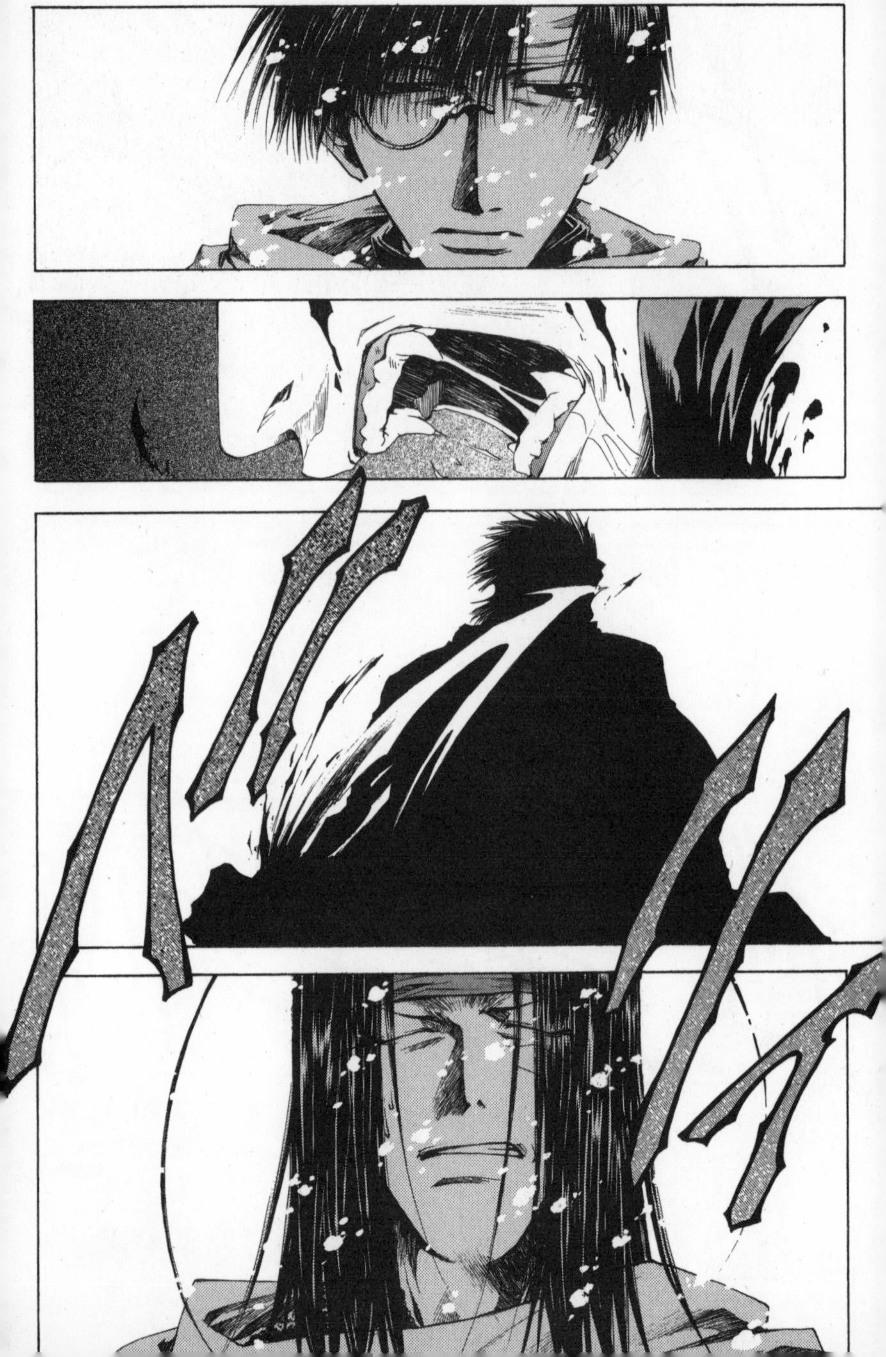

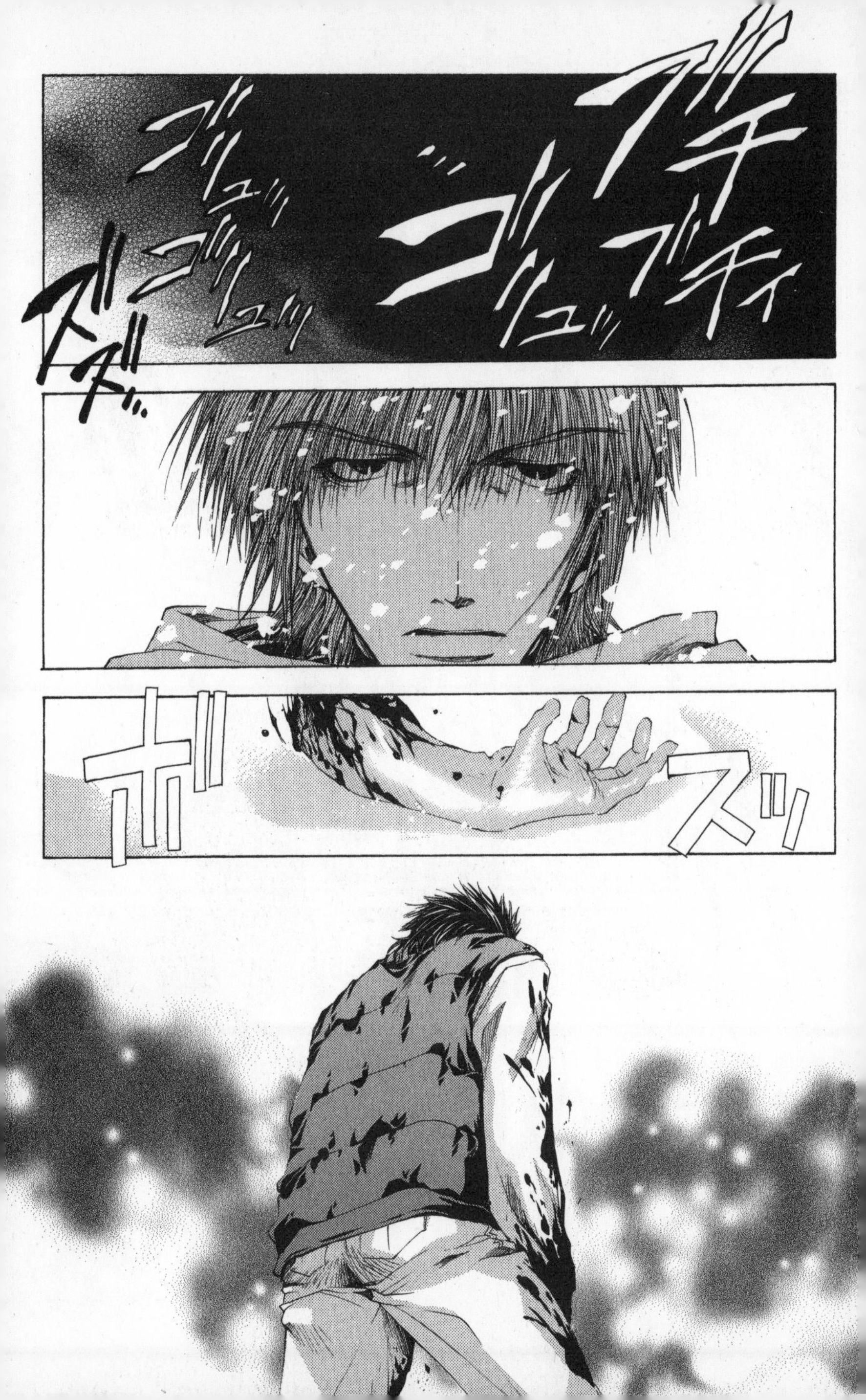
ブチブチィ
ゴリュッ
ブリュッ
ゴリュッ
ズダ…
ボズッ

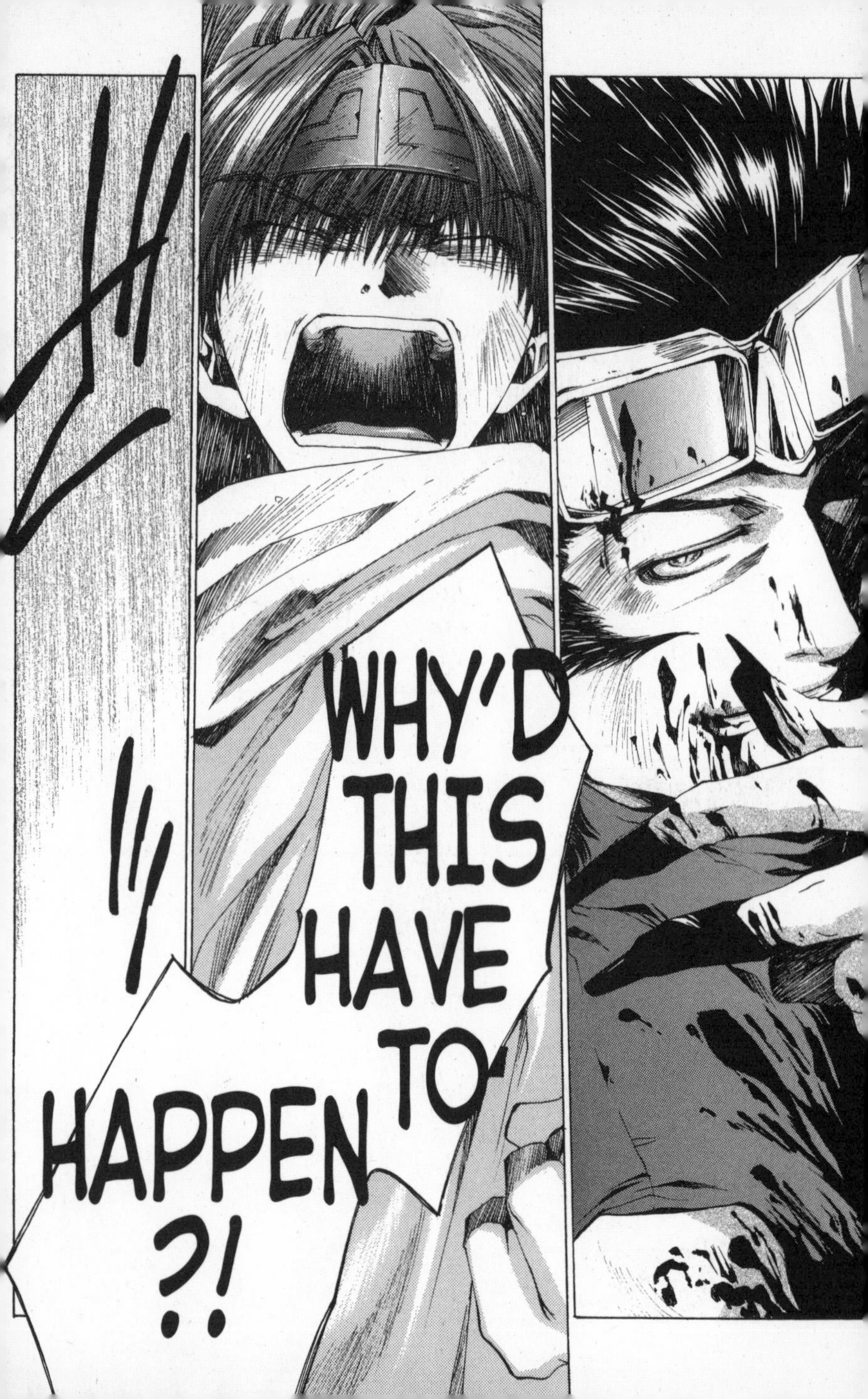
WHY'D THIS HAVE TO HAPPEN ?!

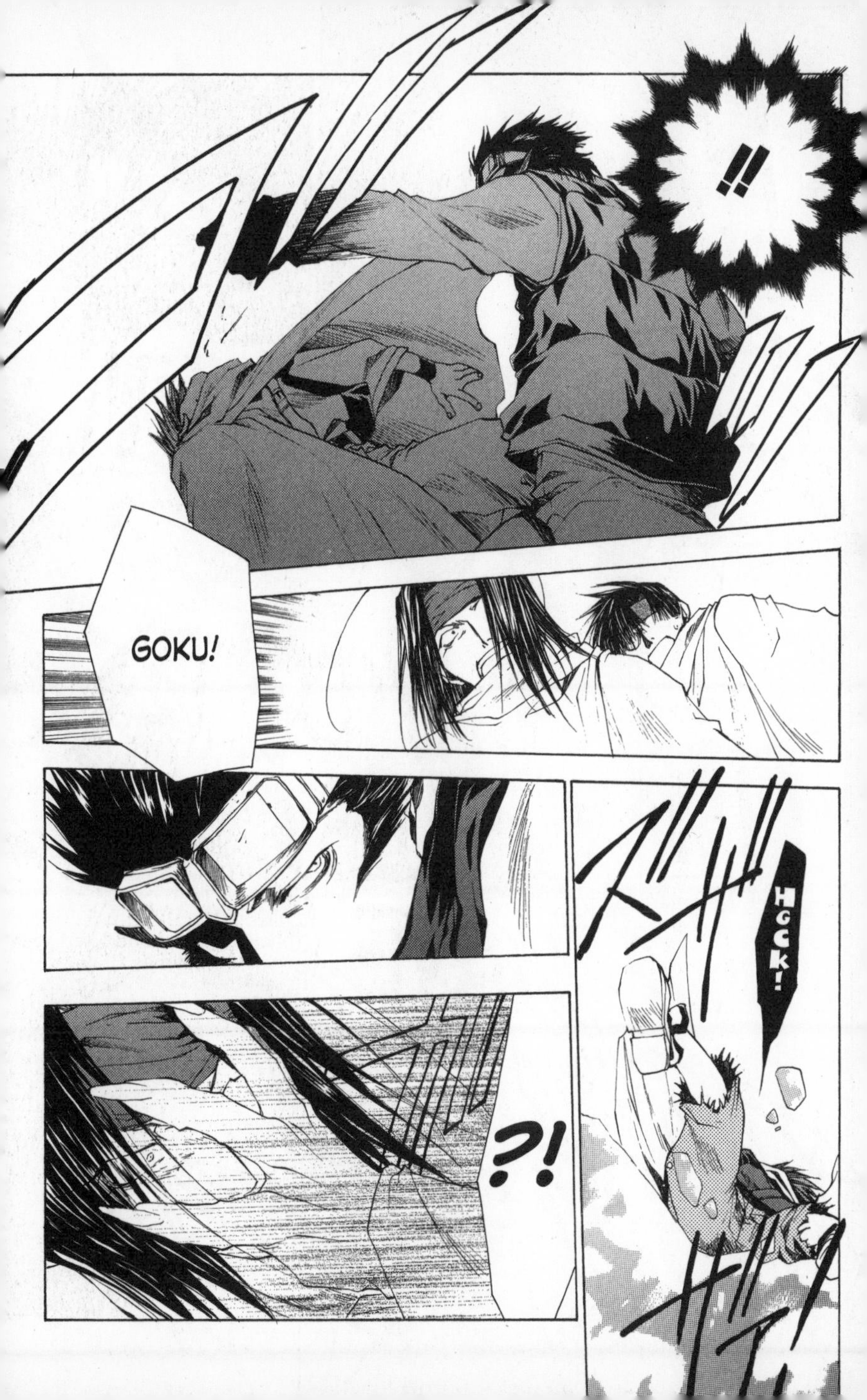
!!
GOKU!
HGCK!
?!

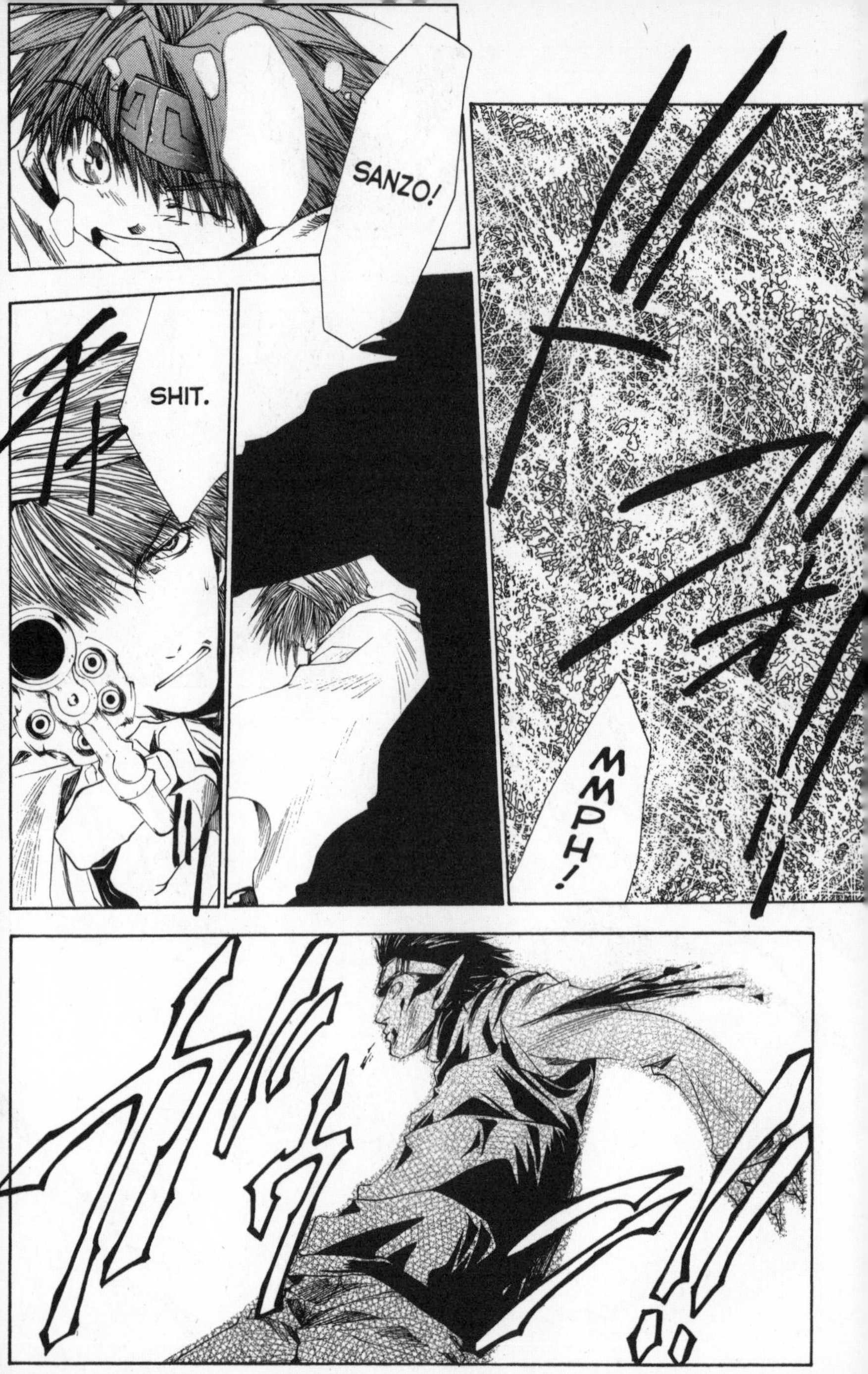
MMPH!
SANZO!
SHIT.

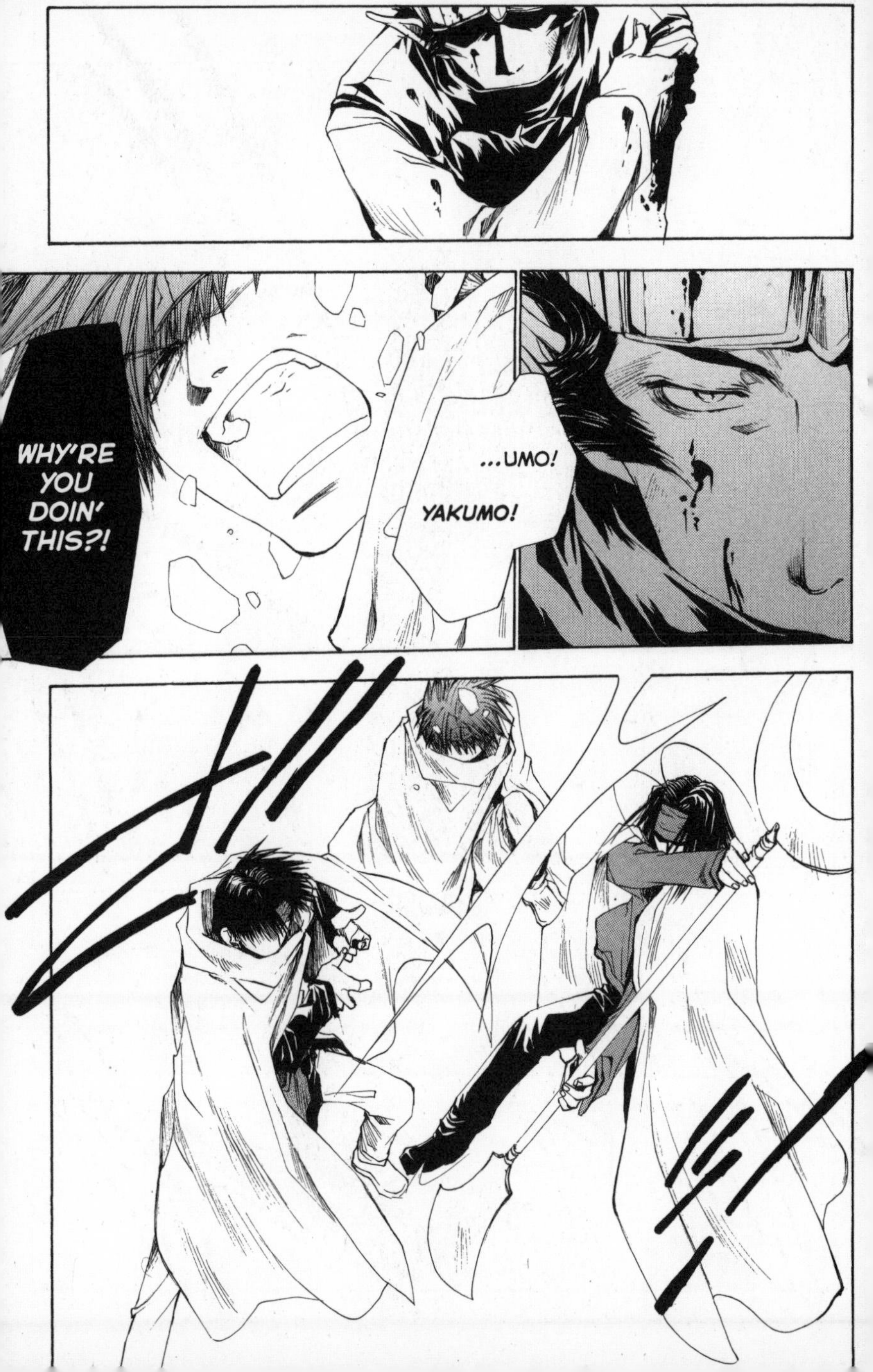
...UMO!
YAKUMO!
WHY'RE YOU DOIN' THIS?!

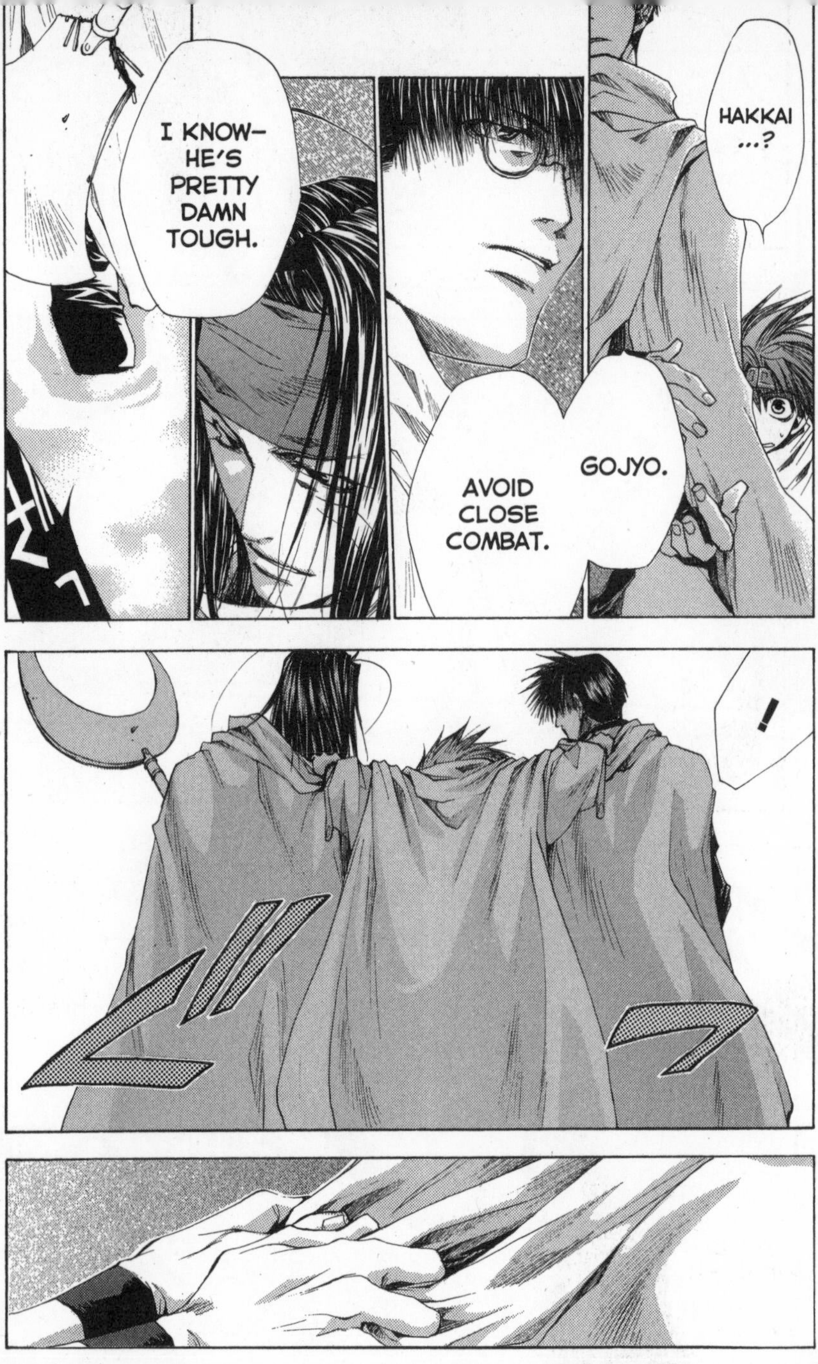
HAKKAI ...?
GOJYO. AVOID CLOSE COMBAT.
I KNOW— HE'S PRETTY DAMN TOUGH.
!

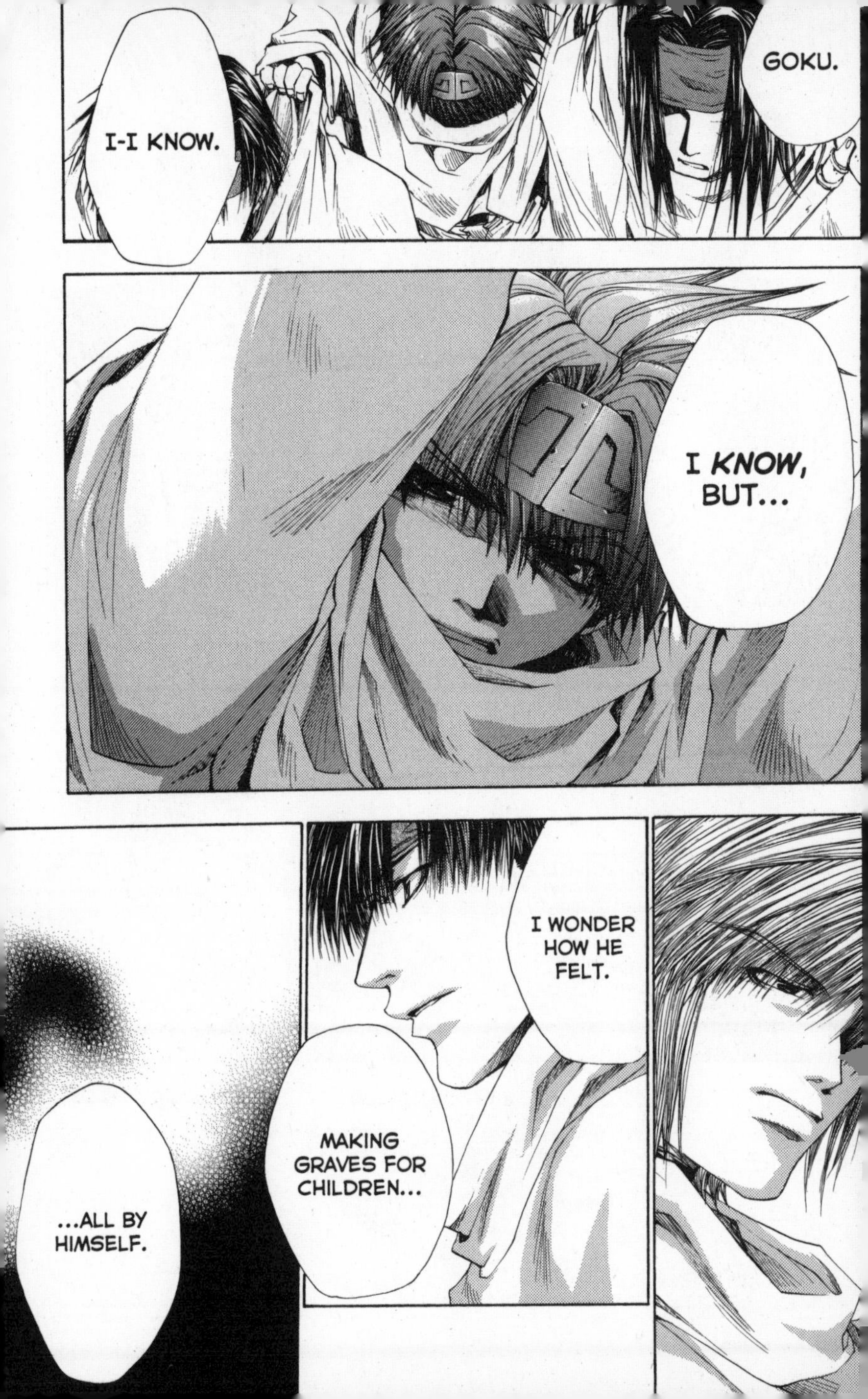
GOKU.
I-I KNOW.
I *KNOW*, BUT...
I WONDER HOW HE FELT.
MAKING GRAVES FOR CHILDREN...
...ALL BY HIMSELF.

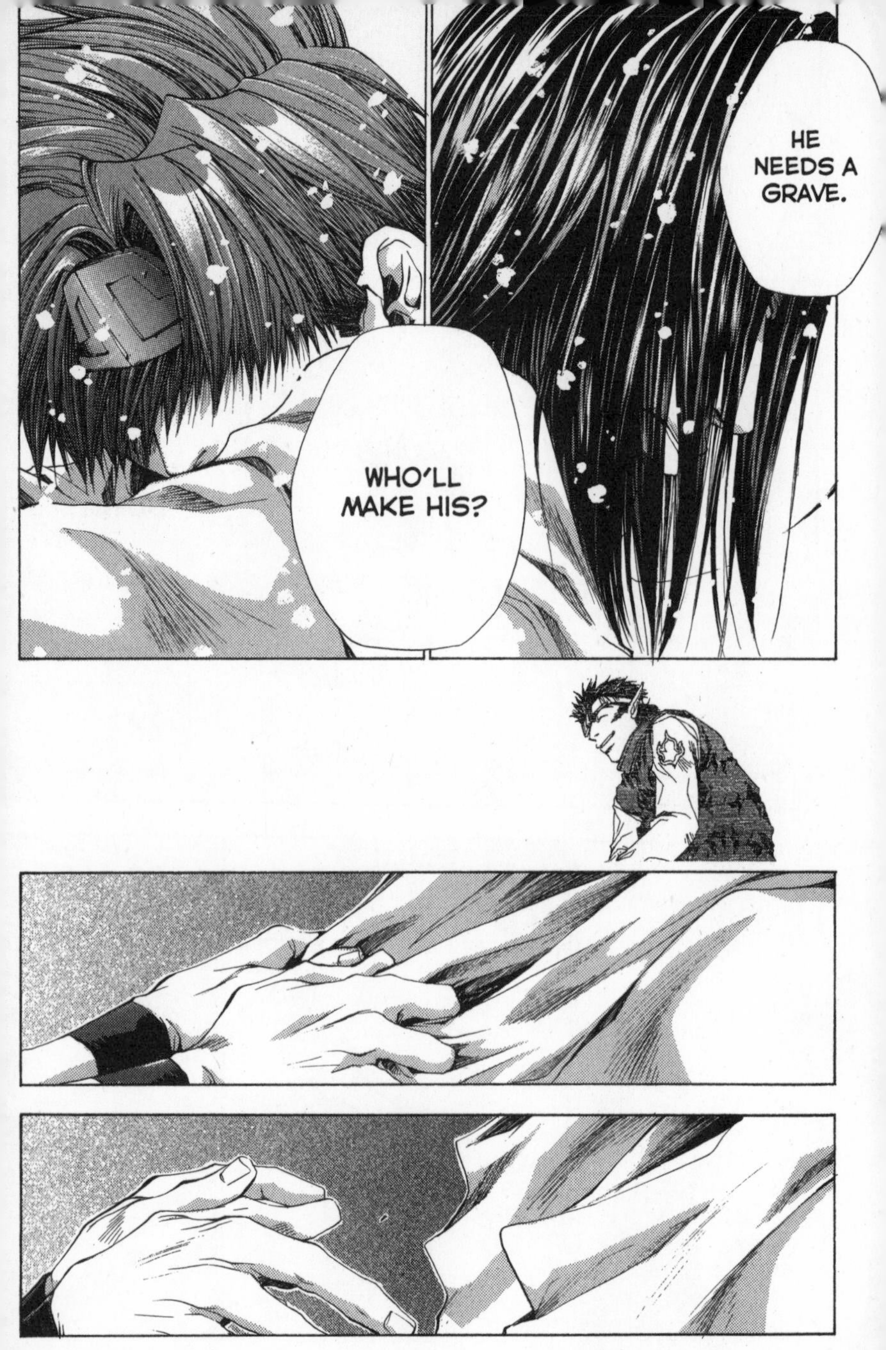
HE NEEDS A GRAVE.
WHO'LL MAKE HIS?

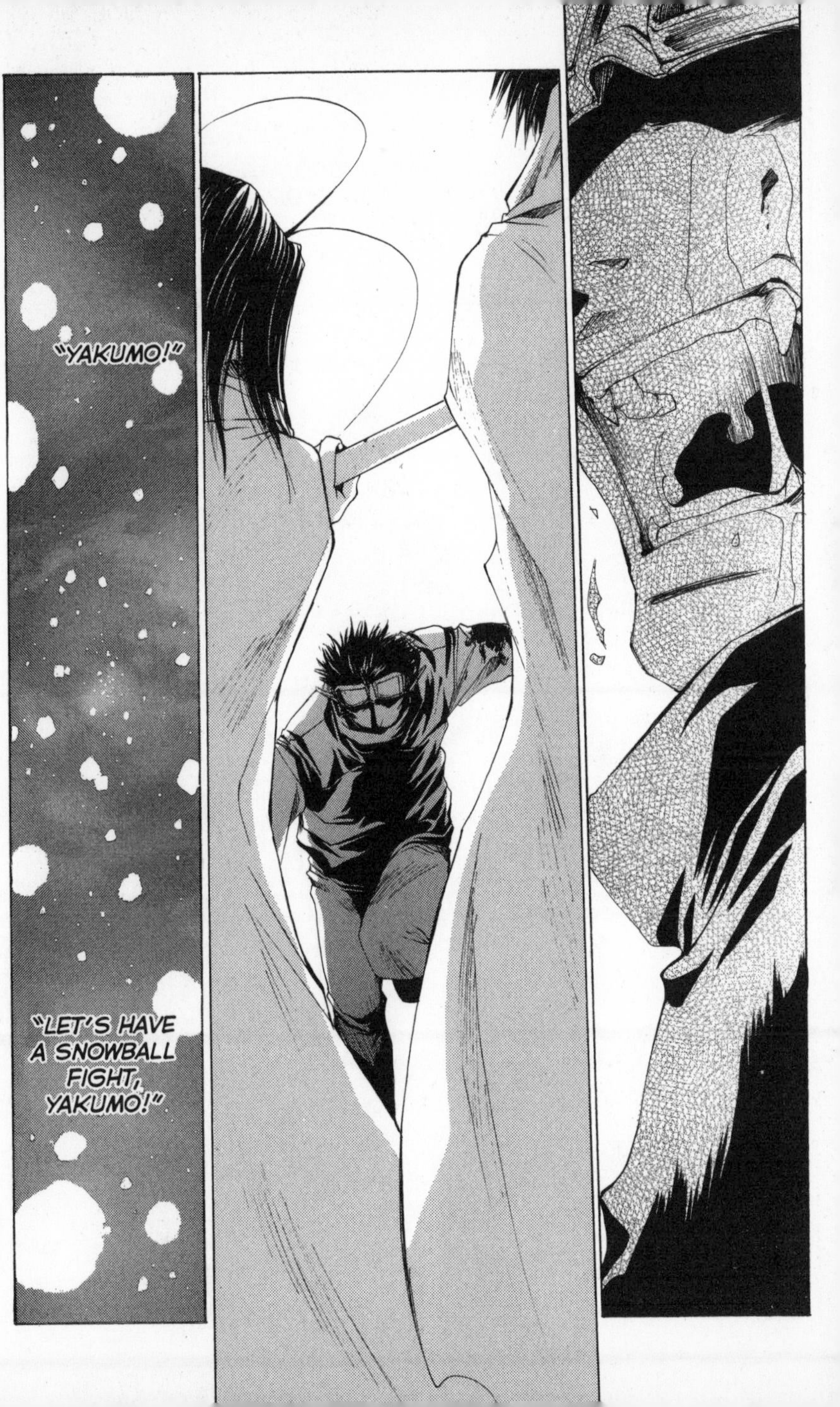
"YAKUMO!"
"LET'S HAVE A SNOWBALL FIGHT, YAKUMO!"

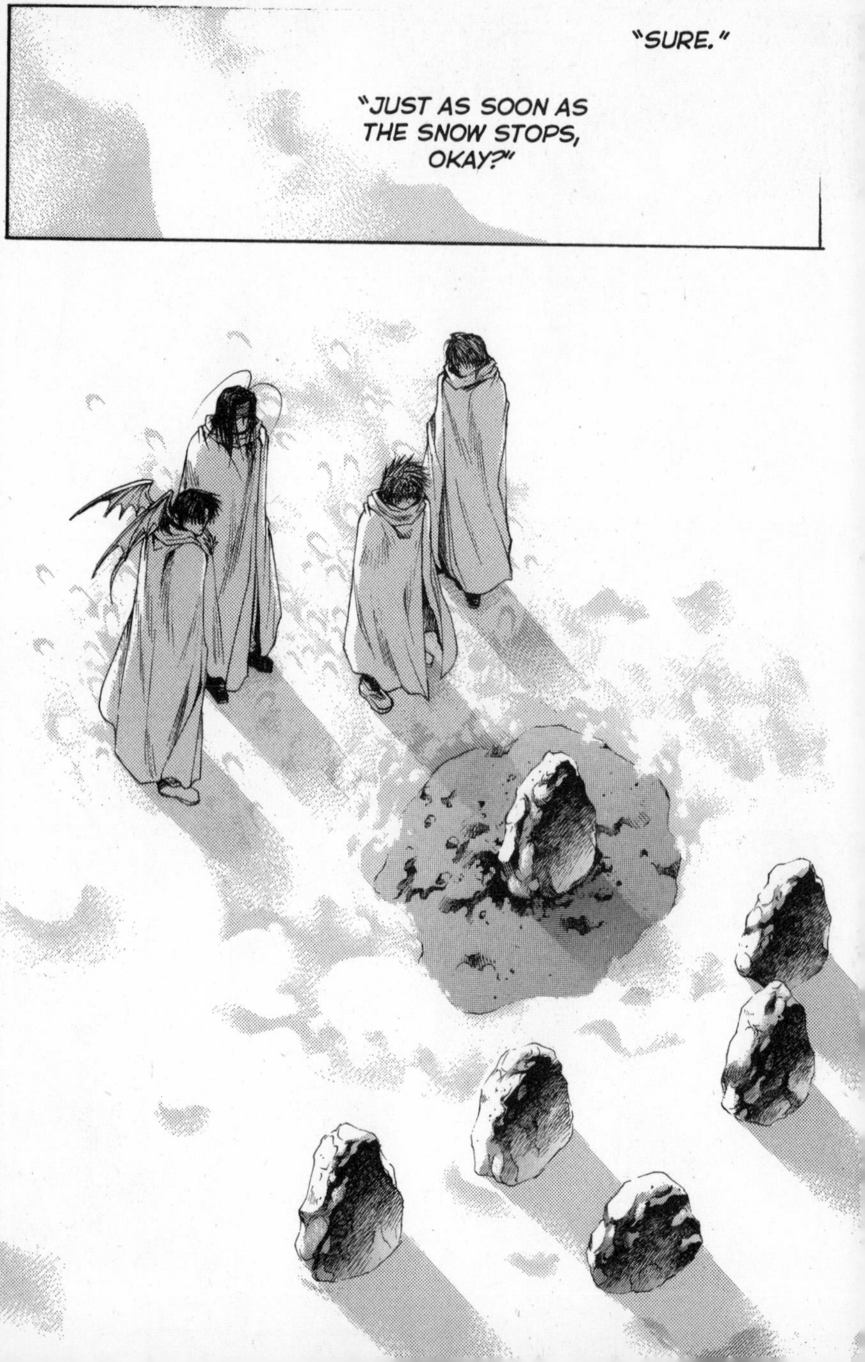
"SURE."
"JUST AS SOON AS THE SNOW STOPS, OKAY?"

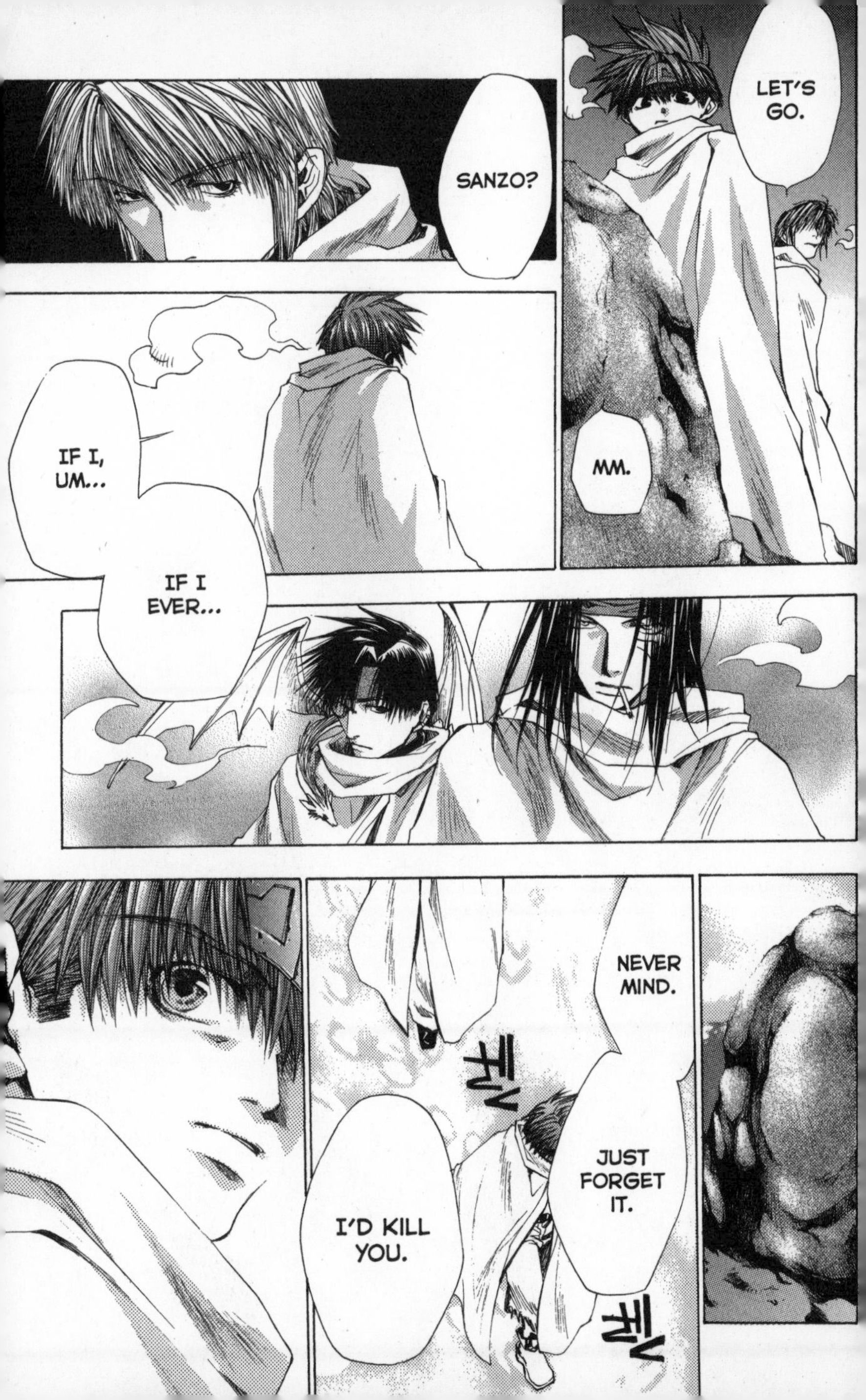
LET'S GO.
MM.
SANZO?
IF I, UM...
IF I EVER...
NEVER MIND.
JUST FORGET IT.
I'D KILL YOU.

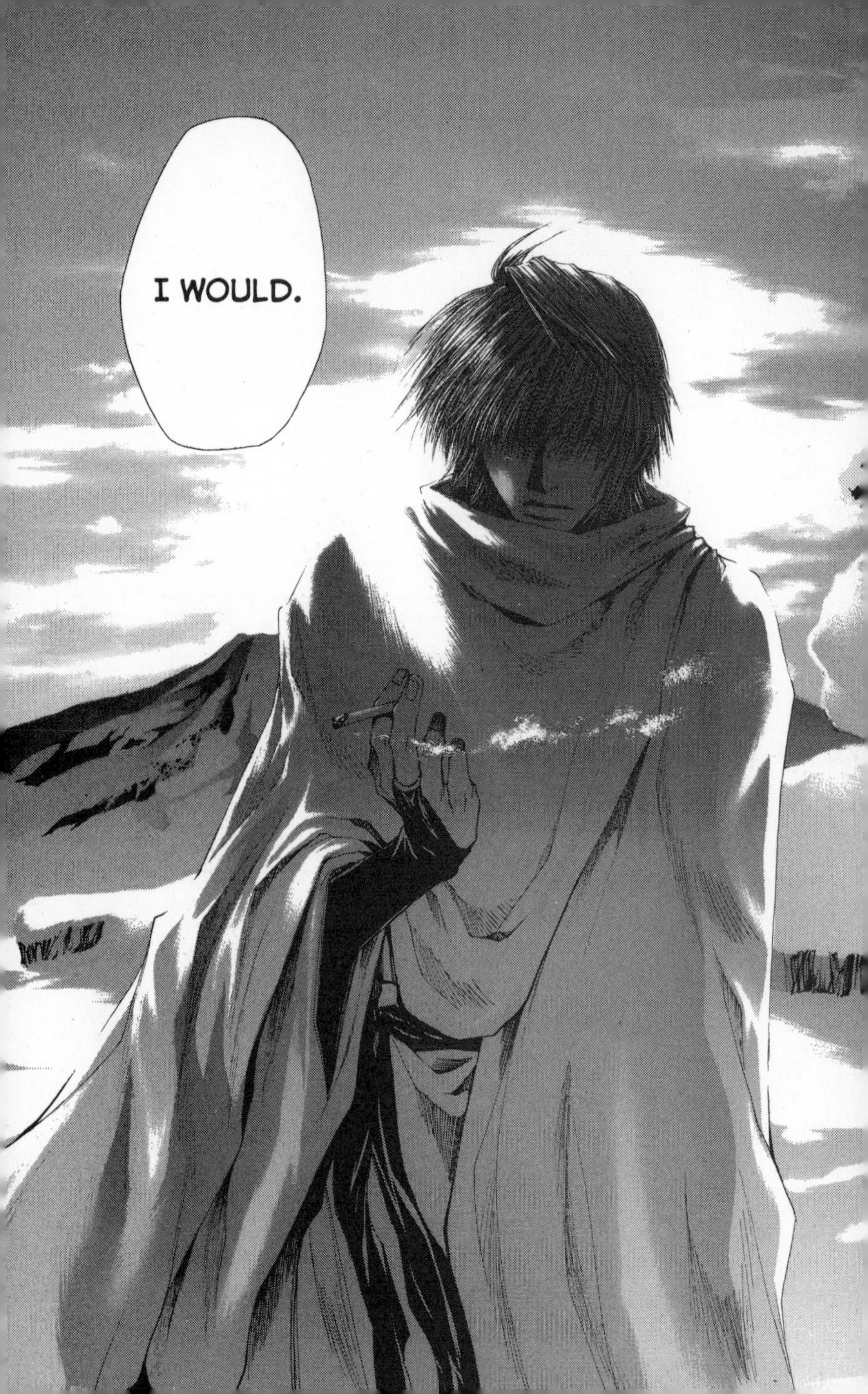
I WOULD.

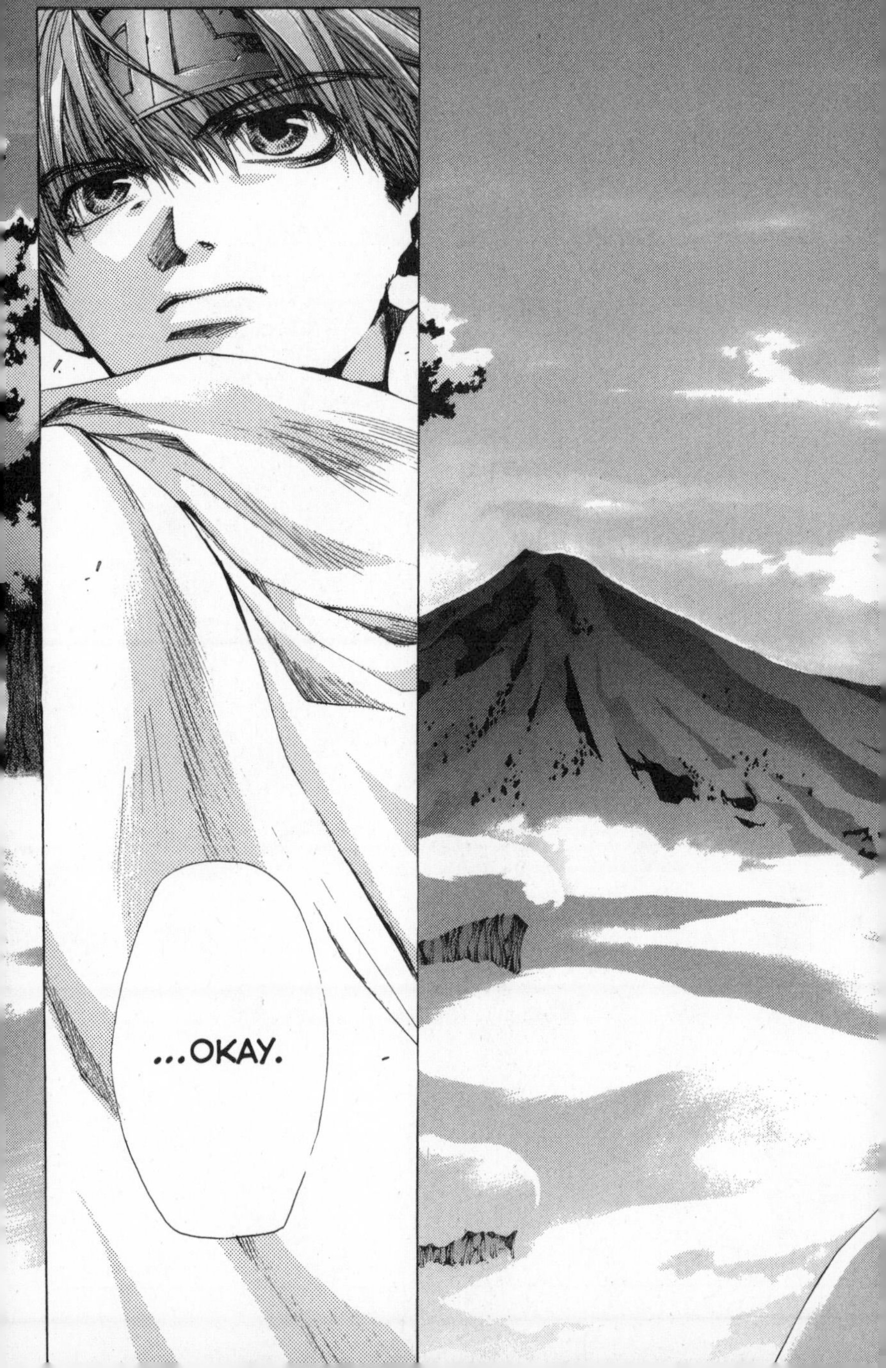
...OKAY.

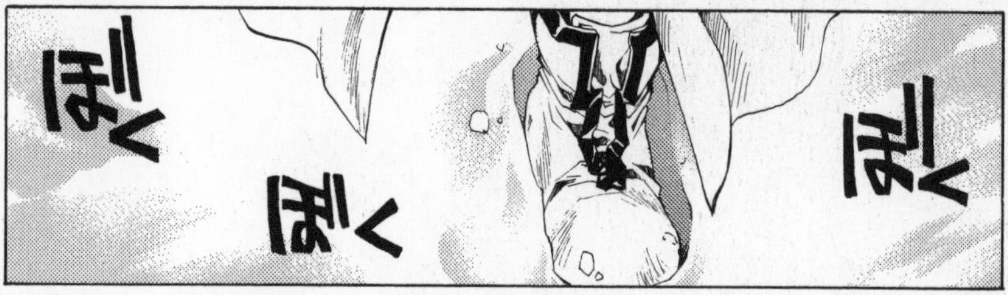
ぼく
ぼく
ぼく
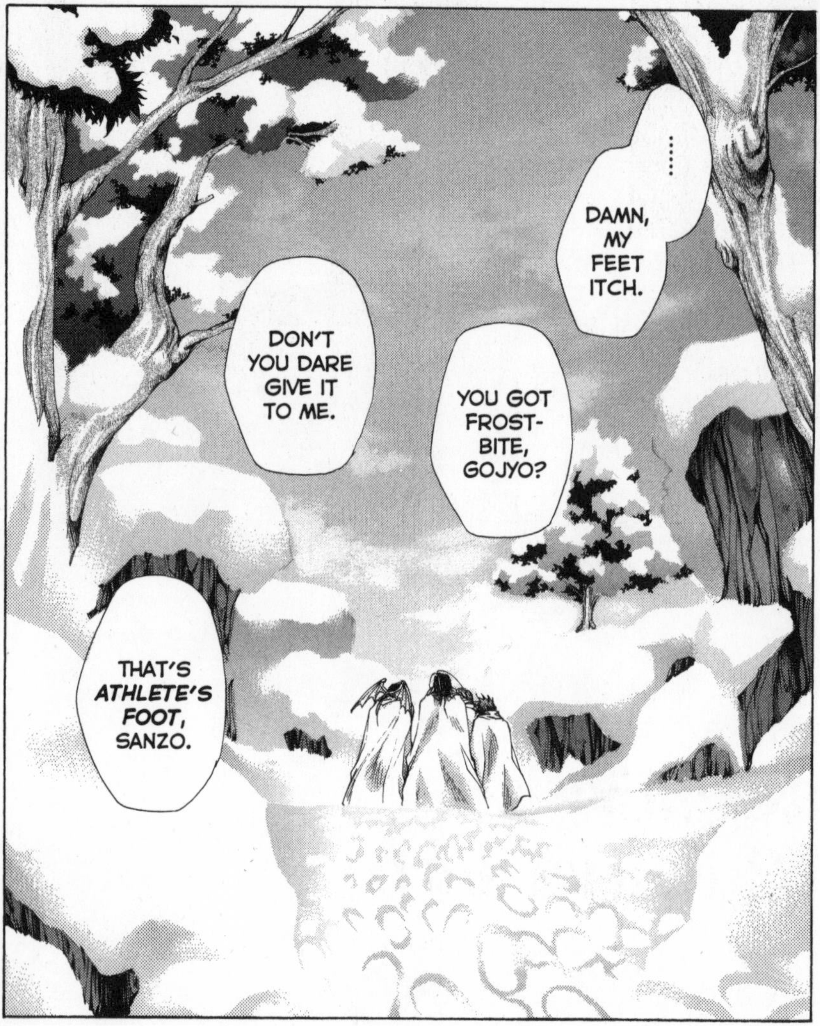
......
DAMN, MY FEET ITCH.
YOU GOT FROST-BITE, GOJYO?
DON'T YOU DARE GIVE IT TO ME.
THAT'S *ATHLETE'S FOOT*, SANZO.

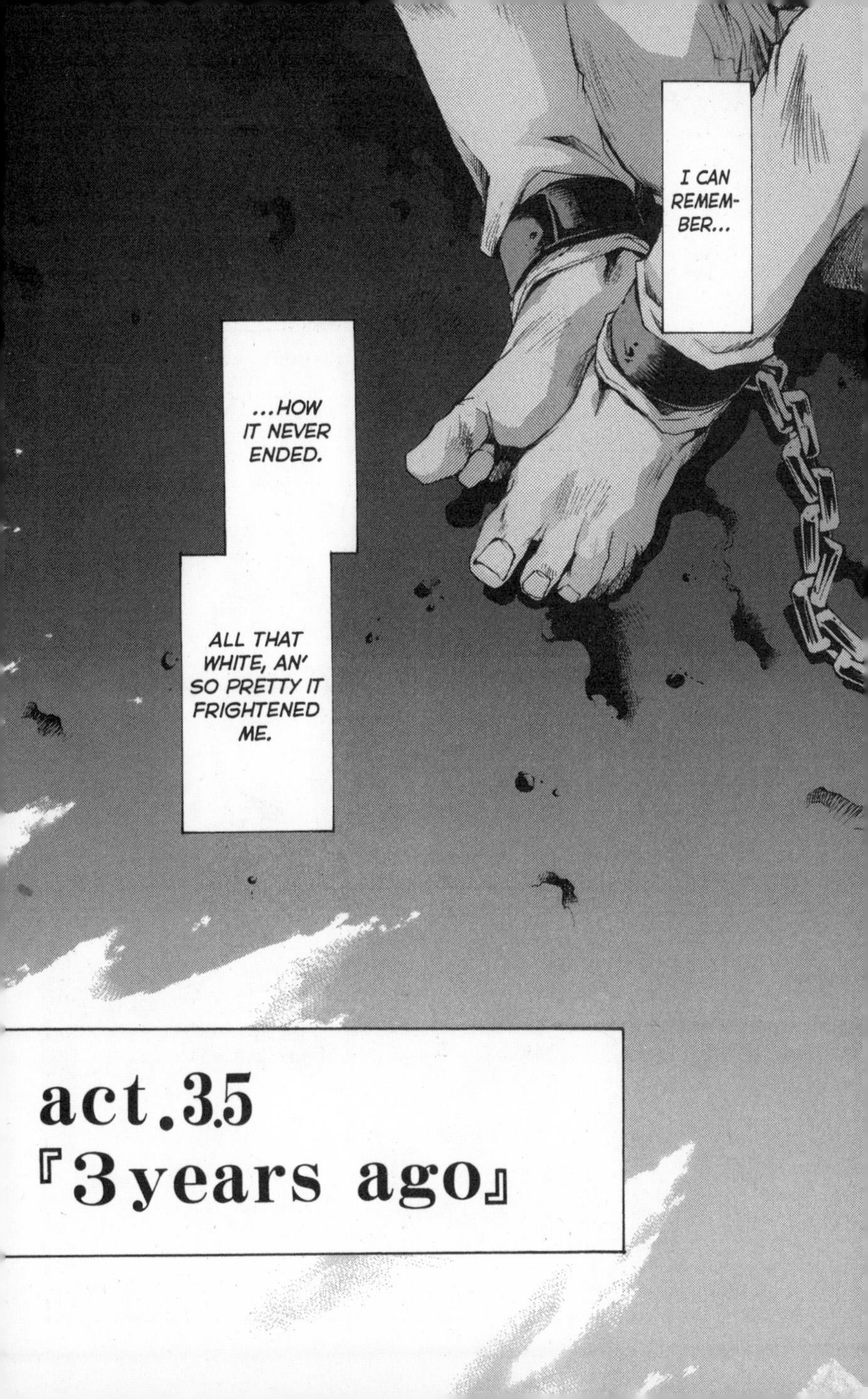
I CAN REMEMBER...
...HOW IT NEVER ENDED.
ALL THAT WHITE, AN' SO PRETTY IT FRIGHTENED ME.
act.3.5 『3years ago』

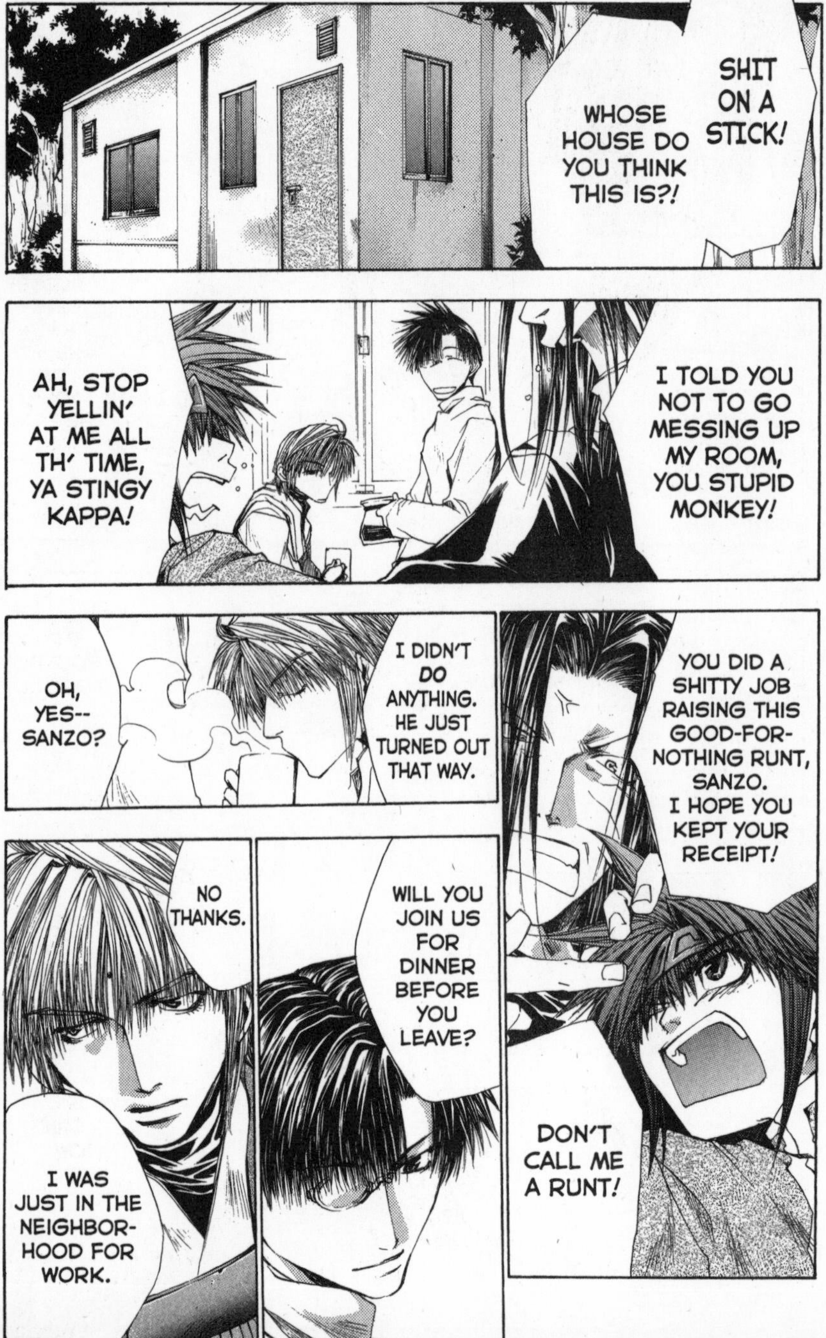
SHIT ON A STICK!
WHOSE HOUSE DO YOU THINK THIS IS?!
I TOLD YOU NOT TO GO MESSING UP MY ROOM, YOU STUPID MONKEY!
AH, STOP YELLIN' AT ME ALL TH' TIME, YA STINGY KAPPA!
YOU DID A SHITTY JOB RAISING THIS GOOD-FOR-NOTHING RUNT, SANZO. I HOPE YOU KEPT YOUR RECEIPT!
DON'T CALL ME A RUNT!
I DIDN'T *DO* ANYTHING. HE JUST TURNED OUT THAT WAY.
OH, YES-- SANZO?
WILL YOU JOIN US FOR DINNER BEFORE YOU LEAVE?
NO THANKS.
I WAS JUST IN THE NEIGHBORHOOD FOR WORK.

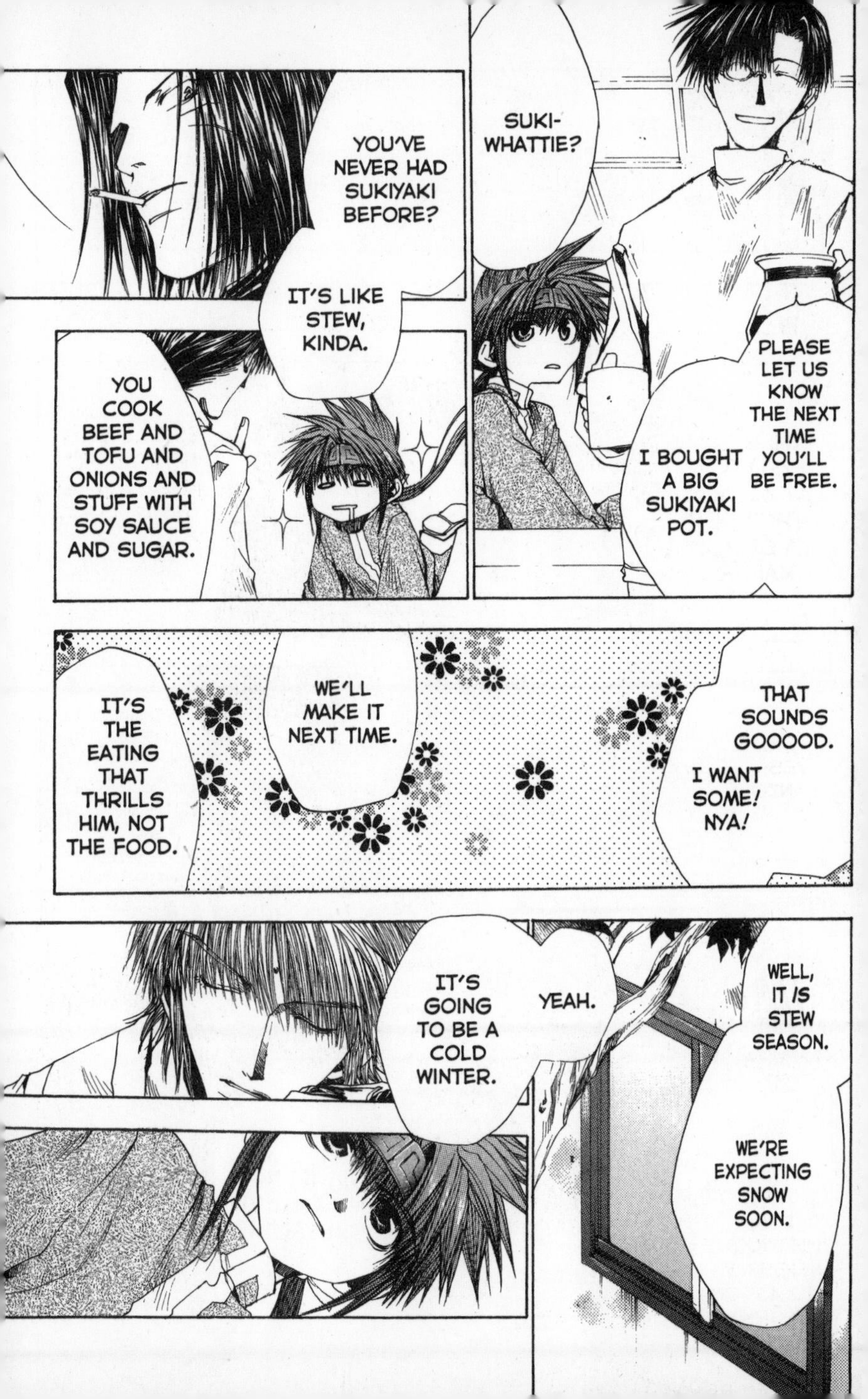
SUKI-WHATTIE?
PLEASE LET US KNOW THE NEXT TIME YOU'LL BE FREE.
I BOUGHT A BIG SUKIYAKI POT.
YOU'VE NEVER HAD SUKIYAKI BEFORE?
IT'S LIKE STEW, KINDA.
YOU COOK BEEF AND TOFU AND ONIONS AND STUFF WITH SOY SAUCE AND SUGAR.
THAT SOUNDS GOOOOD.
I WANT SOME! NYA!
WE'LL MAKE IT NEXT TIME.
IT'S THE EATING THAT THRILLS HIM, NOT THE FOOD.
WELL, IT *IS* STEW SEASON.
WE'RE EXPECTING SNOW SOON.
YEAH.
IT'S GOING TO BE A COLD WINTER.

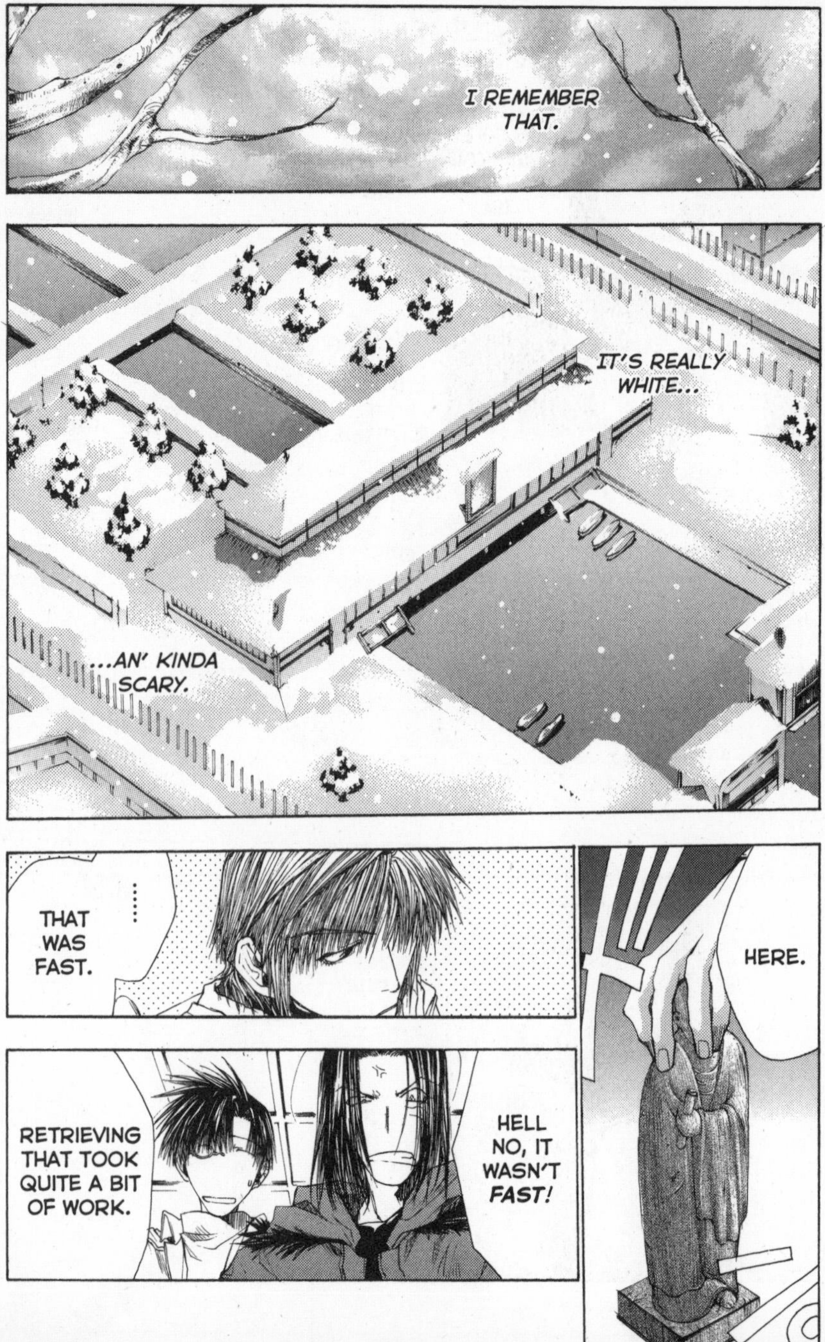
I REMEMBER THAT.
IT'S REALLY WHITE...
...AN' KINDA SCARY.
HERE.
......
THAT WAS FAST.
HELL NO, IT WASN'T FAST!
RETRIEVING THAT TOOK QUITE A BIT OF WORK.

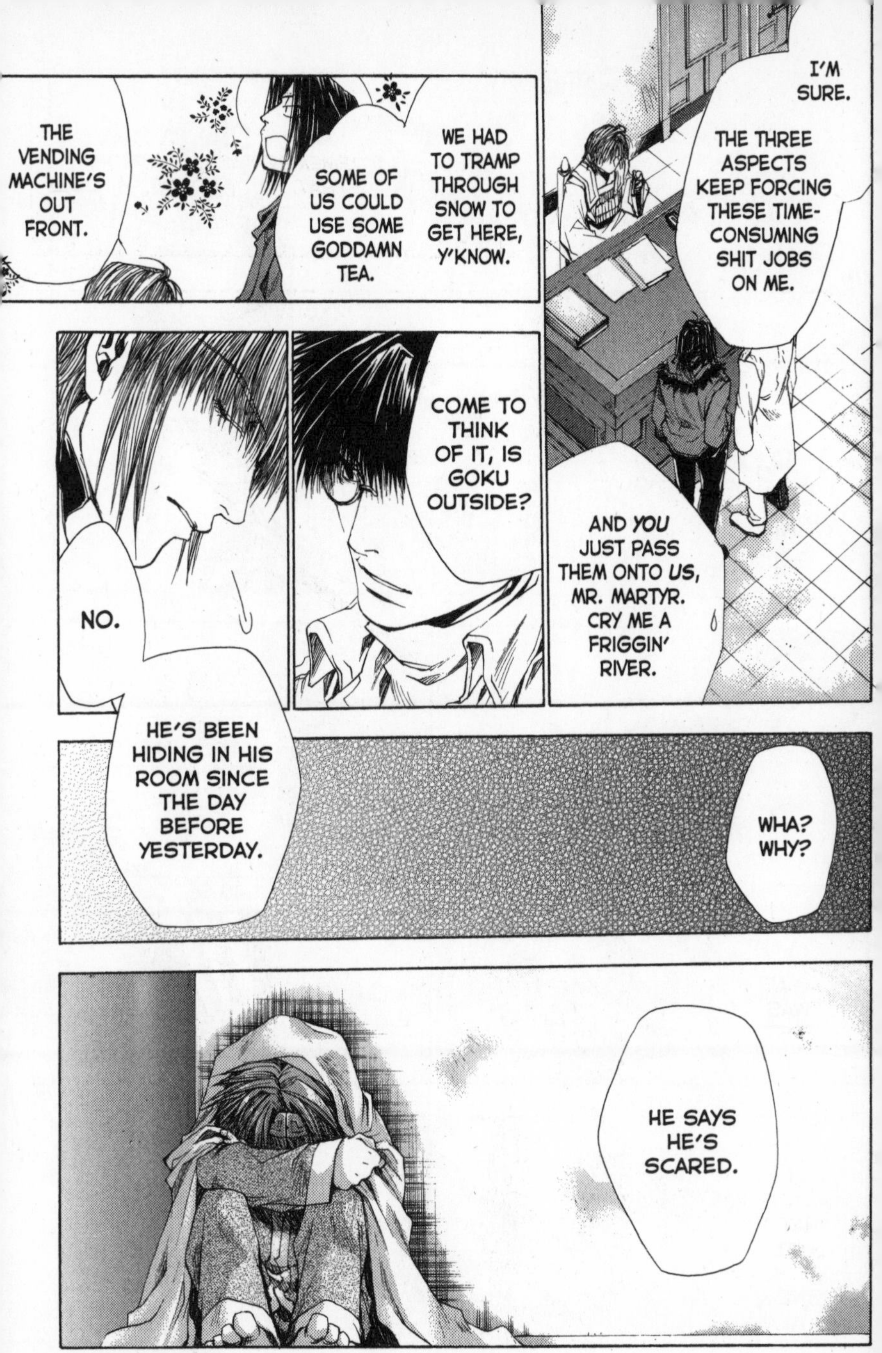
I'M SURE.
THE THREE ASPECTS KEEP FORCING THESE TIME-CONSUMING SHIT JOBS ON ME.
AND *YOU* JUST PASS THEM ONTO *US*, MR. MARTYR. CRY ME A FRIGGIN' RIVER.
WE HAD TO TRAMP THROUGH SNOW TO GET HERE, Y'KNOW.
SOME OF US COULD USE SOME GODDAMN TEA.
THE VENDING MACHINE'S OUT FRONT.
COME TO THINK OF IT, IS GOKU OUTSIDE?
NO.
HE'S BEEN HIDING IN HIS ROOM SINCE THE DAY BEFORE YESTERDAY.
WHA? WHY?
HE SAYS HE'S SCARED.

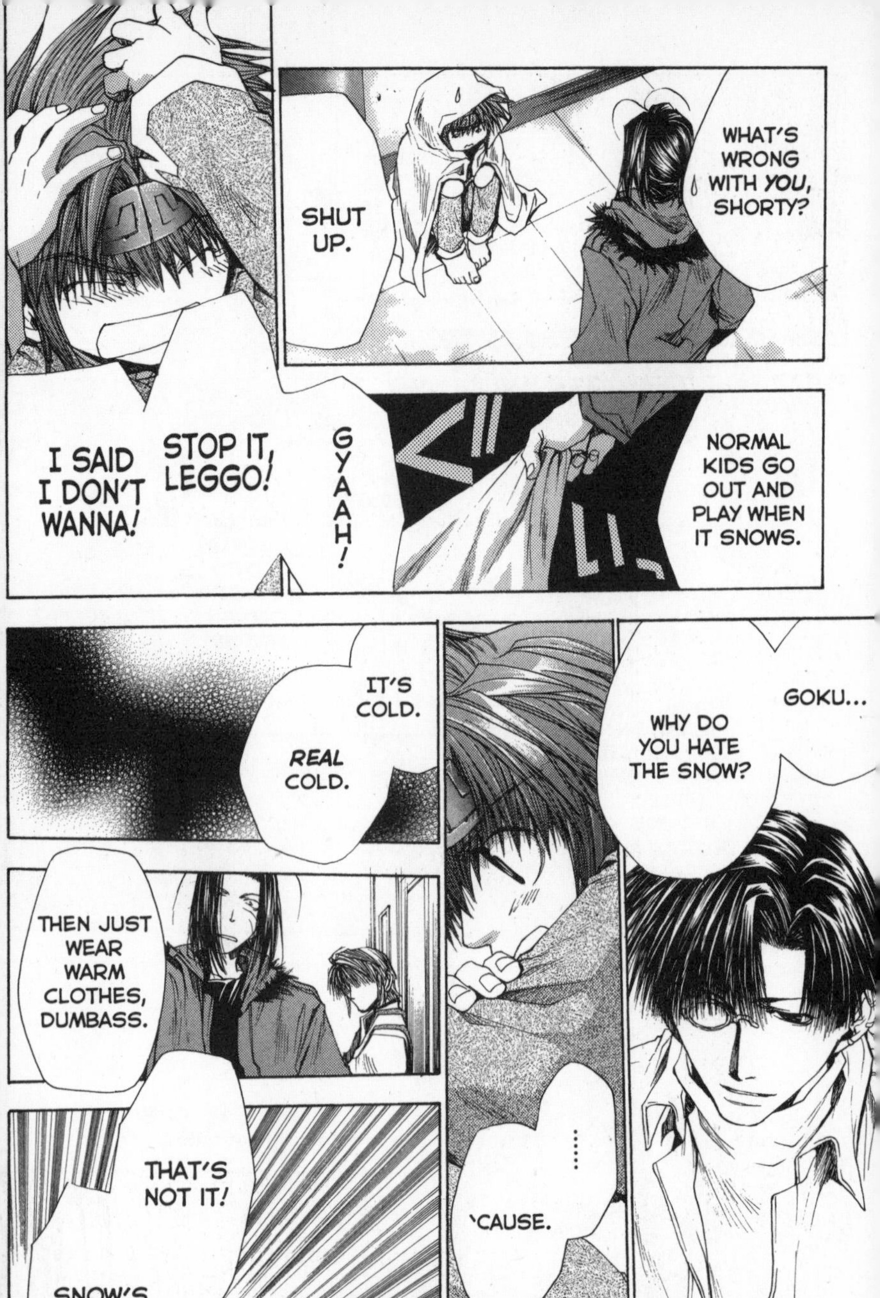
WHAT'S WRONG WITH *YOU*, SHORTY?
SHUT UP.
NORMAL KIDS GO OUT AND PLAY WHEN IT SNOWS.
GYAAH!
STOP IT, LEGGO!
I SAID I DON'T WANNA!
GOKU...
WHY DO YOU HATE THE SNOW?
......
'CAUSE.
IT'S COLD.
REAL COLD.
THEN JUST WEAR WARM CLOTHES, DUMBASS.
THAT'S NOT IT!
SNOW'S BAD!

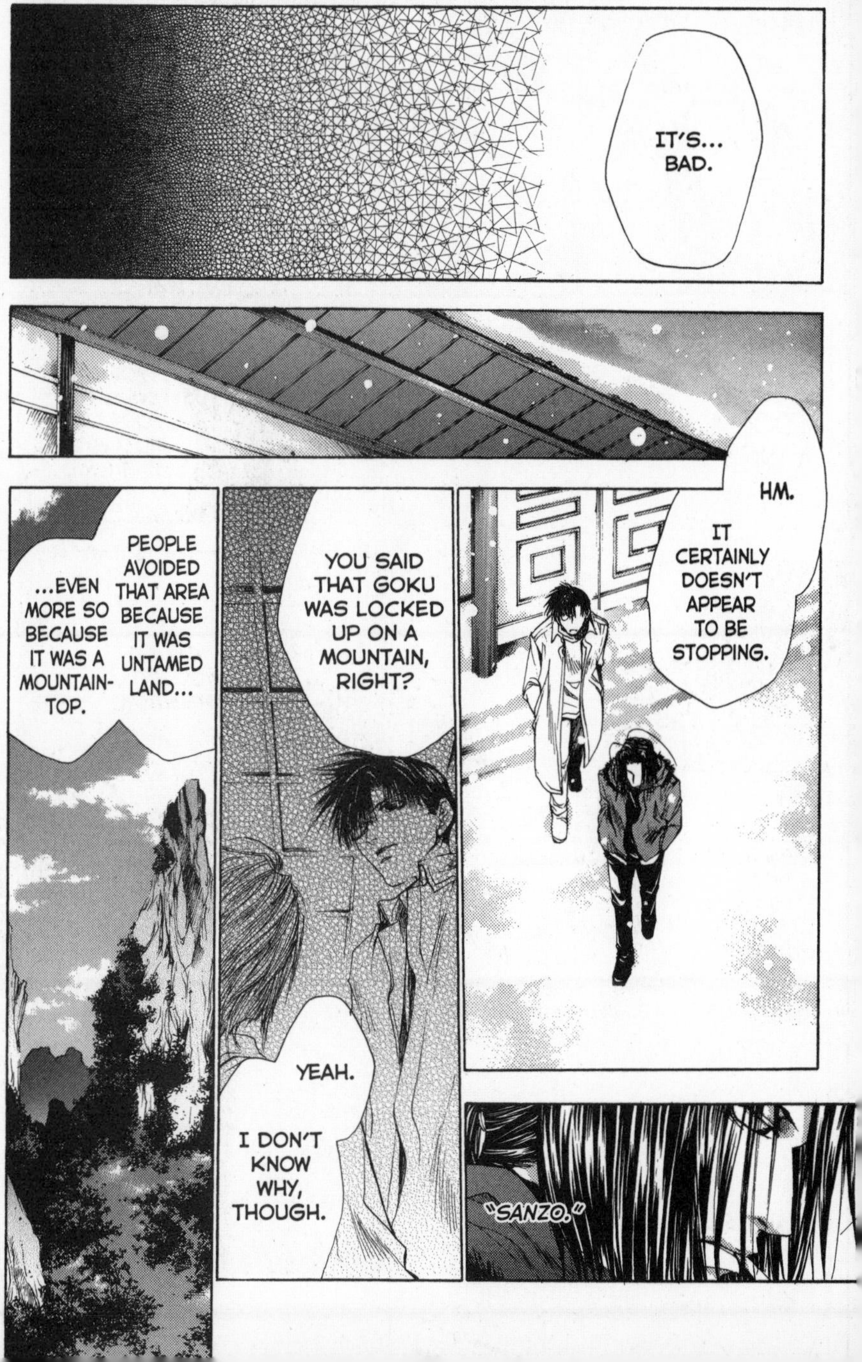
IT'S... BAD.
HM.
IT CERTAINLY DOESN'T APPEAR TO BE STOPPING.
"SANZO."
YOU SAID THAT GOKU WAS LOCKED UP ON A MOUNTAIN, RIGHT?
YEAH.
I DON'T KNOW WHY, THOUGH.
PEOPLE AVOIDED THAT AREA BECAUSE IT WAS UNTAMED LAND...
...EVEN MORE SO BECAUSE IT WAS A MOUNTAIN-TOP.

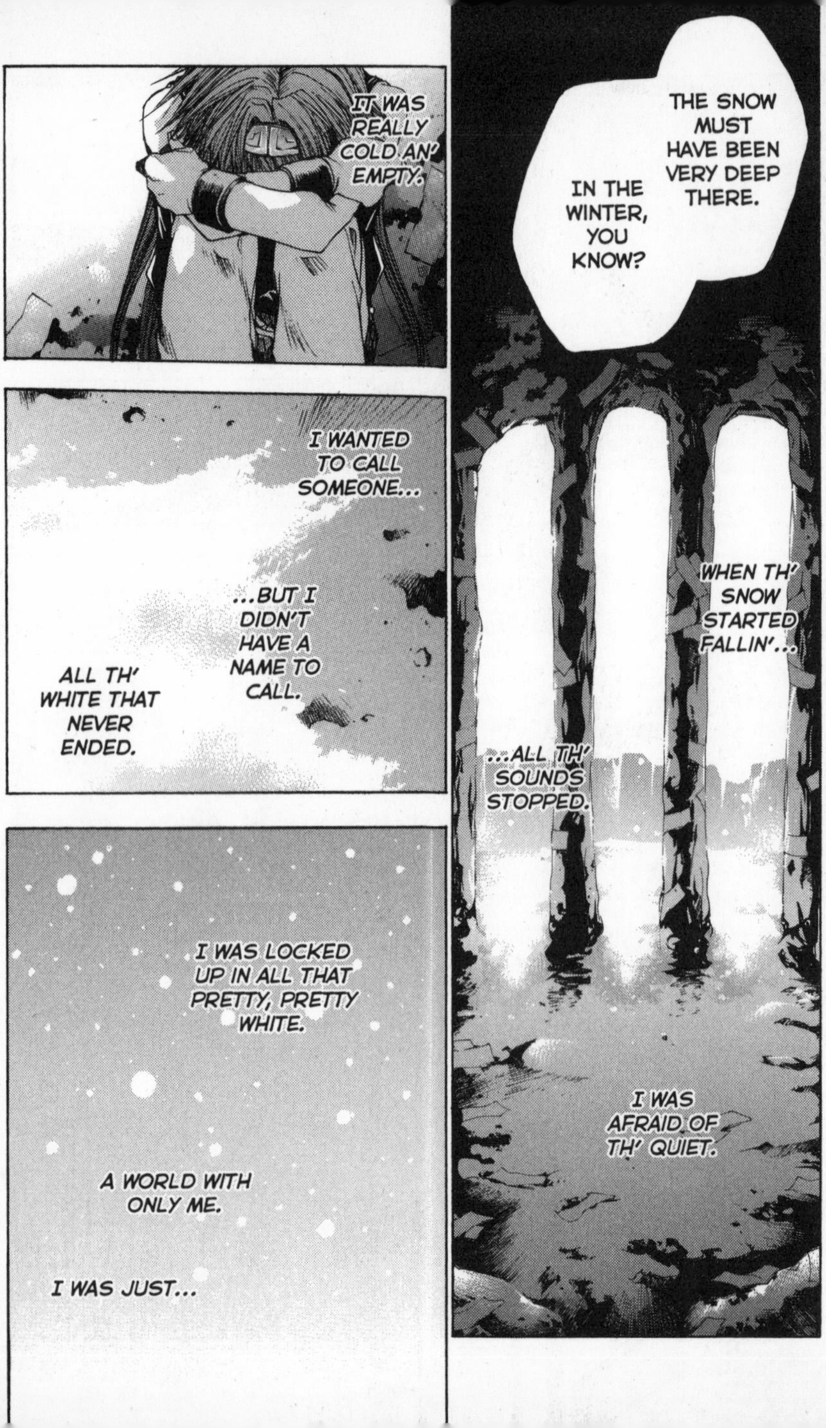
THE SNOW MUST HAVE BEEN VERY DEEP THERE.
IN THE WINTER, YOU KNOW?
WHEN TH' SNOW STARTED FALLIN'...
...ALL TH' SOUNDS STOPPED.
I WAS AFRAID OF TH' QUIET.
IT WAS REALLY COLD AN' EMPTY.
I WANTED TO CALL SOMEONE...
...BUT I DIDN'T HAVE A NAME TO CALL.
ALL TH' WHITE THAT NEVER ENDED.
I WAS LOCKED UP IN ALL THAT PRETTY, PRETTY WHITE.
A WORLD WITH ONLY ME.
I WAS JUST...

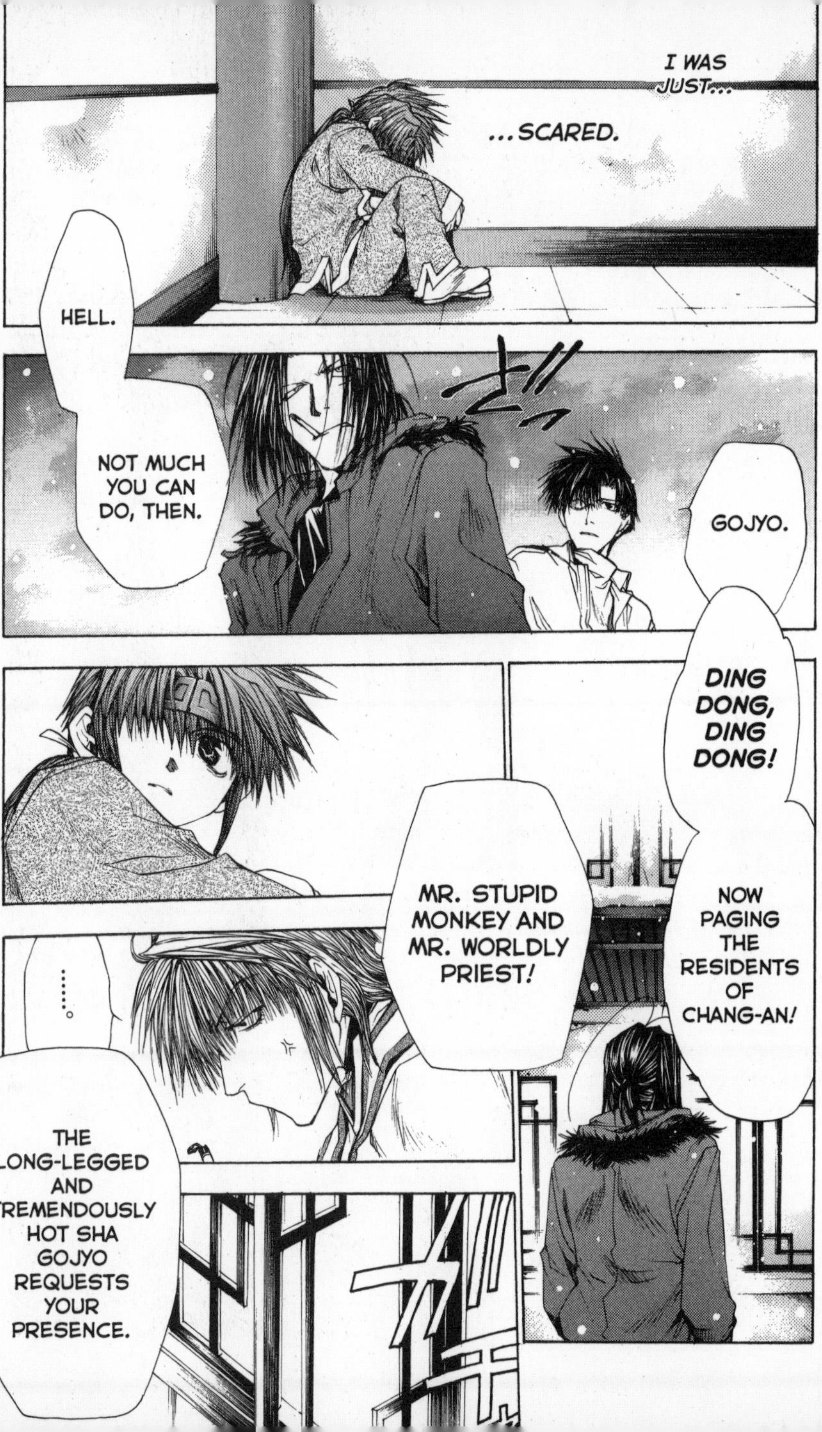
I WAS JUST...
...SCARED.
HELL.
NOT MUCH YOU CAN DO, THEN.
GOJYO.
DING DONG, DING DONG!
NOW PAGING THE RESIDENTS OF CHANG-AN!
MR. STUPID MONKEY AND MR. WORLDLY PRIEST!
THE LONG-LEGGED AND TREMENDOUSLY HOT SHA GOJYO REQUESTS YOUR PRESENCE.
……。

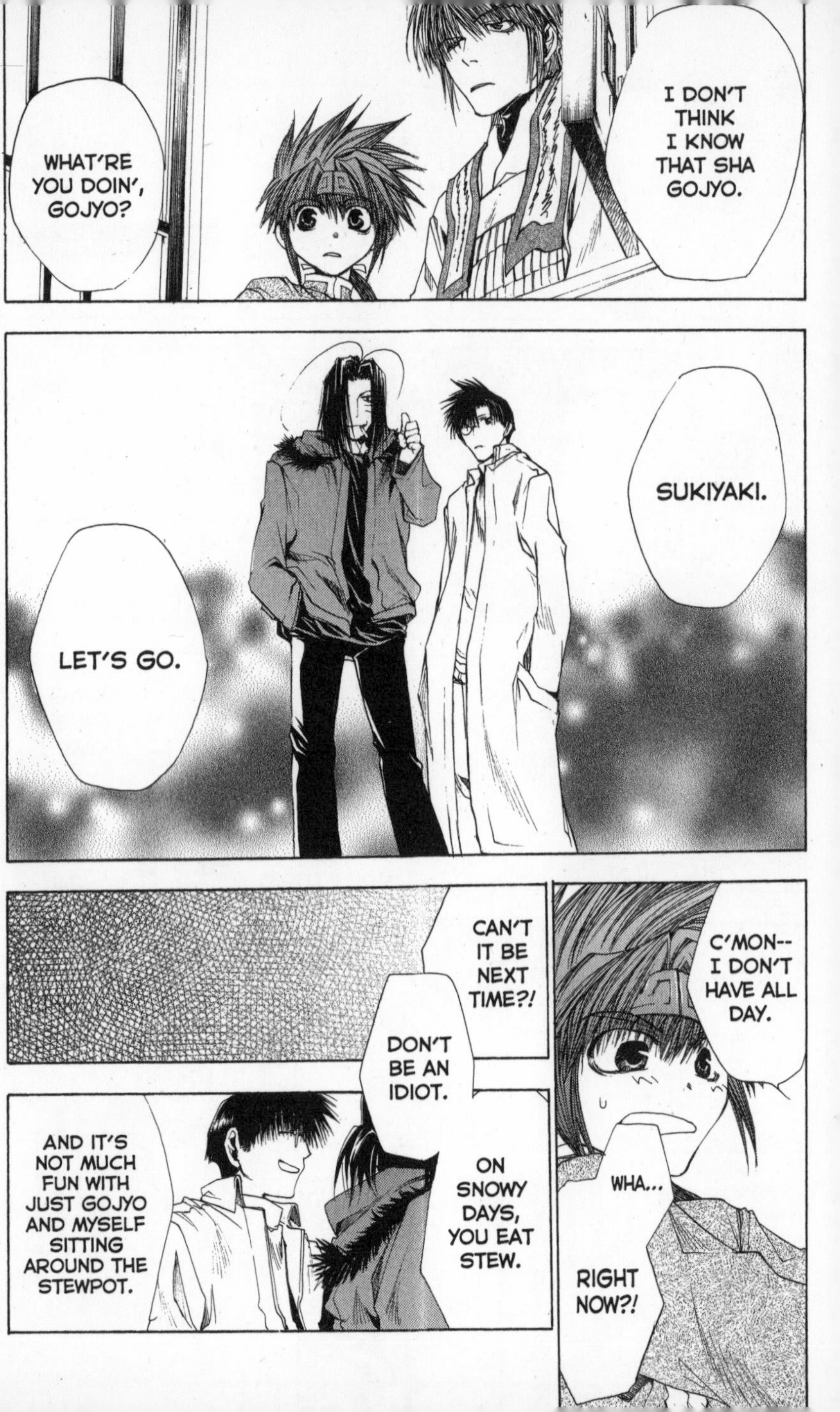
I DON'T THINK I KNOW THAT SHA GOJYO.
WHAT'RE YOU DOIN', GOJYO?
SUKIYAKI.
LET'S GO.
C'MON-- I DON'T HAVE ALL DAY.
WHA...
RIGHT NOW?!
CAN'T IT BE NEXT TIME?!
DON'T BE AN IDIOT.
ON SNOWY DAYS, YOU EAT STEW.
AND IT'S NOT MUCH FUN WITH JUST GOJYO AND MYSELF SITTING AROUND THE STEWPOT.

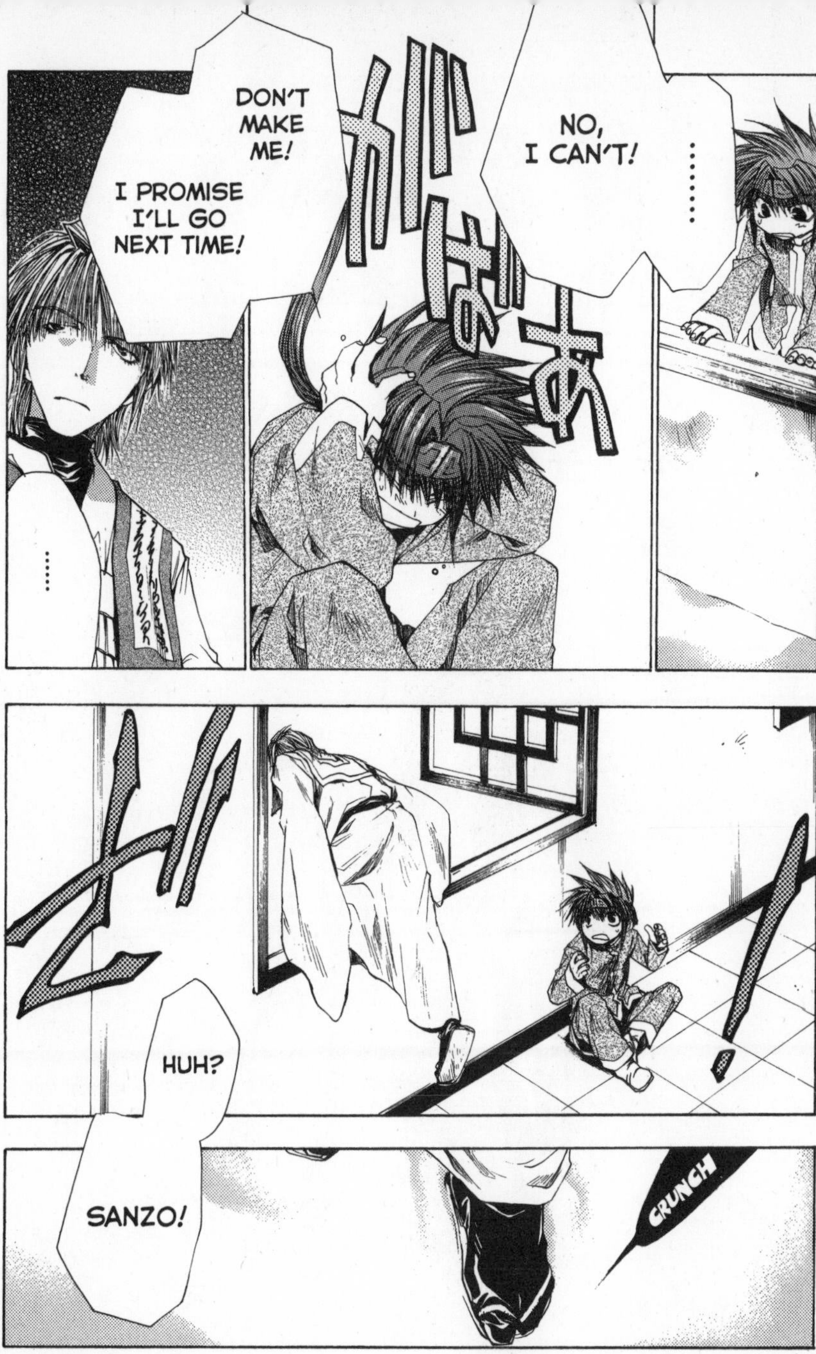
......
NO, I CAN'T!
がばあ
DON'T MAKE ME!
I PROMISE I'LL GO NEXT TIME!
......
HUH?
CRUNCH
SANZO!

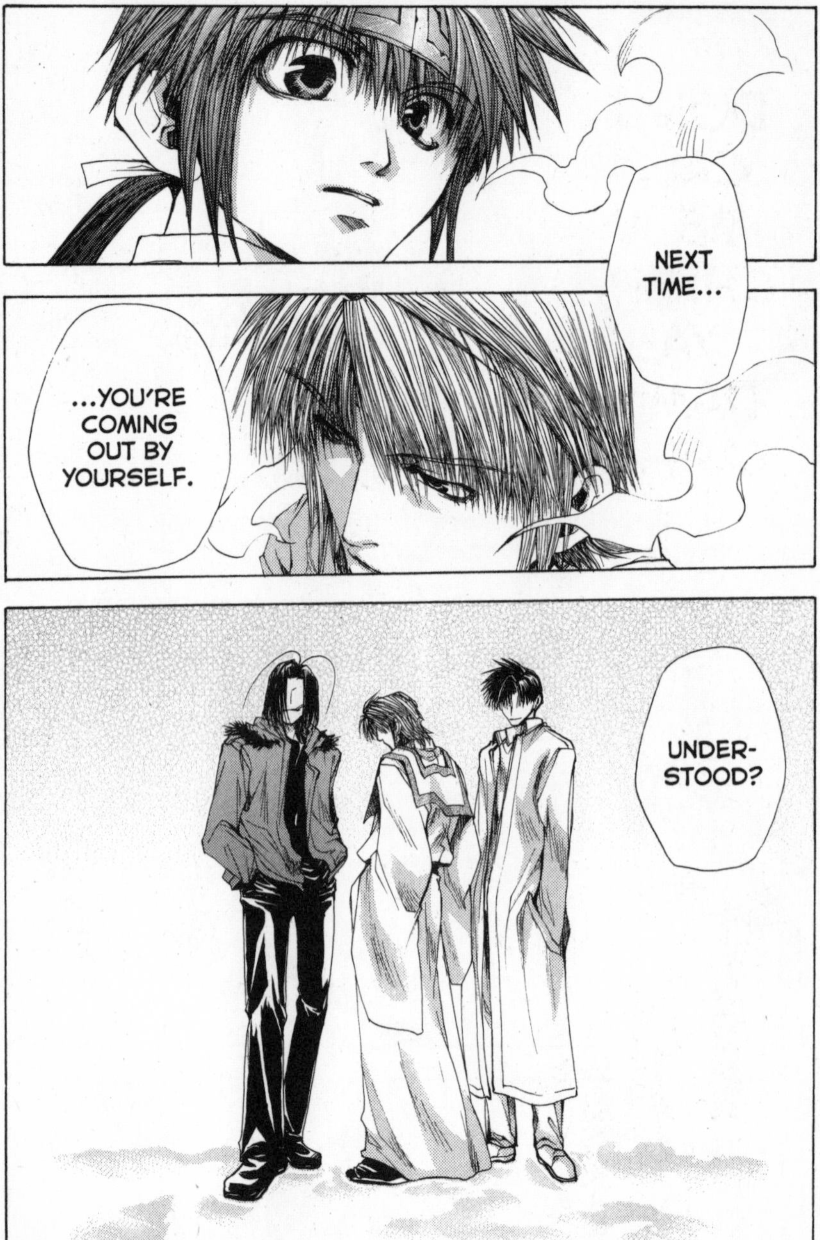
NEXT TIME...
...YOU'RE COMING OUT BY YOURSELF.
UNDER-STOOD?

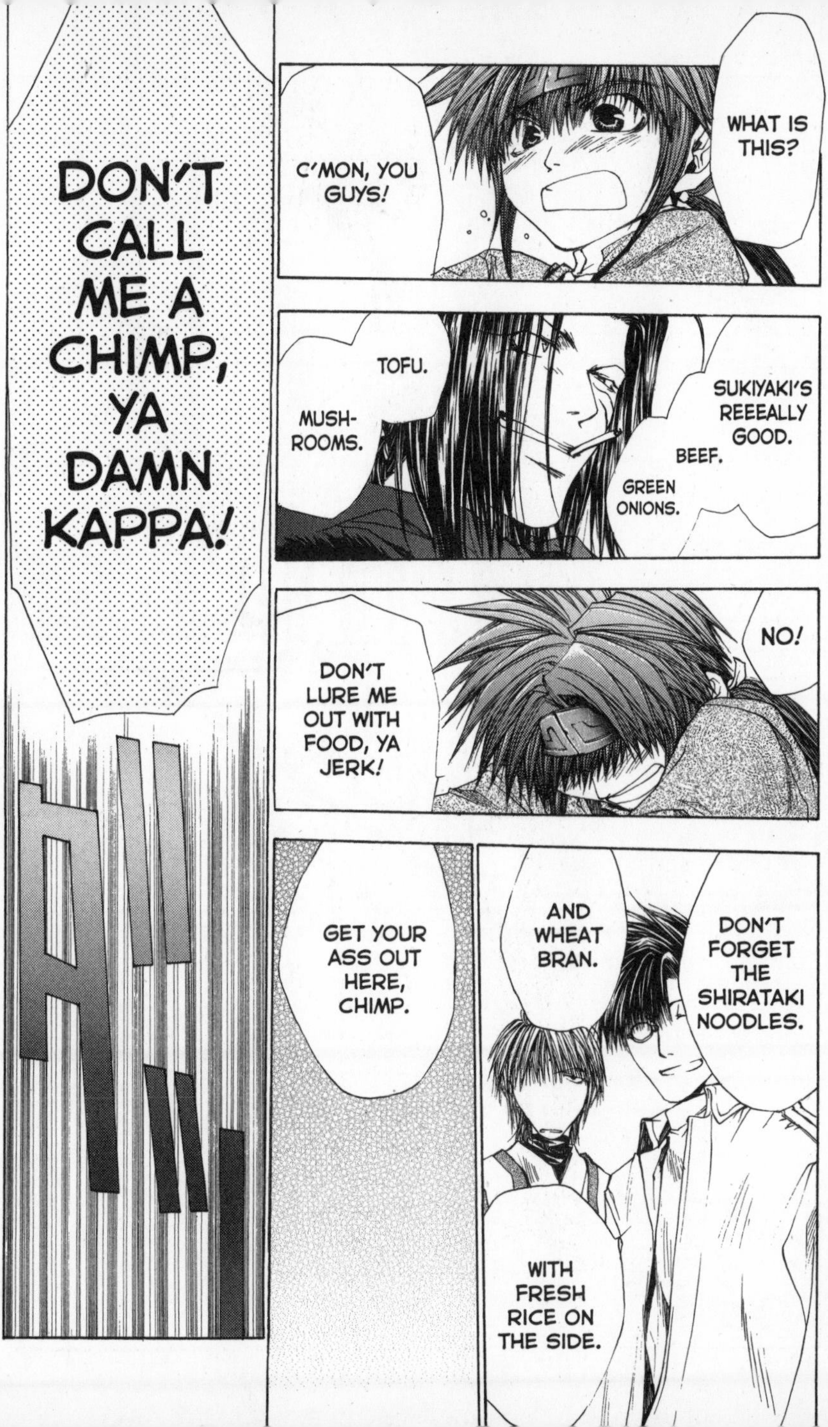
WHAT IS THIS?
C'MON, YOU GUYS!
SUKIYAKI'S REEEALLY GOOD.
BEEF.
GREEN ONIONS.
TOFU.
MUSH-ROOMS.
NO!
DON'T LURE ME OUT WITH FOOD, YA JERK!
DON'T FORGET THE SHIRATAKI NOODLES.
AND WHEAT BRAN.
WITH FRESH RICE ON THE SIDE.
GET YOUR ASS OUT HERE, CHIMP.
DON'T CALL ME A CHIMP, YA DAMN KAPPA!

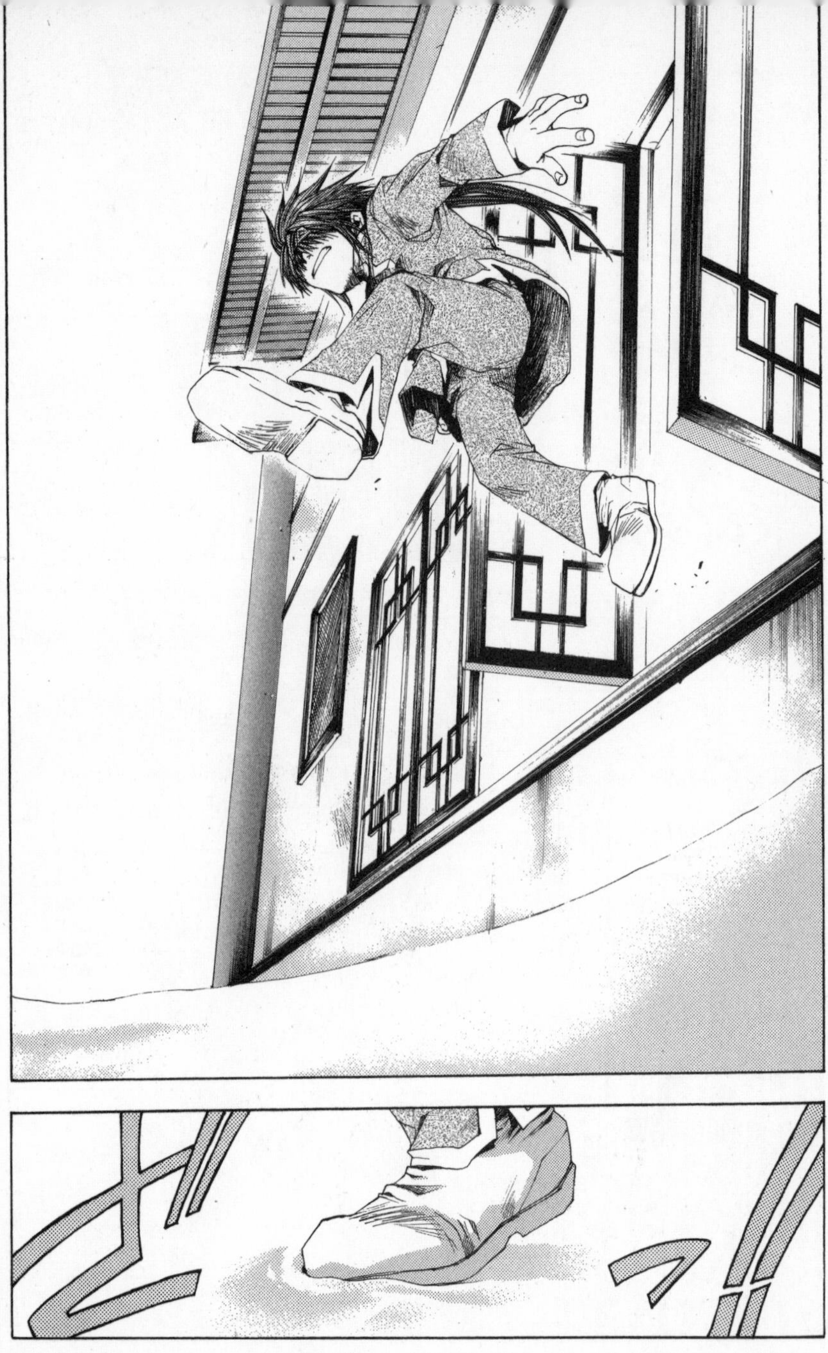

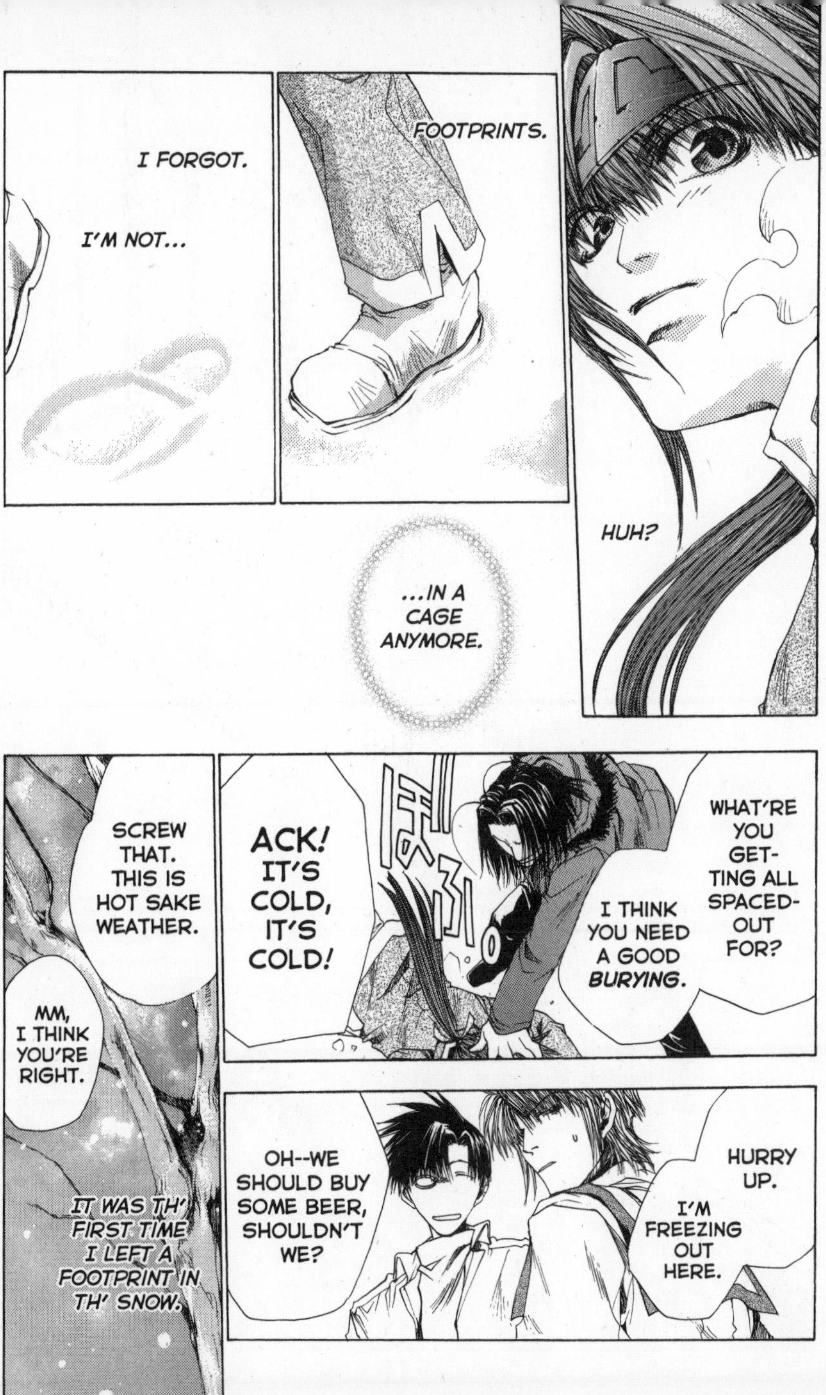
HUH?
FOOTPRINTS.
I FORGOT.
I'M NOT...
...IN A CAGE ANYMORE.
WHAT'RE YOU GETTING ALL SPACED-OUT FOR?
I THINK YOU NEED A GOOD BURYING.
ACK! IT'S COLD, IT'S COLD!
HURRY UP.
I'M FREEZING OUT HERE.
OH--WE SHOULD BUY SOME BEER, SHOULDN'T WE?
SCREW THAT. THIS IS HOT SAKE WEATHER.
MM, I THINK YOU'RE RIGHT.
IT WAS TH' FIRST TIME I LEFT A FOOTPRINT IN TH' SNOW.

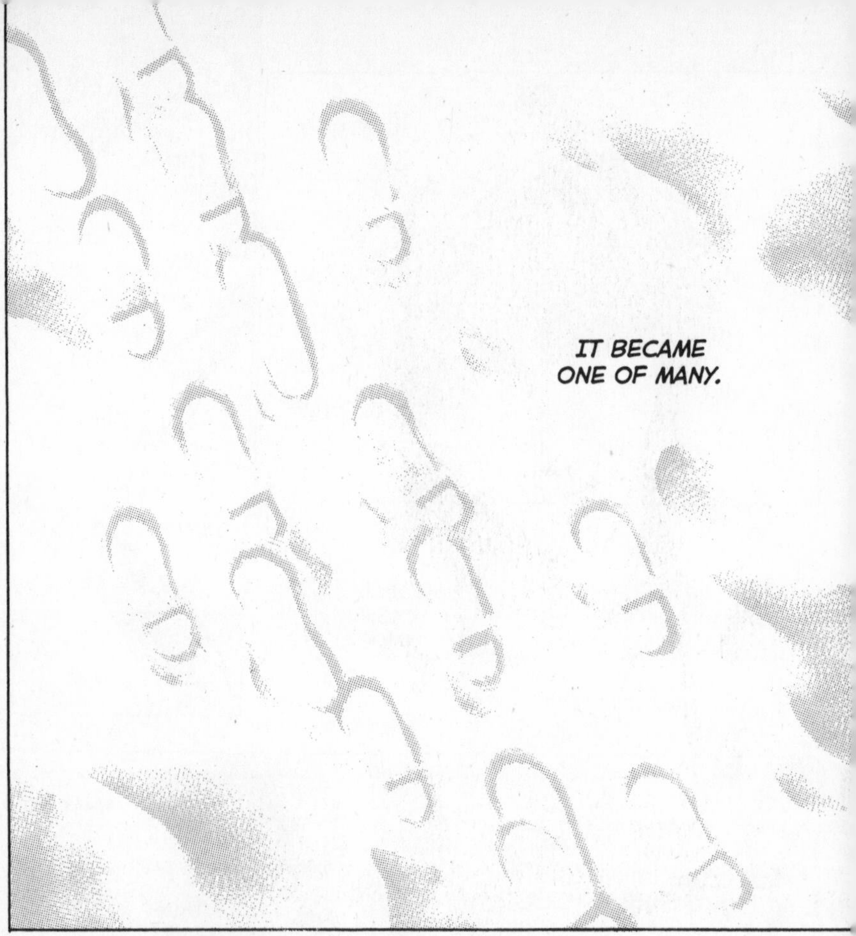
IT BECAME ONE OF MANY.

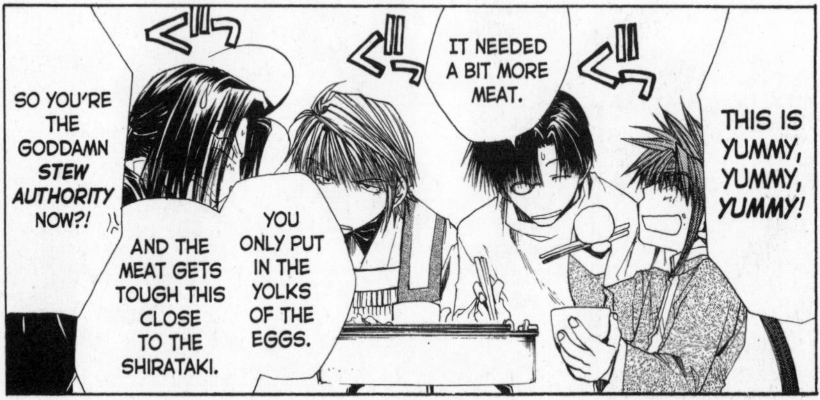
THIS IS YUMMY, YUMMY, YUMMY!
IT NEEDED A BIT MORE MEAT.
YOU ONLY PUT IN THE YOLKS OF THE EGGS.
AND THE MEAT GETS TOUGH THIS CLOSE TO THE SHIRATAKI.
SO YOU'RE THE GODDAMN STEW AUTHORITY NOW?!

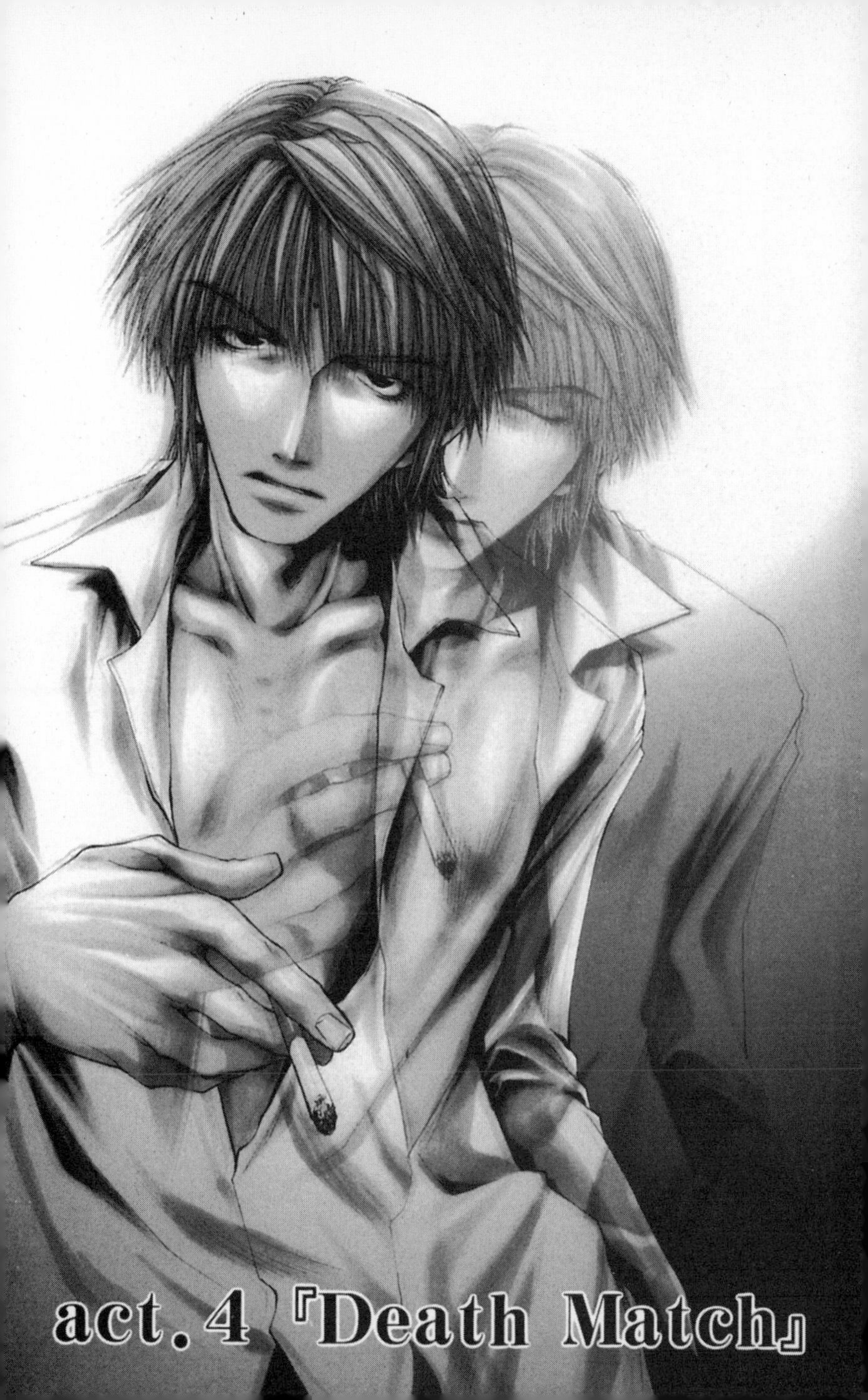
act. 4 『Death Match』

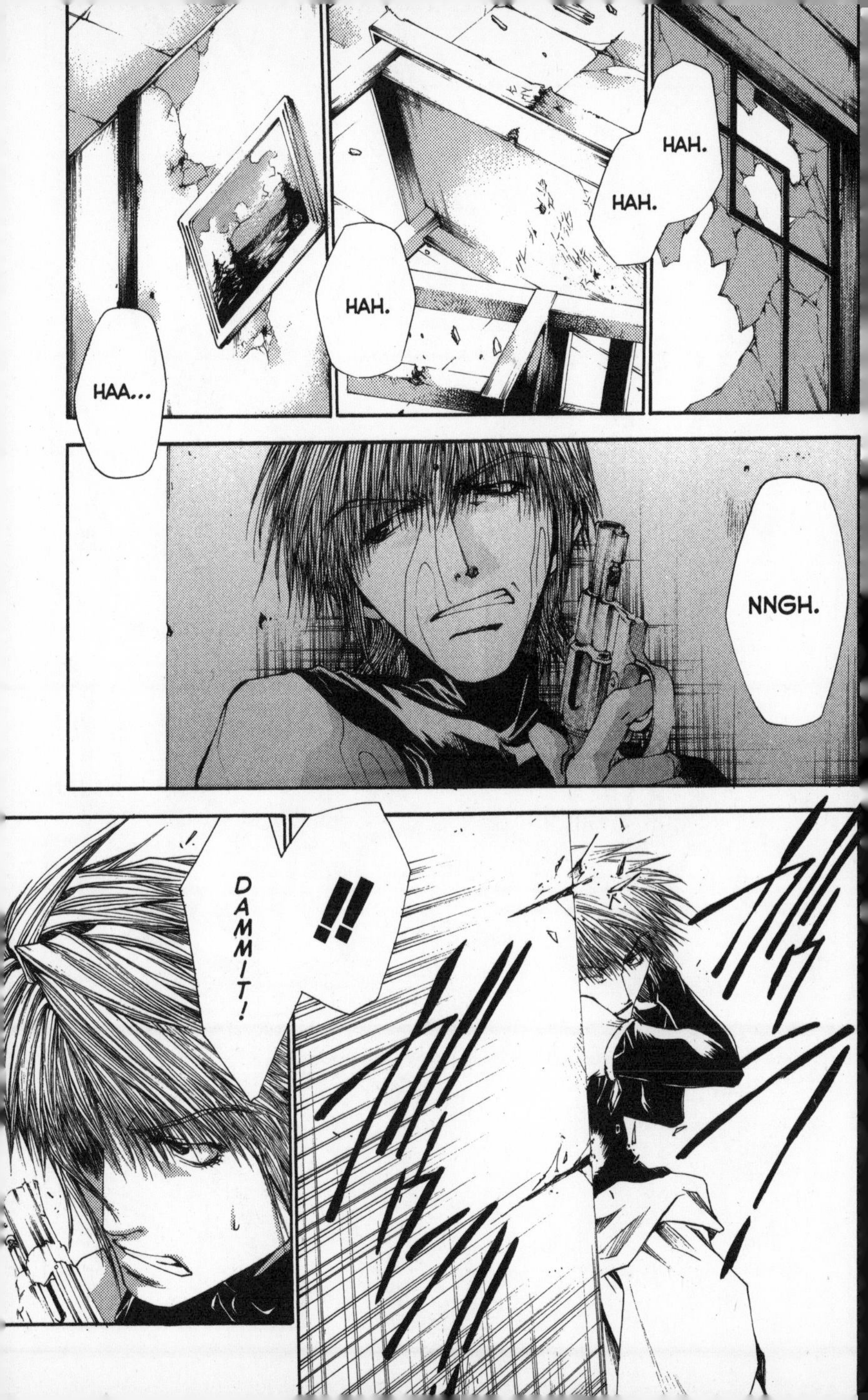
HAH.
HAH.
HAH.
HAA...
NNGH.
!!
DAMMIT!

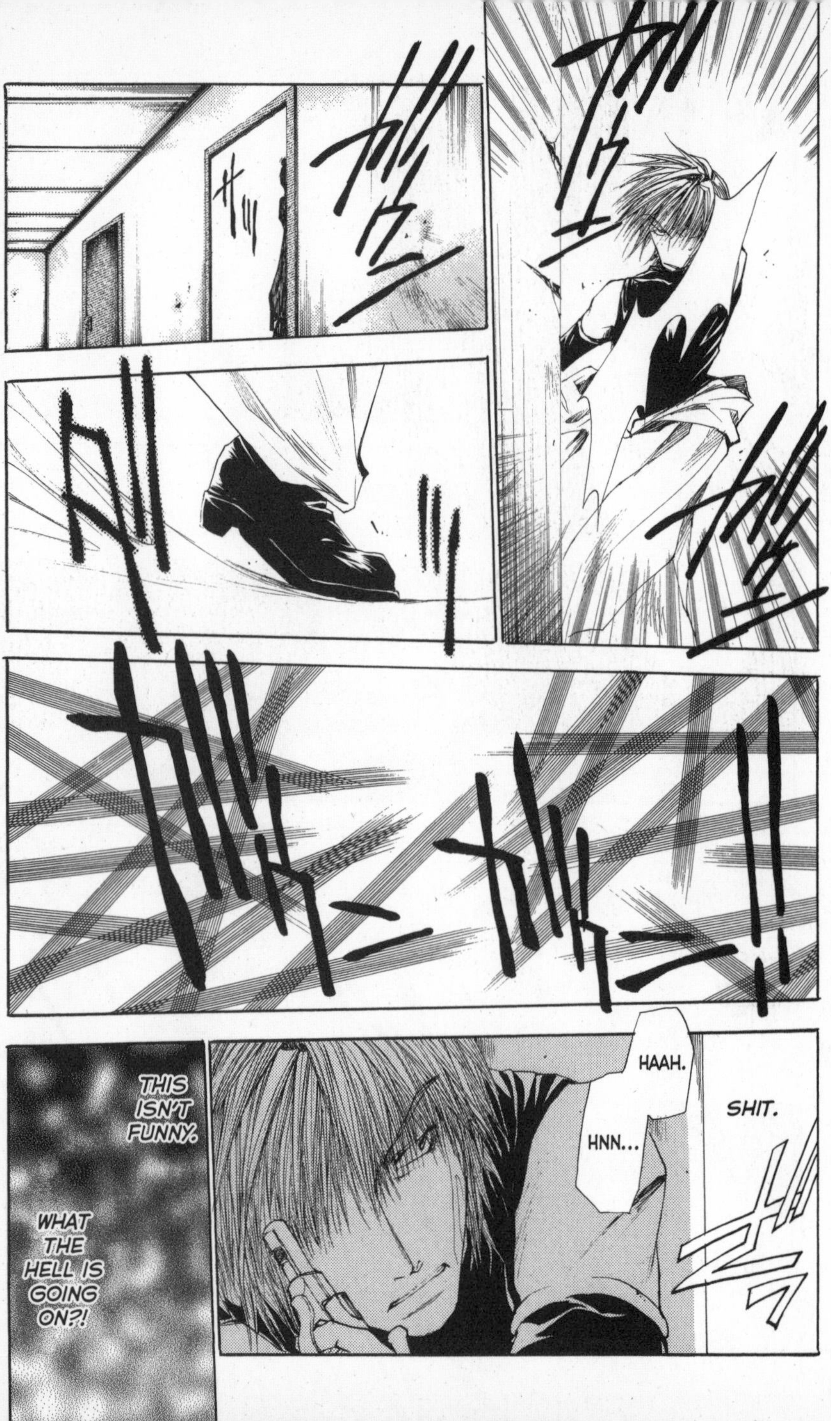
SHIT.
HAAH.
HNN...
THIS ISN'T FUNNY.
WHAT THE HELL IS GOING ON?!

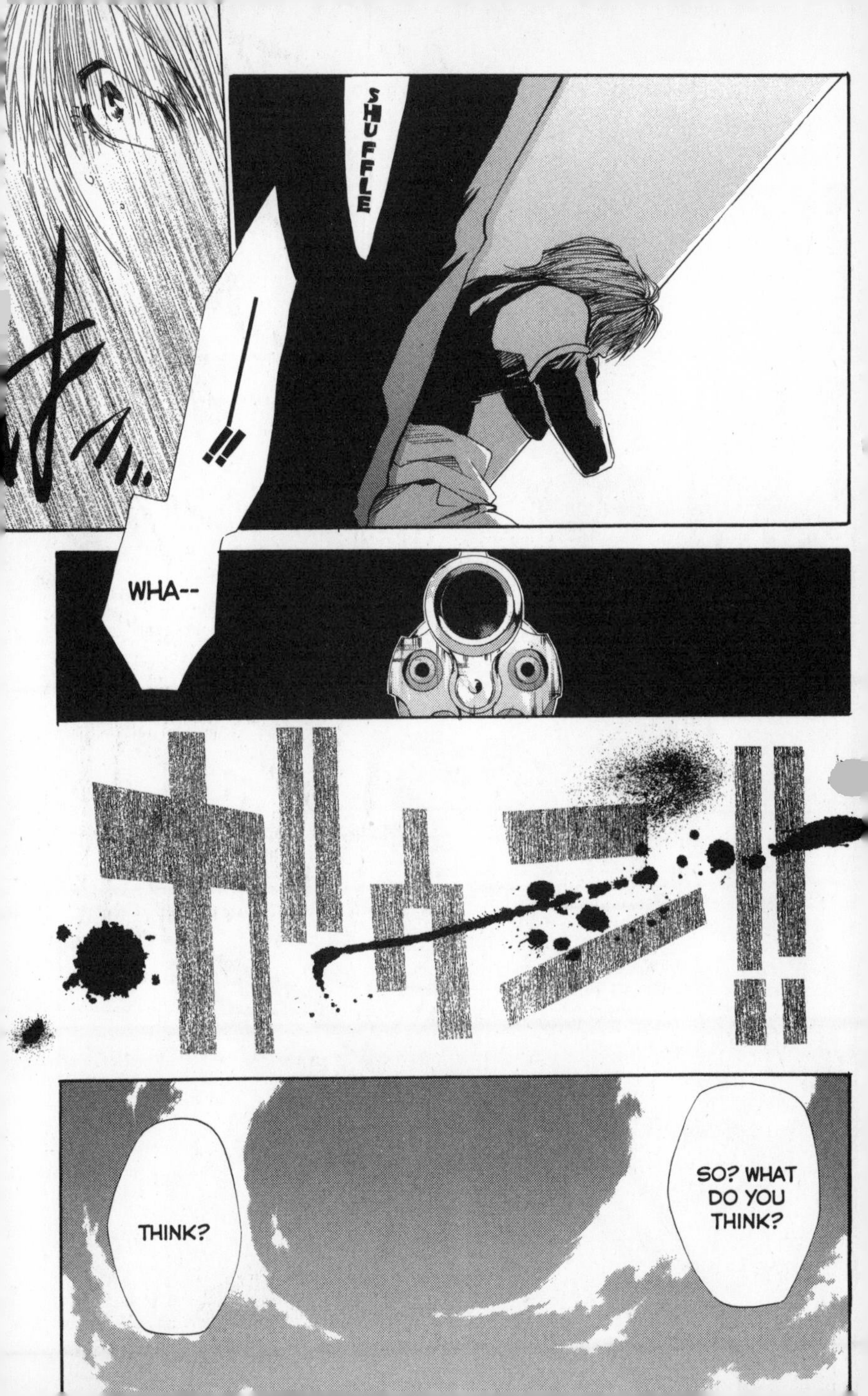
SHUFFLE
—!!
WHA--
SO? WHAT DO YOU THINK?
THINK?

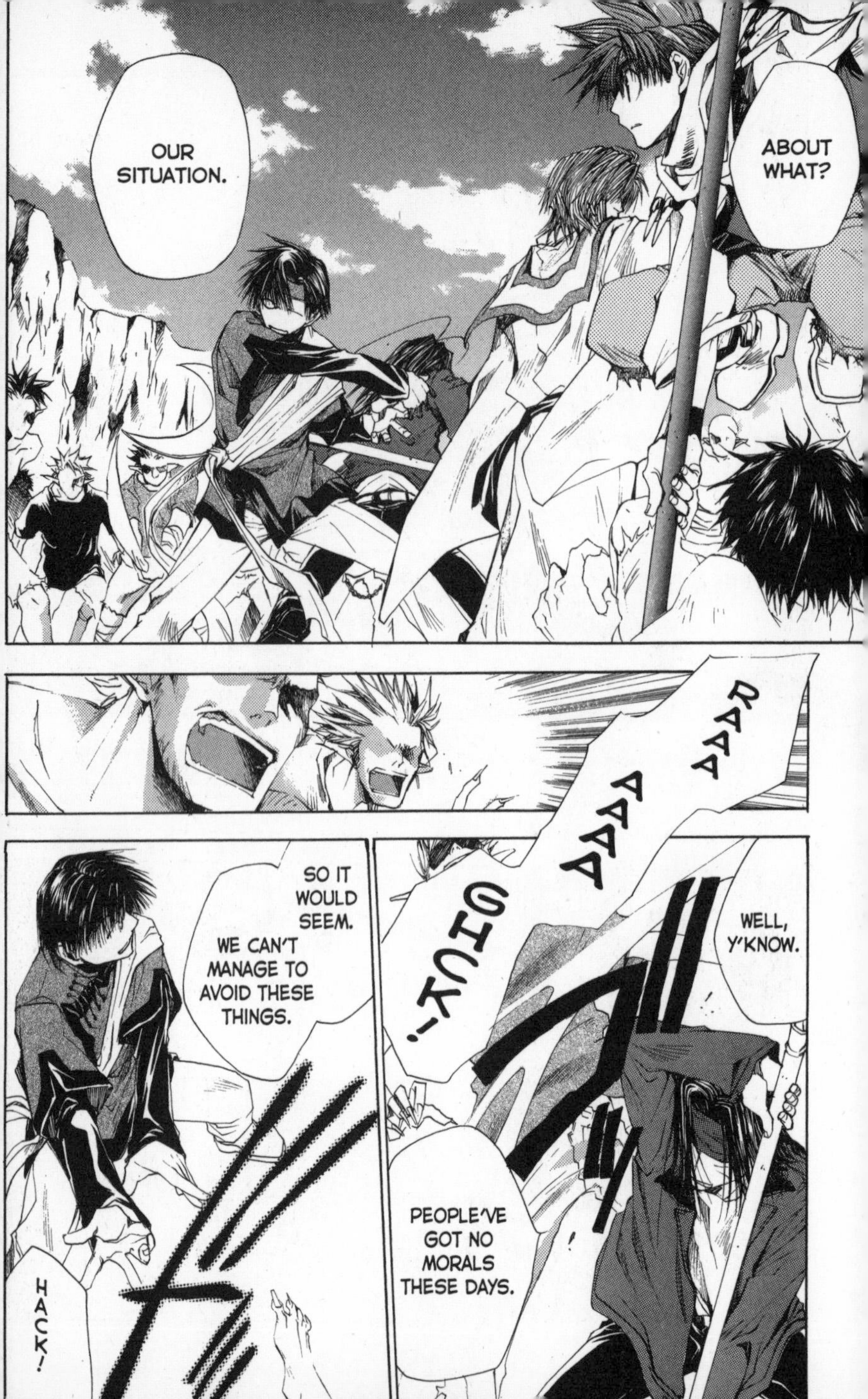
ABOUT WHAT?
OUR SITUATION.
RAAAAAAA
WELL, Y'KNOW.
SHCK!
PEOPLE'VE GOT NO MORALS THESE DAYS.
SO IT WOULD SEEM.
WE CAN'T MANAGE TO AVOID THESE THINGS.
HACK!

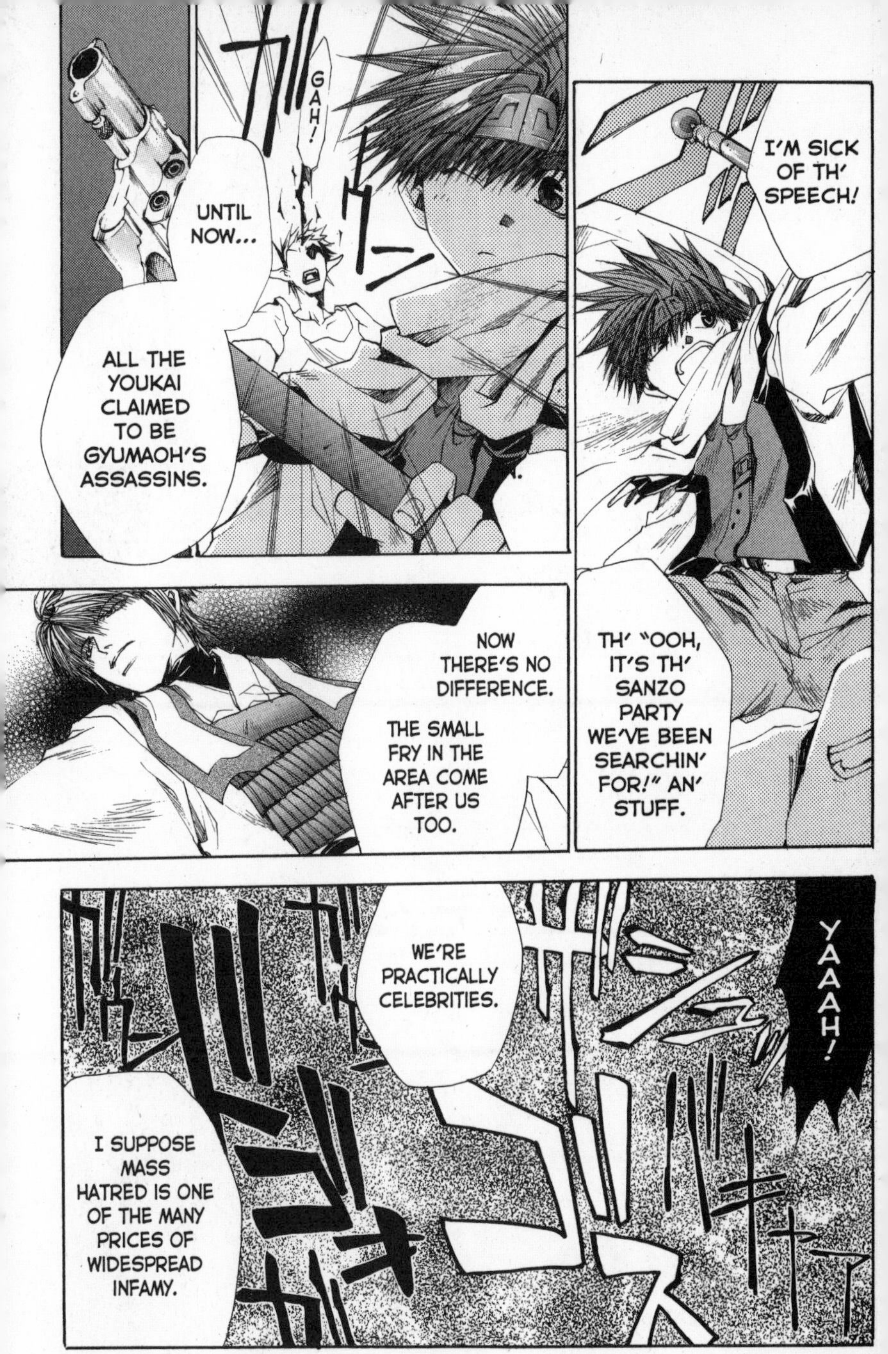
I'M SICK OF TH' SPEECH!
GAH!
UNTIL NOW...
ALL THE YOUKAI CLAIMED TO BE GYUMAOH'S ASSASSINS.
TH' "OOH, IT'S TH' SANZO PARTY WE'VE BEEN SEARCHIN' FOR!" AN' STUFF.
NOW THERE'S NO DIFFERENCE.
THE SMALL FRY IN THE AREA COME AFTER US TOO.
YAAAH!
WE'RE PRACTICALLY CELEBRITIES.
I SUPPOSE MASS HATRED IS ONE OF THE MANY PRICES OF WIDESPREAD INFAMY.

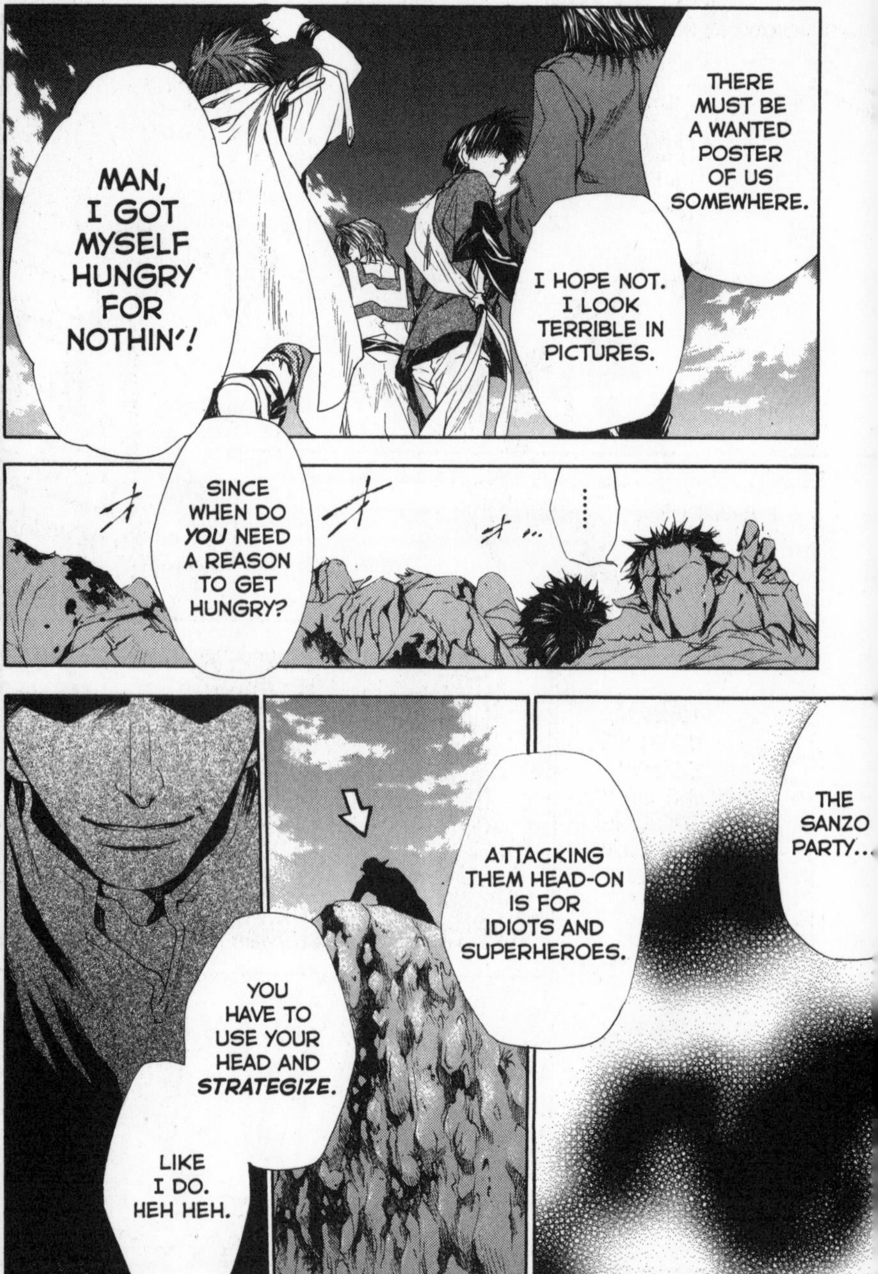
THERE MUST BE A WANTED POSTER OF US SOMEWHERE.
I HOPE NOT. I LOOK TERRIBLE IN PICTURES.
MAN, I GOT MYSELF HUNGRY FOR NOTHIN'!
......
SINCE WHEN DO *YOU* NEED A REASON TO GET HUNGRY?
THE SANZO PARTY...
ATTACKING THEM HEAD-ON IS FOR IDIOTS AND SUPERHEROES.
YOU HAVE TO USE YOUR HEAD AND *STRATEGIZE*.
LIKE I DO. HEH HEH.

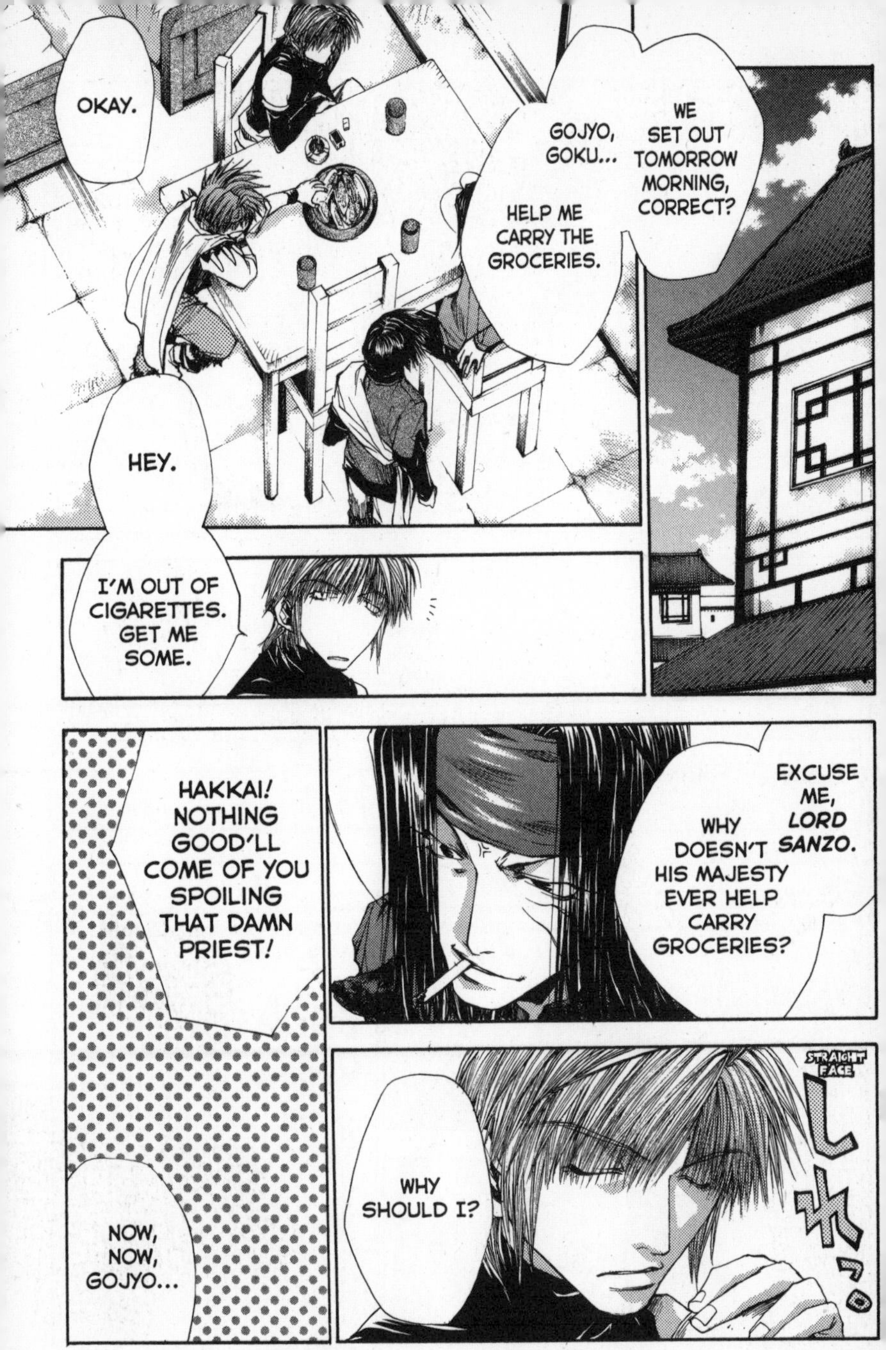

WE SET OUT TOMORROW MORNING, CORRECT?
GOJYO, GOKU...
HELP ME CARRY THE GROCERIES.
OKAY.
HEY.
I'M OUT OF CIGARETTES. GET ME SOME.
EXCUSE ME, LORD SANZO.
WHY DOESN'T HIS MAJESTY EVER HELP CARRY GROCERIES?
STRAIGHT FACE
WHY SHOULD I?
HAKKAI! NOTHING GOOD'LL COME OF YOU SPOILING THAT DAMN PRIEST!
NOW, NOW, GOJYO...

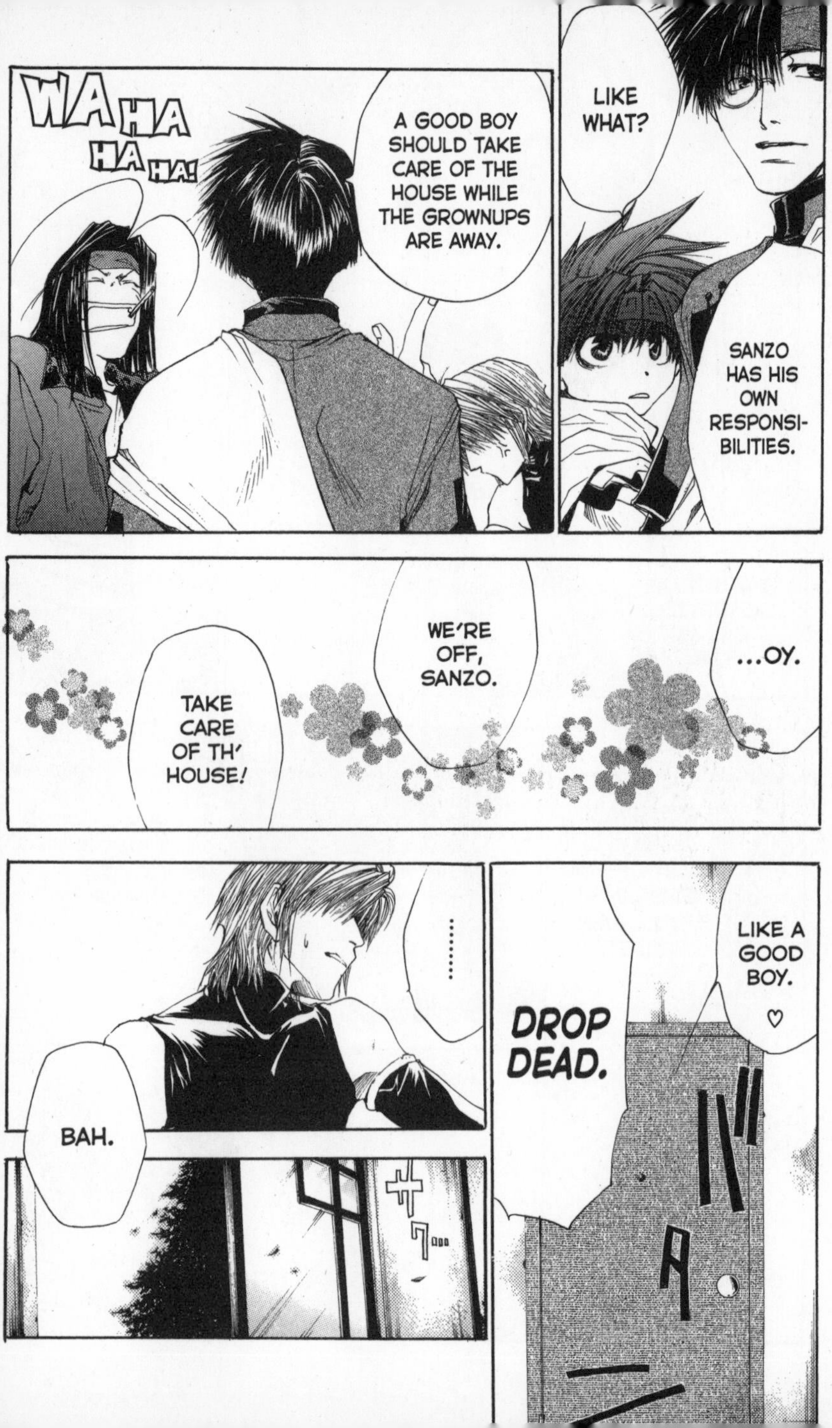
LIKE WHAT?
SANZO HAS HIS OWN RESPONSI-BILITIES.
A GOOD BOY SHOULD TAKE CARE OF THE HOUSE WHILE THE GROWNUPS ARE AWAY.
WAHAHA HAHA!
...OY.
WE'RE OFF, SANZO.
TAKE CARE OF TH' HOUSE!
LIKE A GOOD BOY. ♡
DROP DEAD.
....
BAH.

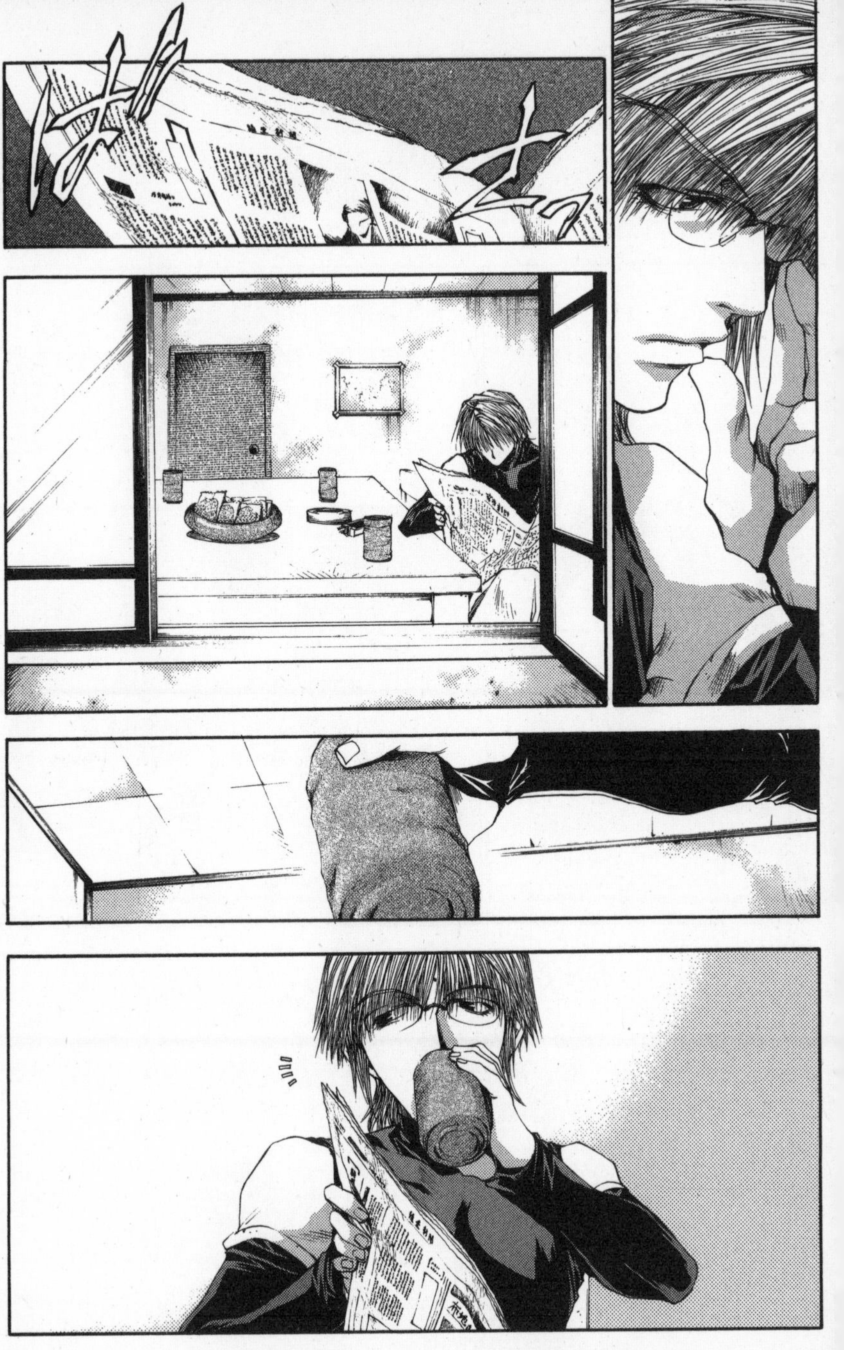
ヌッ
バサ

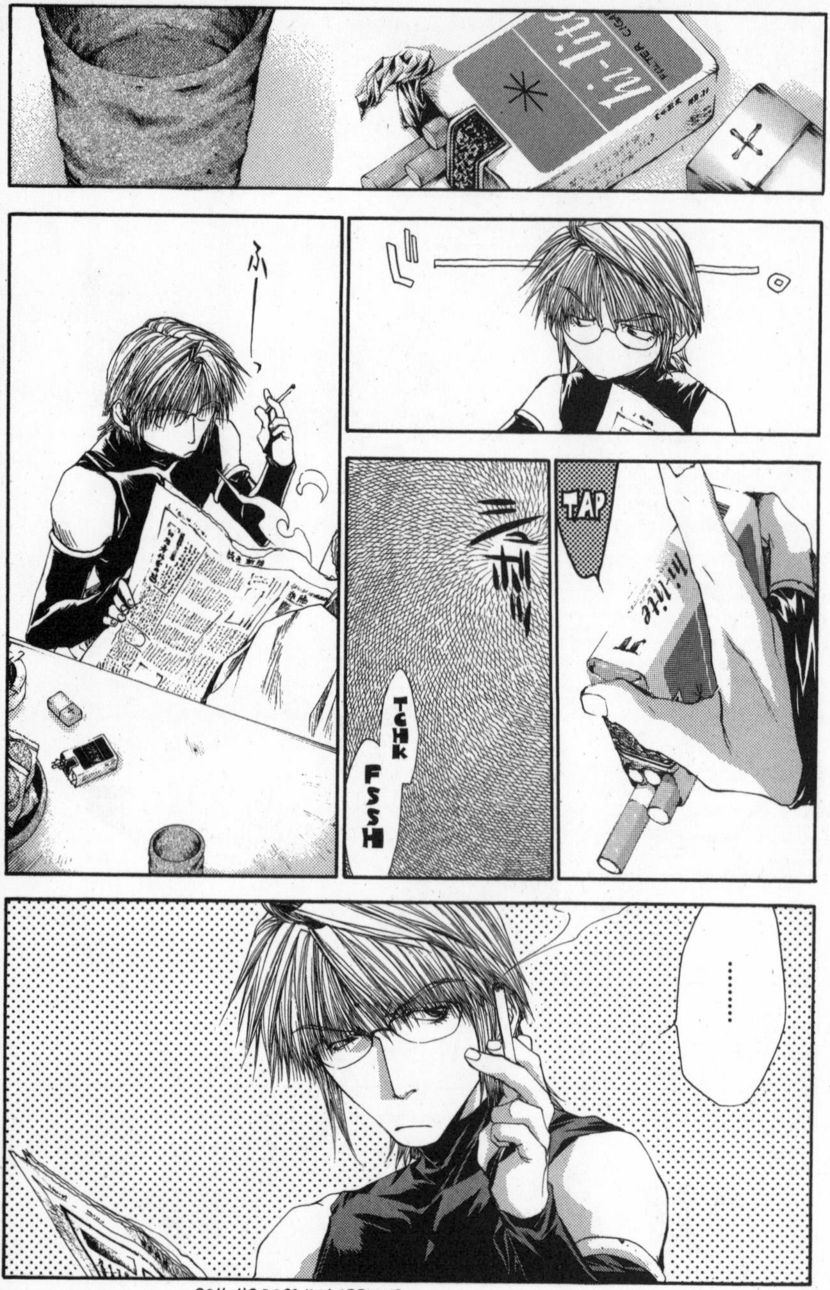
ジーー。
ふーーっ
TAP
TCHK
FSSH
……

OOH. He does not approve.

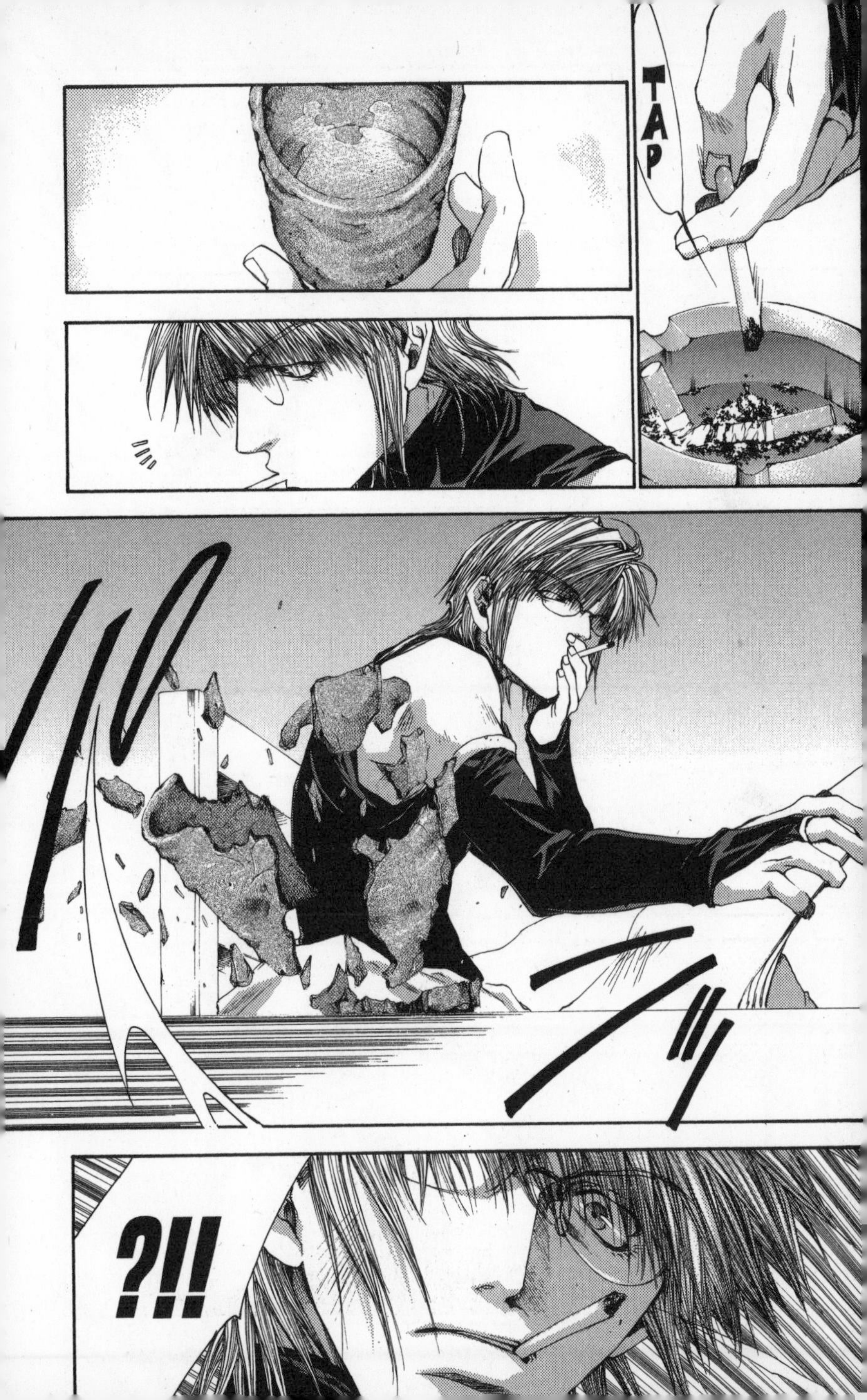
TAP
?!!

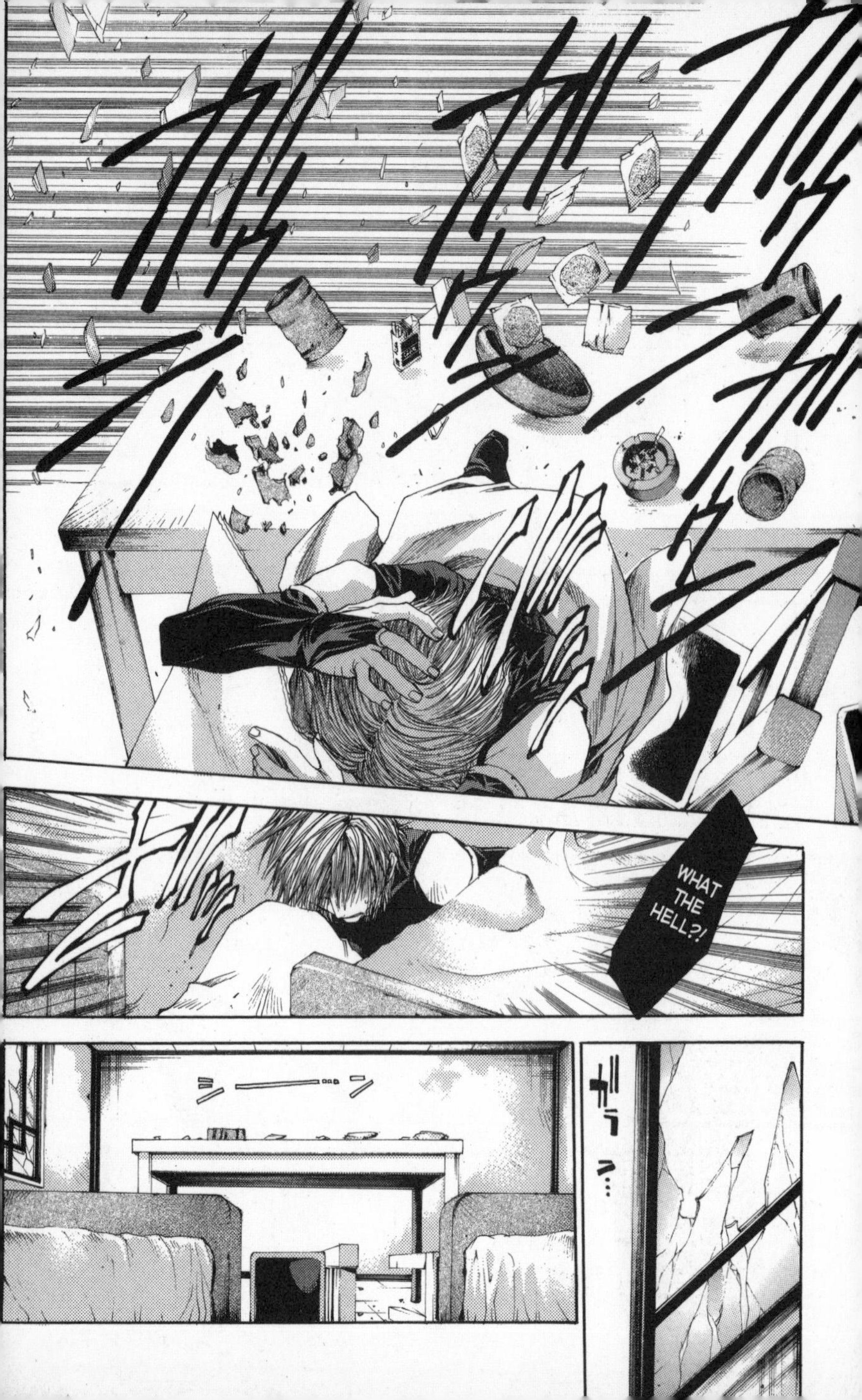
WHAT THE HELL?!

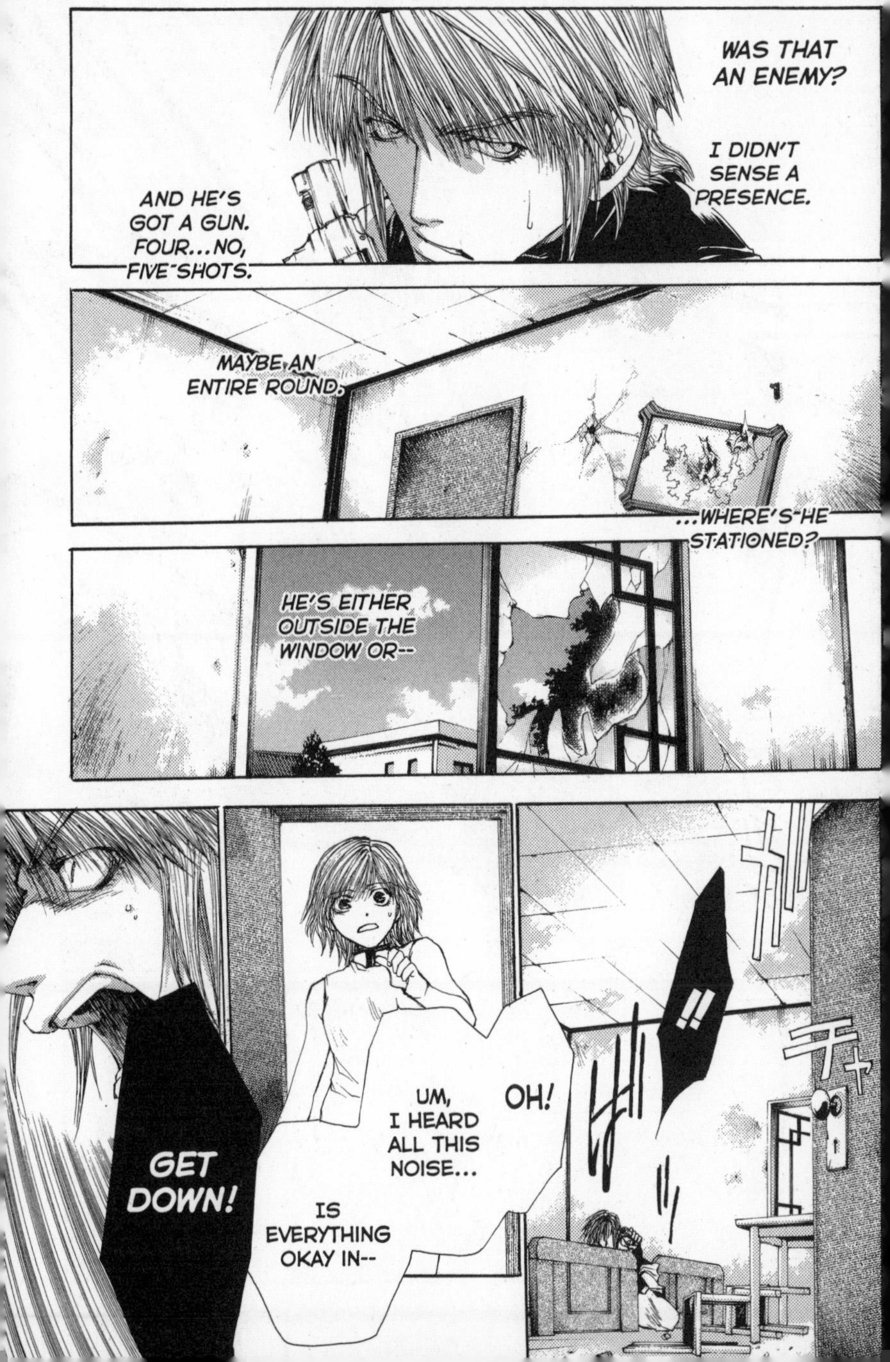
WAS THAT AN ENEMY?
I DIDN'T SENSE A PRESENCE.
AND HE'S GOT A GUN. FOUR...NO, FIVE SHOTS.
MAYBE AN ENTIRE ROUND.
...WHERE'S HE STATIONED?
HE'S EITHER OUTSIDE THE WINDOW OR--
チャ
!!
OH!
UM, I HEARD ALL THIS NOISE...
IS EVERYTHING OKAY IN--
GET DOWN!

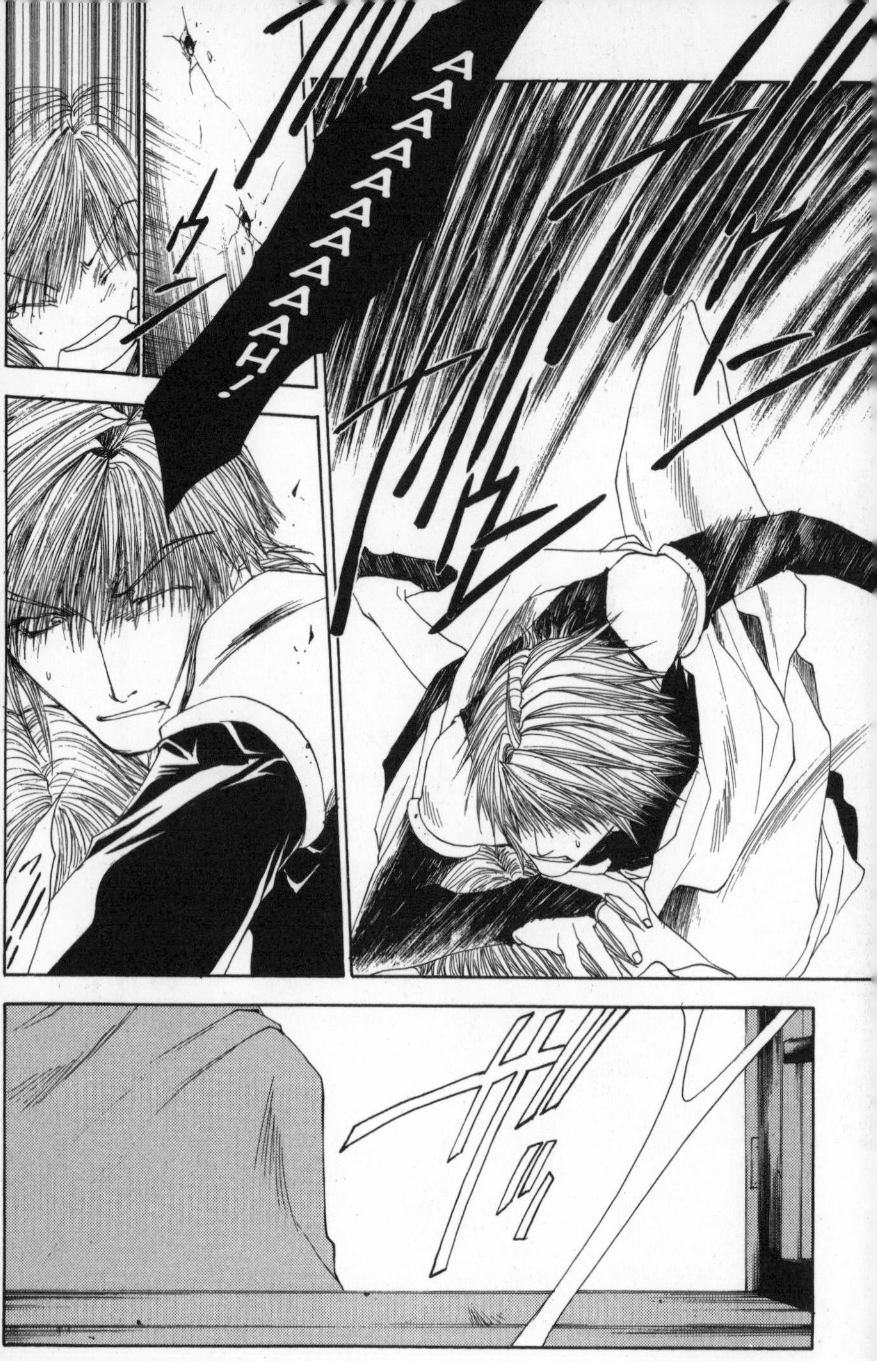
AAAAAAAAAAAH!

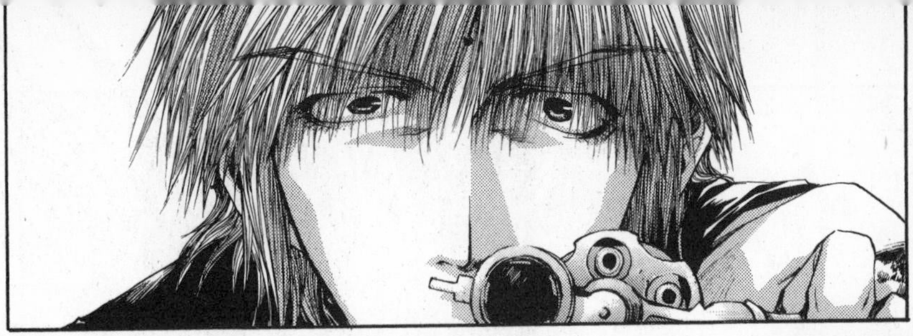
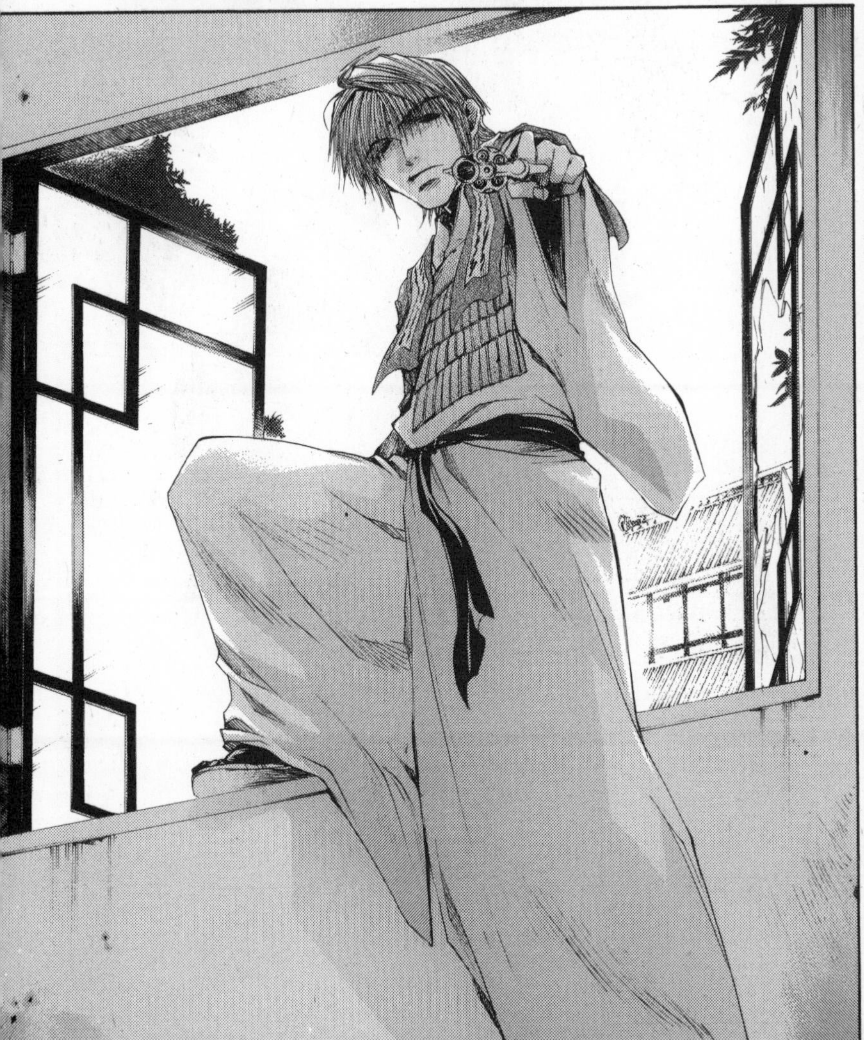

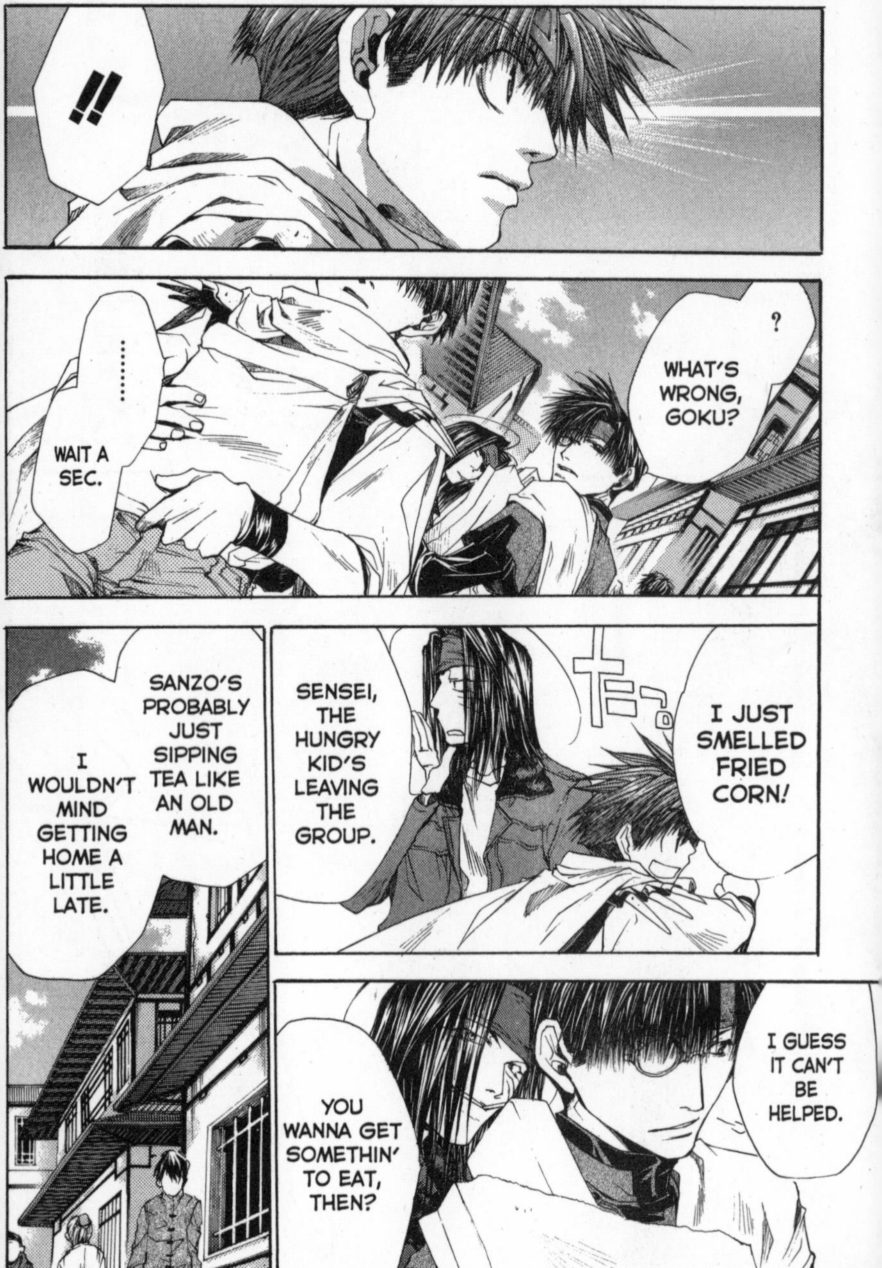
!!
?
WHAT'S WRONG, GOKU?
......
WAIT A SEC.
I JUST SMELLED FRIED CORN!
SENSEI, THE HUNGRY KID'S LEAVING THE GROUP.
I GUESS IT CAN'T BE HELPED.
YOU WANNA GET SOMETHIN' TO EAT, THEN?
SANZO'S PROBABLY JUST SIPPING TEA LIKE AN OLD MAN.
I WOULDN'T MIND GETTING HOME A LITTLE LATE.

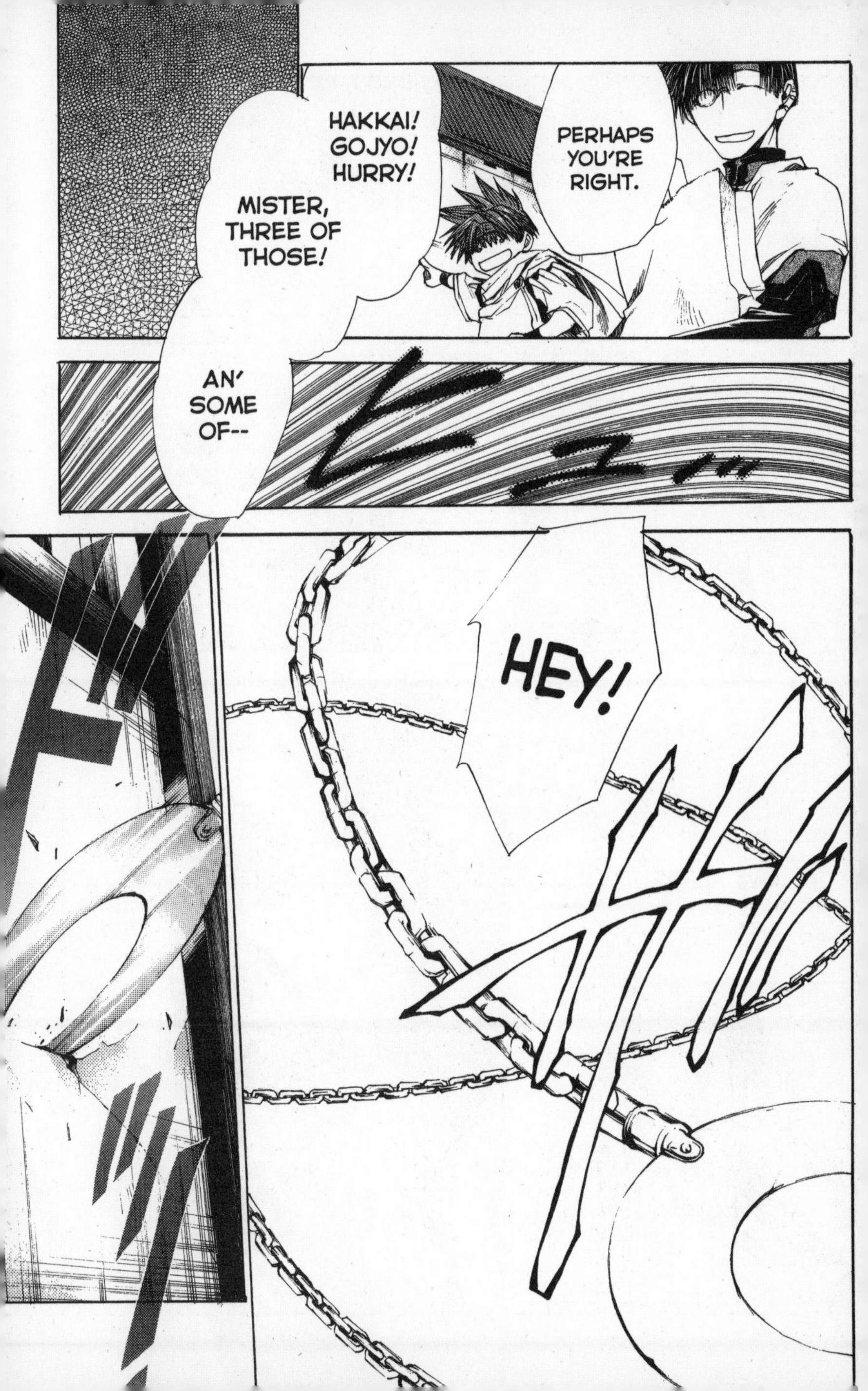
PERHAPS YOU'RE RIGHT.
HAKKAI! GOJYO! HURRY!
MISTER, THREE OF THOSE!
AN' SOME OF--
HEY!

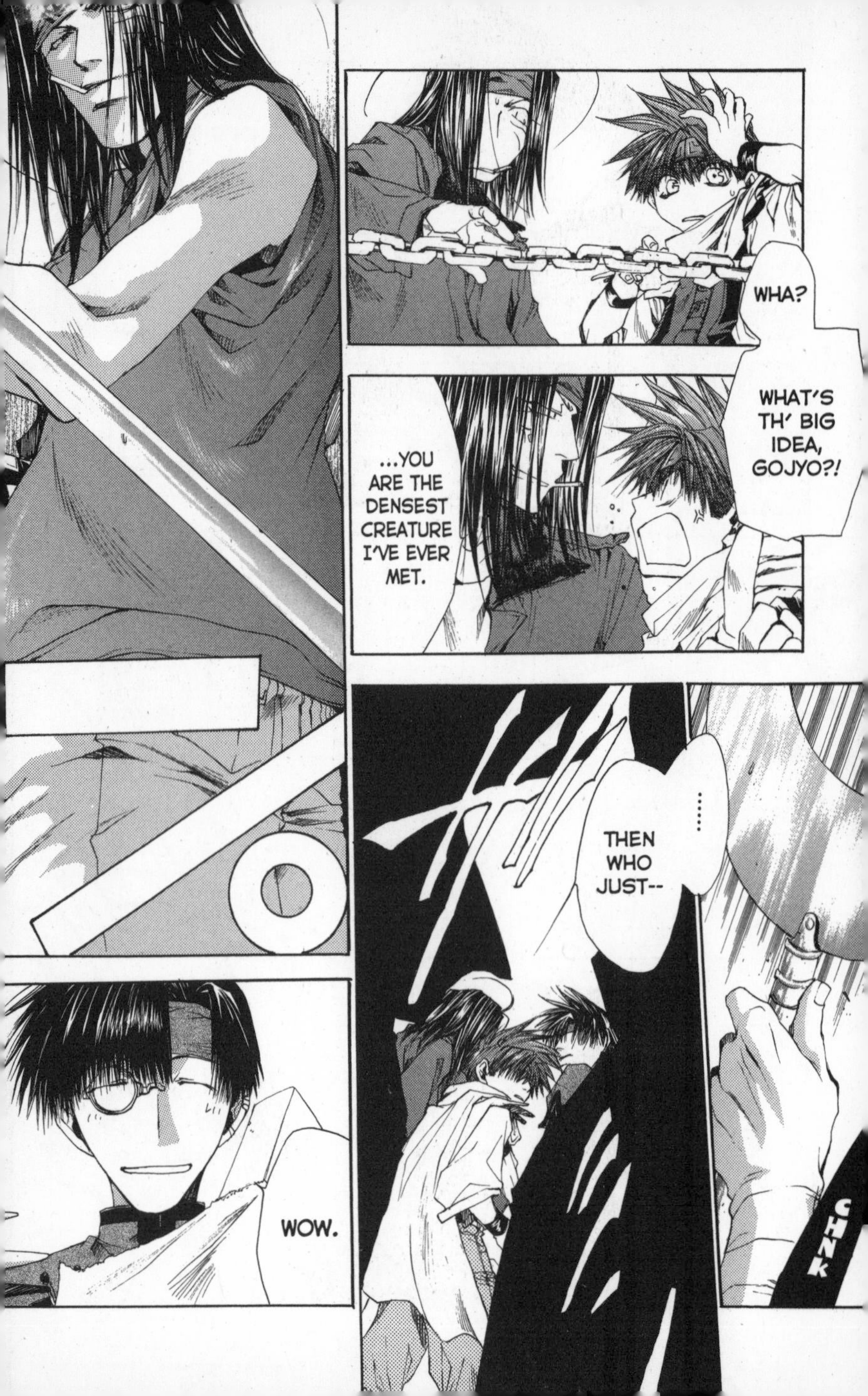
WHA?
WHAT'S TH' BIG IDEA, GOJYO?!
...YOU ARE THE DENSEST CREATURE I'VE EVER MET.
......
THEN WHO JUST--
CHNK
WOW.

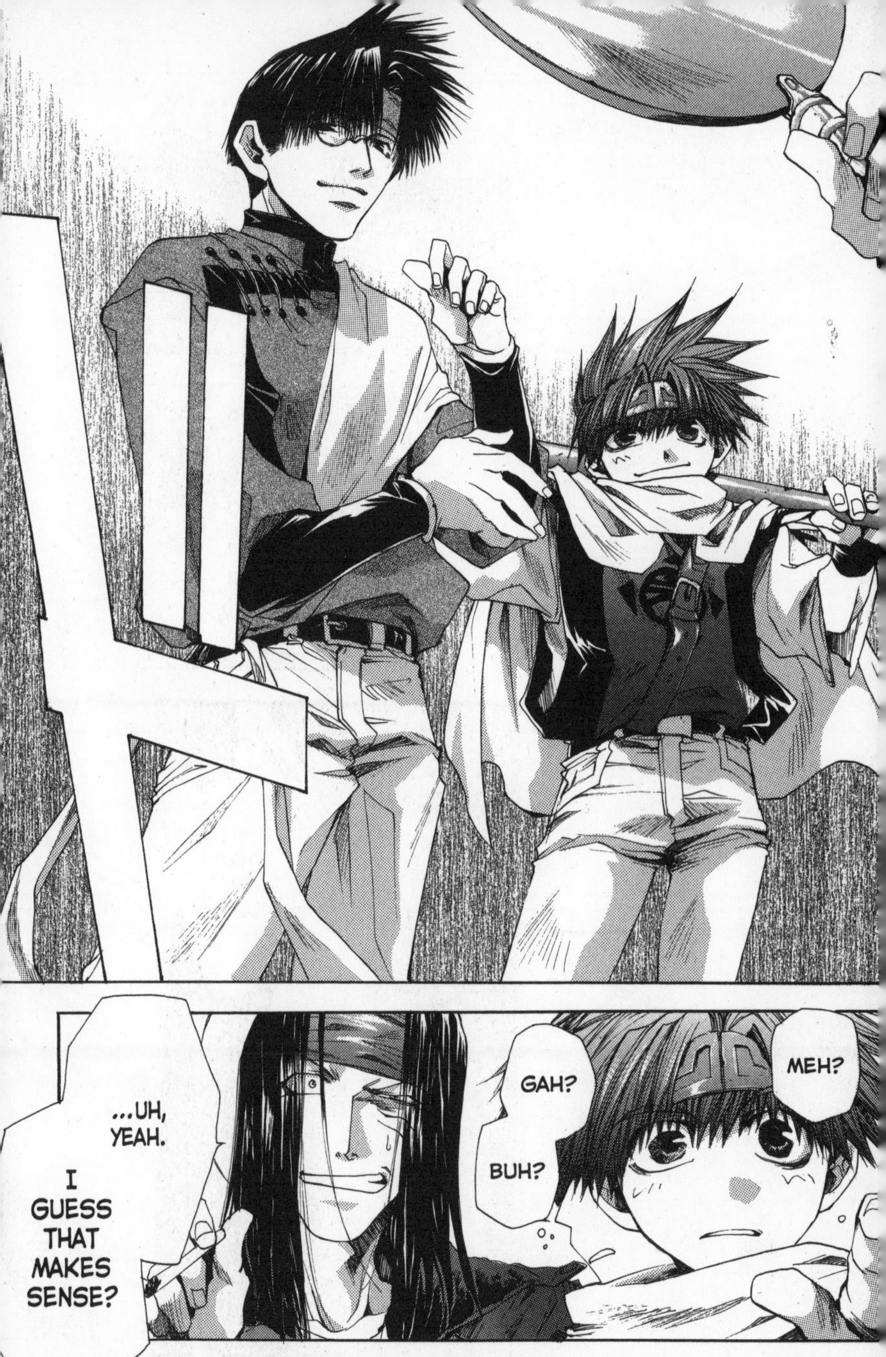
MEH?
GAH?
BUH?
...UH, YEAH.
I GUESS THAT MAKES SENSE?

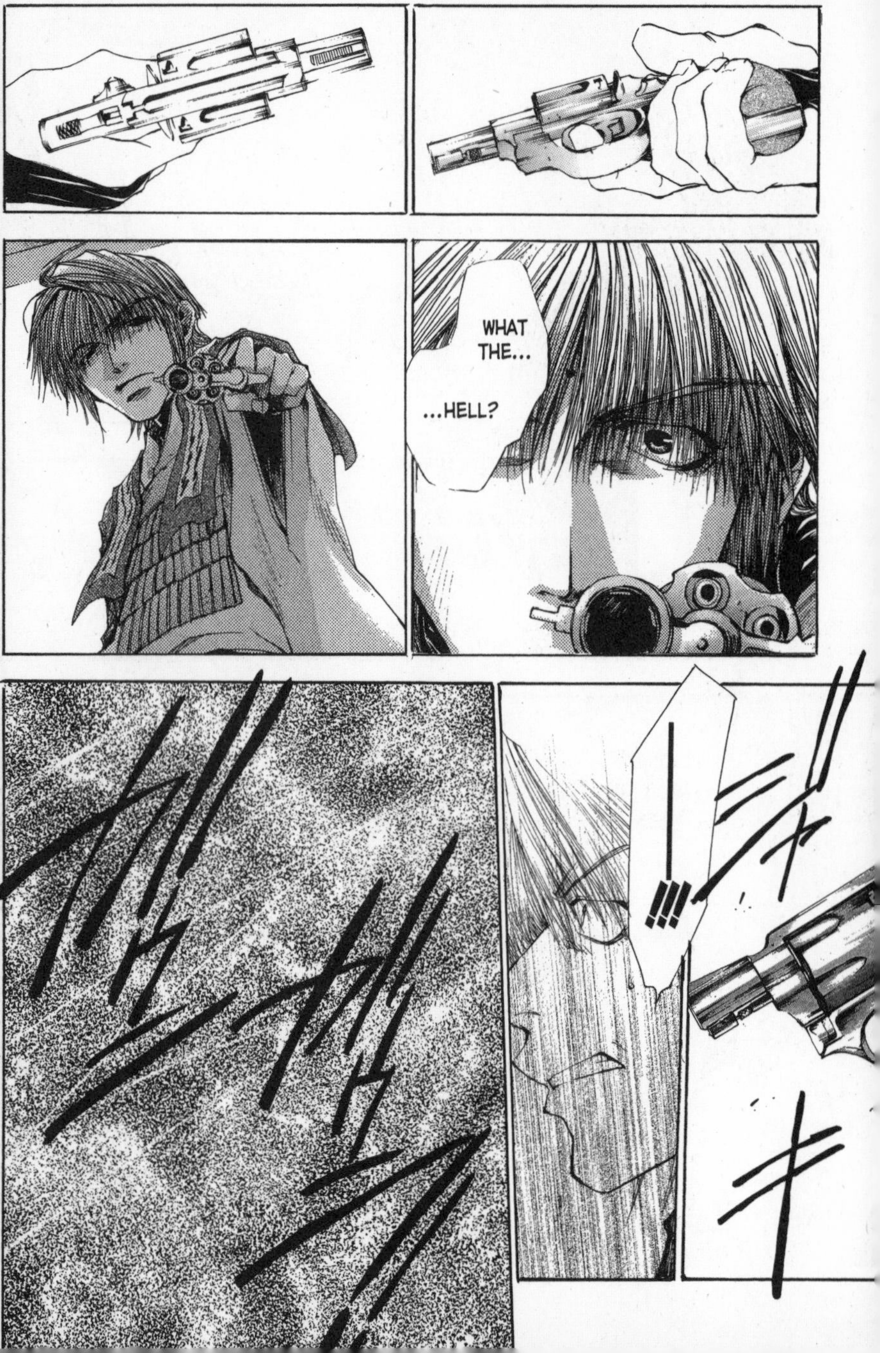
WHAT THE...
...HELL?

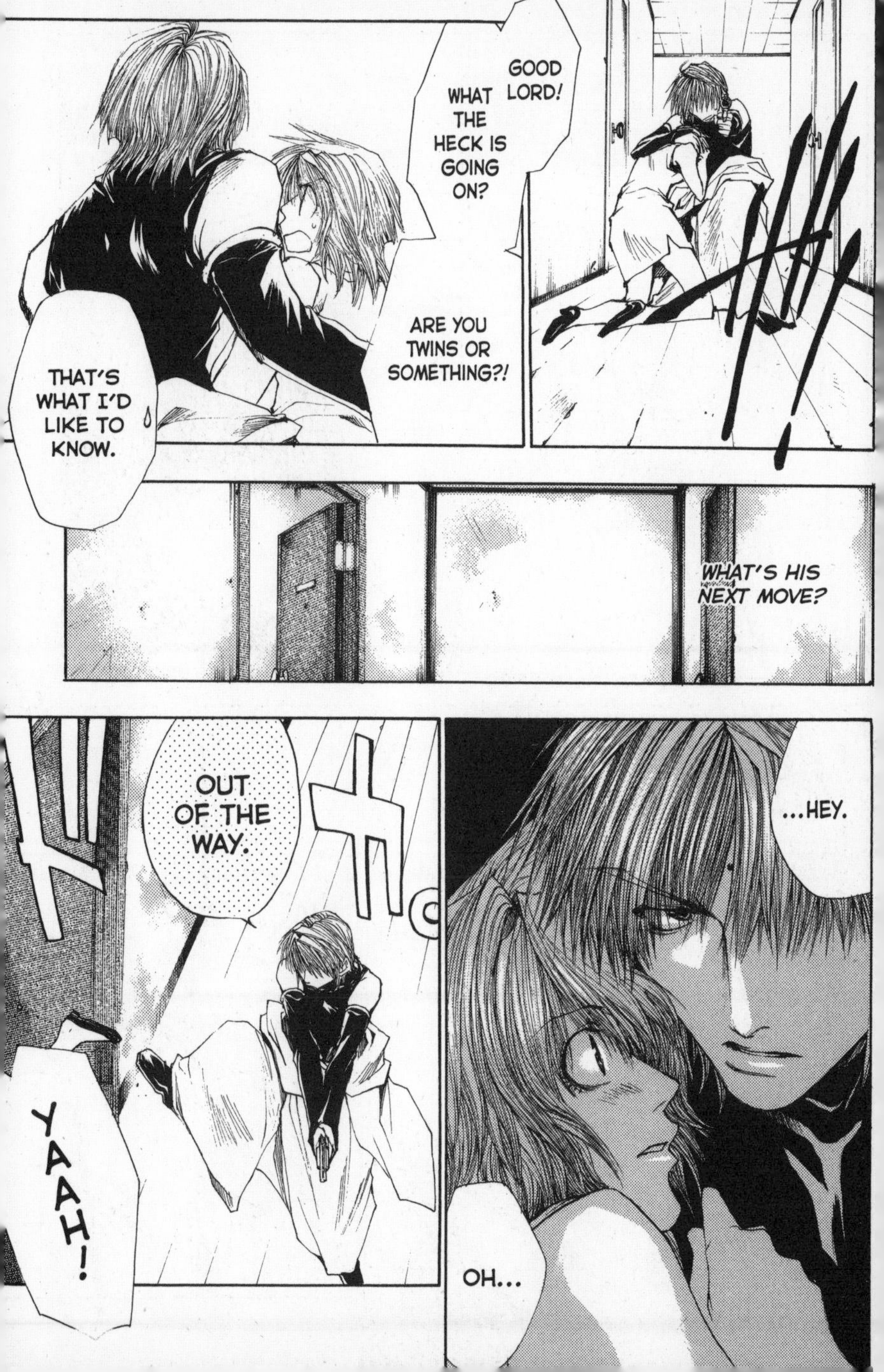
GOOD LORD!
WHAT THE HECK IS GOING ON?
ARE YOU TWINS OR SOMETHING?!
THAT'S WHAT I'D LIKE TO KNOW.
WHAT'S HIS NEXT MOVE?
...HEY.
OH...
OUT OF THE WAY.
YAAH!

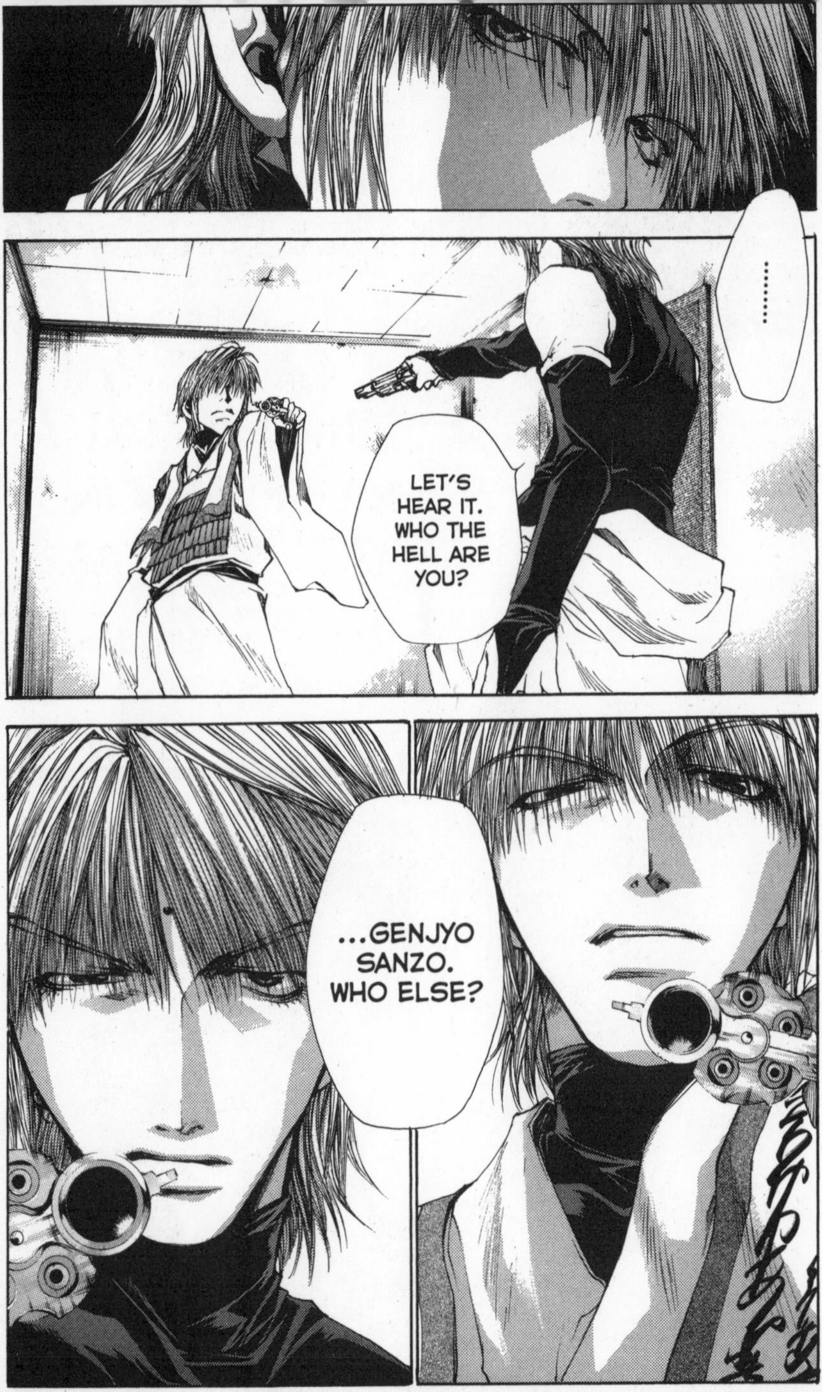
......
LET'S HEAR IT. WHO THE HELL ARE YOU?
...GENJYO SANZO. WHO ELSE?

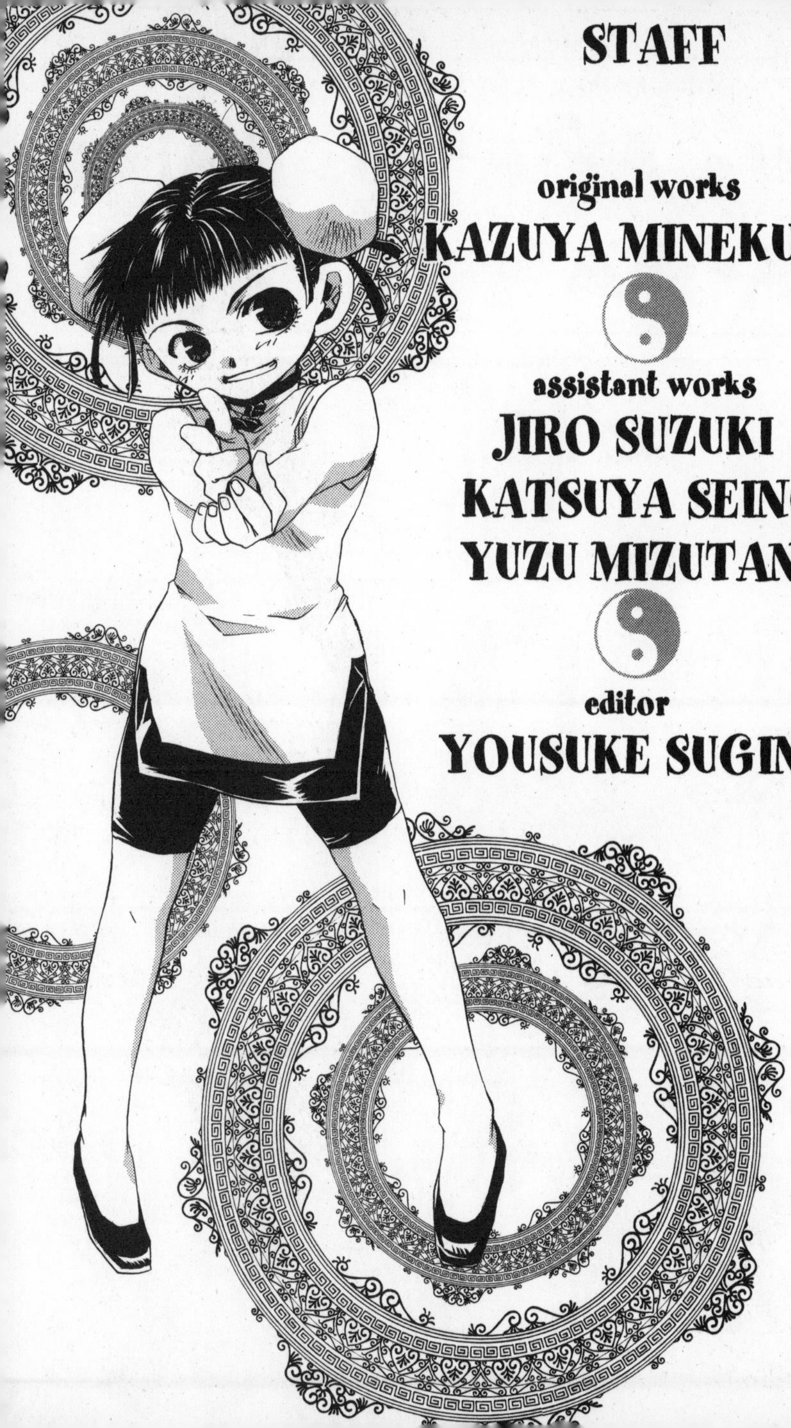

STAFF

original works
KAZUYA MINEKURA

assistant works
JIRO SUZUKI
KATSUYA SEINO
YUZU MIZUTANI

editor
YOUSUKE SUGINO

I'm going to preemptively apologize here. I am so, so sorry.

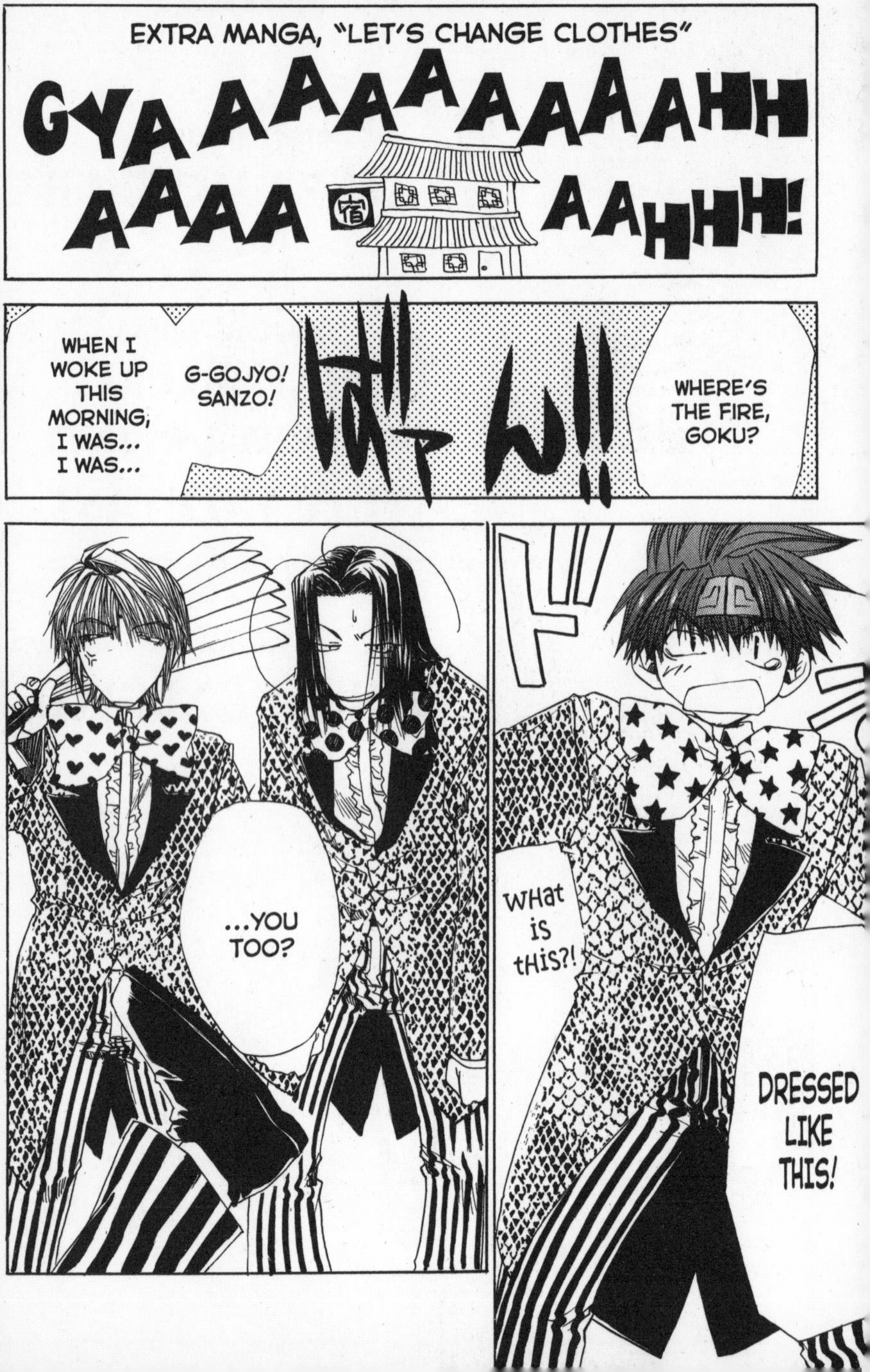

EXTRA MANGA, "LET'S CHANGE CLOTHES"
GYAAAAAAAAAAAHH AAAA AAHHH!
宿
WHERE'S THE FIRE, GOKU?
G-GOJYO! SANZO!
WHEN I WOKE UP THIS MORNING, I WAS... I WAS...
WHAT IS THIS?!
DRESSED LIKE THIS!
...YOU TOO?

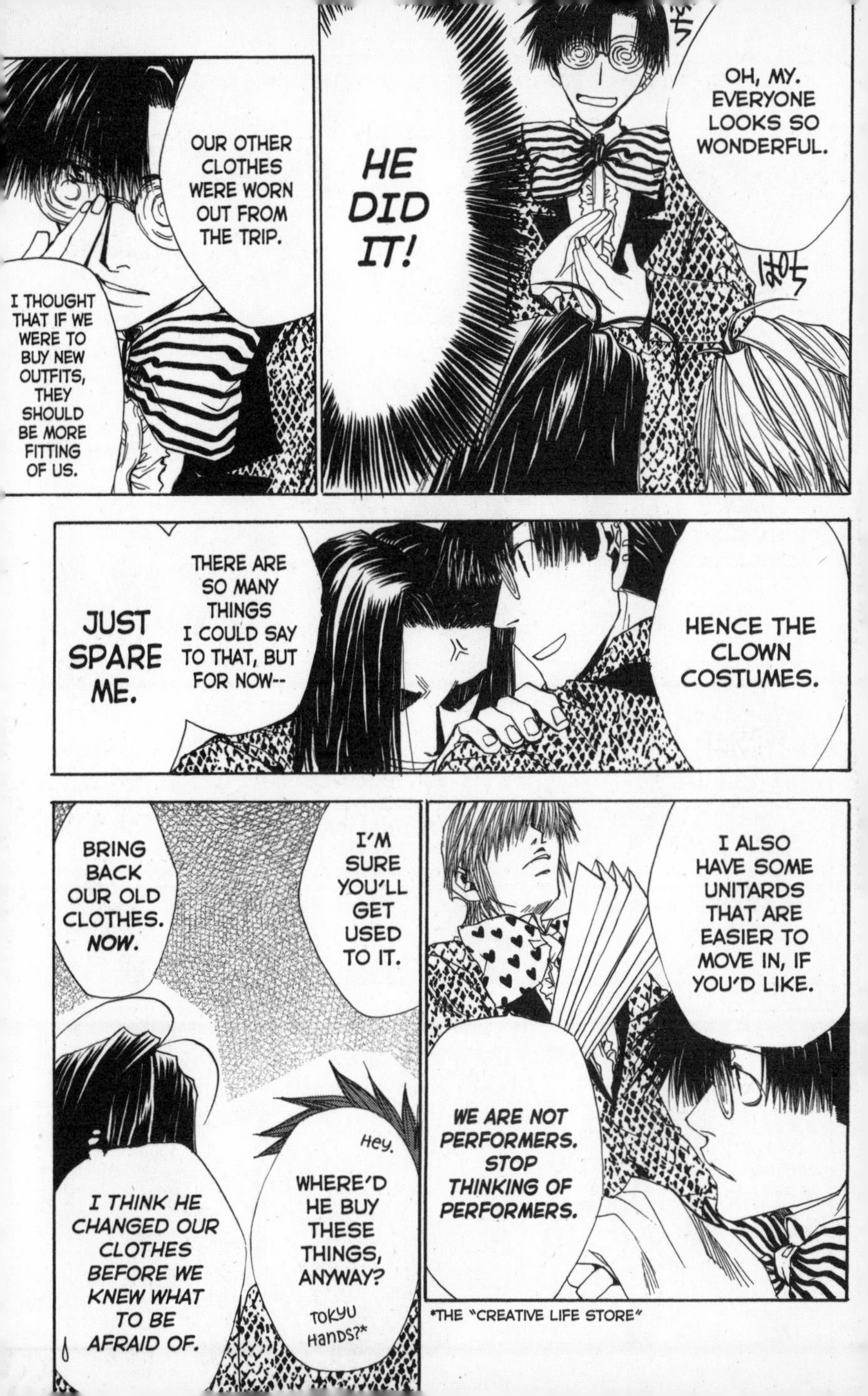
OH, MY. EVERYONE LOOKS SO WONDERFUL.
HE DID IT!
OUR OTHER CLOTHES WERE WORN OUT FROM THE TRIP.
I THOUGHT THAT IF WE WERE TO BUY NEW OUTFITS, THEY SHOULD BE MORE FITTING OF US.
HENCE THE CLOWN COSTUMES.
THERE ARE SO MANY THINGS I COULD SAY TO THAT, BUT FOR NOW--
JUST SPARE ME.
I ALSO HAVE SOME UNITARDS THAT ARE EASIER TO MOVE IN, IF YOU'D LIKE.
WE ARE NOT PERFORMERS. STOP THINKING OF PERFORMERS.
I'M SURE YOU'LL GET USED TO IT.
BRING BACK OUR OLD CLOTHES. NOW.
Hey.
WHERE'D HE BUY THESE THINGS, ANYWAY?
TOKYU HANDS?*
I THINK HE CHANGED OUR CLOTHES BEFORE WE KNEW WHAT TO BE AFRAID OF.
*THE "CREATIVE LIFE STORE"

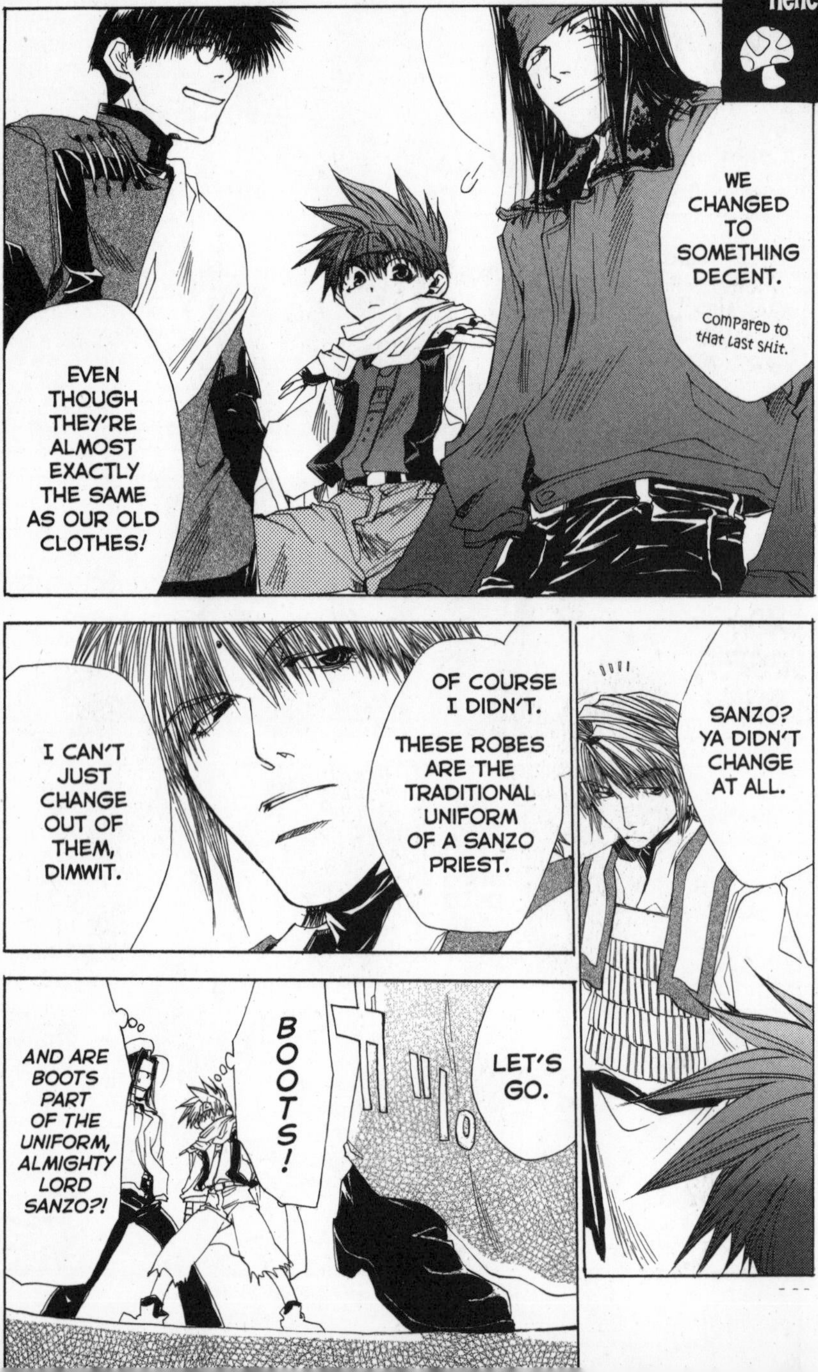
WE CHANGED TO SOMETHING DECENT.
Compared to that last shit.
EVEN THOUGH THEY'RE ALMOST EXACTLY THE SAME AS OUR OLD CLOTHES!
SANZO? YA DIDN'T CHANGE AT ALL.
OF COURSE I DIDN'T.
THESE ROBES ARE THE TRADITIONAL UNIFORM OF A SANZO PRIEST.
I CAN'T JUST CHANGE OUT OF THEM, DIMWIT.
LET'S GO.
BOOTS!
AND ARE BOOTS PART OF THE UNIFORM, ALMIGHTY LORD SANZO?!

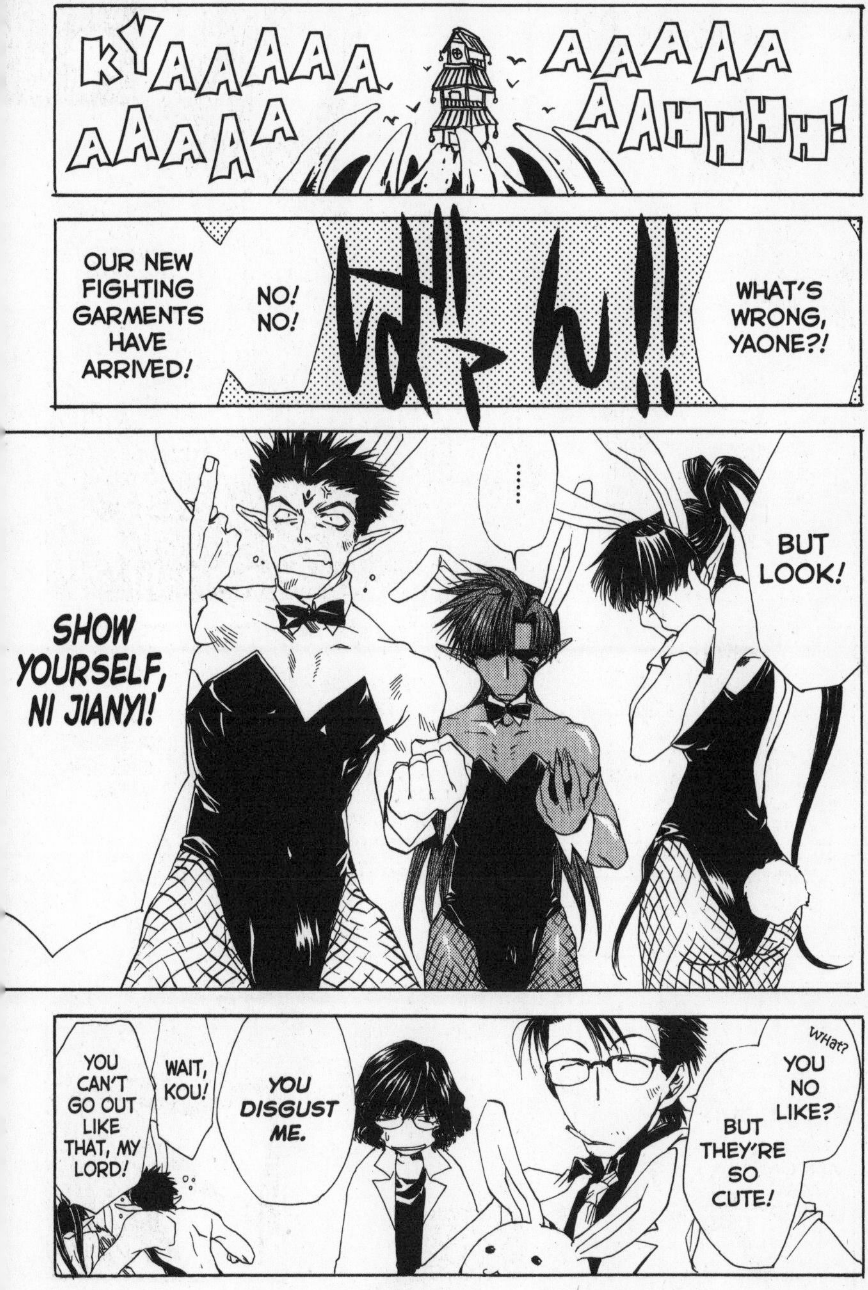
KYAAAAA AAAAA AAAAAA AAHHHHH!
WHAT'S WRONG, YAONE?!
ばァん!!
NO! NO!
OUR NEW FIGHTING GARMENTS HAVE ARRIVED!
BUT LOOK!
......
SHOW YOURSELF, NI JIANYI!
WHAT?
YOU NO LIKE?
BUT THEY'RE SO CUTE!
YOU DISGUST ME.
WAIT, KOU!
YOU CAN'T GO OUT LIKE THAT, MY LORD!

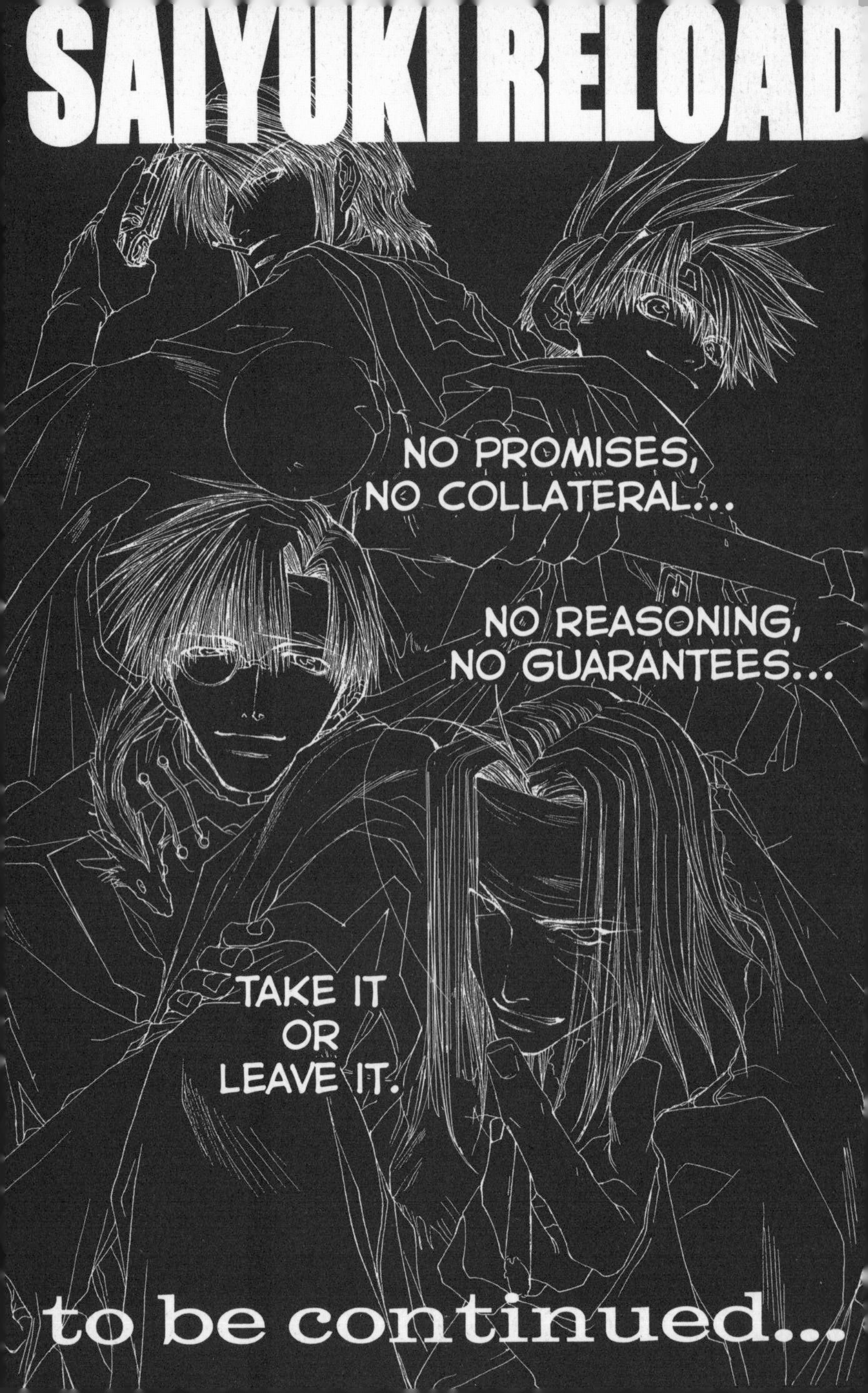
SAIYUKI RELOAD
NO PROMISES, NO COLLATERAL...
NO REASONING, NO GUARANTEES...
TAKE IT OR LEAVE IT.
to be continued...

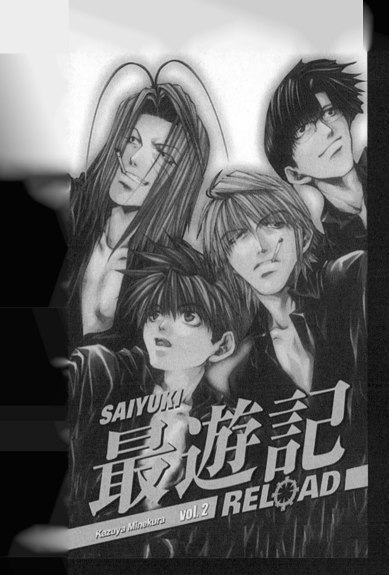

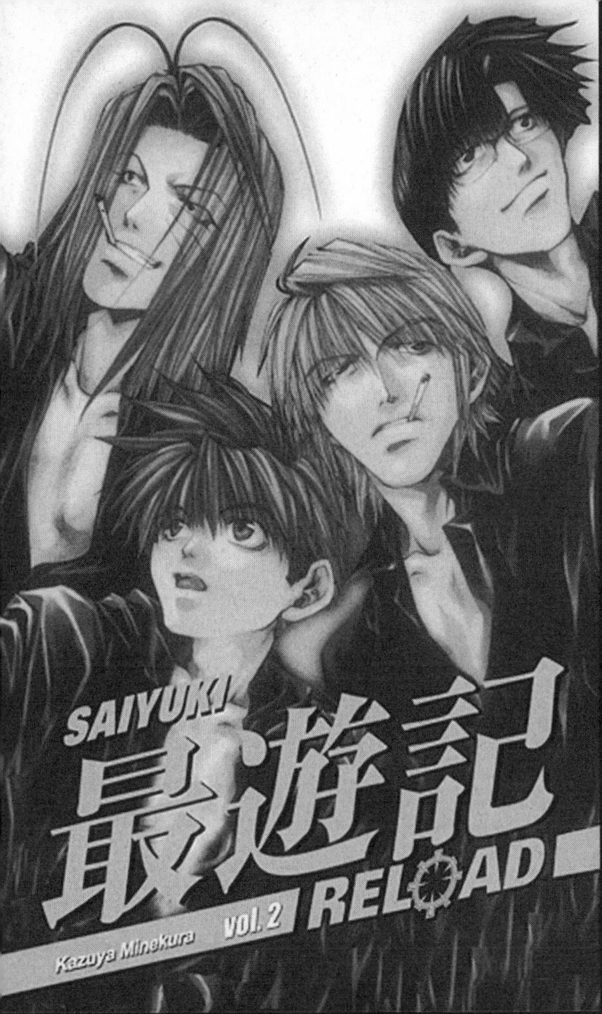
SAIYUKI
最遊記
RELOAD
vol. 2
Kazuya Minekura

t exciting volume, Sanzo faces off against...uh, himself. As if one Sanzo n't enough, now evil doppelgangers of our anti-heroes have shown up, be dispatched, preferably as messily as possible! Then, the progress is further delayed when new villains surface, and an old foe makes a pearance. Yaone and Dokugakuji drag our heroes out of a river just in he new and improved Kougaiji to come along to kick some butt. His soul vith unbelievable strength, Kou now proves to be a challenge for even while his companions wrestle with corporeal demons, Sanzo must face

SOUND EFFECT CHART

THE FOLLOWING IS A LIST OF THE SOUND EFFECTS USED IN *SAIYUKI*. EACH SOUND IS LABELED BY PAGE AND PANEL NUMBER, SEPARATED BY A PERIOD. THE FIRST DESCRIPTION (IN BOLD) IS THE PHONETIC READING OF THE JAPANESE, AND IS FOLLOWED BY THE EQUIVALENT ENGLISH SOUND OR A DESCRIPTION.

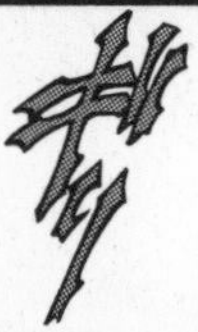

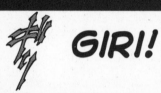

GIRI!

THIS USEFUL SOUND EFFECT HAS A COUPLE OF FUNCTIONS: IT CAN BE EITHER THE SOUND OF GRINDING TEETH OR TWO COMBATANTS STRUGGLING AGAINST EACH OTHER.

1.1	GAUN!!: BANG
11.1	HYOKO.: PEEK
12.3	BOSOX2: MUTTER
12.4	ZUI!: VWP
13.3	HYU.: WHOOSH
13.4	GOSU.: SMASH
13.5	GABAA: GRAB
14.1	GURAA: GURGLE
14.3	KUSU.: HEH
14.4	RUNX2: YAY
16.3	DOON: SHOCK
17.6	PATAN.: SLAM
18.1	GOGOGO: RUMBLE
18.5	SUPAPAAN!!: WHAP
18.6	SHIIN: SILENCE
19.6	GACHA.: CLATCH
20.2	BA!: BAM
21.3	ZAA!: FWOOSH
21.4	DOSAA: KATHUD
21.6	JARI: SKSH
23.3	DA: DASH
23.5	GUI!: GRAB
23.6	DOSAA!: KATHUD
24.3	GO!: WHAM
24.4	DOSAA: THUD
25.5	TAN!: TMP
25.6	HYU...: WHOOSH
26.1	GOPAA!: KAWHANG
26.2	ZA!: WHDD
27.2	HYU.: SWING
27.3	ZASHU!: SLASH
27.6	GAUN!: BANG
29.6	BA!!!: FLUT
34.3	BESHI.: WHAP
34.7	GU!: GRAB
36.1	BOSO: MUTTER
36.2	KAX5: GOBBLE

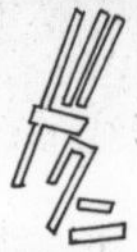

DOKUN!

IN MOST MANGA, A PLEASANT LITTLE "DOKI DOKI" IS THE PREFERRED SOUND FOR HEARTBEATS, BUT IN *SAIYUKI*, THEY NEEDED TO KICK IT UP A NOTCH. "DOKUN" IS THE SOUND OF A PARTICULARLY STRONG HEARTBEAT, USUALLY RESERVED FOR MOMENTS OF EXTREME SHOCK OR DEMONIC TRANSFORMATION.

37.1 PIKU: TWITCH
37.5 GATATA!: SKSH
38.4 ZAWA: MURMUR
41.3 O: RAH
42.1 ZON.: SLICE
43.1 HYU: WHIRL
43.3 DA: BAM
43.4 GOPAA!: KAWHANG
44.2 PASHII: PARRY
44.3 GO!!: THOCK
44.4 KIIII: OONG
44.5 DON!: BAM
45.2 ZASHU: SLASH
45.4 BAKYA!: BASH
46.1 ZA!: WHDD
46.2 GASHAN!: CHAK
46.3 GAUNX2: BANG
47.1 GO!: WHAM
47.2 DOSAA: THUD
47.3 GUSHA: GRIND
48.1 GOPAA!: KAWHANG
50.3 GAKUX2: SHAKE
50.5 GO!.: THWACK
51.2 SHIIN...: SILENCE
53.7 MEKIX3: GROW
54.1 BA!!!: BAM
54.3 BASAA!!: FLAP
55.1 KIKII!: SCREEK
55.3 GYUYRORO!: VROOM
56.1 BURORORO...: RUMBLE
57.5 GABO!: CHOMP
57.7 GU!...: WRENCH
58.1 TO!: JUMP
58.3 ZA!.: WHDD
58.4 DAN!: BAM
60.3 GYAX3: CAREEN
61.1 KIKI!: SCREEK
61.2 BAKYA!: WHANG
61.3 DOGOO: KACRUNCH
62.1 DOSAA: KATHUD
62.2 GEHO!: COUGH
62.3 ZA!: WHDD
66.1 GI!.: SSK
66.2 GAUN!: BANG
67.3 TA!!: DASH
67.7 GURORO...: RUMBLE
68.4 SO!...: TOUCH
69.4 DO!X3: RUMBLE
69.5 DO!X2: RUMBLE
69.6 DO!: RUMBLE
70.2 GUGU: SHOVE
70.4 GUGUGU: SHOVE
70.5 JAKI!: KACHAK
74.6 OOOO...: HOWLING WIND
77.1 BOSU.: SKUSH
78.1 BYUOOO: HOWLING SNOW
78.2 ZAKUX3: SLOG
79.2 BOFU.: BOFF
79.5 ZASU!: SKZSH
80.1 ZASU!X3: SKZSH
80.4 BOSUX2: SKUSH
81.4 BI!: TWING
82.4 BOSUX4: SKUSH
82.5 ZU!: SLIP
83.2 DOX4: CRUMBLE
83.4 BOSA!...: CRUNCH
85.1 PACHIX2: CRACKLE
85.3 YURA...: LEAN
85.5 JAKI.: KACHAK
87.1 NIKOX2: GRIN
87.2 PA!: RELAX
88.1 GOOGAAGOO: SNORE
88.5 BYUOO: HOWLING SNOW
89.3 HYOKO.: PEEK
89.5 WARAX2: SHUFFLE
92.3 O...: HOWLING WIND
94.2 GABAA: POUNCE
94.5 PAAN!!: WHAM
95.6 GA!: GRAB
96.1 ZASHUX2: SLASH
98.3 JAKI!: KACHAK
101.5 GATAX2: SHIVER
102.1 BYUOOO: HOWLING SNOW
103.2 GAKON!: CHOP
103.6 HYOI: YOINK

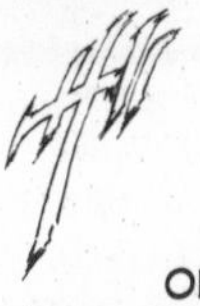

ZAA!

YOU'LL SEE THIS ONE A LOT IN *SAIYUKI*. "ZAA" INDICATES A DRAMATIC APPEARANCE. IF YOU WANT TO MAKE A LASTING IMPRESSION, ALWAYS COME IN WITH A COOL POSE AND A BIG "ZAA!"

104.1 GAKON.: CHOP
104.4 FUU.: PHEW
107.6 ZAKU.: KCH
112.1 ZA!: WHDD
112.2 SU!: SFF
117.1 BYUOOOO...: HOWLING SNOW
117.6 GA: BA
118.1 GAU..N!: BANG
118.2 ZA!X5: WHDD
119.2 OOO...: HOWLING WIND
122.2 ZAA!: WHDD
122.3 ZA!: WHDD
123.1 ZA!: WHDD
123.2 OOO...: HOWLING WIND
123.3 ZAX2: WHDD
123.7 BA!...: BAM
126.2 BYUOO: HOWLING SNOW
126.3 ZA!X2: WHDD
127.3 ZA!!: WHDD
129.1 ZASHU.: SLASH
129.3 BOTAX3: PLUP
129.4 ZASHU: SLASH
129.4 ZAKU!: SOCK
129.4 MEKI: MASH
129.4 BAKII: BASH
129.4 BOKI: BOSH
130.3 BERII: RIP
131.1 BUCHIX2: SNAP
131.1 GORYU!X3: WRENCH
131.1 ZUZU...: SLIP
131.3 BOSU!: THUNK
132.3 ZA!: WHDD
133.1 GO!: WHOCK
133.3 ZUZAZAA!: SLIDE
133.5 GA: SHOVE
134.1 DOGOO!!: KAWHAM
134.4 CHA!: CLICK
134.5 GAUN!!: BANG
135.4 ZA!!: WHDD
136.5 GU!: GRAB
141.6 ZAKUX2: TREAD
144.1 BOKUX3: CRUNCH
148.3 DON.: PLUNK
150.2 GUI!: GRAB
153.2 ZA!: WHDD
153.6 GACHA: CLATCH
155.2 GABAA: SLUMP
155.4 ZA!: WHDD
157.6 DA!: DASH
158.2 ZA!!!: WHDD
159.5 BOFU.: BOFF
160.2 GU!X3: BUBBLE
163.5 GAUN!X2: BANG
164.1 GAUNX2: BANG
164.2 GAUN: BANG
164.2 ZA!: WHDD
164.3 DA!: DASH
164.4 GAUN!X2: BANG
164.5 ZA!: WHDD
165.2 HA!...: GASP
165.4 GAUN!!: BANG
166.3 GO!: WHOCK
166.4 DO!: BAM
167.1 GO!: BWSH
167.2 GAUN: BANG
167.4 ZASHU!: SLASH
167.4 BAKYAA: BASH
167.4 GOSU: KOSH
167.4 GAUNX3: BANG
167.4 DOGOO: KACRUNCH
168.2 OOO...: HOWLING WIND
170.4 BATAN: SLAM
170.6 SAWA...: WHOOSH
171.2 BASA!: RUSTLE
172.2 JII.: STARE
172.4 SHUBO!: FOOM
172.5 FUU!: PHEW
173.4 PAN!: CRASH
174.1 GAUNX4: BANG
174.2 ZA!: WHDD
174.3 GARAN...: CLATTER
174.4 SHII...N: SILENCE
175.4 GACHA: CLATCH
175.4 BA!: WHUD
176.1 GAUNX3: BANG
176.5 ZA!: WHDD
178.3 TA!.: DASH
179.3 HYU...: WHOOSH
179.4 ZA: WHDD
179.5 DO!!: WHOCK
180.4 ZA!.: WHDD
181.1 DON.: BAM
182.5 JAKI: CHAK
182.7 GAUN!X2: BANG
183.1 ZA!: WHDD
183.5 DOKA.: KICK
186.2 BAAN!!: BANG
186.3 DON.: BAM
187.1 PACHIX2: CLAP
188.5 KA!.: TAP
189.2 BAAN!!: BANG

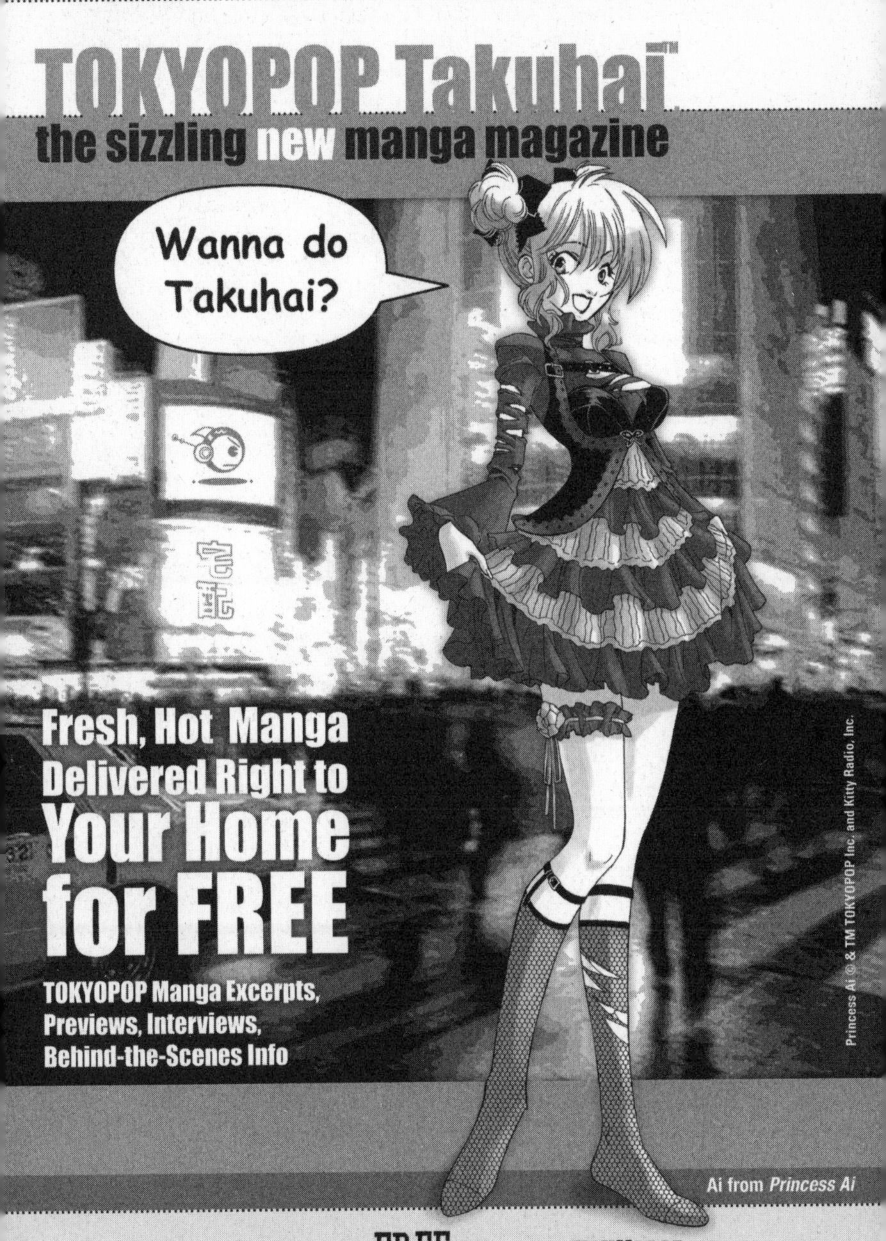

SIGN UP NOW FOR FREE AT: WWW.TOKYOPOP.COM

In the deep South, an ancient voodoo curse unleashes the War on Flesh—a hellish plague of voracious Ew Chott hornets that raises an army of the walking dead. This undead army spreads the plague by ripping the hearts out of living creatures to make room for a Black Heart hive, all in preparation for the most awesome incarnation of evil ever imagined… An unlikely group of five mismatched individuals have to put their differences aside to try to destroy the onslaught of evil before it's too late.

VOODOO MAKES A MAN NASTY!

WAR ON FLESH

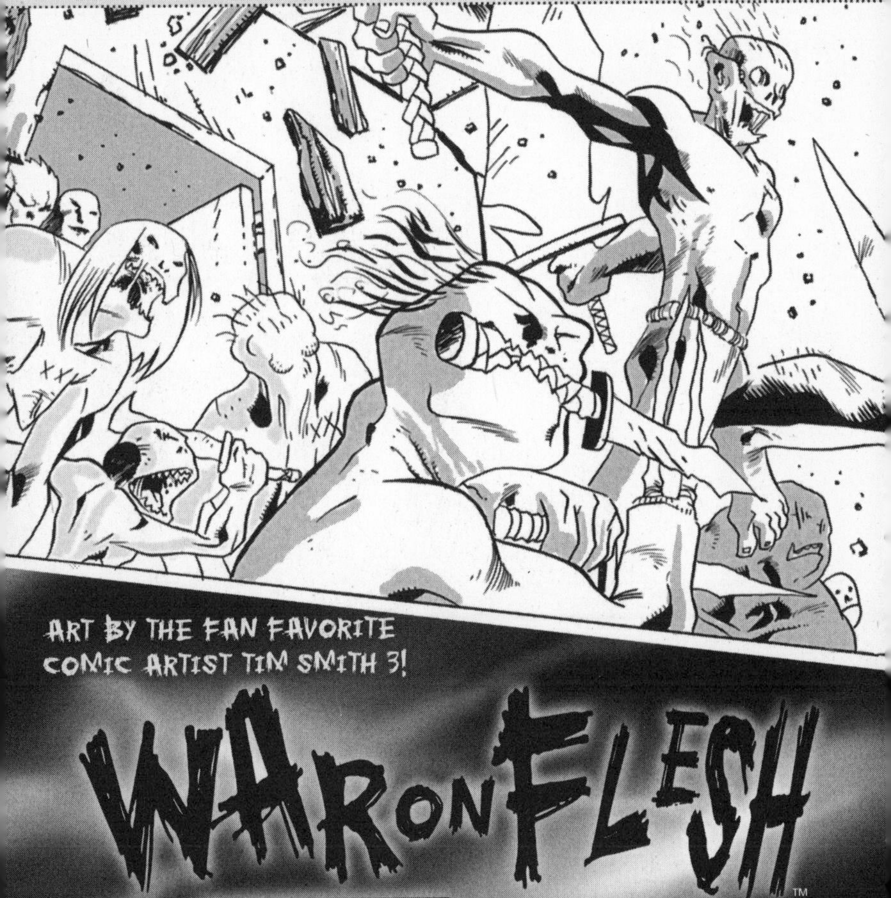

ART BY THE FAN FAVORITE
COMIC ARTIST TIM SMITH 3!

WAR ON FLESH™

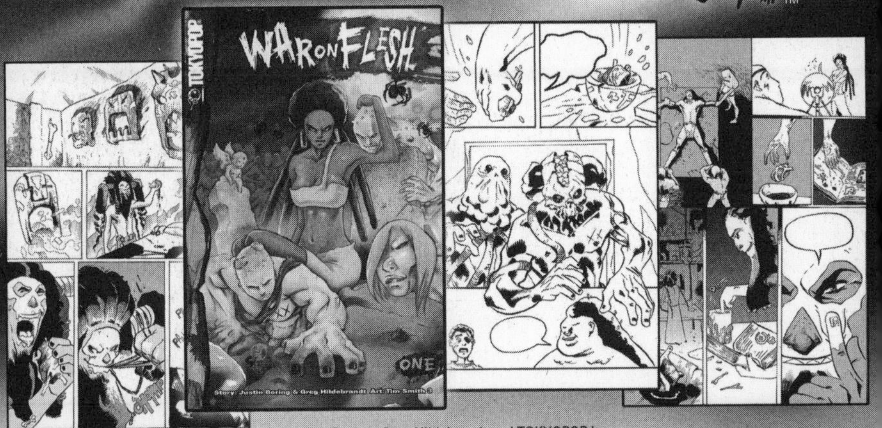
WAR ON FLESH
TOKYOPOP
ONE
Story: Justin Boring & Greg Hildebrandt Art: Tim Smith 3

SPOTLIGHT
TOKYOPOP MANGA SUPPLEMENT

GIRLS BRAVO

BY MARIO KANEDA

T
TEEN
AGE 13+

BOY MEETS GIRL. BOY BREAKS OUT IN HIVES.
BOY STUMBLES ONTO ALIEN PLANET FULL OF GIRLS...

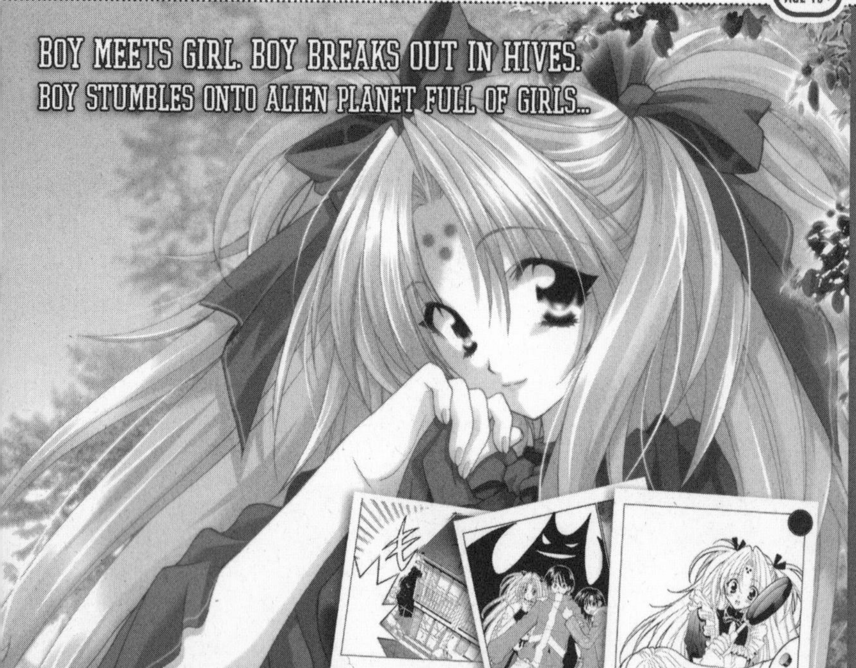

Meet Yukinari Sasaki, an average high school boy who has extreme girl phobia—and an allergic reaction when girls touch him. One day, he befriends an alien named Miharu, who comes from a planet that is inhabited by only women. Remarkably, Yukinari is able to touch Miharu, without breaking out. He returns to his own world accompanied by Miharu, but shortly thereafter, other girls follow them to his world...and his life turns into one big mess!

THE LAUGH-OUT-LOUD MANGA THAT INSPIRED THE POPULAR ANIME ADAPTATION!

FOR MORE INFORMATION VISIT: WWW.TOKYOPOP.COM

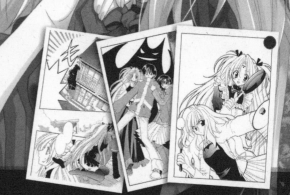

TOKYOPOP SHOP

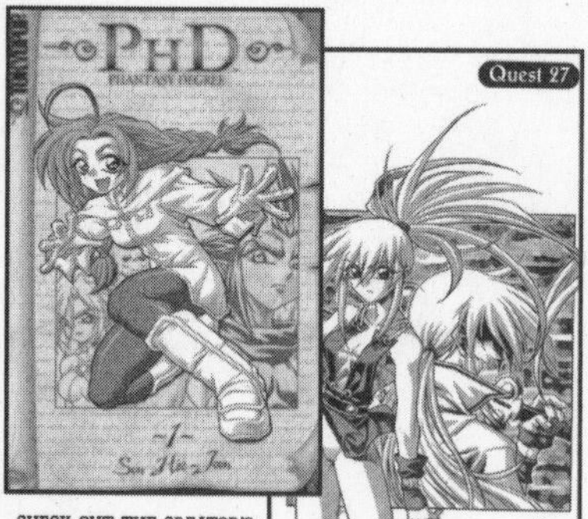
PhD
PHANTASY DEGREE
Quest 27

CHECK OUT THE CREATOR'S *iD_eNTITY*

BY SON HEE-JOON

PhD: PHANTASY DEGREE

So you think you've got it rough at *your* school? Try attending classes at Demon School Hades! When sassy, young Sang makes her monster matriculation to this arcane academy, all hell breaks loose—literally! But what would you expect when the graduating class consists of a werewolf, a mummy and demons by the score? Son Hee-Joon's underworld adventure is pure escapist fun. Always packed with action and often silly in the best sense, *PhD* never takes itself too seriously or lets the reader stop to catch his breath.

~Bryce P. Coleman, Editor

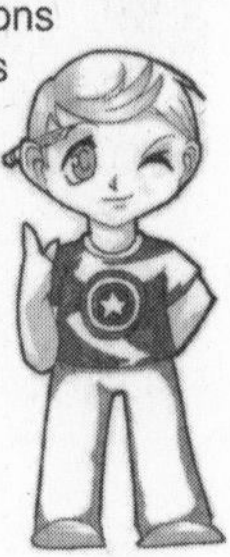

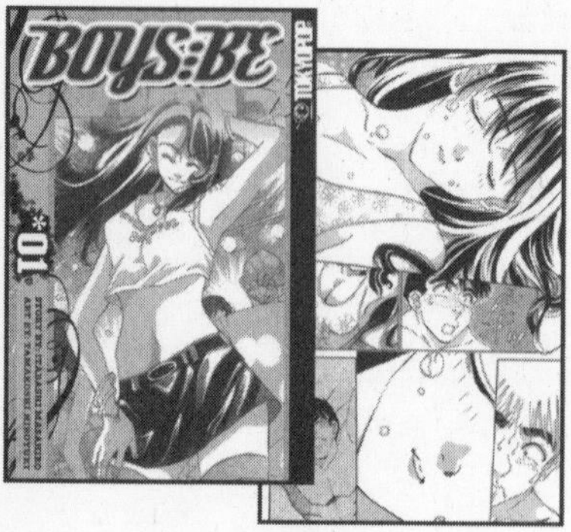
BOYS:BE
01

BY MASAHIRO ITABASHI & HIROYUKI TAMAKOSHI

BOYS BE...

Boys Be... is a series of short stories. But although the hero's name changes from tale to tale, he remains Everyboy—that dorky high school guy who'll do anything to score with the girl of his dreams. You know him. Perhaps you *are* him. He is a dirty mind with the soul of a poet, a stumblebum with a heart of sterling. We follow this guy on quest after quest to woo his lady loves. We savor his victory; we reel with his defeat...and the experience is touching, funny and above all human.

Still not convinced? I have two words for you: fan service.

~Carol Fox, Editor

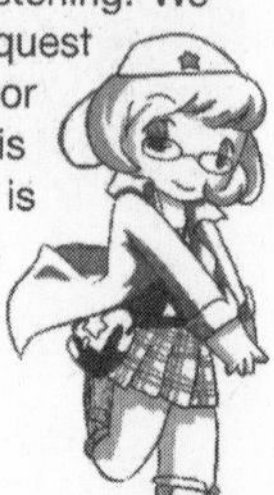

EDITORS' PICKS TOKYOPOP MANGA SUPPLEMENT

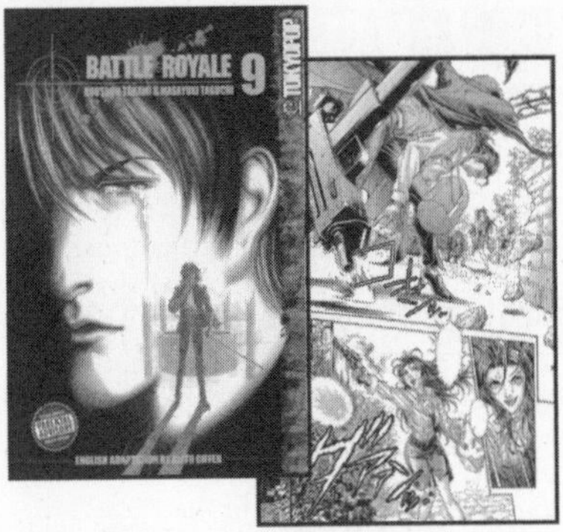
BATTLE ROYALE 9
TOKYOPOP

BY KOUSHUN TAKAMI & MASAYUKI TAGUCHI

BATTLE ROYALE

As far as cautionary tales go, you couldn't get any timelier than *Battle Royale*. Telling the bleak story of a class of middle school students who are forced to fight one another to the death on national television, Koushun Takami and Masayuki Taguchi have created a dark satire that's sickening, yet undeniably exciting as well. And if we have that reaction reading it, it becomes alarmingly clear how the students could be so easily swayed into *doing* it.

~Tim Beedle, Editor

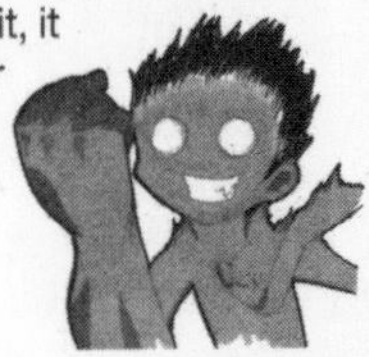

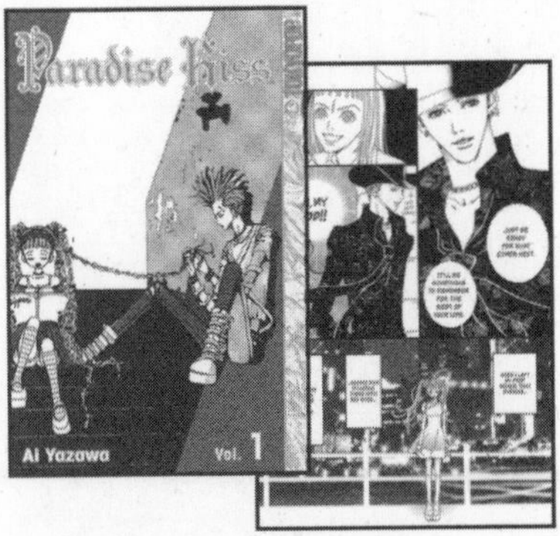
Paradise Kiss
Ai Yazawa
Vol. 1

BY AI YAZAWA

PARADISE KISS

The clothes! The romance! The clothes! The intrigue! And did I mention the clothes?! *Paradise Kiss* is the best fashion manga ever written, from one of the hottest shojo artists in Japan. Ai Yazawa is the coolest. Not only did she create the character designs for *Princess Ai*, which were amazing, but she also produced five fab volumes of *Paradise Kiss*, a manga series bursting with fashion and passion. Read it and be inspired.

~Julie Taylor, Sr. Editor

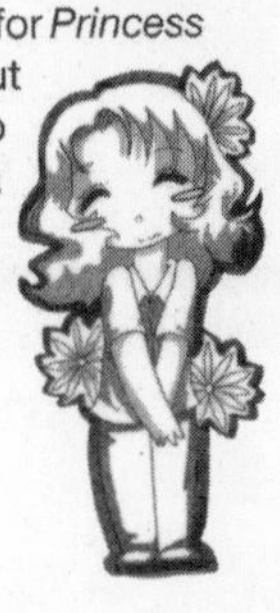

STOP!

This is the back of the book.
You wouldn't want to spoil a great ending!

This book is printed "manga-style," in the authentic Japanese right-to-left format. Since none of the artwork has been flipped or altered, readers get to experience the story just as the creator intended. You've been asking for it, so TOKYOPOP® delivered: authentic, hot-off-the-press, and far more fun!

DIRECTIONS

If this is your first time reading manga-style, here's a quick guide to help you understand how it works.

It's easy... just start in the top right panel and follow the numbers. Have fun, and look for more 100% authentic manga from TOKYOPOP®!